Guaraná

SETH GARFIELD

Guaraná

How Brazil Embraced the World's
Most Caffeine-Rich Plant

The University of North Carolina Press *Chapel Hill*

Set in Arno Pro by Westchester Publishing Services
Manufactured in the United States of America

Library of Congress Cataloging-in-Publication Data
Names: Garfield, Seth, 1967– author.
Title: Guaraná : how Brazil embraced the world's most caffeine-rich plant /
    Seth W. Garfield.
Description: Chapel Hill : University of North Carolina Press, [2022] |
    Includes bibliographical references and index.
Identifiers: LCCN 2022024392 | ISBN 9781469671260 (cloth ; alk. paper) |
    ISBN 9781469671277 (paperback ; alk. paper) | ISBN 9781469671284 (ebook)
Subjects: LCSH: Guarana—Brazil—History. | Guarana—Social aspects—Brazil. |
    Guarana—Economic aspects—Brazil. | Maue Indians—Ethnobotany. | Soft drink
    industry—Brazil—History. | Caffeine—Social aspects—Brazil.
Classification: LCC HD9019.T763 B643 2022 | DDC 615.3/23750981—dc23/eng/20220706
LC record available at https://lccn.loc.gov/2022024392

Cover photo: Guaraná shrub with fruits © guentermanaus/Shutterstock.com.

To Emilia Viotti da Costa, in memoriam

Contents

Illustrations, Maps, and Table

Acknowledgments

Historical monographs are typically single-authored productions, yet their execution relies on an extensive supporting cast. Archivists and librarians organize the jumble known as the past into manuals for the present. Web search engines deliver an emporium of data. Innovations of past and contemporary researchers provide the foundations for intellectual engagement and renewal. Institutions finance the fieldwork and academic leaves that enable research and writing. Editors offer guidelines for publication. Loved ones put up with an author's distractedness. Ranging over several centuries and historiographies, this book reimagines new ways of telling Brazilian history through the trajectory of a material object and its interrelated actor networks. Multiple supporters and guides made this endeavor possible.

Funding for this project came from the University of Texas Faculty Research Assignment, the Lozano Long Institute of Latin American Studies Faculty Research Leave, and the UT Humanities Institute Faculty Fellows Seminar. Summer field research was enabled by the Andrew W. Mellon Foundation Faculty Fellowship in Latin American Studies. I thank the many dedicated archivists and librarians that oversee the collections that I consulted in Brazil, the United States, and Europe.

Given the study's temporal and thematic scope, I leaned on the expertise of a number of colleagues. Barbara Weinstein read the entire manuscript twice, offering incisive comments for abridgment and revision. For more than twenty-five years, I have benefited from her wisdom as a scholar and a mentor and I thank her once more for her generosity and dedication. I am very grateful to James Woodard for imparting his advice on relevant archival collections, without which I could not have completed key sections of this book. Tim Walker generously provided bibliographic and archival tips on the Jesuit and Lusophone trade in medicinal plants. Charles Clement, scientific expert on all things guaraná, offered important clarifications and fact-checking, as did André Luiz Atroch and Cristiane Krug, and Sônia Lorenz shared her deep knowledge of Sateré-Mawé society. I have learned from Teresa Marques's scholarship and her personal communications regarding the history of the Brazilian beer industry. For research assistance during my stay in Belém, I owe a debt of gratitude to Rafael Chambouleyron. For his hospitality during my preliminary research trip to Maués and his commitment to preserving regional history and forms of cultural expression, I will always remember Waldo Mafra Carneiro Monteiro (Mestre Barrô), whose untimely passing is a tragic loss. For her assistance in obtaining images for the book, and for her kindness, I thank Regina Horta Duarte.

My scholarship has benefited from participation in various workshops and conferences. The fellows from the Institute for Historical Studies' yearlong theme, Food and Drink in History—Xaq Frohlich, Laura Giannetti, and Michelle King—inspired me with their work. The series was immeasurably strengthened by the contribution of food historian Rachel Laudan and the various presenters at "The Invention of Food" conference and relied throughout on the invaluable assistance of Courtney Meador. My colleagues Bruce Hunt and Megan Raby allowed me to share my research at an early stage at UT's History and Philosophy of Science series, where I received excellent feedback. As a faculty fellow at the Humanities Institute for the theme of The Humanities in the Environment/The Environment in the Humanities, under the leadership of director Pauline Strong, my scholarship was enhanced by the multidisciplinary perspectives of my colleagues at the University of Texas. I also thank Christopher Dunn and Felipe Cruz for the opportunity to present at Tulane's "Amazônia Ocupada" symposium, and Fred Freitas and Jake Blanc for organizing the conference on the history of Brazil's hinterlands.

For their professional guidance and support, I also wish to thank Bill Balée, William Brice, Patricia Burrowes, Henrique Carneiro, Rosanna Dent, Jane Frank, Virginia Garrard, Paul Gootenberg, Greg Grandin, James Green, Susanna Hecht, John Hemming, Marcio Henrique, Alfredo Kingo Oyama Homma, Roger Horowitz, Jacqueline Jones, Jan McTavish, Victor Nogueira, Suzanne Oakdale, Elizabeth O'Brien, João Pacheco de Oliveira, Heather Roller, Ana Romo, Cassia Roth, Dominici Miranda de Sá, Nelson Sanjad, Lidia Santos, Julia Sarreal, Barbara Sommer, Lena Suk, and Eyal Weinberg. At various stages in the preparation of the book manuscript, I relied on the assistance of Hailey Howe, Ellis Davenport, Timmy Vilgiate, Madeline Olson, and Nicolás Quintero González. For copyediting, I thank Jamie Thaman and Mary Gendron. For design of the book's maps, I counted on Gabe Moss and Madge Duffey. And I extend special thanks to Linda Gill, Melissa Guy, and Ryan Lynch at the Benson Latin American Collection at UT for their assistance with multiple research requests.

The COVID-19 pandemic unfortunately forced me to scrap a field visit to Parintins to meet with members of the Consortium of Sateré-Mawé Producers. I am grateful to Sérgio Garcia Wara for allowing me to interview him via

WhatsApp regarding Projeto Waraná and to learn more about the historical efforts of the Sateré-Mawé to achieve self-determination. Indigenous communities throughout Brazil have suffered unconscionable physical assaults and political smears in recent years under the administration of Jair Bolsonaro. I hope that my work can serve to shed further light on Indigenous history in Brazil and to combat anti-Indigenous racism.

At the University of North Carolina Press, executive editor Elaine Maisner has been an author's dream. She took an eager interest in my work and has provided critical feedback for the book's publication. Over a lengthy career, she put together a formidable list in Latin American history that I am honored to join. I thank as well Debbie Gershenowitz and Andreina Fernandez for shepherding the manuscript to print.

For too many occasions in which this project intruded on evening and weekend time, I appreciate the patience of my family. To my wife, Vivian, thank you for your love and support. After many years, I still count on your critical feedback and your anthropological training as a sounding board for my ideas. To my daughters, Marina and Ana: you are the greatest source of pride and joy. And to my dearest mom and my late father, words cannot even express my gratitude.

This book is dedicated to the memory of my former adviser, Emilia Viotti da Costa. I had the privilege of conducting my doctoral work under the supervision of one of the greatest historians of Brazil. Her trenchant insights and humbling reprimands about historical research and writing still echo three decades later. As a larger-than-life persona and a gift to historians of Latin America, she will always be, in the double meaning of the Portuguese word, *presente*.

Guaraná

Introduction

An Eye on the Past and the Present

"In the ancestral village there lived a virtuous couple who had a young son. A performer of wonders, the boy, by the age of six, was revered by many. Like an angel of peace, surrounded by an aura of joy, the child put an end to feuding, maintaining the unity of his people. Abundant rain nourished plants that had once withered, begging for water. The sick were healed with the touch of his young hand." So begins the Sateré-Mawé's origin story in the Amazon forest as recorded by Brazilian engineer João Martins da Silva Coutinho and published in Rio de Janeiro in 1870.

Roused by jealousy, however, the bad angel Jurupary plotted the young boy's murder. One day, when the child climbed a tree, Jurupary transformed into a snake, grabbed him by the neck, and killed him. When the villagers found the boy, his visage was serene. Eyes wide open, he appeared to be laughing. But despair soon mounted as the boy's death seemingly condemned the community to eternal misfortune. A sudden lightning bolt stilled the people's cries. Then the boy's mother spoke: "Tupã, the beneficent [God], has come to console us from this great affliction, repairing the loss we have suffered. My son will be reborn as a tree that will be our source of food and union, curing us of all bodily ills as well. But it is necessary for his eyes to be planted. And I can't do this, so you must, as Tupã has ordered." With the villagers reluctant to tear out the child's eyes, the elders drew lots. The community's tears watered the planting as the elders stood guard. Several days later, the guaraná bush bloomed.[1] The plant's eyeball-like berries signified the boy's resurrection and the genesis of a Native Amazonian people. The Sateré-Mawé refer to themselves as "the children of guaraná."

In 2014, a century and a half after Silva Coutinho published this myth, the Sateré-Mawé population numbered 13,350. They are one of the largest of the 255 Indigenous groups in Brazil, which total 896,917 individuals, or approximately 0.47 percent of the nation's population, according to the 2010 census.[2] Concentrated primarily on the southern tributaries between the Tapajós and Madeira Rivers on the border of the states of Amazonas and Pará, the Sateré-Mawé are the most populous Indigenous group on the lower Amazon.[3] Most reside in the Andirá-Marau Indigenous Territory, an area of 788,528 hectares ratified by presidential decree in 1986. A smaller group lives

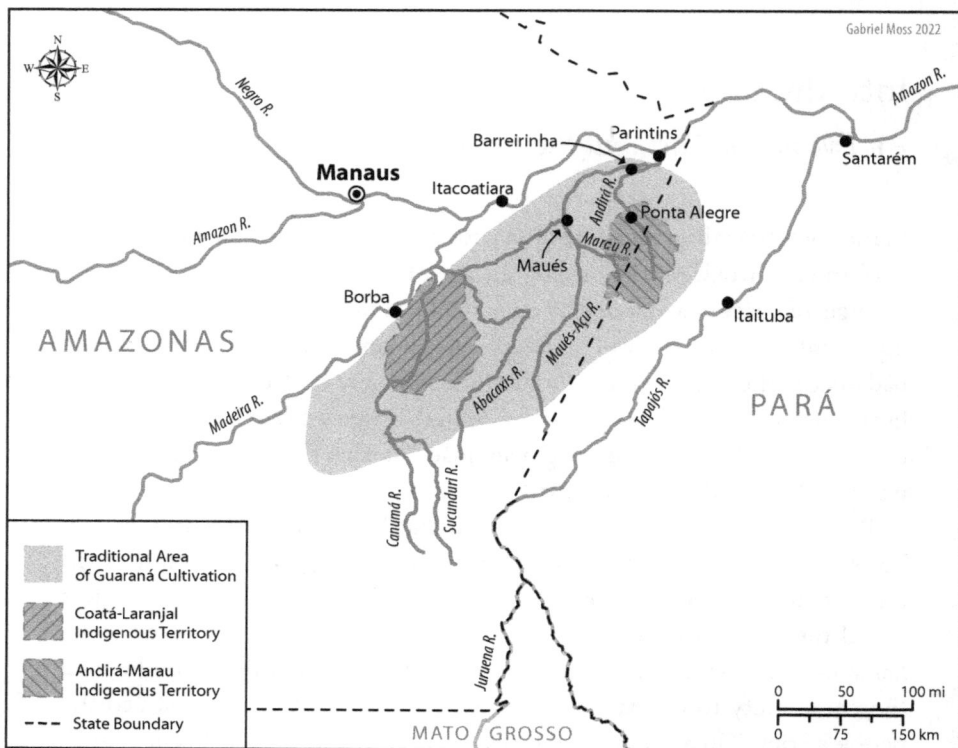

Gabriel Moss 2022

Sateré-Mawé Indigenous territories and traditional area of guaraná cultivation

with the Mundurucu in the Coatá-Laranjal Indigenous Territory near the Madeira River. "In Sateré-Mawé territory nobody will see—at least on a normal day—adult Indians who are naked, painted, or with headdresses," a Brazilian journalist wrote in 2010, dispelling exotic stereotypes. "Flip-flops and color-ful clothing are the rule."[4] For several generations, Sateré-Mawé have also eked out a living in poor neighborhoods ringing Manaus, the capital of Ama-zonas, and in regional towns.[5] The Indigenous communities are marked by traditional clan distinctions as well as religious divisions among Catholics, Seventh-Day Adventists, and Evangelical Protestants.[6]

The Sateré-Mawé language forms part of the Tupi linguistic branch, though it contains distinct vocabulary unrelated to other Indigenous linguis-tic families, as well as many words from *língua geral,* the lingua franca of early colonial Brazil.[7] *Sateré* translates as "fiery caterpillar" and *Mawé* as "intelligent parrot." The group's cultural resilience after more than two centuries of sus-tained contact with Luso-Brazilian society is evinced by a survey from 2003: among more than 1,750 rural households, over 95 percent of the population over the age of five could speak the Sateré-Mawé language, while 36.3 percent lacked proficiency in spoken Portuguese. Indigenous men show greater competence speaking Portuguese and reading and writing in Portuguese and Sateré-Mawé than do Indigenous women, reflective of their higher levels of schooling.[8]

Residents of the Andirá-Marau Indigenous Territory, dispersed over ninety villages in the early 2000s, occupy a sliver of their historic lands.[9] According to Sateré-Mawé accounts, their ancestors lived in the area between the Tapajós and Madeira Rivers, bounded on the north by the Tupinambarana island on the Amazon River and on the south by the Tapajós headwaters.[10] It is estimated that they settled in the region surrounding the Maués and Andirá Rivers between a thousand and two thousand years ago. The area had been densely inhabited by other Indigenous groups, with the presence of gardens of Brazil nut trees pointing to prior histories of crop domestication.[11] Upon passing between the regions of the Tapajós and Madeira, Friar Gaspar de Carvajal, the chronicler of the Europeans' pioneering sixteenth-century expedition down the Amazon, reported seeing villages of warrior women, which he would name "Amazonas" in reference to the Greek myth.[12] The Sateré-Mawé called their homeland Noçoquem (or Nosokem), a land without evil, where lakes and rivers teemed with fish, and forests with animals and plants, a time when "the animals were like people."[13] Nineteenth-century geographers named the Switzerland-sized region delineated by the Amazon, Tapajós, and Madeira, with its networks of rivers, canals, and lagoons, Mundurucânia, in reference to the region's one-time fearsome inhabitants, the Mundurucu. With European conquest, Indigenous peoples would retreat to more isolated upriver and inland regions.[14]

Guaraná, a species of flowering shrubs and lianas in the Sapindaceae, or soapberry, family, is native only to the Maués region of the lower Amazon, the upper Rio Negro, and the Orinoco River of Venezuela. The precise source of such geographic isolation and historic distribution among the regions is unclear.[15] The limited dispersion of many species has been noted in a number of studies of Amazonian botany, particularly for those in specialized habitats, leading some models of phytogeography to suggest a refugia theory that emphasizes the contraction of Amazonian forest environments during the Pleistocene to explain the uneven distribution of certain species, or groups of related species.[16] Guaraná's fruit, of a reddish color when ripe, contains from one to three seeds that are partially enclosed in a starchy white aril and a glossy dark-brown seed coat that resemble a human eyeball.[17] Grown commercially only in Brazil, guaraná is cultivated today by Indigenous and non-Indigenous smallholders as well as on large farms.

In their creation story, the Sateré-Mawé recount their ancestors' transformation of guaraná from one of the Amazon's many botanical creepers battling for the forest canopy to a cultivated bush. The Sateré-Mawé hold a highly credible claim as protagonists in the plant's domestication, which scientists posit occurred prior to the Portuguese arrival to Brazil in 1500; guaraná does not figure, for example, in the myths of the Mundurucu or other Indigenous groups in the region.[18] Over the ensuing centuries, the Sateré-Mawé engaged in continuous domestication of guaraná through consistent use of wild forest seedlings to replace less productive plants—as they do today—thereby ensuring genetic diversity.[19] Indigenous technologies would also turn the plant's caffeine-rich seeds, ensconced within their red-shelled berries, into a foodstuff whose consumption as a beverage sustained distinctive ways of being and doing.[20] In the Sateré-Mawé language, *waraná* signifies the "beginning (*-na*) of all knowledge or explanation (*wará-*)," indicative of the plant's epistemic importance.[21] "It's not simply a fruit for us," stated an Indigenous leader. "It is a sacred plant. It is like a God for us, it has spiritual power."[22]

But then came the *karaiwa*, intent on subordinating the Sateré-Mawé: the slavers, militias, and missionaries who promised reward or retribution in this life or the next; the traders swapping overvalued goods for guaraná to sell in far-off Mato Grosso mining towns; the colonists who produced and marketed the caffeine-rich sticks, albeit of inferior quality; the botanists and chemists disparaging Indigenous scientific knowledge in their pursuit of standardized, universal truths; the pharmaceutical firms that capitalized on Sateré-Mawé know-how; the agronomists who bred their plants; the ethnographers who studied their culture; and the beverage companies that transformed guaraná into a trace ingredient and moniker of Brazil's national soda. In sum, these were the Others with whom Sateré-Mawé communities have engaged in the historical processes of exchange between Indigenous and non-Indigenous populations that have co-produced scientific knowledge of the natural world.[23] Now a historian from the United States has surfaced, guided by the empirical, objectivist methods of an academic discipline (yet no less the product and producer of particular social positions and professional identities), to recount these chapters in guaraná's voyage from Indigenous cultivar and confection to Brazilian national icon.[24]

THIS WORK EXPLORES how a plant that has nurtured the Sateré-Mawé people came to be the namesake ingredient of a multibillion-dollar soft drink industry and the delight of Brazil. Although other "soft drugs"—such as coffee, chocolate, sugar, and tobacco—command pride of place in the "entangled" histories of science, trade, and status in the Atlantic world, we have lacked a full-length historical study of guaraná.[25] And while the ingredient now features in energy drinks worldwide, guaraná soft drinks have not attained the fame of Coca-Cola, whose global brand recognition, owing to U.S. political and corporate hegemony, has generated a number of academic studies.[26] That non-Portuguese-language scholarship would come up short, given guaraná's more renowned peers, is perhaps unsurprising; such is the fate of histories ostensibly confined to the global periphery, in politics as much as in the academy, where standard snipes at relevance in the humanities—"so what?"—are compounded by the condescension of "so, where?"

More perplexing is the dearth of historical studies in Brazil on guaraná, a household name thanks to the soda's popularity.[27] Nationalism has been cultivated worldwide through the consecration of local flora, fauna, and cuisines.[28] In Brazil, African and Indigenous-origin foods have served to showcase so-called racial democracy—a nationalistic credo amply explored in studies of samba, soccer, and Carnival.[29] Guaraná's sidelining in Brazilian historiography, then, prompts further reflection on the academic discipline's epistemic bias. Far from the plantation complex and the transatlantic slave trade, the sustained interventions of colonial and national governments, the economic and academic strongholds of Brazil, and even regional histories dominated by rubber (or, in contemporary ecopolitics, by forests), guaraná never amassed the paper trail in state repositories reflective of larger-scale commercial operations. And unlike cocaine, opium, heroin, and marijuana, guaraná was never criminalized, sparing its consumers stigma and arrest but excluding the drug from the vast documentation of state bureaucracies implicated in the coercive biopolitics of industrial capitalism and the racialized construction of vice in modern societies.[30] Such is the trap of the public archive, the mirror and maker of knowledge and power in society, and the professional historian's building and stumbling block. Not to mention that restricted access to corporate archives ensures the secrecy of more than proprietary formulas.

Guaraná's ties to everyday meanings of development, the polestar of Brazilian politics (and, for many decades, of its historiography), make for a particularly revealing commodity study. If development is defined reductively as an increase in economic products and services, guaraná's massification hits the mark. In the early 2000s, according to one author, Brazilians drank more than seventeen million bottles of guaraná soda daily.[31] And while countless mass-consumed goods are purported deliverers of the health, safety, leisure, and efficiency said to constitute modern homes and nations, not every household item in Brazil is also the namesake of a native Amazonian plant, a symbol of the nation's multicultural heritage, the pride of domestic industry, and the flavor rival to a Yankee juggernaut.[32] A history of guaraná thus allows for the elucidation of race, space, and grace in the making of a national product and project. More broadly, straddling the realms of nature and culture, modernity and tradition, and the public and the private, guaraná upends the conceptual binaries that have informed Western thought and historical writing. Through analysis of missionary accounts, scientific journals, government reports, travelogues, newspaper articles, corporate ledgers, advertising campaigns, ethnographies, and Sateré-Mawé narratives, I have sought to patch together a history of guaraná. Collectively, these form the documentary basis of this study, a vast hunting-and-gathering expedition facilitated by the advent of digital technology, whose enhanced capacity to identify and aggregate empirical data has not so much eliminated power inequalities in the making and writing of history as expanded and diversified approaches to sites of knowledge production.[33]

Given that exchange is a fundamental aspect of human life, and that drugs have long been big business due to their high-value, low-bulk nature, which facilitates long-distance commerce, outsiders' adoption of an Indigenous stimulant would not seem much of an enigma.[34] Proponents of the "biological turn" or "neuro-turn" in historical analysis would correctly peg guaraná's cross-cultural appeal to its analeptic qualities.[35] Guaraná has the highest natural caffeine content of any plant in the world: the yield from its seeds ranges from a low of 2.7 percent (dried weight) to a high of 5.8 percent, or two to five times higher than that of Arabica coffee seeds.[36] A central nervous stimulant, caffeine increases alertness, inhibits fatigue, and suppresses appetite. It is the world's most popular drug, freely available and largely unregulated, whether on the counter in a cup or over it in capsule form, and even injected into children's soft drink beverages. According to a 2001 study, annual global consumption topped 120,000 tons, or enough to fill 260 cups of coffee or tea per year for every human being on earth.[37] Aside from caffeine, guaraná also contains theobromine, theophylline, tannins, saponins, flavonoids (catechins, epicatechins), proanthocyanidins, and trace elements of other compounds.[38] The mix of natural chemicals in guaraná seeds is believed to heighten the stimulant effects over caffeine alone.[39] As an embodied experience, consumption of guaraná has long been a subject of Brazilian popular and medical interest, and its therapeutic benefits have been extensively researched by scientists in recent decades.[40]

Psychoactive drugs such as guaraná are said to sate a seemingly universal human desire for altered consciousness—much like prayer, meditation, music, fasting, sleep, physical exercise, and sex.[41] Yet the meanings enveloping psychoactive substances have varied according to social organization, knowledge systems, technological capacity, cultural tastes, and ideological belief. In the contests over truth and power, the sacred plant-beverage in one culture may be the taboo of another. Islam's proscription of wine contrasts with its centrality in Christian ritual.[42] Missionaries in colonial Latin America condemned Indigenous hallucinogens, in part due to their challenge to wine's primacy in church ceremonies.[43] And in the mid-1940s, guaraná soda companies in Brazil sought to tar a new arrival, Coca-Cola, as a gringo infidel. In other words, the varied social functions, cultural meanings, and ideological workings ascribed to guaraná transcend matters of biochemistry.[44] They are the products of broader histories and the subject of this book.

MATERIAL HISTORIES CAN REVEAL how an object may pass from a confined existence to symbolic appropriation by society, its cultural value calibrated according to a system of hierarchical codes.[45] Indeed, at its core, politics has always been object oriented, assigning arbiters and forums to regulate the interaction of humans and nonhumans.[46] My primary line of investigation explores how a plant intrinsic to Sateré-Mawé kin-based systems and world-making came to be re-signified by new networks of exchange, classification, and accumulation in the context of state expansionism, scientific experimentation, and capitalist development. The book focuses on the interventions of clerics and traders, the technics of scientists, the stratagems of marketers, and the behaviors and tastes of consumers that popularized new forms and uses of the stimulant. I trace the knowledge production and circulation of guaraná in disparate historical eras and situations: from an Indigenous cultivar to a colonial-era missionizing concern and regional trade commodity; from an object of Western scientific study and classification to an Anglo-American pharmaceutical novelty to a mass-consumed soft drink; from a moral crusade and geopolitical agenda to an emblem of Brazilian national development and identity. Mindful of social structure and agency, I foreground the varied historical mediators whose social, material, discursive, and bodily practices have generated knowledge of guaraná.[47]

Bookending this study, a secondary line of inquiry explores guaraná's relevance to Sateré-Mawé cultural survival. Alongside the traditional understandings and uses of guaraná in Sateré-Mawé society, trade with the non-Indigenous enabled the acquisition of Western goods and symbolic power, adapted to

internal social logics.[48] Or as Sérgio Garcia Wara framed his community's contemporary marketing of guaraná: "It's good to see both sides of the coin, for
us to understand first our reality as a people, as well as the educational system of
the government. For us to have two forms of knowledge and to use the knowledge of the white man to favor our people."[49]

Histories of food, marked by cultural exchanges and adaptations, can illu-
minate well the varied meanings ascribed to goods by different social groups,
the spaces and structures that link production and consumption, and the
webs of signification and power in society.[50] Tied to notions of ownership,
organization, status, taste, health, and the body, food practices are intrinsic to
the reproduction and articulation of social orders.[51] Foods evoke strong feelings of what it means to be human—all the more reason why people use them
to communicate messages about race, ethnicity, gender, religion, class, and
other forms of group membership. Beyond biological need, food consumption further signals the capability to control or discipline the body, presenting individuals with a provisional sense of choice and illusion of freedom.[52]

In view of the biogeographical, socioeconomic, technological, cultural,
and political relations that sustain a commodity's trajectory and value, this
history of guaraná employs a mixed and multi-sited approach.[53] It highlights
the causal links, connections, or disruptions among the peoples and places that
shape systemic processes and their relations to differentially positioned subjects.[54] In this integrative method, I have sought to subject the belief systems,
socioeconomic structures, and technoscience of modern populations to the
core cultural analysis traditionally reserved for Indigenous societies. As advocated by Bruno Latour, a "symmetrical anthropology" questions the putative
conceptual divides between nature and society, objects and humans, and
things and signs said to distinguish modern from premodern societies.[55] The
emphasis on subaltern resistance is not so much ignored as subsumed within
broader analytical frameworks of power and subjectivity, namely the sense-
making activities employed by varied social groups within discrete historical
moments.[56] I depart from the anthropological premise that cultures are webs
of meanings spun by and suspending humans and that all knowledge is authenticated and applied according to culturally specific criteria.[57] In this vein,
the study approaches science as a shared form of situated knowledge, a practice and form of communication and symbolic meanings located in discrete
places and times, whose circulation is determined by networks of relations
and struggles over power.[58]

A long-range social biography of guaraná enables broad exploration of the
human impacts on Amazonian ecosystems, the hierarchies of knowledge and

circulation of goods and power in societies, the structuring of social inequalities in Brazil, and development as a political project and embodied practice in Latin America's largest nation.[59] In tracing the interconnections among groups of people, the natural environment, and the stuff and stories that constitute societies, the study contextualizes the day-to-day routines and patterned activities through which social actors reproduce the structural properties of larger collectivities.[60]

This book presents guaraná as a taste of Brazil: a product as well as a projection of the nation's history from pre-Columbian times to the twenty-first century. Structural violence; hierarchies of race, class, and gender; the commodification of nature; and competing regimes of knowledge—legacies of colonialism, Enlightenment thought, and the Scientific Revolution—loom large in the account.[61] But so do their historical permutations in a vast, stratified, multicultural, late-industrializing nation of the Global South. No narrative, of course, can tell "the" story of any nation, since an idea will always command more than one story.[62] Yet as a flash of Indigenous empowerment, a fetish of Brazil's scientific community and agro-industrial economy, a conjurer of myths of race and nature, and a figuration of modernity in the "land of the future," guaraná can provide a sample of what history can do.

CHAPTER ONE

Guaraná

The Roots of History and Myth

Plants formed part of human diet from the early stages of evolution, since *Homo sapiens*, unlike most mammals, are unable to manufacture vitamin C. With the invention of agriculture between ten thousand and twelve thousand years ago, humans began to settle in towns and villages near agricultural fields.[1] Plants provide humans not only with energy through food, and oxygen through photosynthesis, but with clothing, ornamentation, fibers, building materials, and medicines. In the late twentieth century, the World Health Organization estimated that as much as 80 percent of the global population relied on plants directly from nature as their main source of health care.[2] Beyond their importance in material culture, plants are pathways to spiritual transcendence—whether Indigenous peoples' use of entheogens to commune with the supernatural, the incorporation of flowers into funerary rites in Europe and Asia, or the Romantic contemplation of nature. Many serve as the very embodiments of divinities, from the blood of Christ in sacramental wine to the amaranth-based paste that the Mexica ceremonially fashioned into an image of Huitzilopochtli.[3] Consequently, botanist Francis Raymond Fosberg argues, "It is essential that the ethnologist or archeologist who is trying to understand a culture have more than a passing interest in the plants that form a part of the environment under study, and thus enter into the fabric of the culture's existence."[4] Thomas Carlyle may have once lionized the "Great Men" of history, but it is time to look to plants, great and not-so-great, as markers of human experience and cultural diversity.[5]

In traditional communities, human relationships with plants tend to be more explicit due to the closer link between production and consumption. Ethnobotanical studies document Indigenous peoples' vast knowledge and use of plants—the incontrovertible link between cultural and biological diversity.[6] Research among the Bororo of Mato Grosso, for example, found that the Indigenous could name at first glance 85 percent of the plants found in an area of three square miles of tropical savanna; they also identified all but two of the two hundred specimens gathered by the scientists.[7] Likewise, in a two-year study initiated in 1987 in the state of Amazonas, Brazilian scientists cataloged 196 medicinal plants used by traditional and Indigenous communities.[8] And in studies of the Ka'apor and Tembé of Brazil and the Panare of Venezuela by William Balée and Brian Boom, respectively, 76.8 percent of local plants were used by the former, and 48.6 percent by the latter.[9] Of course, in the city as in the forest, humans are plants' dependents as much as their disseminators. The so-called distinction between culture and nature attributed to Enlightenment thought is mere invention of the "moderns," since all societies are constituted by the integration of the human and nonhuman worlds.[10]

Unlike guaraná, most plants never make it to a pantry, since humans have incorporated less than 1 percent of the estimated tens of thousands of edible species into their diets.[11] Three plants—rice, maize, and wheat—make up 60 percent of the world's food energy intake, a testament to monocropping in sustaining expanding global populations while also reducing biodiversity, impoverishing the human diet, and generating environmentally unsustainable practices.[12] In the realm of tropical botany, guaraná likewise stands out. Occupying 6 percent of the globe's surface, tropical rain forests contain the greatest diversity of flora: among the earth's approximate 390,000 species of plants, an estimated 35,000 to 50,000 are found in the Amazon rain forest.[13] A sample plot of one hectare of tropical rain forest may contain up to one hundred tree species of twenty centimeters or more in diameter and a vast array of plants of nutritional, medical, and utilitarian value.[14] Yet according to one survey, of more than five thousand plants in the Amazon of seeming commercial potential, relatively few have been systematically studied by outsiders.[15] Five centuries after the Iberian arrival in the Americas, under 2 percent of the Amazon's plant species were tested for pharmacological activity.[16] According to another study from 1999, Western scientists had cataloged the phytotherapeutic qualities of merely three hundred Amazonian species. Then again, only an estimated 5 to 15 percent of all higher plants worldwide have been systematically investigated for their medicinal properties, of which approximately just two hundred are used in Western medicine.[17] Guaraná, on the other hand, has been the subject of over two hundred scientific studies.[18] It is one of only a handful of Amazonian plants that is a household name in Brazil.

Amid the environmental legacies of colonialism, guaraná's triumph resonates. With European settlement of the New World and the introduction of livestock, plantation crops, and exotic plant species, many Amerindian crops became marginalized or neglected.[19] Indigenous ecologies of knowledge—expressions of epistemological and cultural diversity—were suppressed.[20] And the trend continues: in the contemporary Amazon, cattle ranchers fell vast tracts, replacing species-rich forests of some 450 large trees per hectare (and over 150 different species) with one cow per hectare.[21] Throughout the Americas, demand for traditional Indigenous foods has waned since European colonization due to economic conditions, cultural attitudes, expanded urbanization, and the disappearance of ethnic groups with command of botanical knowledge.[22] Of course, a number of crops in cultivation in the Americas in 1492, such as corn, potatoes, and cassava, now represent key global food staples. Moreover, increased foreign demand facilitated by economic and infrastructural improvement allowed other Indigenous plants, such as agave, cacao, coca, pineapple, and the prickly pear (for the processing of cochineal insects), to be transformed into commercial agriculture in the Americas, although at the cost of specialization in production and abandonment of other species.[23] Native cultivars also survived due to culinary preferences, as well as Indigenous communities' practice of raising introduced crops and livestock for market while continuing to cultivate traditional plants.[24]

Guaraná's survival mirrors that of its domesticators, the Sateré-Mawé. It has been estimated that by the mid-twentieth century, the pre-Columbian population of the Amazon region had been reduced by some 90 to 95 percent.[25] Centuries of colonial violence and epidemic disease transformed onetime large, hierarchical, regionally integrated societies to small-scale autonomous communities.[26] Given the reduction of Brazil's Indigenous population to 500,000 by the early 1980s, compared to an estimated five to six million in Greater Amazonia prior to European contact (and perhaps as high as eight to ten million), the Sateré-Mawé may be viewed as survivors of genocide.[27]

Indigenous ways of knowing and producing guaraná, the basis for subsequent Western appropriation and modification, present a necessary starting point for historical inquiry. Key to this chapter's analysis is the locality of all knowledge systems and their social infrastructures, which must be explored without privileging one form of comprehending the natural world over another.[28] An examination of Indigenous processes of collection and dissemination of knowledge of the natural world is also fundamental to rendering more holistic, integrated, and global histories of science.[29] While fine-grained historical reconstruction of Indigenous understandings and uses of guaraná is crimped by the evidentiary rules of an academic discipline that enshrines literacy and its attendant structures of power, we can turn to plant genetics, paleoecology, and archaeobotany; Sateré-Mawé narratives and anthropological "upstreaming"; and colonial-era and nineteenth-century chronicles to provisionally map this section of the itinerary. Detailing the plant's behavioral ecology is first in order.

LIKE THE SATERÉ-MAWÉ ORIGIN STORY, ours begins with a plant and its discovery and transformation by an Indigenous people. Such outsider inquiries have their own distinct lineages. In 1874, for example, Franz Keller-Leuzinger, commissioned by the Brazilian government to study transport conditions on the Madeira River, the largest tributary of the Amazon, pondered the origins of a regional addiction: How had Indigenous peoples discovered guaraná, whose "stimulating effects" turned so "indispensable" to both Native and non-Native? Had a famished hunter tried the unpalatable seeds and discovered that they "strengthened and refreshed him," the German engineer asked, analogizing the reported discovery of coffee berries' hidden pleasures by the legendary Ethiopian goatherd Kaldi.[30] Keller-Leuzinger's attribution of ethnopharmacology to happenstance rather than the careful observation and testing more akin to science is standard fare in Western renditions of Indigenous knowledge production—as if mastery in the manufacture and application of a drug did not require extensive botanical knowledge, technological experimentation, and the memorialization and transmission of know-how.[31] Still, his well-founded curiosity regarding the drug's materialization from Amazonian flora invites a broader reflection on the origins of guaraná's propagation and transformation.[32]

For decades, environmental historians have striven to temper anthropocentric narratives that overlook or minimize the causality of the nonhuman natural realm in understanding the past. Adopting a "plant's-eye view of the world" to sustain a historical drama would be narratively challenging, but stage directions would entail less waiting in the wings (or "vegetating") than immersion and full exposure in the world, or, in the words of one philosopher, "metaphysical mixture."[33] The emerging fields of plant behavioral ecology and multispecies anthropology have posited that plants exhibit perceptual awareness and learned behaviors; are able to acquire, remember, and learn information from their surroundings; and can communicate through and alter underground fungal networks that transfer water and minerals among species. Lacking mobility for defense or reproduction, plants communicate within and between species through displays of shapes and colors and the emission of chemicals to attract pollinators and repel predators.[34]

As a monoecious species, with either pistillate or staminate flowers produced by a given plant on a specific day, guaraná depends on cross-pollination to set fruits. During anthesis, or the flowering period of the plant, which occurs between June and September, guaraná's floral scent serves as a form of chemical communication for nocturnal bees that act as pollinators. Diurnal bees, the main agents of pollination, are attracted by sight and subsequent awareness to the plant's nectar and pollen, as are other opportunistic insects (such as ants, moths, butterflies, and beetles).[35] For its phytochemical architecture, or chemical defense, caffeine distribution in guaraná's organs and tissues protects it from attacks by insects and herbivores. The alkaloid is found in guaraná's leaves, stems, husks, and seeds, with the latter two containing the highest concentration.[36] In contrast, the aril's lack of caffeine, or of theobromine and theophylline, facilitates seed dispersal; in accessing the plant's sugars, large birds such as toucans and guans ingest the seeds without breakage to avoid alkaloid intoxication, dispersing them intact upon expulsion.[37]

Guaraná's biochemistry has also ensured devotion and dissemination by humans. Caffeine, also known as trimethylxanthine, is a chemical that occurs in more than sixty plant species. The xanthine-related plant alkaloids, containing a nitrogen in a closed ring of atoms, produce similar physiological reactions.[38] Xanthines inhibit the enzyme phosphodiesterase, which increases the body's basic energy units—cyclic adenosine monophosphate—with a subsequent release of endogenous epinephrine in the blood. This results in the direct relaxation of the smooth muscles of the lungs' bronchi and pulmonary vessels, leading to stimulation of the central nervous system and induction of urination, coupled with increased digestive tract activity, greater gastric acid secretion, and a weak positive chronotropic and isotropic effect on the heart. Overdose may cause tachycardia, convulsions, restlessness, tremors, nausea, and vomiting, while withdrawal often precipitates punishing symptoms.[39]

Plants rouse people's sensory experiences of taste, touch, smell, sight, and hearing, just as they respond to the human touch.[40] The four most popular addictive substances—coffee, sugar, tobacco, and alcohol—derive from plants whose chemicals have coaxed humans into repurposing their entire planet through colonialism, slavery, warfare, and deforestation.[41] A rather hefty price to satisfy a drag, sweet tooth, or caffeine high. Dating to Middle English, the etymological origins of *ambush* underscore the wooded backdrop of a surprise attack, but it is time to see the plants themselves as the agents of stealth. Contending with fainter sunlight beneath the canopy, and soils limited in water and nutrients, flora in tropical forests vie with their neighbors for access to limited resources.[42] From a "plant's-eye view of the world," certain contestants in the struggle of natural selection have flourished thanks to a human hand, often one feeding a human mouth.[43] Guaraná's history is one such tale of seduction, transformation, and symbiosis, what novelists might call a love story. Its protagonist attracted humans with a figurative eye and bewitching chemistry. Its primeval setting is the tropical forest of the Amazon and the Orinoco, landscapes animated not only by Indigenous peoples' myths but by their conquerors' as well.

FOR MILLENNIA, Amazonian populations have altered the natural habitat through a range of strategies applied to the exploitation of both wild and managed forest food resources.[44] While the extent of pre-Columbian transformation of Amazonian landscapes is debated, plants domesticated by ancestral Native peoples are more likely to be dominant in Amazonian forests, while those forests more proximate to archaeological sites often contain a greater number and array of domesticated species.[45] Anthropologist William Balée coined the term "cultural forests" to denote Indigenous peoples' historical modification of Amazonian landscapes.[46] Although the Amazon contains vast plant and animal resources, cycles of greater abundance of fish in the dry season and of fruit during the wet months led Native populations to concentrate resources by sowing the seeds for food, medicinal, and utilitarian plants in places of greater accessibility.[47] It has been estimated, for example, that the Kayapó moved plants over a territorial area the size of western Europe.[48] In procuring plant resources through foraging, humans began to alter the landscape before systematic cultivation occurred, while creating the necessary opportunities for sedentism and domestication to develop.[49] Human intervention created favorable conditions for plant growth by clearing forest vegetation that competed for light and nutrients through the practice of swidden agriculture, enhancing the nutrient-poor soil with ash. Moreover, on the floodplains adjacent to the main waterways, rich alluvial soil encouraged the germination of commonly used food plants.[50] Anthropogenic concentrations of fruit trees, whether the product of past sedentary or nomadic groups that discarded seeds of edible fruits, resulted in the alteration of alpha diversity.[51]

In the archaeology of the Americas, the Formative period was marked by historical processes in which groups that specialized in hunting and gathering began to depend on foodstuffs that were available or storable for a substantial portion of the annual cycle. Sedentism and consumption of plant foodstuffs were intimately linked through selection of preferred attributes and modification of habitats; the intensification of agricultural production facilitated population growth and more complex social organizations. Manioc's high-starch content, adaptability to low-nutrient acid soils, and longer-term underground storage capacity, for example, were particularly important to sedentarism and population growth. Even in the poorest ecosystems of the Amazon, a mix of fish, manioc, and fruit could support sedentary lifestyles.[52]

Anthropogenic soils (or anthrosols) in the Amazon, known as *terras pretas* or *terras mulatas* in Brazil, are viewed as evidence of pre-Columbian sedentism and agricultural intensification. Amazonian dark earths have been shown to contain large quantities of black carbon deriving from charcoal produced during pre-Columbian settlements, their intra-site concentrations presumably linked to the presence of houses, middens, and other areas of activity associated with old villages. They also contain fragments of microscopic bone, ceramic vessels, and baked clay. The levels of soil enhancement or enrichment suggest in-site burning associated with cooking and smoking, pottery manufacture that mineralized nutrients in plant matter and raised soil pH, and waste management production that produced ash and charcoal, contributing to organic matter retention.[53] Widespread along Amazonian rivers, including the Amazon proper, Madeira, Tapajós, Xingu, Trombetas, and many others, dark soils offer indirect evidence of historically intensive cultivation and dense human settlement.[54] All this suggests that Amazonian soils do not constitute an inherent restriction to the historical emergence of agricultural societies—"a counterfeit paradise" incapable of sustaining dense populations—and that domestication and crop intensification may have relied on the cumulative effects of Indigenous communities on the landscape. It also debunks the myth of pristine nature in the Amazon.[55]

At the time of European conquest, Indigenous peoples of Amazonia had domesticated 138 different plants, 63 of which were fruits. Among these cultivars were cassava, pineapple, cacao, peach palm, and guaraná. Aside from carbohydrate-rich tubers and tree fruits, lowland cultivators depended on fishing and hunting for their main dietary inputs of protein and fat.[56] The complex labor-intensive system of agroforestry that ensued, comprising home gardens, swiddens, and managed fallows, integrated multiple crops into an ecological unit and harvesting of forest products that offered yearlong benefits to the local community.[57] Across time, Native Amazonian agroecological practices have tended to conserve botanical complexity and have been less environmentally destructive than the monocropping characteristic of Western agriculture.[58]

The restorative qualities of guaraná most likely induced the Sateré-Mawé to domesticate the plant. In the wild, the vine can sprout tendrils of up to ten meters in the presence of supporting trees, its prized seeds achingly far from human reach.[59] Sateré-Mawé elders estimate that their ancestors domesticated guaraná some half a millennium earlier, a century so or prior to the arrival of the Portuguese in Brazil in 1500. Historical ecologists and plant geneticists note that the lack of molecular genetic variability observed in the

sorbilis variety among samples collected in three areas of Amazonia, including Maués, and the fact that other Tupi groups in the vicinity do not value
guaraná as much as the Sateré-Mawé, may support this contention.[60] Sateré-
Mawé agriculturists today still collect wild guaraná seedlings from the forest
for cultivation in their fields.[61] Planting the seedling "sons" from the "mother"
vines ensures that the *wará* (knowledge), contained only in the latter, will be
retained in the offspring's seeds, whose consumption will ensure that the
Sateré-Mawé will maintain their heritage as "the children of guaraná."[62]

As Manuela Carneiro da Cunha notes, plant "domestication" by Native
Amazonians did not imply or result in an evolution from foraging to an agriculturalist way of life. In practicing swidden agriculture, marked by itinerant or
shifting cultivation and high forest regeneration through the management of
fallows, lowland Indigenous populations resisted subjection to absolute domestication. The system to cultivate manioc, for example, which required opening
up at least one new field annually and relocating every few years as gardens
ranged too distant from villages, ultimately induced territorial movement. The
alternative of foraging, hunting, and fishing served as a further deterrent to per-
manently settling down—that is, from turning the agricultural domesticator into
the domesticated agriculturalist. The fluidity between agriculture and foraging,
which continues to characterize many lowland Amazonian Indigenous lifestyles,
defies Western evolutionary models of "progress."[63]

SINCE HUMANS RELY ON TECHNOLOGIES of preparation and preservation
for their foods, aside from those eaten raw, the culinary arts transcend the history of agriculture.[64] Native Amazonian domestication of bitter manioc, for
example, would not have sustained their communities without the perfection
of a complex processing technology to detoxify the tuber. The challenge to
ensure guaraná's year-round consumption, defying the patterns of seasonal
fruiting and rapid spoilage by microorganisms, likewise entailed an ambit for
Indigenous scientific experimentation. To avert fermentation, the Sateré-Mawé
pulped the harvested seeds of the cherry-sized fruit and then pounded them
with their feet or large pestles in a small solution of water. The compact paste
was then shaped into round or cylindrical masses of about eight to ten inches
in length and hardened by smoke to expel moisture that might contribute to
spoilage. Smoking typically made use of *murici* wood that imbued the final
product's signature aroma.[65] It is worth noting historical mention of alternative
forms of preparation by other Indigenous peoples. On a voyage up the Orinoco River in Venezuela in 1800, naturalists Alexander von Humboldt and
Aimé Bonpland described the guaraná (locally termed "cupana") beverage of

the Native populations as a saffron-colored fermented drink made with manioc.[66] In Venezuelan territory, the Maku did not toast the seeds of cupana but rather ground them into a mush mixed with cold water.[67]

Sateré-Mawé technologies, harnessed to a labor-intensive process of production, aimed to surmount environmental challenges: well-smoked sticks of guaraná enjoy an extended shelf life between annual harvests, unlike whole seeds or powders prone to mold and deterioration in the Amazonian tropical lowlands.[68] Thus another chapter unfolded in humankind's incessant efforts to expand access to foods across time and space.[69] On an ontological level, as Lévi-Strauss argued, cooking serves to communicate the so-called division between culture and nature through which human societies are said to sustain their organizational categories, since animals display no such arts in the consumption of food.[70] For Terence Turner, Native Amazonian populations have understood culture as neither excluding nor suppressing natural processes but rather retaining and reproducing them through the generative potential of production.[71]

Sateré-Mawé expertise in processing guaraná ensured the product's broader geographic circulation. In the pre-Columbian Amazon, guaraná most likely served as an important good exchanged among Indigenous peoples, as the biological complexity of the tropical forest and the far-flung distribution of species favored extensive trade networks.[72] Ethnographers have noted the presence of seeming Arawak and Carib elements in the material culture and ritual practice of the Sateré-Mawé, suggestive of histories of interethnic exchange.[73] In addition, observers long ago reported that guaraná's commercial success owed to specialty in manufacture rather than the purportedly exclusive soil properties of the lower Amazon's Maués region. As a traveler to Amazonas in 1891 noted: "Not everyone, nevertheless, knows how to duly make guaraná, and those in the know recognize this after preparation."[74] Indeed, the robust trade in guaraná in the Maués region, manufactured by both Indigenous and non-Indigenous populations by the mid-nineteenth century, contrasts sharply with that of the Rio Negro and Orinoco. In his late eighteenth-century travel account, naturalist Alexandre Rodrigues Ferreira noted that the inferior processing of the Rio Negro product, allowing the seeds to mold before arriving at market, was spurned by traders in Belém.[75] And although British botanist Richard Spruce reported in 1852 that the Barré on the Rio Negro, who had migrated from downriver, also manufactured guaraná, it had all but disappeared as a regional commercial crop by the twentieth century, as well as in the Orinoco region, notwithstanding the local plant's larger fruits and seeds.[76]

While the absence of detailed written colonial-era accounts of guaraná cultivation and manufacture preclude deeper historical examination, twentieth-century ethnographers can shed greater light on more recent Sateré-Mawé modes of production and the worldviews they embody and sustain. In her 1992 study, anthropologist Sônia Lorenz noted that Sateré-Mawé men selected seedings between one and four years old from the forests (also referred to as "children of guaraná"), replanting them in groups of two at the beginning of the rainy season in upland soils nearer to their homes, with stalks intersecting to maximize fruit production. Each pair was spaced three meters apart to facilitate harvesting and the eradication of weeds.[77] Ethnologist Manoel Nunes Pereira had observed decades earlier that a shaman officiated at the planting of guaraná and also undertook ceremonies to ensure a favorable harvest.[78]

As fruit production is annual, with the first yields occurring in the fourth year subsequent to planting and more bountiful after the sixth, during the October–December harvest season the Indigenous pick bunches before their husks open.[79] Since guaraná plants exhibit significant lack of uniformity in fruit maturation, a single plant may be harvested ten to twenty times during this period.[80] As Lorenz documented, Sateré-Mawé men and children of both sexes manually remove the seeds, washing and cleaning off their white coating. The seeds are then roasted, preferably in clay ovens, and rotated with shovels or sticks for several hours. Afterward, the roasted seeds (known in Portuguese as *guaraná em rama*) are placed in a bag and beaten and the inner seeds removed for grinding in the mortar, with the slight addition of water. Once the seeds have been pounded into a doughy substance, the *padeiro* (baker) shapes the mass into *pães de guaraná*, as the "loaves," or sticks, are known. The planting, harvesting, grinding, molding, and smoking of guaraná are all exclusively adult male activities. The lone role for Sateré-Mawé women in this stage of processing entails washing the loaves prior to smoking to even the surface for curing. Lorenz posits that the assignment may reflect the symbolic importance of Onhiamuaçabê, the female protagonist in the myth of creation.[81] Placed on a rack over a light flame in the smokehouse to harden, the loaves are inspected daily for two months to avoid the formation of cavities or bubbles (*poca*) that would facilitate mold. The final product, resembling a narrow salami in shape and color, is then ready for consumption or marketing.

The processing (*fábrico*) of guaraná coincides with the rainy season, beginning in October and November and ending in March with completion of the smoking. Aside from the harvesting and the washing of seeds, contemporary production by the Sateré-Mawé is largely household based.[82] Guaraná harvesting and processing enact gendered and age-based divisions, while the beliefs and rituals surrounding the origins and consumption of the beverage reflect patterns of Indigenous thought and practice.[83]

The earliest published eyewitness description of Sateré-Mawé communal consumption of the guaraná beverage, which the Indigenous call *çapó*, dates to 1872. It is a short passage from botanist João Barbosa Rodrigues's report of his travels along the Tapajós River, in which he visited an inland Sateré-Mawé village comprising twelve houses. From daybreak until five in the afternoon, he wrote, a succession of Indigenous women grated guaraná at the center of a large hut. Others sewed nearby, while men swayed in their hammocks smoking *tauari* cigars. When the beverage was prepared, the villagers approached with smaller drinking gourds in their hands. The community members repeated the patterns of consumption throughout the day.[84] Other nineteenth-century chroniclers likewise noted that the Indigenous might consume only guaraná for days, exhibiting robust health.[85] Such reports jibe with colonial-era accounts noting Indigenous peoples' general disinclination to mix food and beverages in their meals.

Twentieth-century documentation of the communal consumption of *çapó* bears many resemblances to Rodrigues's description. Preparation of the drink is undertaken exclusively by females, generally the wife or the young daughter of the chief, or *tuxaua*. Nowadays she is referred to by the Portuguese term *aguadeira* (waterer), due to the processing method: with the loaf immersed repeatedly in a water-filled gourd, the grater scrapes the guaraná with a slab of basalt, forming a viscous substance that she dissolves by submerging her fingers in the liquid.[86] Once prepared, the solution is diluted with water and stored in another gourd.[87] All the implements used—from the bench supporting the grater to the gourd and its support—bear symbolic attributes.[88] For example, the *patawi*, a stand on which the gourd rests during the preparation of the drink, is metaphorically compared to the *tuxaua*, who sustains Sateré-Mawé communities.[89]

As with modes of production, cultural modifications surrounding *çapó* consumption are challenging to track over time. For example, when did the preparer of the beverage gain the Portuguese denomination of *aguadeira*? Indigenous cultural expression is not immutable, and Native Amazonians, particularly Tupi peoples, have viewed the incorporation and adaptation of the Other as a form of cultural regeneration. Still, the presence of non-Western beliefs and practices linked to the beverage, notwithstanding centuries of interethnic contact, suggests deep endogenous roots and continuities.

Nunes Pereira, who visited Sateré-Mawé villages in 1939, noted that the Indigenous viewed guaraná as a talisman that spread joy and encouraged hard work. The *tuxaua* Manuel Francisco da Silva told him that guaraná brought rain, success in war and love, protection from storms, and prospects for good health.[90] Gabriel Alvarez's ethnography (2009) likewise highlighted Sateré-Mawé belief that collective consumption ensured a community's prosperity and happiness. It was also believed to inspire eloquence and truth-telling at communal ceremonies, eliciting words of honor to be upheld and transformed into action.[91] Hence, guaraná lubricates the council meetings of adult men, where the Sateré-Mawé *tuxaua*, seeking to organize work parties (*puxiruns*) for agricultural harvests or construction, must exhibit leadership skills through counsel, conciliation, and generosity.[92] In a society divided by clans, consumption of guaraná has aimed to solidify communal bonds and consensus through "good words" (or *sehay wakuat* in the Sateré-Mawé language).[93]

Drinking of *çapó*, unaccompanied by food, also adhered to a ritualized order, according to these later ethnographic studies. The gourd containing the grated guaraná circulated to all attendees, each taking a sip (ideally an even number of times and passed to the right) and saving the last for the chief. Symbolically, the drink thus became infused with the intent of the drinkers, with the chief, as the final consumer, embodying the motivations of each of the participants. In this capacity, guaraná functions as a persuasive arm or symbolic adhesion, a reconciliation of competing factional interests in a kin-based and largely politically egalitarian society.[94]

In Sateré-Mawé households, the ritual surrounding the preparation and consumption of *çapó* resembles that of council meetings.[95] According to twentieth-century ethnographic accounts, the female head would hand the *çapó* to her husband, who would take a small sip and pass the beverage to others, giving priority to elders and esteemed visitors, typically in a straight line rather than a circle, each drinking from the same gourd. These might include relatives or friends from other locales or villages on hand to help with collective labor.[96] No one would refuse the drink, nor down the remainder before resupplying the host, for only he could end the session, either by taking the final sip or ceding that role to a family member with the exhortation of "*wai'pó*" or "*olha o rabo*" (watch the tail). As the beverage would circulate, the grater continued to rasp the guaraná mass, dissolving the powder in water upon the gourd's return for redistribution in another of several rounds.[97] In domestic settings, where the Indigenous consumed guaraná collectively several times a day, *çapó* might be paired with tobacco smoking in the form of a large cigar rolled in tree bark known as *tauari* (similar to Rodrigues's description) and used to channel intent for specific objectives; the practice, known as "blowing guaraná" (*soprar o guaraná*), might be used to ensure, say, the success of a son or son-in-law on a hunt. The Sateré-Mawé also employed the plant's flower, bark, and roots to prepare other beverages, but these carry less value and symbolic importance than the *çapó*.[98]

Guaraná has featured prominently as well in Sateré-Mawé dietary prescriptions and rites of passage, although the absence of written documentation bedevils recovery of pre-Columbian understandings of health and disease, including valuation of guaraná's therapeutic properties. In the early nineteenth century, Karl von Martius reported that expectant Sateré-Mawé parents limited their diets to guaraná, mushrooms, and ants. The Bavarian naturalist noted as well the consumption of guaraná during the monthlong fast following the death of the *tuxaua*.[99] Anthropological studies conducted in the 1920s and 1930s by Curt Nimuendajú and Nunes Pereira, respectively, noted that expectant parents continued to follow the aforementioned diet, as well as cutting their arms and legs with a rodent's tooth or a toucan's bill and rubbing the ashes of the genipap fruit into the wounds. To facilitate childbirth, the woman's hips were bathed beforehand in the ashes of paca skulls or bird eggshells mixed with water. Afterward, the mother adhered to a postpartum rest period of a month, while the father restricted his diet to porridge (*mingau*) and guaraná.[100] Nunes Pereira also reported that the Sateré-Mawé mocked *civilizados'* belief in guaraná's aphrodisiac qualities; the Indigenous had more faith in the sting of the taoca ant—whose effects lasted twenty-four hours—for enhanced sexual performance.[101] In the 1980s, anthropologist Anthony Henman asserted that the Sateré-Mawé continued to practice diet modification for many reasons —disease, menstruation, pregnancy, childbirth, death, preparation before hunting—with the ideal of a "light body" achieved through dietary restrictions and an increase in stimulant consumption.[102] The beverage is also consumed during the *waymat*, a traditional communal masculine rite of passage in which young men's hands are repeatedly stung by dozens of venomous bullet ants (*tocandiras*) to test their courage as future warriors and providers.[103]

Guaraná commands a hallowed place in Sateré-Mawé oral collective traditions, or *sehaypot'l*, in which narrators and guardians of cosmological knowledge create sacred bonds with members of the community through formally structured narratives that include obligatory silences, contemplation of common values, and respectful assent.[104] The story of the origin of guaraná is also engraved on one side of the *porantim*, a one-and-a-half-meters-high piece of wood resembling an oar or a war club (the other side features the myth of war). Carved on the larger side with rhombs, points, and bands in bas relief painted in white, the *porantim* is referred to by the Sateré-Mawé as their constitution or bible (a "*patente*," or document) rather than a physical weapon, upholding political and religious functions. In times past, the chief would read the *porantim*'s text to settle a dispute or to summon a communal work party (aided by the consumption of *çapó*), but knowledge to recite the text has been lost more recently.[105] Thus, beyond its importance as a comestible, guaraná assumed for the Sateré-Mawé a metaphysical significance, an affective mechanism for suturing communal life, a distinctive way of being.[106]

AN ANALYSIS OF GUARANÁ'S ORIGINS, as recounted in ethnographic accounts subsequent to Silva Coutinho's nineteenth-century report, yields further insights into Indigenous cosmologies and histories. According to the story recorded by Nunes Pereira in 1939, the young boy whose eyeballs would give rise to the plant was murdered by his uncles. The boy's mother, Onhiamuaçabê, had lived unmarried with her two brothers, Ocumáato and Icuaman, in the enchanted land of Noçoquem, where she had planted a Brazil nut tree. Reliant on Onhiamuaçabê's knowledge of plants and their remedies, her older brothers feared she might abandon them to live with a snake that had impregnated her. Following the birth of her son, Onhiamuaçabê was expelled by her brothers, but as soon as the boy could speak, he wished to eat the Brazil nuts planted by his mother. Upon his return to Noçoquem, the animal guardians of the tree—the agouti, the macaw, and the parakeet—informed his uncles, who ordered them to kill him. As the boy descended the Brazil nut tree, they decapitated him with a cord. Hearing her son's cry, Onhiamuaçabê proclaimed: "It was your uncles that ordered that you be killed. They thought you'd be a poor little thing (*um coitadinho*) but you will not be." Resolutely, she first buried her son's left eye, but the plant that germinated was poor, or "false guaraná." The right eye, however, grew into "true guaraná." Presaging the boy's return, she exulted: "You, my son, will be the greatest force of Nature; you will do good for all men; you will be great; you will free men from some sicknesses and cure them of others." Then she gathered his other body parts, smeared them with "a magic plant" that she had chewed and lubricated with her saliva, and buried her son. Soon a guaraná plant began to grow and flourish. Subsequently, she opened the grave and a child, the first Sateré-Mawé ancestor, emerged; it was Onhiamuaçabê's son, who had been resurrected.[107]

The story of guaraná's transformation from a human eyeball encapsulates a common belief along Native Amazonian peoples in the transmutability of beings and the interchangeability among living things during primordial times. As Fernando Santos-Granero notes, "The notion that in mythical times, all things were human—or appeared to each other as human—constitutes one of the most widespread Native Amazonian mythemes. In times of indifferentiation, the predecessors of all living beings—humans, animals, plants, and spirits, but also a variety of objects—shared the primordial mythscape with powerful creator gods, cultural heroes, or mischievous tricksters. This idyllic existence, Native Amazonians say, came to an end due to the fallibility of the ancient people, at which point emerged the different categories of beings that populate the world nowadays." Santos-Granero notes that according to Native peoples, this emergence was not a straightforward process. It involved "multiple metamorphoses, by which primordial people passed through different modalities of existence before acquiring their (more or less) definite form. It entailed processes of bodily deconstitution and reconstitution marked by extreme forms of interspecific permutation of body parts, including artifacts that were formerly body parts and body parts that were formerly artifacts." In other words, the coming into being of the present-day world was "the product of the transformation of existing things."[108] According to the Sateré-Mawé myth, the eyeballs of the primordial being brought forth the guaraná shrub, while his body parts gave rise to the koata monkeys and the peccaries, as well as the first human couple.[109] Or as the myth of origin of animals recorded by Nunes Pereira in 1939 opens: "In the beginning of the world all of the animals were people like the [Sateré] Maués."[110] In sum, as anthropologists Carlos Fausto and Michael Heckenberger argue, Indigenous history in Amazonia is more accurately conceived of as the outcome of socioeconomic interactions between different types of persons, human and nonhuman, that reaffirm the process of transformation. The making of historical agents depends on "the fabrication of people's agential capacities through involvement in shamanic and ritual practices."[111]

Guaraná's tale of origin also encapsulates the hierarchies (older brothers) and organizational axes of conflict between affines (nephews and maternal uncles) in Sateré-Mawé society. A patrilineal, patrilocal society, the Sateré-Mawé social structure is divided into *ywãnia*, which can be understood as clans, oriented by exogamous marriages. Clan names reflect Native belief in their descent from animals and plants: Sateré (fiery caterpillar), Waraná (guaraná), Akuri (agouti), Awkuy (howler monkey), Nhap (wasp), As'ho (armadillo), Ywaçai (açai), Iaguaretê (jaguar), Moi (snake), Hwi (hawk), Piriwato (large rat), Akyi (bat), Uruba (vulture), Nhampo (forest bird). As noted, the term *Mawé* means intelligent parrot.[112] According to Sateré-Mawé myth, clans originated with the appearance of a jaguar-monster that threat-ened to destroy primordial mankind. An elderly woman managed to slay the beast, bestowing the names of animals and plants on survivors, which gave rise to the exogamous groupings. Although the perils of primeval times had been overcome, the clans soon descended into internecine conflict.[113] Women play an important part in transforming relationships of opposition into alli-ance, a role indexed in the origin tale by Onhiamuaçabê.[114]

Anthropologist Terence Turner has argued against viewing Indigenous South American myths as merely a passive device for classifying historical "events" but as "a program for orienting social, political, ritual, and other forms of historical action."[115] Like other forms of history, myths are simulta-neously discourses of identity, attributing meaning in the past to a structured present and wielding potent symbols for political mobilization.[116] They are also not incompatible with more "dynamic" or "objectivist" means of under-standing processes of change, as both forms of historical consciousness can occur simultaneously and complementarily in the same society or narra-tive.[117] Nor are Indigenous myths necessarily devoid of relevant scientific content. As plant geneticists noted in 2010, the *sorbilis* variety of guaraná cul-tivated by the Sateré-Mawé is a high-level polyploid, with 210 chromosomes rather than the standard 24 for the genus. It differs from the other guaraná varieties that grow wild in the Sateré-Mawé territory, with the former readily distinguishable morphologically by its larger fruit and seeds and its brightly colored fruit case.[118] This discovery led molecular biologists to believe that the Indigenous peoples who first domesticated guaraná may have encour-aged the cultivation of a plant with a significant number of chromosomes.[119] In other words, the ancestral woman of Sateré-Mawé myth recognized that a special type of guaraná had become available to her, as distinct from the more common and less useful "false guaraná," and planted it for the benefit of future generations. Through domestication a new species emerged, charac-terized by interspecific hybridization followed by chromosome doubling and resulting in the formation of allopolyploids, or what the Indigenous refer to as the "true guaraná."[120] In this sense, the Sateré-Mawé origin story of guar-aná resembles what Darwin described in *On the Origin of Species* as the pro-cess whereby plants in the wild offer new qualities that human actions then allow to survive and prosper.[121]

It would be reductive, however, to subject Sateré-Mawé understandings of guaraná, and Indigenous knowledge systems more broadly, to Western scien-tific standards. The distinction between science and other knowledge sys-tems purportedly characteristic of modern Western culture is alien to many traditional societies, which evince a mixture of what the former might consider rational, empirically based knowledge and mystical beliefs.[122] Lowland Indigenous peoples have viewed the forest cultivated by spirits, animals, "mothers," and even other plants as a landscape organized and shared by other sentient beings, with rules and restrictions on use by humans.[123] As cultural expressions of ways of encountering the natural world, with implications of how humans might interact with particular environments, traditional knowledge systems are critical to the preservation of ethnic and biological diversity.[124] Sateré-Mawé understandings of guaraná reflect such distinct structures of seeing and being in the world.

UNDER LUSO-BRAZILIAN DOMINATION, guaraná would also allow for new forms of cross-cultural exchange. In the Tapajós-Madeira region, Amerindian spatial and political activities had shaped regional patterns of pre-Columbian trade and warfare that would articulate with new agents of Portuguese colonialism in the Amazon, whose fulcrum of power lay in Belém.[125] Amid colonial encounters in which power was wielded by the sword and the pen, guaraná's circulation was contoured by violence, coercion, (mis)communication, and adaptation. As the battle for bodies and souls raged in the Amazon, Portuguese colonial authorities situated guaraná in alternative networks of knowledge and commercial exchange, ampler in geographic scope and institutional power. This was a global empire, where the trade in goods and knowledge anchored a vast colonial enterprise across far-flung territories.

On the colonial and nineteenth-century Amazon frontier, a "middle ground" where Native peoples and Luso-Brazilians traded and raided, guaraná cemented new relationships and hierarchies, offering prospects for transformation to Indigenous and non-Indigenous alike.[126] In these points of intersection, meanings were fractured by extant cultural frameworks.[127] The historical formation of Brazilian society owes to such interethnic exchanges and the boundaries and tensions they never erased.

CHAPTER TWO

Colonial Missions
Remaking Plants and People

The New World's luxuriant flora evinced for early Portuguese chroniclers divine providence and untold wealth—foundational myths of Brazilian society.[1] Planter Gabriel Soares de Souza's *Tratado descritivo do Brasil* (1587), for example, spotlighted Indigenous medicinal plants, such as passion fruit, pineapple, copaiba, jaborandi, and ipecacuanha.[2] A century later, Jesuit Simão de Vasconcelos boasted of Brazil's "treasure of medicinal virtues that God placed in this part of the world."[3] Although overshadowed initially by Portuguese interest in Asian maritime trade, Brazilian botany would animate colonial imaginaries of Edenic realms.[4] This fascination with botanical richness persists: present-day scientists cite Brazil as one of seventeen countries that constitute 70 percent of the earth's biodiversity.[5] Condemnations of Indigenous peoples' purported degeneracy and the insalubriousness of the tropics also stretch back to colonial European chroniclers.[6] Reconstructing the historical contexts of guaraná's early cross-cultural circulation can reveal conflicts and exchanges that shaped social hierarchies and the transmission of knowledge in Amazonian society under Luso-Brazilian rule.

Guaraná's first known non-Indigenous author was a Jesuit, the religious order preeminent in Amazonian affairs from the seventeenth to the mid-eighteenth century. "The Andirazes have among their bushes a small fruit they call guaraná, which they dry then step on, afterwards out of which they make balls that they value the way the whites value their gold and scraped with a small stone that they rub in a gourd of drinking water," wrote Father João Felipe Bettendorff, a septuagenarian who served as the head of the Colégio de Santo Antônio in São Luis, Maranhão, where the colony's elite young men were educated. "It gives so much strength that when the Indians go to hunt, from one day to another, they are not hungry. Aside from making one urinate, it takes away fever and headaches and cramps. Of its use in urinating, I am sure; of the others, I am not certain, only of what is commonly said."[7] The short passage, written between 1694 and 1698 in *Crônica da missão dos padres da companhia de Jesus no Estado do Maranhão* (and only published in 1910), presents the earliest European description of guaraná, its mode of consumption, and its reputed pharmacological properties. Bettendorff had become acquainted with the substance on a 1669 visit to a mission on Tu-pinambarana Island, which congregated several Indigenous groups, including the Sateré-Mawé, in the strategic interfluvial location framed by the Amazonas, Madeira, and Tapajós Rivers. Colonial sources seemingly identified the Sateré-Mawé by various names: Mabué, Mangués, Magueses, Jaquezes, and Maraguá. Given that the Sateré-Mawé traditionally dwelled along the Andirá River, ethnographer Nunes Pereira contends that the term "Andirazes" likely refers to the group as well. At the time of his fieldwork in 1939, Sateré-Mawé still lived near the Andirá and rasped guaraná with a palm-sized stone they called *ué-y*, unlike the "*civilizados*," who used the bristled hyoid bone of the sturgeon-like pirarucu fish to prepare the beverage.[8]

During Bettendorff's thirty-seven years in northern Brazil, his under-staffed mission confronted Indigenous resistance, settler revolt, and a small-pox epidemic.[9] Amid ubiquitous conflict in the Amazon—between Europeans and the Indigenous, settlers and missionaries, humans and nature, and God and the devil—Bettendorff undoubtedly took solace in divine grace and Jesuit rectitude.[10] He also comprehended Native peoples' indispensability to the knowledge and extraction of forest resources, agricultural production, river-ine transport, civil construction, military defense, and domestic service in the region—in other words, the success of European colonization. And he knew well the importance of the healing arts for the propagation of the gospel. He also wrote at a time when Portuguese authorities, stung by territorial losses in Asia to the Dutch, looked to the botanical bounty of the region, then called the Estado do Maranhão e Grão-Pará, as a surrogate.[11]

Colonial missionary accounts were calls to faith and action. Bettendorff's showcasing of ethnographic and botanical knowledge, along with clerical martyrdom and masculine risk-taking, angled to enlist royal support and novitiates for the Amazon mission of the Society of Jesus.[12] In affirming Jesuit awareness of guaraná's uses, the chronicle aspired to convey tropical abundance and command over fugitive landscapes and communities. Medicinal plants, wonders of God's creation, also offered "new" drugs for the Jesuits' global pharmacological inventory and fonts of revenue, healing, and hope where none were assured nor undisputed.[13] Medicine in colonial Brazil was a contested field among professional doctors, folk healers, religious leaders, family members, and patients.[14]

Bettendorff's writings, in sum, signaled guaraná's insertion into Western networks of knowledge and power that emerged with the centralization of European states and expansion of empires, the spread of Christianity, and the globalization of science. As an expansionary religion, Christianity integrated

and sought to control vast bodies of knowledge that linked the natural and social worlds, with networks of transmission transcending state borders and continents. Due to its associations with economic transformation and social
control, science garnered the support of influential patrons, expanding in its
own networks of communication and institutions across Europe and its colonies. Modern science, born out of the social and epistemic evolutions bred by
the expansion of states and religion and self-organizing networks of professionals operating within differential institutional scales and hubs, reinforced the
conditions for the growth and circulation of knowledge.[15] It drew on Indigenous knowledge of the natural world, which expanded European understandings of botanical history and medicine beyond biblical notions of the natural
world or pharmaceutical practices rooted in the classical texts of Dioscorides
and Galen, the Islamic tradition, and Persian and Indian medical expertise.[16]

European chronicles provide less of a window into Brazil's Indigenous past
than a screen. Like the broader Western historical archive, they brim with
bluster and bias, both willful and inadvertent, and gaping silences.[17] Although Bettendorff referenced guaraná's Indigenous denomination, for example, he omitted discussion of traditional cosmological meanings.[18] He
obscured Native understandings of sickness and health through a passive
voice, attributing guaraná's reputed therapeutic properties to "what is commonly said" and the personal avowal of its diuretic qualities. And his moral
judgments of the Indigenous abound elsewhere in his writings: "Few are in-
terested in doctrine and holy things, negligent with respect to God and salvation, stupid, imbeciles, brutes, and almost with an innate tendency for inertia
and immorality."[19] But Bettendorff's account—and colonial-era historiography more broadly—also indicates the entanglement of Indigenous lifeways
and landscapes in the broader Atlantic world owing to violence, commercial
exchange, and Native peoples' strategic initiatives.[20] In tracking Sateré-Mawé
engagement with Luso-Brazilian society during the Jesuit's lifetime and the
century-and-a-half following his death, this chapter also shines light on the historical processes by which an autonomous Amazonian people came to
be reconfigured as "Indians," and their hallowed plant, a "backland drug." Mapping guaraná's colonial and early nineteenth-century trajectory reveals historically intertwined networks of trade, knowledge, and power in the Amazon.

BORN TO A WEALTHY FAMILY in Luxembourg in 1625, Johannes Philippus
Bettendorff was educated in philosophy at the University of Cuneo, civil law
at the University of Trier, and theology in France.[21] In 1659, shortly after his
ordination, he was posted by the Jesuit superior general to the Portuguese

Amazon in response to the appeal for backups by Antonio Vieira, the superior of the Jesuit mission in the Estado do Maranhão e Grão-Pará. Native conversion officially legitimized Portuguese colonization of the New World, and missionaries also ministered to the spiritual care and education of the colonists.[22] Bettendorff made his way to Lisbon to learn Portuguese and to study the Tupi language through a grammar book compiled by Jesuit Luis Figueira. In November 1660, he set sail for São Luís, arriving in January of the following year.[23]

As a frontier bordering Spanish, French, and Dutch possessions and threatened by British interlopers, the Amazon region represented a vulnerable flank of Lisbon's New World colony. The crown's establishment of the Estado do Maranhão e Grão-Pará in 1621 as an independent administrative unit reflected the difficulties of intracolonial communication and trade with eastern Brazil due to wind and ocean currents. Forest products, dispersed over vast, undefended territories, formed the basis of the region's economy.[24] Absent Indigenous labor, European ambitions in the Amazon would collapse. As the Overseas Council stated to the Portuguese king in 1645: "It is impossible to cultivate and fructify the lands of these captaincies without Indians."[25] As such, the regimentation of Indigenous laborers, both free and enslaved, became highly contentious among colonial authorities, missionaries, settlers, and Native peoples themselves. Aside from brief intervals in the seventeenth century, Indigenous enslavement remained legal in Portuguese America, predicated on the notion of a "just war" or a ransoming (*resgate*) of captives held by rival tribes.[26] For peaceful relations, the Portuguese relied on military alliance, gift giving, and negotiation, while Native peoples sought to carve out spaces of relative autonomy.[27]

For the Jesuits, Indigenous practices such as cannibalism, polygyny, and ceremonial intoxication implicated in wars of revenge revealed the devil's work.[28] Yet in the missionaries' eyes, such depravity stemmed from the historic deprivation of divine grace.[29] Redemption loomed through the church, requiring missionaries' unflagging vigilance in the face of Indigenous inconstancy and backsliding.[30] The intended transformation was more than spiritual, as missionaries aspired broadly to Europeanize Native peoples. Nomadism should give way to settlement, foraging to agriculture, itinerancy to regimented labor, dispersal to concentration, shamanistic practices to Christian healing, and varied kinship patterns to monogamous patriarchal families.[31] In a gradualist approach to conversion, certain Indigenous customs might be respected in order to earn trust.[32]

Missionaries offered moralistic justifications for their oversight of Indigenous affairs—a dominion bitterly resented by colonists and erratically mediated by the crown.[33] Since arriving in 1653 in São Luís as superior of the Jesuit mission, Antonio Vieira denounced Indigenous enslavement as anathema to the Portuguese Catholic mandate to spearhead universal conversion of the heathens.[34] The Jesuits' moral outrage dovetailed with the logistic challenges of indoctrinating Indigenous villagers brutalized by slaving raids and long-term labor drafts. Vieira successfully lobbied to outlaw Indigenous enslavement in 1652, amended the following year, due to settler opposition, to authorize Jesuit oversight of the process. In 1655, the crown further granted the Jesuits control over the spiritual and temporal administration of the Indigenous, including primacy over other religious orders.[35] Over the next six years, Vieira attempted religious conversion by "descending" Indigenous peoples to mission villages in the vicinity of Belém and São Luis as well as founding upriver missions.[36] As he would later crow: "And these today are the beasts that, instead of taking our lives, welcome and venerate us as did the lions to Daniel."[37] Violent, lazy, superstitious, undisciplined, and puerile: Indigenous peoples received a characterological verdict from colonial agents that history has never fully commuted.[38]

A Daniel for the lions' den: such was Bettendorff's casting call. First came missionary service near Belém, ministering to local residents and learning *língua geral* for communication with the Indigenous population. As the first permanent missionary for the region extending from Gurupá westward, Bettendorff founded in June 1661 a mission at the mouth of the Tapajós, today the city of Santarém. In the multiethnic Tapajós-Madeira region, dominated by the Tupinambá, Tapajó, and Iruri, relations among Indigenous peoples were marked by warfare and enslavement, cultural and commercial exchange, and geographic mobility. The incursion of the Jesuits and whites into the lower Tapajós, fanning out over the next decades to the lower Madeira and regional tributaries, served to transform the area. With the Tupinambá and Tapajó extinguished as ethnically distinct peoples, groups such as the Sateré-Mawé, Mundurucu, and Parintintin strove for self-determination through warfare, relocation, and strategic engagement with whites.[39] A 1691 map by Bohemian Jesuit Samuel Fritz, sent by the Spanish Crown downriver to expand missions toward the Rio Negro, placed the Mabués and Maraguaz (which historians presume are references to the Sateré-Mawé) on the western bank of the lower Tapajós, once a stronghold of the homonymous Indigenous nation.[40]

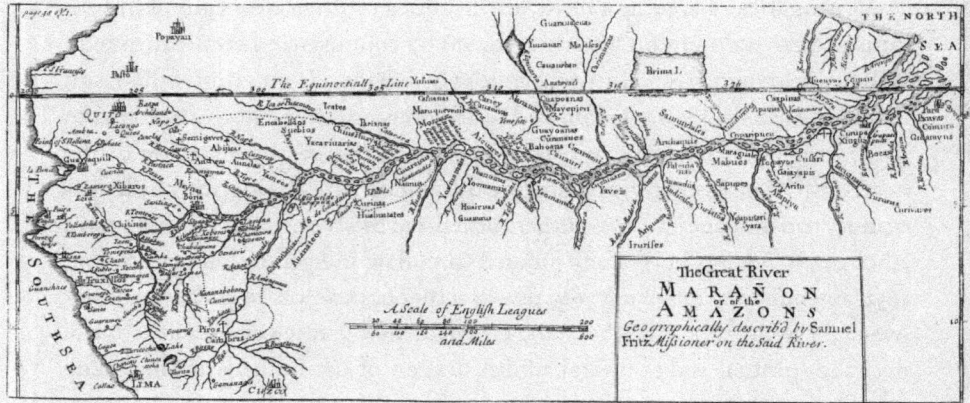

The Great River Marañon or of the Amazons Geographically Describ'd by Samuel Fritz, Missioner on the Said River, 1711–12. Bohemian Jesuit Samuel Fritz, dispatched to the Amazon by the Spanish Crown in 1686 to contain Portuguese advances beyond the Rio Negro, most likely drew up the original map in 1692–93 after navigating the Amazon River in its entirety. In the territorial disputes between the Iberian empires as well as among religious missions, physical occupation through the submission of Indigenous populations was key to sovereignty claims. Herman Moll, *Atlas Geographus: or, A Compleat System of Geography, Ancient and Modern*, Vol. 5 (London: J. Nutt, 1711–12). Map 2550, Maps Collection, The Latin American Library at Tulane University. Courtesy of The Latin American Library, Tulane University.

As Jesuit influence spread in the Tapajós region over ensuing decades, contact with the Sateré-Mawé expanded. Mission villages (*aldeias*) represented sites of convergence and conflict between European and Indigenous ways. Whereas missionaries aimed to reorient Indigenous trade networks, labor systems, and kin relations to the benefit of the church and the crown, Native regional systems sought to preclude or temper outsiders' incursions.[41] Permanent resettlement often proved elusive in light of Indigenous peoples' subsistence strategies, kin networks, heavy-handed treatment, and exposure to epidemic disease.[42] Bettendorff noted, for example, that a mission set up in 1696 among the Maraguazes was far from ideal, since "the land, water, and air in that area were not good." While he boasted that "in the surroundings there are various nations that can only be reduced to Our Faith, becoming domesticated little by little," the location presumably boded ill for long-term settlement.[43]

Missionary control of Indigenous labor also rankled colonists. As Bettendorff sneered, the settlers "wish to live the law of the nobility and be waited upon in Pará, when most of them in their homelands served others, and even

less so themselves."[44] Shortly after founding the Santarém mission, Bettendorff and his peers came under settler attack. In May 1661, during the Feast of
the Holy Ghost, residents of São Luís arrested the local Jesuits and those in
nearby missions; a month later, Belém's townspeople followed suit, demand-
ing the missionaries' expulsion from the colony.[45] In September 1661, Vieira
and his brothers from São Luis were deported to Portugal. After weeks spent
hiding in the forest, Bettendorff and Brother Gaspar Misch sought refuge at
the Gurupá fort but were seized by a delegation from Belém's town council
and likewise banished. Bettendorff's ship took on water and was allowed to
return to Belém, where he suffered house arrest for three months until his
release.[46] Bowing to colonist pressure, a royal law of 1663 repealed Jesuits'
temporal administration of the Native population as well as their spiritual
monopoly.[47] The exiles were permitted to return to Brazil, with the exception
of Vieira.

In September 1668, Bettendorff became the director (superior) of the mission of Maranhão. In this capacity, he undertook an official visit to the
mission villages of Pará, reaching the westernmost tip at the island of Tu-
pinambarana near the mouth of the Madeira River in September 1669. It was
here where he encountered guaraná, according to his late seventeenth-
century *Crônica*. In the intervening three decades, Bettendorff had witnessed
the fluctuations in royal policies toward Native Amazonians. Following the
1680 passage of two laws inspired by Vieira—which abolished Indigenous
slavery, invested Jesuits with sole authority of regrouping Native peoples into
aldeias, and allocated exclusive rights to the importation of enslaved Africans
to a Portuguese commercial firm—the residents of São Luís once more re-
volted. In 1684, rebels led by Manuel Beckman held twenty-seven Jesuits
under house arrest before herding them onto two ships bound for Portugal.
European pirates attacked one vessel near Ceará, torturing the priests and
setting them adrift in a flimsy canoe. Exiled on the other ship, Bettendorff
eventually made his way to Portugal to plead the Jesuits' case before the
crown.[48]

In 1686, Pedro II promulgated the Regimento das Missões, legislation that
restored temporal jurisdiction over Indigenous villages to the Jesuits, but in a
concession to the settlers, a subsequent law legitimized Native enslavement
through just wars or ransom (overseen by Jesuits). In 1692, the governor of
Maranhão, Antonio de Albuquerque Coelho de Carvalho, declared a just war
on the Sateré-Mawé and other Indigenous groups in light of the "audacity of
the jungle Indians, who lacked due respect for the whites who passed through

their lands without attacking them."[49] In line with his conciliatory policy toward the settlers, Bettendorff acceded, loath to "cause great hatred to the Company [of Jesus]." When canoes with one hundred whites and two hundred Indigenous left Belém "with great applause" to undertake the offensive, Bettendorff dispatched Padre Miguel do Aragão to assist with the sacraments to the Natives. The colonists enslaved several Sateré-Mawé and treated others as freedpersons (*forros*) under the condition that they serve white employers for five years and be moved downriver lest they remain in their territories as "sworn enemies of the Portuguese." Bettendorff noted that Captain Major Hilario de Souza, governor of Pará, had made excellent returns on his investment of 16,000 cruzados in the operation.[50]

During Bettendorff's tenure in the Amazon, Sateré-Mawé communities confronted enslavement, missionizing, commercial exchange, and disease. In this context of violence and negotiation, the Sateré-Mawé trade in guaraná extended beyond pre-Columbian circuits. In referencing guaraná, Bettendorff's chronicle sought to project Jesuit authority over Amazonian landscapes and populations. While Pedro II's decree earlier that decade restricted Jesuit jurisdiction to the southern bank of the Amazon River and its interior and allotted missions to the north—as well as newer missions on the Madeira and Negro Rivers—to the Franciscans, Mercedarians, and Carmelites, the Society of Jesus preserved twenty-eight missions, those more integrated into the economic life of the colony.[51] By 1714, the Jesuits ministered extensively to communities on the Maués River, a likely epicenter of the Indigenous group.[52] By 1730, the mission on the Andirá River reportedly had a multiethnic population of 495, of whom a majority appear to have been Sateré-Mawé.[53]

BETTENDORFF'S ACCOUNT OF GUARANÁ REFLECTS Portugal's preeminence in the early modern commercialization of tropical medicinal plants, a global exchange in which the Jesuits played a key role. As historian Timothy Walker notes, Portugal's colonial empire in South America, Africa, and Asia allowed for a vast appropriation and dissemination of botanical drugs and knowledge.[54] Under a royal edict during Portugal's union with Spain (1580–1640), for example, the Hapsburg monarchy selected emissaries to investigate the Native use of medicine. "Recognizing how this and other kingdoms will benefit from the news, communications and commerce of some plant [*sic*], herb, seeds and other medicinal things that may lead to the cure and health of human bodies," the crown "decided to sometimes send one or many protophysicians to the provinces of the Indies and the adjacencies."[55] Botanicals shipped from Brazil included cacao and cocoa butter (for skin ailments), ipecacuanha (an emetic), cinchona bark or quina (to treat malaria), jalapa (a purgative), copaiba (for gonorrhea), and sarsaparilla (for syphilis and skin disease).[56] Fruits such as cashews, guava, pineapple, and pitanga (Surinam cherry) were transplanted across the Portuguese empire, just as mango, star fruit, and jackfruit came from India to South America.[57]

Through the distribution of materia medica and medical texts, Portuguese colonial therapeutics spread across early modern Europe.[58] Scientific observations circulated in manuscript form, unintended for medical authorities outside the Lusophone world or for the general public, symptomatic of Portugal's efforts to sequester knowledge of its Brazilian and overseas territories.[59] A recent study has found, for example, that guaraná was one of 129 native Brazilian species (belonging to 36 taxonomic families) with putative effects on the central nervous system mentioned in historical sources from the sixteenth to the nineteenth century.[60] The contributions of Lusophone medical investigation and practice, whose intercontinental networks preceded and exceeded Portugal's European rivals during the early modern period, is a vital chapter in Western medical history.[61] The Portuguese colonial drug trade was also indissociable from hierarchies of knowledge and power; in a competitive therapeutic market, missionaries and medical doctors aimed to sever Indigenous healing arts from their cosmologies, or in clerical derogation, from "witchcraft" and "superstition."[62]

Alongside the Santa Casa de Misericórdia—a global Portuguese charitable religious institution—the Jesuits pioneered the early exchange of medicinal plants and knowledge between the New and Old Worlds through their networks of medical facilities.[63] In colonial Brazil, the Society of Jesus took a deep interest in gathering and prescribing simples for the care of Indigenous peoples, settler populations, and military garrisons, and for export to Portugal and its overseas territories. In conjunction with the cult of the saints, medical treatment promised healing for the sick; ecclesiastics in the colonies, as in Europe, combined therapeutic and spiritual care. Although the latter was paramount, the body demanded succor as the repository of the soul, while illness could be seen as punishment for sin. As a tool of overseas evangelism, the healing arts were included in the Jesuits' training before they departed Europe.[64]

By the mid-eighteenth century, the Jesuits had established over thirty apothecaries in Brazil. Adjoining their architecturally imposing colleges, the apothecaries dispensed drugs for profit to support the order's evangelization. Stocked with native and Old World simples (the latter predominant), theirs were often the only ones in cities or villages.[65] The eighteenth-century inventory of the

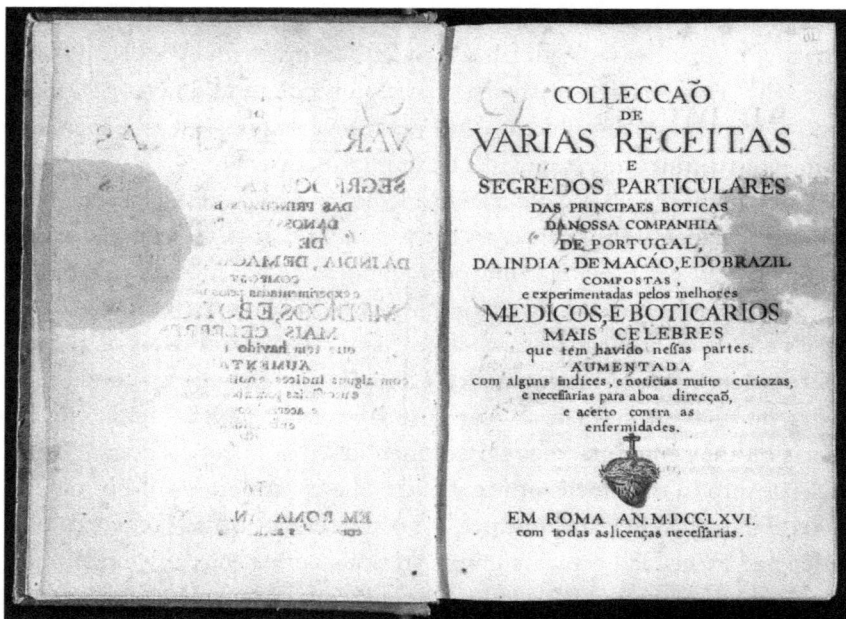

Collecçaõ de varias receitas e segredos particulares das principaes botanicas da nossa companhia de Portugal, da Índia, de Macáo, e do Brazil (Collection of various recipes and private secrets of the main botanicals of our company in Portugal, India, Macao, and Brazil). Jesuit remedy book compiled from Lusophone world, Rome, 1766. The collection of remedies, "composed and tested by the best doctors and most celebrated apothecaries" from the Society of Jesus in Portugal, India, Macau, and Brazil, reflects the importance of the Portuguese Empire and the Jesuit order in the early modern global exchange of botanical and medical knowledge. Manuscript Opp. NN. 17. ©Archivum Romanum Societatis Iesu.

apothecary (*botica*) of the Colégio of Maranhão, for example, included furnaces, stills, and instruments to produce drugs according to the Galenic method.[66] In 1760, the shelves of the apothecary of the Colégio of Pará, inferior to that of Bahia and Rio, stocked more than four hundred drugs and twenty medical tomes, as well as flasks, pots, basins, mortars, weights, scales, and stills.[67] Professional and domestic medicine at the time principally utilized leaves, roots, seeds, and bark, which were ground, macerated, or infused.[68]

Through missionaries, health practitioners, and traders, Brazilian botanicals circulated in the colony's backlands in travelers' trusty wooden medicine chests and by ship to Portuguese dominions spanning four continents.[69] Historian Vera Regina Beltrão Marques found numerous plants of Brazilian origin in a review of eighteenth-century pharmacopoeia in Portugal, although licensed physicians and folk healers preferred familiar European remedies.[70] In his unpublished "História pharmaceutica das plantas exóticas," written in Portugal in 1777, Benedictine monk-pharmacist João de Jesus Maria described guaraná as a dark red, aromatic "composition" of varied shapes made by the "tame Gentiles of Pará," which he indicated for gastrointestinal headaches, hemorrhagic diarrhea, urinary incontinence, and fevers from "the heat of the sun."[71] In Brazil, native botanicals permeated the colony's official and vernacular medical culture, offered up in apothecaries, barbershops, bakeries, and goldsmiths' workshops.[72]

In adopting Native American flora, official European medicine typically recast Indigenous beliefs and therapeutic practices through the lens of classical knowledge and Christian cosmology.[73] Portuguese doctors held that disease resulted from a lack or an overabundance of one or more bodily humors, with their cures centered on restoring deficit or suppressing excess. Conditions could be stabilized through diet and regimen, focusing on the patient's personal habits, climatic exposure, professional activities, sexual behavior, clothing, and hygiene. For European physicians and missionaries, a good drug did not directly cure the disease but served to reinstate equilibrium to the humors.[74] Thus, Jesuit João Daniel's eighteenth-century account, *Tesouro descoberto no Rio Amazonas*, hailed guaraná as an arm against "gas, pain, and colic cause by minimum heat." The missionary, who lived for over fifteen years in the Amazon prior to his eviction in 1757 (and two years before the expulsion of the Jesuit order from Brazil), touted the plant as a remedy for dysentery and "heated blood," and a "cordial coolant for fevers," while noting that it contributed to "a lack of sleep." Emphasis on blood temperature and bodily equilibrium reveals the drug's re-inscription in a humoralist framework and the characteristic omission of Indigenous cosmological and etiological understandings. Daniel's massive inventory of the region's flora and fauna, written while incarcerated in Lisbon from 1757 until his death in 1776, also evinced missionaries' unrelenting quest to transform the Amazonian jungle into a garden. He touted guaraná as "one of the most unique species in those lands and therefore a worthy plant to be cultivated in orchards, vegetable patches [*hortos*], and gardens, as the Indians do, who despite being so uninterested in the cultivation of plants, hold it in such high esteem that many cultivate it in their plots [*roças*]."[75]

According to Hippocratic environmentalist understandings of health, New World ailments also purportedly differed from those of Europe due to the quality of air, soil, and water, and were best treated with native plants.[76] In 1735, for example, Luis Gomes Ferreyra, a Portuguese physician in gold rush–era

Minas Gerais, extolled native plants for curing local illnesses.[77] Likewise, Friar
Caetano Brandão, a Portuguese who served as the bishop of Pará in the 1780s,
remarked, "It's better to be treated by an Indian from the backlands who tends
with the most unrestrained instinct than by a Lisbon doctor."[78] In any event,
the scarcity of "Lisbon doctors" and the high cost and spoilage of European
drugs in Brazil meant that the staunchest skeptic of Indigenous medicinals
might succumb to need. Ravaged by smallpox, dysentery, typhoid, malaria,
syphilis, leprosy, and ancylostomiasis, colonial populations had their fair share
of misfortunes as well as theories regarding their origins and cures, with even
the wealthiest patient turning to an Indigenous or African remedy. Cases
brought before the colonial Inquisition reveal that both elites and commoners
embraced spiritual and healing practices, derived from fusions of popular Ca-
tholicism and Indigenous and African beliefs, to restore the broken harmony
from evil spells presumed to beget physical suffering.[79]

In this sense, Bettendorff's reference to guaraná reflected the church's appropriation of an Indigenous medicinal in the contest over healing, faith, and
power. Embracing Indigenous therapeutic practice, Europeans deprecated
Native cosmological beliefs.[80] The church punished divination, diabolism,
and shamanic healing while attributing curative power to the mediation of
saints. Medical doctors slammed Indigenous "superstitions" while upholding
Christian exorcism's health-giving effects. [81]

Bettendorff recounted one such conflict over plants and power involving
the Sateré-Mawé. Following the relocation of a group of Maraguazes to the Jesuit college's plantations at Mamayacu in the early 1690s, Bettendorff paid a
visit. He encountered an infirm woman whose husband's lack of support
purportedly led her to the village. After several days under missionary tutelage, Bettendorff deemed the woman "well-prepared in doctrine and repen-
tant and equipped with all of the necessary actions for baptism," but his plan
floundered when "Indians of her nation," offering her some gourds with "porridge and mush," beckoned her to the forest. Bettendorff urged the woman to
follow God's words, which she heeded, but she died shortly thereafter.[82] It is
unclear if the "porridge and mush" contained guaraná. Bavarian naturalist
Karl von Martius noted in 1819 that Sateré-Mawé shamans prepared a guaraná
paste.[83] Bettendorff's account suggests the importance of plants in the Jesuits'
tug-of-war over Indigenous bodies and souls, just as Martius indicates their
ultimate shortfalls. In the early part of the twentieth century, anthropologist
Curt Nimuendajú likewise noted the Sateré-Mawé belief in "witchcraft" and
their reluctance to take the medicines of "*civilizados*" due to their fear of spells.

Communities had ample knowledge of medicinal plants and animal products, and shamans (*painim*) consumed a strong manioc drink (*tarobá*) to undertake therapeutic care. Nimuendajú mentioned one legendary nineteenth-century chieftain and shaman, Uaciri-pot, who could capture "the mother of sickness" through conjuring and gestures.[84] Similarly, Sateré-Mawé elders told Nunes Pereira in 1939 that their ancestors had used *paricá* in ritual dances and smoke blowing, although shamans had since substituted cachaça and cannabis to commune with aquatic, celestial, and terrestrial beings.[85]

Following the Jesuit expulsion in 1759, the Portuguese Crown sought expanded botanical-medical knowledge and commercial export of natural products from Brazil, India, and Africa.[86] Under the auspices of Sebastião Carvalho e Melo, the Marquis of Pombal—a proponent of mercantilism and scientific education as tools of statecraft—the Royal Botanical Garden of Ajuda was founded in Lisbon in 1768, led by Paduan botanist and University of Coimbra professor Domenico Vandelli. In 1783, the crown dispatched a scientific expedition headed by Brazilian-born, Coimbra-educated naturalist Alexandre Rodrigues Ferreira to the captaincies of Grão Pará, Rio Negro, and Mato Grosso to survey the region's marketable resources, agricultural potential, and demography in order to facilitate Portuguese colonization. Over the course of his nine-year "philosophical journey," Ferreira described and remitted to Lisbon thousands of natural and ethnographic specimens in boxes, barrels, and flasks, including guaraná.[87]

In 1796, the crown established a royal garden in Belém (vying with a sister institution in neighboring French Guiana) to acclimatize commercially lucrative Asian plants and to inventory local flora with similar attributes.[88] During the late eighteenth century, the secretary of the Estado dos Negócios da Marinha e Domínios Ultramarinos instructed the governors of the northern captaincies of Brazil to send specimens to the Botanical Garden at Ajuda and the Royal Cabinet of Natural History and to report on natural products of potential economic value.[89] In February 1778, the governor and captain general of the Estado do Pará, João Pereira Caldas, sent samples of guaraná to the colonial council in Lisbon.[90] In the late 1790s, Diogo de Sousa, the governor of Maranhão, commissioned several descriptive works of commercially promising flora, including two folios of watercolor botanical illustrations and one manuscript describing the plants' uses; among the fifty-five species, primarily of medicinal importance, was guaraná.[91] Following the transfer of the Portuguese monarchy to Rio de Janeiro in 1808, Father Manuel Aires de Casal availed himself of the newly installed royal printing press to publish a chorographic study of

Brazil (1817), noting that among guaraná's various fabled qualities, "the surest is to banish sleep."[92]

GUARANÁ'S CIRCULATION in the Portuguese colonial world held varied meanings for its protagonists. Luso-Brazilians who traded tools, trinkets, and foodstuffs aimed to secure Indigenous conversion, resettlement, and allegiance. For Tupi peoples, the exchange of goods, beyond the acquisition of utilitarian objects and strategic alliance, may have signified transformation through the internalization of the Other.[93] Anthropologist Eduardo Viveiros de Castro's historical ethnography of the Tupinambá posits that colonial interactions with Europeans were marked by both receptivity and recalcitrance, deriving from the desire to be like the Other but on one's own cultural terms. Tupinambá cosmology viewed humanity as a condition, rather than a nature, in which relations to others prevailed over being and substance. The European arrival offered the Tupinambá an opportunity to transform themselves through a relationship with powerful foreign messengers—just as they had previously shared their world with gods, affines, and enemies, and had subordinated figures of alterity to internal social logics. For Indigenous peoples, the exchange of goods did not always reflect gullibility or dissimulation but an assertion of power through incorporation of externalities.[94] Pacts with the Portuguese, or the absence of concerted Indigenous opposition, reflected the initiatives of communities or factions for self-determination rather than necessary admission of political defeat or territorial surrender.[95] Forts, trading posts, and missions offered potential tactical or material support, opportunities for transformation and regeneration instead of sites of subjection. In these spaces, Indigenous and colonial regional systems commingled and collided.[96] Various ethnographic studies have underscored Indigenous historical understandings of "pacification" as their people's victory over whites.[97]

The documentation of the Sateré-Mawé's interethnic contact under Portuguese and early Brazilian rule, although scattered and skewed, reveals conflicts bred of competing understandings and objectives. Guaraná factors as both frame and flashpoint in Sateré-Mawé engagement with dominant society, emblematic of the Indigenous agency that contoured historical processes of European colonization of Amazonia.[98] Bettendorff, for example, noted only partial success in resettling the Maraguazes downriver, notwithstanding exhortations to leave "the land of Egypt" to become "children of God and free from the attacks of their enemies." A group of 67 Maraguazes did relocate, although the missionaries had hoped to establish a village of 250 households.[99] In the 1990s, Sateré-Mawé oral histories celebrated those ancestors who abandoned the Mamayacu village at the Jesuit's Santo Alexandre school in 1692. In their memorialization, an ancestral woman exhorts her brethren to abandon the mission and to return to their traditional lands, where the stool to prepare *çapó* had been left behind.[100] Archaeologists have noted the cultural importance of seats and benches in tropical forest cultures, often viewed as symbols of stability and wisdom and links to the spiritual world, and closely associated to the consumption of particular ritualistic substances.[101] Critically, as a history recounted by Sateré-Mawé in the 1990s amid sociopolitical marginalization, the narrative linked contemporary struggles to ancestral resistance in which women, as preparers of the guaraná beverage, served as guardians of tradition. Well into the twentieth century, Sateré-Mawé communities pressured or prohibited women from speaking Portuguese in order to limit contact with outsiders.[102]

Following the Jesuit expulsion, historical documentation registers sporadic conflicts involving the Sateré-Mawé. Traveling through the Tapajós region between 1762 and 1763, bishop of Belém João de São José de Queirós da Silva reported on several victims, including the *paulista* João Portes, "cruelly killed" by Sateré-Mawé after they had promised relocation and "submission to the Catholic faith."[103] The bishop also noted that following commander Jeronimo José de Carvalho's drubbing of a Sateré-Mawé member of a collecting band at the Praia da Tartaruga (Turtle Beach), the victim's companions vowed to kill the assailant after downing guaraná in "a ceremony indispensable to their meeting for war and other serious matters." Carvalho avoided an untimely end by loading the soldiers' rifles and distributing sugarcane brandy, derided by the cleric as the "divine drink" of the Indigenous and whites of Pará.[104] For the Sateré-Mawé, exploitation fueled resistance, with guaraná serving as a fortifier for battle.

To reduce the Sateré-Mawé to "necessity," thereby forcing relocation to official villages, Pará governor Athaide Tevé banned trade altogether with the Indigenous group in 1769.[105] Recounting his voyage downriver from Barcelos to Belém the previous year, Father José Monteiro de Noronha noted the density of Indigenous populations in the Abacaxis, Canumá, and Maué River regions, with the latter possessing "abundant clove and excellent guaraná."[106] Trade with Indigenous peoples had aimed to induce rather than forestall acquiescence to Luso-Brazilian domination. In response, Tevé's edict turned the Sateré-Mawé's "drug" into contraband. As Francisco Xavier Ribeiro de Sampaio, the magistrate and general intendant of the captaincy of São José do Rio Negro, explained in 1774–75: "The [Sateré-]Maués are valiant, with them we had trade that is now prohibited, following the lack of good faith,

with which these Indians behaved, and because of the deaths that they caused
to some *cabos* [heads of collecting expeditions] of this trade, which showed
what little use to us was their friendship."[107] For Portuguese colonial authorities, an Indigenous people's aversion to religious conversion, labor drafts, or
territorial surrender—the colonial triad of Native Amazonian population
management—signified a lack of "friendship" or betrayal.[108]

Following the Treaty of Madrid (1750), as Portugal sought to promote the
occupation of territory formally ceded by Spain, Indigenous groups along
the Madeira and Tapajós Rivers and their tributaries increasingly sparred
with Luso-Brazilian settlers and militias. Conflicts with the Mundurucu, first
appearing in colonial documents in 1768, pepper official correspondence; attacks by the Indigenous headhunters on the lower Tapajós were met by
Portuguese policies of armed conflict and compensatory integration. Subsequent to a peace treaty in 1795, Mundurucu allied with the Luso-Brazilians
in combating the Mura and other hostile Indigenous groups.[109] Like the
Mundurucu—their neighbors and erstwhile enemies—the Sateré-Mawé pursued peace with Luso-Brazilians sometime in the final years of the eighteenth
century. In 1798, José Rodrigues Preto and Luiz Pereira da Cruz founded
the settlement of Luzéa (today the town of Maués) on the right bank of the
Maués-Açu River at the site of a former Jesuit mission, congregating some
243 Sateré-Mawé and Mundurucu families.[110] As *sertanistas*, or backland adventurers who often had a military background, Preto and Cruz established
personal or kin-based ties to Amerindian groups to secure labor and goods.[111]
In 1811, Carmelite missionary José Alvares das Chagas founded a mission on
the left bank of the Canomá River in the Tapajós region, offering another
mode of Indigenous integration.[112] In 1823, the village of Itaituba was founded
on the Tapajós River, and by 1828, four hundred Sateré-Mawé had settled
there.[113]

Whereas colonial documents often presented peacemaking as surrender, Indigenous contact strategies entailed military alliance against rival
groups, access to broader trade networks, and expectations of gifts and ac-
commodations.[114] On their 1819 visit to the Tapajós, Bavarian naturalists Johann Baptist von Spix and Karl von Martius hailed the Sateré-Mawé as an
"important and industrious nation" with "peaceful disposition towards the
merchants that seek them out." Alongside their renowned preparation of guaraná, the Sateré-Mawé excelled, in the naturalists' eyes, as collectors of sarsaparilla, clove, palm wax, and fiber, and as manufacturers of wooden bows and
feathered arrows, which they traded for hoes, axes, knives, salt, and cloth.[115]
In the town of Vila Nova da Rainha, Spix and Martius reported, many

Indigenous arrived in small boats, each with four rowers and laden with cargo, to sell guaraná and manioc flour.[116] Another early nineteenth-century report noted that the Sateré-Mawé had received guns, powder, and lead shot, notwithstanding an official ban on firearms to Indigenous peoples.[117] And a bishop in Pará noted in 1846 that an Indigenous *tuxaua* had told the directors of one of the villages that he planned to travel to Belém with "ample manioc flour and guaraná to 'buy a priest.'"[118] Native peoples' understandings of trade with Luso-Brazilians, mediated by distinct cultural expectations, held forth alternative outcomes from interethnic exchange.

Spix and Martius described as well the pervasive use of state coercion toward the Amazon's Indigenous population. As Martius noted, "News of my arrival spread terror among the neophytes of the kindly priest, who assumed I had arrived to conscript them for public service. Recently, despite the protests of the vicar, the recruitment had begun of a certain number of Mundurucu for forced labor each trimester, causing the Indians to become difficult and to threaten returning to the forest." Martius fretted that the large number of Indigenous peoples at the religious missions demanded "certain precautions."[119] His concern proved prescient. In 1823, the residents of Vila Nova da Rainha (today Parintins) complained that the Sateré-Mawé, "unsteady" in their embrace of "the religious, political and social realms of the State," had attacked white residents and pillaged their property. Nine years later, driven by rumors of their impending enslavement, Indigenous fighters under the command of chief Manoel Marques killed over thirty soldiers and white settlers (mainly Portuguese) in the village of Luzéa.[120] But the Sateré-Mawé's gravest showdown with agents of dominant society awaited the postindependence era.

In 1835, an intra-elite political feud that erupted in Belém soon devolved into a large-scale popular uprising, pejoratively deemed the Cabanagem, in reference to the rebels' cabanas, or shacks. The Amazon's downtrodden, squeezed by labor drafts and the expansion of cacao estates, placed their own spin on contemporary catchwords of "liberty" and "rights."[121] Many Sateré-Mawé joined their ranks. Chief Chrispim de Leão, for example, mobilized his community to destroy nearby settlements, and although he died in battle, his followers besieged Vila Nova da Rainha, forcing residents to flee downriver to Óbidos.[122] When the Cabanos surrendered to government forces in 1840, thousands had been killed or dispersed in the bloodiest regional revolt in Brazilian history. Prince Adalbert of Prussia, who visited Pará in 1842, speculated that the pre-Cabanagem population of sixty thousand *índios aldeados* (Indians settled in villages nominally under state authority) had been halved.[123]

The Sateré-Mawé paid a heavy price for joining a rebellion that regional elites cynically cast as a race war.[124] In 1837, government commander Ambrósio Ayres (nicknamed Bararoá) noted that the Cabano stronghold in Luzéa was "completely struck today and today is a pile of ashes, the defeated rebels will lose their hope of reuniting, all of their spots are extinct and garrisoned by legal forces."[125] In the revolt's aftermath, the provincial labor draft of the Guarda Policial and Corpo de Trabalhadores snatched many Indigenous men from their communities. In 1846, three Sateré-Mawé chiefs complained to the Pará governor about violence at the hand of interim inspector Manoel José Plácido.[126] Settlement also expanded in the Maués region. In the 1850s, Amazonas provincial president João Batista de Figueiredo Tenreiro Aranha noted that the mission at Andirá, refounded by Capuchin friar Pietro di Ceriana and home to over five hundred Sateré-Mawé, resembled more of a town (*vila*), with its numerous white farmers and their enslaved Black workers.[127] In 1850, British naturalist Richard Spruce described Luzéa as "a place of growing importance with church and chapel, with several white residents and a few shops."[128] Such was the backdrop of the Amazonian Indigenous population's reduction from majority to minority by the mid-nineteenth century.[129]

Retreating from lands on the banks of the Tapajós, Sateré-Mawé communities established villages inland (or in the forest "center," in their words), availing themselves of large numbers of palm trees and animals near the headwaters of smaller rivers and narrow igarapés with swift waters.[130] Late nineteenth-century observers would describe the Sateré-Mawé as neither a canoeing people nor good swimmers but as energetic and fast walkers.[131] In 1862, the president of Pará, Araújo Brusque, claimed there were 9,907 Mundurucu and 5,657 Sateré-Mawé on the Tapajós River, the latter distributed among four villages along the banks and another twenty-eight inland. Both Indigenous groups, he noted, traded copaiba oil, guaraná, clove, tobacco, cotton, and *cumaru* with "*civilizados*" but were frequently cheated by river traders, spent little time in their villages to avoid abuse, and responded violently to harassment of their womenfolk.[132] An 1858 report on Indigenous catechism noted that the Sateré-Mawé came to town only twice a year, when the priest oversaw religious festivities. According to one of their chiefs, there were fifty settlements along the Guaranatuba River, some harvesting more than twenty arrobas of guaraná annually, which they traded with river peddlers, whom officials blamed for corrupting the Indigenous with "bad ideas."[133] Among Indigenous Amazonians, social fission also served as a means to avoid conflict and restore social harmony disrupted by disputed access to resources, competition over women, accusations of sorcery, and factional power struggles.[134]

Although settler violence and epidemic decimated many Indigenous nations in Brazil, others became, in historian John Manuel Monteiro's words, "colonial Indians": ethnically distinct subordinate populations, reshaped by Iberian legal and cultural norms.[135] There were many variations of "colonial Indians"—guides, rowers, healers, warriors, cooks, concubines, servants, artisans, traders—who differed in value for the Luso-Brazilian colonizers. Yet social boundaries maintained by dominant actors to assert political control and cultural superiority constituted the common colonialist logic of incorporation with differentiation. For their part, Native peoples' readjustment of hegemonic frameworks and resistance to deculturation resulted in ethnic transformation rather than erasure. Brazil's "colonial Indians" were no less "authentic" as Indigenous peoples than their forebears for having assumed trappings of European Catholic culture; they were merely different.

As an Indigenous foodstuff, guaraná would undergo a concomitant process of colonial reordering. Although guaraná retained distinct meanings and uses for the Sateré-Mawé, the plant acquired newfound range and significance under Luso-Brazilian dominion as an object of knowledge, exchange, and consumption. As dominant actors resituated guaraná in new frameworks of knowledge and trade, Sateré-Mawé reckoned both with the plant's traditions and transitions. If Sateré-Mawé would become "colonial Indians," guaraná would become a colonial medicament—or, in the regional parlance, a backland drug (*droga do sertão*). In his 1774–75 account, for example, Francisco Xavier Ribeiro de Sampaio wrote, "The Maués are famous for their manufacture of their celebrated, extremely cold beverage guaraná, which is already consumed in Europe and which has some renowned virtues, as well as dangers in its overuse." Sampaio extolled the drug as a cure for "light diarrhea, headaches and urinary diseases," but claimed its overuse caused insomnia and even impotence in some. While the non-Indigenous colonial populations had begun to consume the beverage sweetened, he noted many residents in Pará indulged in the drink "all the time, and without sugar, like the Indians, and very bitter."[136] Eighteenth- and nineteenth-century historical documents do not mention outsiders' consumption of guaraná in the communal fashion of the Sateré-Mawé, presumably shunned as unhygienic.[137]

BETTENDORFF'S CHRONICLE SIGNALS the re-embedding of guaraná in Western networks of trade and knowledge. Just as missionizing, state violence, and exploitative systems of labor and exchange served to turn the Sateré-Mawé into "colonial Indians," so too did guaraná become a commodity increasingly configured to colonial social relations and world-making. For the Sateré-Mawé, guaraná would sustain memories and acts of community belonging while contouring new forms of intercultural exchange amid marked imbalances of power.[138] In the Indigenous adaptation to Luso-Brazilian hegemony, guaraná served as an object of empowerment and contestation, an agent of ethnic continuity and transformation. Its consecration in Sateré-Mawé myth and social practice symbolized Indigenous ways of knowing the natural world and the shared interpretive frameworks that made the past meaningful and guided contemporary actions. Its broader circulation in Western networks also undergirded Indigenous incorporation of outsiders' goods and knowledge.

In grounding Brazilian exceptionalism in putative interracial harmonies, Gilberto Freyre and other twentieth-century nationalist thinkers have offered the nation's multicultural foodways as evidence.[139] Brazil's food system was predominantly Indigenous during the first two centuries of Portuguese colonization.[140] Yet unlike Freyre's (literally) sugar-coated narrative of Brazilian nation-building, this chapter's analysis of guaraná's early cross-cultural circulation indicates no such romance. Rather, the historical record highlights tensions in overlapping and contested spheres of ethnic influence. While guaraná remained central to Sateré-Mawé ways of being and becoming, outsiders clamored for the plant's transformation and commercialization in the name of science, progress, and Brazil's (geo)political advantage.

CHAPTER THREE

Silva Coutinho's Plant

Nineteenth-Century Science and Amazonian Geopolitics

On December 10, 1865, a group of illustrious passengers set sail on the warship *Ibicuhy* from Manaus to Maués, heartland of the guaraná trade. As head of the foreign scientific expedition aboard, Swiss-born Harvard professor of zoology and geology Louis Agassiz, founder of the university's Museum of Comparative Zoology in 1859, had been traveling in the Amazon for four months. In gathering scientific specimens, he aspired to "illustrate the natural history of the uncivilized races," while making Europe's natural history museums "tributary" to his own. By pressuring Brazilian authorities, he hoped to open navigation on the Amazon River to ships from non-bordering nations, barred at the time of his visit due to fears of U.S. expansionism. And by documenting the natural history of the Amazon—particularly its geological formation and distribution of freshwater fish—he aimed to defend his creationist theories.[1]

Since the publication of Charles Darwin's *On the Origin of Species* in 1859, Agassiz had inveighed against the transmutation of species, positing that God had created similar species suited to particular local environments. Evolution, he contended, had occurred through great catastrophes, such as flood or glacial action, that had periodically destroyed life on earth. Past and present species were not linked; God had created the latter anew, while variations within species represented different stages of growth or cycles of development.[2] Following a series of lectures at the Lowell Institute in Massachusetts in 1863–64, in which Agassiz affirmed that an investigation of the Amazon basin would reveal the glacial action that had destroyed life on all continents, Boston businessman and anti-Darwinist Nathaniel Thayer offered to sponsor an expedition to Brazil.[3] The Harvard professor assembled a team of scientists, student interns, and volunteer aides, and with free passage on a Pacific Mail steamship, the delegation arrived in Rio de Janeiro in April 1865. Agassiz was accompanied by his wife, Elizabeth Cary Agassiz, a longtime collaborator in his scientific research, an innovator in female education, and future first president of Radcliffe College.

In Brazil, Louis Agassiz counted on backing at all levels. Emperor Dom Pedro II supplied the steamship and appointed João Martins da Silva

Members of the Thayer expedition, Brazil, 1865. Brazilian engineer João Martins da Silva Coutinho (standing, right) served as the Harvard University expedition's guide in the Amazon. Jacques Burkhardt (seated on bench, second from right) was the collecting mission's scientific illustrator. Also featured in the photograph is William James (seated on the floor), a Harvard medical school student at the time, who later became a pioneering figure in the United States in the fields of psychology and philosophy. Ernst Mayr Library and Archives of the Museum of Comparative Zoology, Harvard University.

Coutinho, a major in the Brazilian Army Corps of Engineers, as the expedition's guide. Amazonas provincial president Epaminondas de Mello directed locals to assist the delegation (and accompanied the Agassizes to Maués). Church superiors instructed parish priests to aid the foreigners.[4] A distinction of "civilized" nations that nineteenth-century Brazilian statesmen coveted, scientific investigation enabled an inventory of the Amazon's natural endowment. For scientists on the global periphery, connections with European and North American colleagues could facilitate international recognition.[5]

Much has been written on the Agassizes' Amazon journey of 1865–66 and its historical context. We know that Louis Agassiz's interest in Brazil dated back nearly four decades to his days as a twenty-year-old student of natural history and medicine at the University of Munich. Between 1817 and 1820, his professor, botanist Karl Friedrich Philipp von Martius, trekked alongside zoologist Johann Baptist von Spix over sixteen thousand miles, from Rio de Janeiro to Belém and up the Amazon River by canoe, collecting thousands of plants and animals. Following Spix's death in 1826, Martius invited Agassiz to research and catalog an extensive collection of Brazilian freshwater fish, which resulted in Agassiz's first publication—and his lifelong fascination with Brazil.[6]

Agassiz's journey followed in the footsteps of a number of European and U.S. naturalists and explorers who traveled to the Amazon basin between the 1820s and 1860s. With the transfer of the Portuguese Crown to Brazil in 1808 and independence in 1822, colonial regulations that had restricted foreigners from engaging directly in commerce and exploration in the Amazon were dismantled.[7] The arrival of the steamship on the Amazon River in 1853 reduced the duration and vulnerability of transport due to the fluctuations of wind (for sailing vessels), the muscle power and temperament of rowers, and the treachery of currents.[8] Thanks to the introduction of Wardian cases—botanical boxes that began to circulate in the 1830s—naturalists could also ensure greater survival of flora on long sea voyages for transplanting to foreign botanical gardens and commercial nurseries.[9] In turn, a new species washed up on the banks of Amazonian rivers—the foreign naturalist—to survey regions and assess natural resources; collect and commercialize specimens in the name of science and trade; deploy natural history as social metaphor and political ideology; and convert mundane diary-writing into enthralling narrative.[10] Like Agassiz, they stuffed their nations' emergent natural history museums with tropical specimens to document the processes of human evolution (facilitated by discoveries in the fields of geology and paleontology in the 1830s and 1840s and reorientations in anthropology), eager to validate scientific truths, titillate public interest, and flex political power.[11] Mundurucu scepters, hoods, and feathered garlands dazzled exhibition visitors in Vienna, Munich, and Berlin.[12] The giant Amazonian water lily that bloomed in 1850 at the Royal Botanic Gardens at Kew from seeds dispatched by Royal Geographical Society emissaries (from Guyana) gained a newfound scientific name, *Victoria amazonica*, honoring the British queen.[13] Imperial dreams came in many shapes and colors.

Brazil's importance for Agassiz's theories of racial science has also been widely explored. As a proponent of polygenism, he deemed Blacks, whites, and Indigenous as different species deriving from disparate moments of divine creation, divided by natural hierarchies, and tailored to distinct ecological zones.[14] Agassiz defended segregation in the antebellum United States and opposed racial mixture, or "hybridism," which he argued had resulted in degeneration and infertility.[15] Brazil's multiracial population, in his assessment, demonstrated that the "natural result of an uninterrupted contact of half-breeds with one another is a class of men in which pure type fades away as completely as do all the good qualities, physical and moral, of the primitive races, engendering a mongrel crowd as repulsive as the mongrel dogs."[16] Through a photographic series of naked and semiclothed subjects taken prior to his departure from Manaus, while awaiting the replacement of pickling alcohol, Agassiz sought to document the purported degeneracy of Brazil's racially mixed population as a cautionary tale for postbellum America.[17] And while Agassiz urged Brazilian statesmen to mine Indigenous peoples' extensive botanical knowledge, he insisted that a "better class of immigrants"—Americans or Britons, who would not degrade themselves as the Portuguese "to the social levels of the Indians"—oversee the planting of crops and forest products "barbarously" collected by the local population.[18] U.S. ambassador extraordinaire James Watson Webb's 1862 proposal for the mass relocation of freedpeople to the Amazon as a solution to prospective racial "contamination" in the United States and northern Brazil's labor shortage, while rejected by the Brazilian government, undoubtedly appealed to Agassiz, with its consignment of Blacks to physical labor in tropical regions.[19]

Louis and Elizabeth Agassiz's coauthored travelogue, *A Journey in Brazil* (1868), has also been analyzed by scholars. Aimed at readers seeking greater knowledge of natural history and "exotic" faraway lands, the book, largely adapted from Elizabeth's diary, splices picturesque observations of Brazil's natural landscapes and social customs with her husband's intermittent racist diatribes.[20] In traveling with her husband, Elizabeth Agassiz was a rarity among elite women in the Amazon, whose "benighted, colorless, crippled lives," in her words, owed to relentless scrutiny and enforced seclusion.[21] On his 1868 journey, James Orton noted, "On no Amazonian steamer did we meet with a lady passenger."[22] Like other nineteenth-century U.S. and European travel accounts, prejudice toward the supposed deficiencies of tropical peoples permeates the writing, yet Elizabeth Agassiz also expressed admiration for Indigenous adaptation to the natural environment and denounced their exploitation at the hands of whites.[23] The study belongs to a rich historical genre of travel literature animated by outsiders' observations and biases.[24]

There is one seemingly narrow question concerning the Agassizes' journey, however, that historians have not addressed: In a region as large as the

Amazon, why was the Thayer expedition headed to the heart of guaraná territory, a trip that entailed certain risks? To reach Maués, Captain João Gomes de Faria would need to cut from the Amazon River through the Paraná Ramos, a channel unknown to steam navigation.[25] In 1852, the imperial government had granted an exclusive thirty-year concession to the Companhia de Navegação e Comércio do Amazonas, established by Brazilian entrepreneur Irineu Evangelista de Souza, the baron of Mauá, to operate steamships in the Amazon.[26] In addition, Brazilian warships, such as the *Ibicuhy*, cruised the largest rivers. Admirers marveled at the social transformations in the vessels' wake: from the camphene-lit, macadamized roads in Belém that allowed scores of imported American coaches to haul passengers around town, rather than the traditional hammocks, to townspeople's attentiveness to "the latest Parisian fashions, instead of going about in stockingless feet, wooden clogs, and shirt sleeves."[27] While the Amazon and the Madeira were navigable by steam throughout the year (the latter, until the Santo Antonio falls, some 168 leagues from the headwaters), other tributaries were bedeviled by waterfalls or seasonal ebbing that snarled transport from August to December. Captains plying these waterways knew that beaching might delay travel for days as passengers and crew pulled with ropes; transported cargo to flat-bottom vessels, rafts, and other smaller boats; or awaited the rising water from the rains.[28]

Louis Agassiz offered his explanation for the itinerary. Situated among the vast network of rivers connecting the Madeira and the Tapajós with the Amazon, the Maués region's geographic distribution of fish species would prove his point about the Creator's design.[29] By showing how "every hydrographic basin has its own inhabitants, more or less different from those of any other basin," he planned to demonstrate the separateness of Amazonian fish species (due to natural catastrophes) rather than the variability among species central to the theory of natural selection.[30] Yet this origin of the journey is questionable; although Elizabeth Agassiz was the Amazon adventure's principal scriptwriter, and Louis its headliner, the set designer was engineer João Martins da Silva Coutinho, their official guide, who presumably chose the scenery. The Brazilian engineer did not keep a diary or publish his own travelogue, but his terse reference in a report to the minister of agriculture, commerce, and public works is suggestive: the trip to Maués was not undertaken "only in the interest of science" but "of the province" as well.[31] An opaque statement, but we know from the engineer's writings that he championed the guaraná trade as critical to regional development. A tall order for one specimen, yet perhaps one worth diverting a steamship with a high-profile foreign delegation to unplumbed waters to study and spotlight? In traveling to Maués, Silva Coutinho likely had a plant in mind for the Agassizes, in both senses of the word. As this chapter argues, Brazilian engineers, botanists, physicians, and geologists, tied to the nation's emergent scientific institutions, had their stay and say in the backlands too, imprinting a nationalistic stamp on geographic exploration, specimen collection, ecological conservation, and comparative ethnology.

Silva Coutinho knew well the chasm that separated the linearity of the map from the sprawl of vernacular practice in the Amazon. In 1866–67, Pará's estimated population of 350,000 (325,000 free and 25,000 enslaved) spread over a province of 39,925 square leagues, while in Amazonas an estimated 100,000 persons (95,000 free and 5,000 enslaved) were sprinkled over 71,800 square leagues.[32] Hostile Indigenous peoples, runaway slave communities, peripatetic river dwellers, murky state boundaries, and watery worlds of riotous flora vexed government authorities. To "civilize" the *sertão*, or the backlands, better understood as an imagined racialized space than a determinate ecosystem or geography, Brazilian reformers trumpeted the modernization of agriculture and transportation and the influx of immigrants.[33] The vulnerability of the hinterland at the outbreak of the Paraguayan War (1864–70) reinforced the mission's urgency. Imperial authorities enlisted the natural sciences—zoology, botany, astronomy, and ethnology—in order to expand knowledge, trade, and state power.[34]

In a largely agrarian nation, where elites touted physiocratic ideals and the doctrines of comparative advantage, the plans and plants of the Brazilian empire often intertwined.[35] Imperial iconography included depictions of fruits, trees, and tropical products to signal the fertility and economic potential of the territory, while nationalist thinkers invoked nature as destiny.[36] As this chapter explores, Silva Coutinho attributed a key role to guaraná in the Amazon. As the "heart of the trade" on the Madeira and the Tapajós, two large tributaries of the Amazon that flowed northward through the province of Mato Grosso, guaraná served as an agent of national integration.[37] Guaraná also epitomized a purported pathway to commercial agriculture and sedentarization of the regional labor force. And as a crop cultivated and traded by the Sateré-Mawé, guaraná conveyed Native Amazonian potential. In other words, while serving as a guide for the Harvard expedition, Silva Coutinho advanced the geopolitical agendas of the imperial government and its nascent scientific institutions to map territories and waterways, regiment Indigenous and rural workers, colonize frontiers, commercialize natural resources, and demarcate and defend international borders.

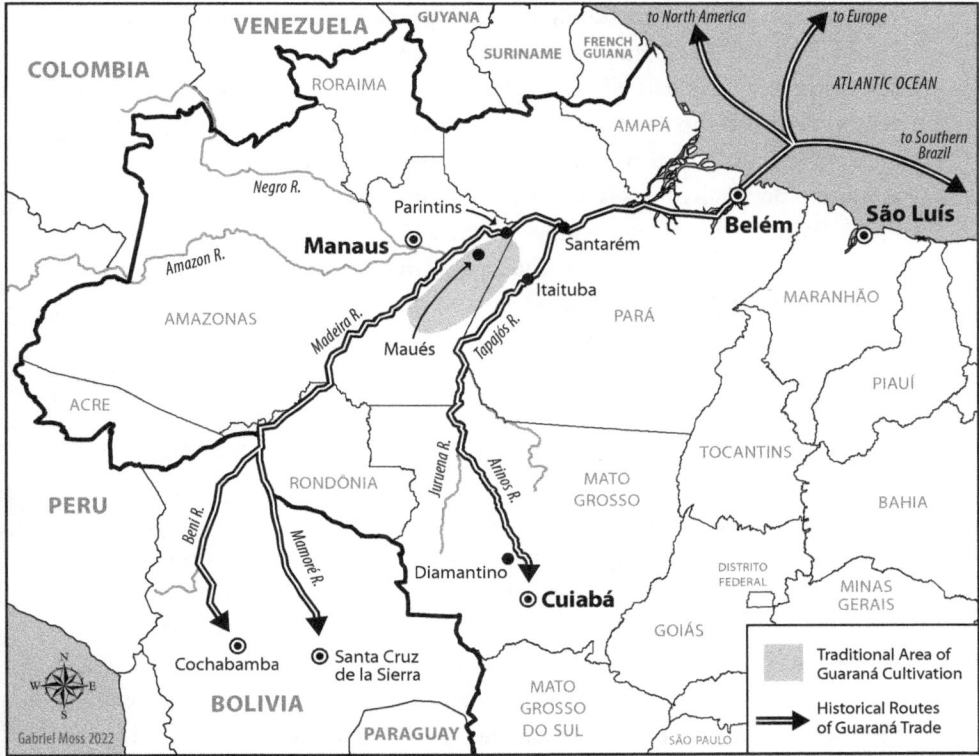

Historical routes of guaraná trade

As scientists, Silva Coutinho and Louis Agassiz had a common goal to order the natural world through experimentation, measurement, and classification. Both sought to regiment landscapes and peoples through "objective" and "universal" forms of knowledge. When Agassiz fumed that local fishermen, who viewed river dolphins as shape-shifting enchanters, had cut off the fin of a specimen intended for his museum to serve as their therapeutic treatment and amulet, Silva Coutinho would have likely concurred that native "ignorance and superstition" would obstruct science from accessing "the riches" of Brazil.[38] In 1868, Agassiz copublished an article with Silva Coutinho in the *Bulletin de la Société géologique de France* in which the Harvard scientist championed Amazonian glacial drift by referencing his Brazilian colleague's geological findings. While I have been unable to ascertain the latter's personal beliefs regarding creationism, thinkers in the Iberian Atlantic initially received Darwinist ideas with considerable skepticism, particularly those who were more politically conservative and religiously devout.[39]

Yet exchanges between foreign and Brazilian scientists could be tense, marked by the disparagement or misattribution of local knowledge and ensuing resentment.[40] Agassiz, for example, scoffed that offerings at the local fish market surpassed the specimens at the National Museum, Brazil's principal nineteenth-century institutional space for science.[41] In a lecture of June 1865, naturalized Brazilian geologist Guilherme Schuch de Capanema—who trained in Saxony, was a founding member of the Rio-based natural history organization Sociedade Vellosiana de Ciências Naturais, and conducted years of geological research in Brazil—charged that the materials labeled as glacial drift by Agassiz, after only a month's stay, had resulted from the decomposition and weathering of local bedrock. Capanema defensively insisted that "among ourselves [Brazilians] there is some [scientific] study."[42] In *A Estátua Amazônica—Comédia Archeológica* (1851), Manoel Araújo Porto Alegre, head of the ethnographic subsection of the National Museum, satirized foreign naturalists' pompousness.[43] In this vein, Silva Coutinho had rebutted the French Société de Géographie's smear of Amazonian insalubriousness by compiling a statistical comparison of mortality rates in Europe and in Pará's Bragança region.[44] Silva Coutinho also rejected the logic of Agassiz's racial science for Amazonia: frontier colonization was best left to the Brazilian "man from the south," who would better withstand its climate and customs.[45] Many of Brazil's men of letters repudiated the "harder" forms of scientific racism articulated by Agassiz in favor of interracial mixture and the "whitening" of the Brazilian population.[46] In sum, if Brazil represented a laboratory for foreign naturalists, national scientists clamored for recognition as producers of knowledge.[47]

As historian Mary Winsor notes, scientific research, an intellectual agenda to provide answers for future development, is empowered as much as circumscribed by the institutions, laboratories, museums, universities, networks, and readers that underwrite it.[48] Silva Coutinho's decision to lead the Thayer expedition to Maués reflected the commission of science to Brazilian nationalism. In acquiring and disseminating knowledge of the cultivation, processing, and commercialization of guaraná, he aimed to advance economic botany, socioenvironmental engineering, and Brazilian geopolitical advantage in the Amazon. Yet how did the engineer come to believe that guaraná could reshape the Amazon's future? The answer requires further investigation of Silva Coutinho's world and that of his beloved plant.

BORN IN THE PROVINCE of Rio de Janeiro in 1830 to an elite family, Silva Coutinho graduated with a degree in engineering from the Escola Militar in

1851. Entering the Army Corps of Engineers, he drew up plans for the defense of the northern borders of Brazil and was later promoted to the rank of major.[49] Leaders of the newly created province of Amazonas tapped Silva Coutinho for various exploratory missions on the Tapajós, Madeira, and Purus Rivers to assess hydrological conditions and identify areas rich in rubber trees and other natural resources. He was also entrusted to report on the Indigenous populations and zones for future colonization, and to map alternative trade routes to Mato Grosso and Bolivia in order to stem Amazonas's isolation and commercial subordination to Belém, the Atlantic world's port of entry for the Amazon.[50] Due to their technical competence in civic architecture, waterfront construction, urban defense, surveying of backland regions, and mapping of borderlands, military engineers had long overseen a number of public projects in the Amazon, particularly in the aftermath of the Treaty of Madrid (1750) and the Treaty of San Ildefonso (1777), which settled the boundaries between Spain and Portugal in South America.[51] During the long rule of Dom Pedro II (1840–89), Brazilian engineers spearheaded various efforts to map national territory and to integrate transportation networks, proffering technical solutions for political problems.[52]

Like many Amazonian explorers, Silva Coutinho experienced numerous hardships. In surveying the Madeira on the *Pirajá* steamship to the Santo Antonio waterfalls and upriver by canoe with a crew of twenty-two Indigenous soldiers, Silva Coutinho confronted a treacherous two-hundred-kilometer stretch of rapids and waterfalls to reach Guajará-Mirim on the Mamoré River. His team repeatedly fell into the water, lost their supplies, dodged an artillery of driftwood (whose hulking presence lent the Madeira River its name), ran out of wood for the steam engine, and beached due to the inexperience of a local guide. Silva Coutinho himself took ill with "cerebral congestion."[53] Yet from his extensive travel and array of local informants, Silva Coutinho came to possess and produce broad geographic, botanical, and ethnographic knowledge about the Amazon. Between 1857 and 1866, he published eight works on the rain forest, including epidemiological reports, navigation and colonization surveys, and studies of forest commodities, such as sarsaparilla, rubber, cacao, and guaraná.[54] He also learned to communicate in *língua geral* and compiled copious notes on Indigenous nations—including those still uncontacted—and their use of plants as medicines, dyes, and poisons.[55]

Silva Coutinho's investigations may be situated in the institutionalization of scientific practice in imperial Brazil. In the absence of universities, these networks comprised the National Museum, founded in 1818 in Rio de Janeiro (then known as the Royal Museum), which emerged as the premier scientific institution in Brazil for the study of natural history, with research divisions by midcentury in comparative anatomy, zoology, botany, agriculture, mineralogy, geology and physical sciences, archaeology, and ethnology.[56] The Instituto Histórico e Geográfico Brasileiro, founded in 1838, promoted knowledge of Brazil's human and natural history through cartographic and field studies, ethnographic reports, and archaeological investigations.[57] The Sociedade Auxiliadora da Indústria Nacional (SAIN), an independent advisory organ of the state created in 1827, encouraged agricultural and technological innovation as well as natural resource and export diversification. SAIN worked closely with the Imperial Instituto Fluminense de Agricultura (IIFA), founded in 1860 in Rio de Janeiro as an experimental school for the domestication or acclimatization of plants and agricultural modernization.[58] And the Rio de Janeiro Botanical Garden, established in 1808 with the arrival of the Portuguese Crown, cultivated medicinal plants and other economically promising flora, both domestic and exotic.[59]

Silva Coutinho had collaborated with a number of these institutions and initiatives—including the Comissão Científica de Exploração in northeastern Brazil (1859–61), the first wholly national scientific expedition—surveying landscapes and collecting botanical, geological, and ethnographic specimens.[60] For Brazil's First National Industrial Exposition, organized in 1861 by the SAIN and the IIFA at Rio de Janeiro's Polytechnic School, Silva Coutinho formed part of Amazonas's organizing committee, responsible for selecting the regional flora and fauna that would join goods from across the empire for exhibition in a symbolic show of national communion.[61] Guaraná and many other Amazonian objects also featured among the fifteen hundred natural specimens at Brazil's stand at the International Exhibition in London that year.[62] That this Brazilian polymath and explorer extraordinaire of the Amazon is less known than contemporaneous European naturalists in the region owes to a historiography that long overlooked the production of scientific knowledge in Latin America.[63] Official obfuscation of Indigenous and Black leadership in backland expeditions—Manoel Urbano da Encarnação, an Afro-Brazilian, guided Silva Coutinho on the Purus—is another chapter primed for historical revision.[64]

It was in July 1863, on a voyage to the upper Tapajós to devise plans for a military or settler colony at Mambuai, that Silva Coutinho traversed the Maués region, assisted by the elderly Sateré-Mawé chief Vicente in exchange for hatchets.[65] The engineer liked what he saw. Smallholders cultivated and marketed guaraná, sustaining interregional trade networks.[66] The land boasted fertile soil, a more concentrated population, and Indigenous peoples with productive and patriotic promise. To facilitate the trade in guaraná with Mato Grosso's capital, Cuiabá—a primary destination—Silva Coutinho sought a route that might bypass the falls on the upper Tapajós, navigable by steamboat only as far as Itaituba. After traveling from Tatú on the Carauahy River, an arm of the Maués, on a four-day journey to the banks of the Tapajós, he proposed the construction of a road to shorten the distance.[67] He also tried an overland route favored by some Mato Grosso merchants from Mambuai to the affluents of the Uaranatuba, and then by canoe to the Maués River. But the journey had lasted ten days due to limited access to labor—only four Sateré-Mawé would assist him, and this required generous compensation—and the scarcity of foodstuffs.[68] Guaraná now beckoned Silva Coutinho back to Maués, this time with a foreign scientific expedition in tow, to promote a geopolitical project for frontier development.

FOR SILVA COUTINHO, guaraná's importance in the commercial trade of Amazonas and Pará with Mato Grosso and Bolivia rendered the plant a strategic resource. A landlocked borderland giant with a mid-nineteenth-century population of fifty-three thousand, or one inhabitant per twenty-two square kilometers (excluding uncontacted Indigenous peoples, estimated at twenty-four thousand by one observer), the central-western province of Mato Grosso epitomized for Brazilian statesmen the curse of geographic isolation, arduous transport, and sparse (or, more accurately, unwilling) labor.[69] Since the early eighteenth century, when São Paulo slave raiders discovered gold in the Guaporé basin and extended the Portuguese presence far beyond the legally sanctioned boundaries with Spain—formally recognized under the principle of uti possidetis in the Treaty of Madrid—Mato Grosso was linked tenuously to Luso-Brazilian centers of trade and political power.[70] In the eighteenth century, Paulistas plied multiple rivers and an overland trail before reaching Cuiabá, a mining town reassigned in 1817 as the capital of Mato Grosso.[71] An alternative overland route, the Estrada de Goiás, linked São Paulo to Cuiabá until the mid-nineteenth century, when Indigenous attacks increasingly hampered passage.[72] Prior to the Treaty of Madrid, the crown prohibited fluvial trade between Pará and Mato Grosso to stanch a rush to the gold-mining districts and the flow of contraband, and although subsequently legalized on the Madeira (1752) and the Tapajós (1790), multiple waterfalls and Indigenous attacks bedeviled transit on both waterways.[73] By the early 1860s, the volume of Mato Grosso's northern trade plummeted once the Paraguayan government allowed Brazilian ships sailing from the Atlantic coast to cross its territory via the Paraguayan River to reach Cuiabá.[74]

Guaraná remained one of the principal products sustaining Mato Grosso's trade with the northern Amazonian region, providing a critical source of provincial tax revenue.[75] As a Diamantino official reported in 1857: "This year we joyfully saw all of the crews that traveled to Pará return home safe. The guaraná imported to our province is more than 200 arrobas [about 6,400 pounds] and the town council never earned as much money for the treasury as this year." Municipal authorities had sponsored a ten-day festival of Senhor Divino Espírito Santo the previous month, followed by two weeks of horseback riding tournaments, parades, and "dances and more dances." "Only as of yesterday," the official signed off, "did I rest from celebrating so much, to send you the news."[76] Guaraná had enabled the merrymaking and presumably the writer's stamina as well.

Indeed, consumption of the stimulant in Mato Grosso was widespread, notwithstanding the relatively high price.[77] Joaquim Ferreira Moutinho, a Portuguese merchant who lived in Cuiabá from 1851 to 1868, reported that residents of the provincial capital drank the beverage early in the morning in bed and several times throughout the day: two spoonfuls, grated with a metal file or dried pirarucu (fish) tongue, mixed with four spoonfuls of refined sugar in fresh water (the latter, in short supply during the dry season). With enslaved women key to the provisioning of food and domestic services in Cuiabá and other urban centers in mid-nineteenth-century Brazil—in 1862, the enslaved in Mato Grosso's capital numbered 4,100 of a total population of 11,000—preparation of guaraná in better-off households would have fallen to this demographic sector.[78] Moutinho calculated that a family of four that consumed eight cups a day committed to spending a hefty 240 réis. Then again, his reference to the high cost of food in town suggests the appeal of an analeptic and appetite suppressant, not to mention the fact that caffeine's deserters suffer punishing withdrawal symptoms.[79] Silva Coutinho asserted that the population would sooner dispense with meat and flour than guaraná, though the poor could only hope for some sprinkles.[80] The engineer's observation that regional demand for guaraná exceeded that in Amazonas (except among the Sateré-Mawé), where the mestizo population favored coffee and a homemade "coarse chocolate," validates the anthropological assessment that the symbolic value of a good is often related to the amount of resistance overcome, both monetary and spatial, for its acquisition.[81]

According to botanist Richard Spruce, guaraná was sold in Cuiabá primarily in taverns.[82] The town of twelve thousand in the mid-1860s contained over 160 of them (nearly half its commercial establishments), where free and enslaved men and women socialized; cachaça lubricated merrymaking

Smoked guaraná stick and dried tongue of pirarucu fish. For a century and a half, Mato Grosso was the primary destination for commercial guaraná, where it was transported in the form of smoked sticks, rasped with the dried tongue of the pirarucu fish or a metal file, and mixed with cold water for consumption. Photograph by Jose Miguel Martinez-McIntosh of materials in author's collection.

and brawls; and gold, victuals, and dry goods were traded (or contrabanded). According to the census of 1872, Cuiabá had a population of 1,394 enslaved and 5,585 free *pardo* and Black residents, representing 63 percent of the total population. Research on taverns in Cuiabá operating between 1848 and 1888 has found that 35 percent were female owned, many most likely by free Black women.[83] At the establishments, guaraná might be purchased in powder, carefully weighed to a grain, or in cold beverages known as *ponches* for 80 to 120 réis a piece.[84] Mining economies have long nurtured trade in stimulants, energizing an overwhelmingly male workforce confronting physical exhaustion and life-threatening danger.

Residents of Cuiabá reportedly carried guaraná in powdered and solid form, along with the beverage's accoutrements—special glasses, silver spoons, and metal files for rasping—whenever they ventured far from home.[85] Then again, given the hazards of Amazonian travel, an energy boost could never hurt, as explorer William Chandless's frightful 1869 journey on the Madeira attested. To expedite a six-week, seven-hundred-mile voyage upstream, the

Briton accepted a tow from a small steamboat, but strong river currents and the captain's poor navigation caused Chandless's canoe to take on large amounts of water. At nighttime, his terror worsened at the prospect of being dragged over or under a projecting tree or through the bushy *goiabaranas* lining the shore. Distrusting his oarsmen, a desperate Chandless spent the night bailing water, fortunately finding the stamina: at four in the morning, he grated and drank guaraná, "which banished alike sleep and fatigue, and enabled me with freshness of body (and, I hope, to some extent, of mind) to watch this coming-on of day."[86]

Life was hard in Mato Grosso. Declines in mining by the mid-1860s left ipecacuanha and animal skins as the province's main exports. In 1867, a smallpox epidemic linked to soldiers in the Paraguayan War claimed six thousand lives in Cuiabá, or half the population.[87] As Spruce noted, guaraná was valued as an antidiarrheal and generally viewed as "a preventive of every kind of sickness, and especially of epidemics, rather than an antidote against any."[88] Consumption of the beverage, however, further signaled a celebration of life and the networks that sustained it. According to Silva Coutinho, Cuiabá's residents considered guaraná the best present that a host or sojourner could offer.[89] As Karl von den Steinen, a German ethnologist and explorer, reported in 1884: "The social life is the nice part about Cuiabá. One celebration follows another and one is received well everywhere. On a morning visit, one receives, as a welcoming gesture, a glass of liqueur, generally home-made and very good, or guaraná, with an innocent flavor, or pure homemade aguardente, made from sugar."[90] In a town where married elite women were largely confined to homemaking, and public diversions restricted to churchgoing, celebrations of saints' days, moonlight serenades, singing and musical recitals, taverns, and gambling, personal reputation was a premium, reinforced through lavish social displays of generosity and gratitude. After all, everyone knew and gossiped about each other's business, with much "free time" afforded by the lack of steady work. On visits to family and friends, the wealthy made sure to wear their finest—men in overcoats in the sweltering heat and women in silk dresses and black mantles to cover their faces—while even poor women dressed up in cambric, tarlatan, and silk. Much was for show, since many residents, buried in debt, owned not much more than the clothes on their back.[91]

Guaraná arrived in Cuiabá via a tortuous journey. Boat crews would set off typically in December from Diamantino, a settlement 30 leagues (over 100 miles) from Cuiabá; walk overland some 40 kilometers to Rio Preto; and then descend the Arinos, Juruena, and Tapajós Rivers. In their canoes made of one large trunk (*ubás*) and bearing an average of 400 arrobas (about 12,800 pounds) of merchandise, they confronted over thirty waterfalls. The trip to Itaituba (270 leagues from Rio Preto) lasted thirty days, and to Santarém, farther down the Tapajós, forty. On overland routes to reach Indigenous villages, the Sateré-Mawé served as guides. The trip home lasted between two to five months on average. Manioc and corn planted in cleared forest on the outbound journey offered fresh provisions to the expeditionaries on their return.[92]

Rewards for merchants were potentially handsome. In 1866, for example, guaraná sold for 50$000 (50 mil-réis) per arroba (32 pounds) in Maués, 200$000 in Diamantino, and an average of 240$000 and up to 300$000 in Cuiabá, reaching as high as 500$000 after the Paraguayan invasion.[93] According to Silva Coutinho, Cuiabanos set up residence on the Tapajós near Itaituba, planting guaraná, "disciplining the Indians," and selling the drug to traders who came downriver from Mato Grosso. In a report from the 1870s, botanist João Barbosa Rodrigues wrote of a "Cuiabá mulatto" near Mambuai whose "immoralities and villainy had succeeded in dominating and enslaving a large number of Indians who work to augment his fortune."[94] Other traders penetrated the territory of the Sateré-Mawé, usually through the Jacaré basin, in an effort to acquire guaraná directly.[95] Decades later, an elderly backwoodsman told botanist F. C. Hoehne of his many trips from Cuiabá to Maués around 1870, where profit accrued from the exchange of artifacts, alcohol, and other objects "worth a pittance" for guaraná."[96] Sateré-Mawé guaraná, colloquially called *guaraná das terras*, was considered superior to the non-Indigenous *guaraná da Luzeia* due to the manner of harvesting and processing; the adulteration of the latter product with manioc flour was also not unknown.[97] Although the Indigenous producers' take on the trade is hazier, an 1864 account by Amazonas provincial president Adolfo de Barros Cavalcanti de Albuquerque Lacerda of a recent encounter with Sateré-Mawé in Manaus offers a clue. The group's chief wore a "striped cotton shirt and blue pants," each equivalent to the price of an arroba of guaraná, which the shocked governor blamed on traders' exploitation of Indigenous peoples' "instinctive vanity." Beyond elite discomfort at Indigenous finery or supposed gullibility, the report reveals Sateré-Mawé leaders' acquisition of valued commodities through commercial exchange.[98]

On the Madeira River, the thriving guaraná trade extended into Bolivia. Although the origins of the transborder commerce are murky, Spix and Martius reported that by 1819, the stimulant had found a market in the provinces of Moxos and Chiquitos.[99] By 1864–65, about seventy Bolivian boats

Bolivianische Bootsleute (Indianer) vom oberen Rio Madeira.

Indigenous Bolivian Rowers Embarking from the Port of Manaus, c. 1867. The photograph by
German commercial photographer Albert Frisch was part of a series of images from an
Amazonian venture that sought to capitalize on outsiders' fascination with the region.
Courtesy of the Archive of the Leibniz Institute for Regional Geography, Leipzig.

descended the Madeira annually to Serpa (today Itacoatiara), near the mouth
of the river, carrying hides, jerky, tallow, cacao, tobacco, and sugar, and acquiring guaraná in Maués for their return.[100] After the Brazilian government
opened up the Amazon to foreign ships in 1867, Bolivian merchants had
greater access to imported trade goods, with the official value of Brazilian
commerce with Bolivia along the Madeira that year registered at $43,000.[101]
One decade later, engineer Franz Keller-Leuzinger remarked that boats on
the Madeira carried large amounts of guaraná, as there were many in Santa
Cruz de la Sierra and Cochabamba "who prefer all the rigors of fasting to ab-
stinence from their favourite beverage," which sold for as much as 30 francs a
pound.[102] When the Thayer expedition disembarked in Maués after nearly a
full day of travel (and successful passage through the Ramos channel), Eliza-

beth Agassiz expressed astonishment at encountering groups of Indigenous Bolivians, who had lit large campfires on the town's sandy beach to deter jaguar attacks and hawked fine cotton twill robes to the arrivals. Silva Coutinho explained that the Bolivians had braved the Madeira's roaring cataracts in primitive craft to obtain guaraná.[103]

For Silva Coutinho, the severing of the River Plate-Paraná-Paraguayan River route to Cuiabá during the Paraguayan War underscored the necessity of securing interprovincial transport on the Madeira and Tapajós. The latter waterway, he argued, was critical to national cohesion, while the Madeira, "belonging solely to Brazil," entailed more than a "natural route" for interregional integration, since Bolivia's need for an Atlantic outlet would mean "all of their trade becomes ours."[104] During the mid-eighteenth century, the Madeira's importance as a bulwark against Spanish penetration spurred official missions to fortify the Portuguese presence through exploration, mapping, and settlement.[105] More recently, Brazil's undefended border with Bolivia had been the subject of a confidential 1859 report by a government official involved in demarcation of the international boundary, who warned that Chuquisaca residents boasted of overpowering Mato Grosso's "small population and scant armed forces" with militias from Santa Cruz de la Sierra.[106] In fact, fearing Bolivia's possible wartime alliance with Paraguay, Brazil signed the Treaty of Ayacucho in 1867, granting the Andean nation recognition of a swath of territory in the northwestern Amazon. Guaraná's importance to interprovincial trade in the heartland inspired Silva Coutinho's visions of caffeine-coursing arteries of the Madeira and Tapajós sustaining Brazil's appendages.

Like Silva Coutinho, a number of prominent nineteenth-century Brazilian men of state and science championed the improvement of inland transportation and "uplift" of rural populations.[107] Congressman Aureliano Cândido Tavares Bastos, favoring interregional trade between Pará and Mato Grosso to free the latter province from dependency on the River Plate nations, backed Silva Coutinho's proposal for a road connecting the upper Tapajós to Maués.[108] In *Navegação interior do Brazil* (1869), army engineer Eduardo José de Moraes bemoaned too the nation's maritime overreliance and sponsorship of European immigration rather than the construction of roads, canals, and improved river transport to integrate the western points of the Brazilian empire and interlink the Amazon and the River Plate.[109] Imperial statesmen's dream of connecting the two river basins, forging an "Island Brazil" whose aquatic boundaries would "naturalize" international borders and enable circumnavigation of national territory, accentuated the importance of mastering Mato

Grosso's hydrography.[110] Thus, in buttressing commerce in Brazil's heartland, guaraná appealed to Silva Coutinho as more than an economically valuable plant. Guaraná strengthened the networks linking Mato Grosso to Amazonas and Pará in a regional integration plan that gained new geopolitical urgency during a wartime crisis.

IT WAS NOT ONLY the guaraná trade's function that pleased Silva Coutinho but its structure. Since the colonial period, the Amazonian commercial economy had pivoted on the extraction of forest and river products. Laborers scoured vast regions in pursuit of marketable commodities, to the chagrin of reformers and missionaries who decried the socioenvironmental costs of "nomadic" lifestyles.[111] While commercial agriculture was not unimportant in the Amazon's economic history—cacao, a plant native to the region and its lead eighteenth- and early nineteenth-century export, was extracted in the forest but also cultivated from Parintins to Monte Alegre as well as near Santarém—its scope remained limited.[112] In 1853, Amazonas's main "industries," according to provincial president Herculano Ferreira Penna, were pirarucu (a sturgeon-like fish sold both fresh and salted); turtle butter (used for illumination as well as seasoning); tree tow for caulking; and medicinals such as cloves, copaiba, and sarsaparilla. In addition, extraction of wild rubber had risen since Charles Goodyear's development of the vulcanization process in 1839 expanded industrial applications.[113] Five crops dominated commercial agriculture in Amazonas—cotton, cacao, coffee, tobacco, and guaraná—while staples such as rice, beans, and manioc flour were imported to meet local demand.[114]

The export of forest products invigorated the financially strapped provinces of northern Brazil: public revenues in Amazonas, for example, quintupled from 1852 to 1860 and increased more than eightfold over the following decade, boosted by the opening of the river trade to steam and foreign vessels.[115] Wild rubber exports skyrocketed with the bicycle craze in the 1880s, transforming Manaus and Belém, regional hubs of the trade, into cosmopolitan cities with opera houses, streetcars, electric lights, and imported luxury goods. Nevertheless, a number of public officials in the Amazon consistently assailed the reigning economic model for sacrificing "orderly" settlement and resource conservation.[116] How would the region progress, the Amazonas secretary of education fretted, when fewer than four hundred students enrolled in school—alongside a shortage of teachers—because fathers took their children on monthslong collecting trips, where they learned to row, fish, smoke, and drink, rather than to read or write?[117] With the "proportionate ease of subsistence" afforded by the riverine ecology, groused army captain Lourenço da Silva Araújo e Amazonas, how could Amazonian towns be assured steady supplies of food?[118] Villages besieged by encroaching forest due to the unavailability of labor beheld dilapidated churches, brickyards, sawmills, cemeteries, jails, and ports—teetering symbols of order and authority.[119] That river dwellers who did "nothing for themselves or for the state" defied elites' regimentation only amplified the sermonizing.[120] That foreigners and immigrants dominated mercantile firms in the Amazon also raised nationalist hackles.

Silva Coutinho viewed extractivism as Amazonians' Faustian bargain. As the former provincial director of the Public Lands and Colonization division of Pará, he saw the Land Law of 1850, devised to privatize land and incentivize agricultural production, vitiated by a labor "shortage" that devalued property titles. He bewailed ecological devastation as tantamount to killing the goose that lay the golden eggs: the hatcheting of copaiba trees for their therapeutic oil; the smashing of turtle eggs for food and oil; the depletion of riverbank sarsaparilla, whose long roots, unearthed by teams of workers between January and March, were indicated for skin ailments, rheumatism, and venereal disease.[121] For cost-effectiveness, why not cultivate the latter alongside staple crops rather than catapult laborers into the jungle? With the burgeoning wild rubber trade damaging the trees on the river islands near Belém through overtapping and *arrocho* (compression with a thick vine to squeeze latex from incisions made at the tree top), tappers would expand the arc of destruction up the Madeira and the Purus, he feared.[122] Lured by profits chanced from forests and rivers, extractivists surrendered the stability of their homes, the honor of their families, the comforts of religion, the rule of law, and the promise of formal education for lives blighted by physical debilitation and vice.[123] "Don't be deceived by the startling progress of Pará," he warned. "It is fictitious and baseless and will end unless the government takes measures."[124]

Silva Coutinho extolled commercial agriculture as the "true source of the nation's wealth."[125] And the Amazon had a cash crop that represented a "true antidote against the plague of extractivism": guaraná.[126] In an article published subsequent to the Thayer expedition's visit to Maués, he reported that the cultivated plant yielded fruit after three to four years, with a well-treated bush producing eight pounds annually. Aside from occasional pruning, the only expense entailed the harvesting and confection of the drug. He noted that the high prices for guaraná, which tripled between 1862 and 1865, had encouraged the local population to adopt a "morally and economically" pleasing industry.[127] Indeed, according to the Companhia de Navegação e

Comércio do Amazonas, guaraná sold for 30$000 (30 mil-réis) per arroba in 1867, or ten times the price of cacao and three times the price of rubber.[128]

Silva Coutinho did not count on guaraná alone to wean the Amazon from extractivism. The stimulant was lucrative, but steamships on the Amazon River carried only 1,374 arrobas annually in the late 1860s, in comparison to over 300,000 arrobas of cacao and over 125,000 arrobas of rubber. In light of the growing global demand for latex, he advocated settlement on the Madeira through the concession of titles to public lands, payable after twenty years, where families could plant rubber trees and food crops and graze cattle.[129] On the Purus, he likewise called for planting rubber and sarsaparilla and for steamship service to facilitate trade.[130] Yet Silva Coutinho attributed special importance to expanding and improving the trade in guaraná. The "people and the government," he explained, "ought to look to the guaraná bush" not simply "as an instrument of financial profit" but as "a symbol of civilization in this part of Amazonas." If only other Amazonian regions possessed an equivalent plant, he lamented.[131]

Silva Coutinho believed that you are what you grow. Whereas extractivism entailed human prostration before the realm of nature, agriculture signified the conquest of space, a hallmark of cultural advancement and moral superiority.[132] He dismissed the possibility that a mixed economy based on extraction of natural resources and subsistence agriculture, calibrated to seasonal variations in river volume and rainfall and the adaptations of flora and fauna, might grant greater autonomy through selective integration into commercial markets as well as insurance against environmental calamity. He could not countenance that geographic mobility stitched together the social networks of Amazonian communities in culturally meaningful ways. Nor would he publicly admit that for poorer Amazonian men, a fixed residence was an open invitation to an army dragoon and other forms of state-sanctioned violence: with the outbreak of the Paraguayan War, the Brazilian army dispatched press gangs to small towns and Indigenous villages in the Amazon, rounding up hundreds of poor men who were shackled and handcuffed in crowded prisons and transported by steamship (including the *Ibicuhy*) to Belém and on to the battlefront.[133] That's why the Agassizes noted canoes mainly rowed by women, who mourned the near collapse in turtle fishing and manioc flour production due to the conscription or flight of their menfolk.[134]

Historiographical treatment of Silva Coutinho as a proto-environmentalist, based on his abhorrence of extractivism, might be more shaded.[135] The engineer foreshadowed important components of Brazilian developmentalist policy over the next century and a half in promoting commercial agriculture and mechanization, cattle ranching, colonization, and modernized transport in the Amazon. He sought to turn nature into a frontier, transforming labor power, facilitating the flow of goods, and constituting state sovereignty.[136] He viewed the Amazon's human ecology and natural landscape as both inspiration and impediment for national progress. And he disregarded poor river dwellers' well-founded apprehensions that "modern" technologies harnessed to state power might bring new horrors. As the Ministry of Agriculture, Commerce, and Public Works cheered in 1867 with the opening of the Amazon River to foreign navigation, the region had been "delivered to modern industry, its immense natural wealth . . . no longer belong[ing] solely to the savage Indian."[137] But neither is a fully revisionist narrative, with its potential for declension and anachronism, the main objective in detailing the engineer's boosterism of guaraná. Rather, it is to elucidate how the meanings that Silva Coutinho invested in the plant inhered to the world that he inhabited and sought to change. In this context, the engineer's rendering of guaraná history as emblematic of Indigenous nationalistic promise can also be understood.

BRAZILIAN HISTORIOGRAPHY HAS NOTED Indigenous peoples' significance for imperial state formation and nineteenth-century nation-building. To root nationalism in time and territory, ethnographic studies of the Instituto Histórico e Geográfico Brasileiro (IHGB) lauded ancestral Indigenous bravery as constitutive of Brazilian cultural stock.[138] Some elites studied Tupi and included Indigenous imagery in their coat of arms.[139] Archaeological remains were scrutinized for supposed linkages to ancient Mediterranean civilizations.[140] As Brazil lacked monumental pre-Columbian architecture, nationalist thinkers touted Indigenous sophistication in the forest and fields and in the kitchen to counter European colonial ideologies. To promote colonization and resource extraction, the IHGB investigated the agricultural and botanical knowledge of the Indigenous, whose mastery of "natural products" even their detractors acknowledged.[141]

To be sure, the most blessed Native for elites was bygone, as dominant nineteenth-century ideologies throughout the Americas slated Indigenous peoples for disappearance, whether through physical elimination or cultural assimilation.[142] The noble savage's ideological foil in Brazil was the "Tapuia," the generically named foes of the coastal Tupi and the Portuguese, tarred by Spix and Martius as the "declared enemies of the immigrant, at times attacking and persecuting him, while at others, sensing their inferiority, fleeing from any contact with the European."[143] Advocates of eliminationism included Portuguese prince regent Dom João VI, who declared a "just war" on the Botocudo people; half a century later, Brazilian diplomat and historian Francisco Adolfo de Varnhagen urged force against the Indigenous and compulsory labor as recompense for their captors.[144] The imperial Brazilian state, however, officially endorsed a more conciliatory Indigenous policy. The Regulamento das Missões of 1845 entrusted lay directors with the provincial and local administration of Indigenous villages but authorized missionaries to provide religious and educational assistance.[145] In practice, violence, fraud, and co-optation continued as day-to-day strategies for controlling Indigenous labor and land.[146]

Members of the dominant society assessed Native Brazilians according to presumed productive, commercial, and military advantage. For Amazonian statesmen, the mid-nineteenth-century Indigenous "question" was particularly fraught due to the regional labor shortage. In 1858, the president of Amazonas deemed Indigenous peoples as the province's "only hands" for the foreseeable future, until the groundwork for colonization had been laid.[147] Likewise, in opposing the navy's proposed recruitment of Indigenous men, Pará congressman Bernardo de Souza Franco emphasized their regional importance as boatsmen and traders.[148] Many Indigenous peoples continued to elude state control entirely in the Amazon, with assaults on settlers and river travelers commonplace, alongside revenge attacks by colonists.[149]

During the 1860s and 1870s, a number of Amazonian reformers extolled the Mundurucu and the Sateré-Mawé as "model" Indigenous populations, in part for their involvement in the guaraná trade. In 1866, Amazonas Director of Indians Gabriel Antonio Ribeiro Guimarães praised the Sateré-Mawé, "who cultivate guaraná and today make the wealth of the Municipality with this name," and the Mundurucu, "who likewise plant guaraná and are very hard-working, light, and warrior in spirit."[150] In *O vale do Amazonas* (1866), Tavares Bastos likewise hailed their industriousness, noting that "the banks of the Tapajós and its vicinity are occupied by many catechized Indians; of these the Maués and Mundurucus tribes are well known."[151] A decade later, Rufino Luiz Tavares's survey of the Tapajós listed two exceptions to the "indifferent and ambitionless Indians": the Mundurucu, "useful, intelligent, friends of the whites and dedicated manioc famers," with an estimated population of ten thousand; and the Sateré-Mawé, "tame, highly industrious and the only cultivators and processors of guaraná, although false and slightly perverse in character," numbering some four thousand.[152] Based on his visit to a Sateré-Mawé village in 1872, botanist João Barbosa Rodrigues, the future director of Rio's Botanical Garden, characterized the Indigenous people as "proud, industrious, spirited, and independent."[153] That judgment was rendered after he had also measured their skulls in the craniometric studies of purported racial aptitude dear to nineteenth-century scientists and natural history museums worldwide.[154]

As a proponent of Indigenous integration, Silva Coutinho proclaimed, "The Indian is good, docile, and amenable to civilization." Merely "a child, nothing more, nothing less," Indigenous peoples could not be abandoned to their "savage instincts" in the forest, the nation deprived of "useful sons."[155] Like other nineteenth-century *indigenistas*, Silva Coutinho upheld the virtues of Native peoples, particularly those with agricultural vocations and dispositional labor.[156] Topping his list were the Mundurucu, a "loyal and honorable" people who lived better than most of the population of Amazonas, in his estimation. For their domestication and cultivation of guaraná, the Sateré-Mawé also merited acclaim; only the history of white violence, dispossession, and swindling explained why some remained "perfidious in their heart" while "docile in their physiognomy."[157] Likewise, in 1876, military general and former provincial president José Vieira Couto de Magalhães posited that guaraná exemplified the sophistication of Indigenous food science. Couto de Magalhães, who upheld Indigenous peoples as symbols of national identity and promoted their conversion into colonists and laborers through education, noted, "Till today that plant that is richer in theine than tea or coffee is cultivated exclusively by them, and from whose fruit is prepared the sticks (*bastões*) of guaraná, making the Maué tribe, who live in the Tapajós valley, famous among all others for the excellence of this product, which is beginning to gain a following in European markets."[158]

Through his ethnographic writings, Silva Coutinho also introduced Brazilian readers to the rich cultural worlds of Native Amazonian peoples. In his article on guaraná, he recounted the "beautiful and sublime" myth of the plant's origin and Sateré-Mawé ethnogenesis (presumably conveyed to him by an Indigenous informant), thereby glorifying Brazil's multiethnic heritage. Yet the Sateré-Mawé's story also revealed the purported illogic of Indigenous understandings of the natural environment, or according to the engineer, "the imagination of a people in its infancy, heated up in the equatorial sun."[159] In other words, Silva Coutinho's claims to scientific expertise entailed the disparagement of Indigenous knowledge intrinsic to postcolonial hierarchies of power. "History" posited a division between the human and the natural worlds, the agency of human actors, the chronological sequence of events, and the celebratory march of scientific progress.[160] Silva Coutinho's retelling of the Sateré-Mawé creationist myth, recounted in this book's introduction, nationalized Indigenous folklore while underscoring the importance of "civilizing" the backlands.

Nineteenth-century Latin American scientists were not only encumbered with mapping territories and studying natural resources; they were also "professional explainers," offering reassurance or reproach to foreigners and compatriots alike regarding their countries' futures.[161] Guaraná caught Silva Coutinho's fancy as a means to this end: a formula for regional integration, an "antidote" to extractivism, a marker of Indigenous potential and Brazilian distinction. Born from his elite upbringing and education, professional experience, and years of travel in the Amazon, Silva Coutinho's scientific nationalism placed him both at one and at odds with foreign colleagues and Amazonian locals. In insisting on guaraná's importance to sustainable development and Brazilian geopolitical primacy in the South American heartland, Silva Coutinho had a lot of explaining to do. The audience just needed to listen.

THE THAYER EXPEDITION SPENT EIGHT DAYS in the Maués region. Aside from the main town, they visited two Mundurucu and Sateré-Mawé villages nearby. At the first, Mucajatuba, they were welcomed by a group of fifty, under the leadership of the elderly chief Vicente, who had accompanied Silva Coutinho on his 1863 Tapajós journey. At the village at Paricatuba, only two Indigenous came aboard the ship. Agassiz added another seventy species of fish to his collection from the Maués segment of his journey.[162] In total, the expedition would remit eighty thousand Amazonian objects to Harvard, including clippings of guaraná and a figurine molded from the paste. Examination of the Brazilian specimens, aside from the fish, was never systematically undertaken.[163]

In *A Journey in Brazil*, published in Boston in 1868 (in France the following year, and in Brazil only in 1938), Elizabeth Agassiz noted of guaraná: "It is said to have medicinal properties also, and is administered with excellent effect in cases of diarrhea. In certain parts of Brazil it is very extensively used as well as in Bolivia, and will, no doubt, have a wider distribution when its value is more generally known." Of Maués, she wrote, "Those who know of its history speak of it as one of the most promising of the Amazonian settlements, and as having a better moral tone than usually prevails." Of the Madeira's geopolitical importance, she likewise parroted her guide: "It seems strange, when this river is the highway of commerce from Bolivia, Matto-Grosso, and through Matto-Grosso from Paraguay to the Amazons, that the suggestion made by Major Coutinho in his interesting account of his journey on the Rio Madeira, has not been adopted. He says that a road carried along the shore of the river for a distance of forty leagues would obviate all the difficulty and danger of this arduous journey."[164] Silva Coutinho had achieved a public relations breakthrough.

For his part, the engineer submitted a report to the minister of agriculture, commerce, and public works on "guaraná and other products from the province of Amazonas," along with thirteen packages containing mineral and botanical samples, including flowers, seeds, and sticks of guaraná. Silva Coutinho urged the minister to plant the seeds at Rio's Botanical Garden to encourage propagation throughout Brazil and to dispel doubt surrounding guaraná's cultivability outside Maués or under the care of "*civilizados.*" Citing rising French demand for the drug to treat neuralgia, he also suggested exporting dried seeds to bypass the intricate processing method.[165] In 1870, Silva Coutinho published a study on guaraná in the *Revista Agrícola do Instituto Fluminense de Agricultura*, the first full-length article dedicated to the plant.[166] As the secretary of the Brazilian Commission to the Centennial International Exhibition in Philadelphia in 1876, he promoted the product "richer in caffeine than tea, maté, coffee leaves and roasted coffee."[167] In this way, Silva Coutinho aspired to achieve socioeconomic development and state sovereignty on the Amazonian frontier.

The modernization of the guaraná trade, however, eluded Silva Coutinho during his lifetime. Foreign markets continued to crown coffee, the nation's decades-long leading export, king. Furthermore, the boom in latex production conspired against an overhaul of the Amazon's extractivist economy. By 1881, crude rubber exports from Pará were valued at over six times that of cacao and nearly one hundred times that of guaraná.[168] As Silva Coutinho had feared, rubber fever swept the Madeira over the next decades, facilitated by the regular steam service introduced on the river in 1873.[169] The rubber trade also came to dominate the Tapajós. João Barbosa Rodrigues noted that by 1872, commerce in guaraná between Itaituba and Mato Grosso had diminished due to the increased extraction of rubber and diversion of labor.[170] The influx of migrant tappers overran Sateré-Mawé villages, while French geographer Henri Coudreau claimed on his 1895–96 Tapajós journey that even "the Maués, onetime major producers of guaraná, have nearly completely abandoned this work for rubber." He estimated that the total amount of guaraná produced by the Maués region did not exceed one hundred arrobas (1,500 kilos).[171] While rubber's advance up the Madeira and Tapajós solidified trade and transportation, linking Mato Grosso and Bolivia with Brazil's northern provinces and the international market, Silva Coutinho watched another extractive economy siphon labor and resources, upending plans for "orderly" settlement. With Paraguay's wartime defeat and the resumption of regular steam service to Cuiabá via the Paraguayan River in the 1870s, guaraná could again more easily reach the Mato Grosso capital through the Atlantic and

River Plate route. Years later, Claude Lévi-Strauss noted that coastal steamers brought guaraná from Manaus and Belém to Rio de Janeiro, from where it was shipped to Cuiabá, relegating the Tapajós trade to a "heroic and already forgotten past."[172]

Indeed, many of the best-laid plans of nineteenth-century Brazilian engineers for agricultural modernization, transportation overhaul, and frontier colonization ran aground in a slavocratic, latifundia society committed to a monocrop economy.[173] In the case of guaraná, small-scale growers continued to control production as part of mixed subsistence, foraging, trade, and communal practices—the "routinism" of Brazilian agriculturists decried by modernizers.[174] From his 1872 journey on the Tapajós, João Barbosa Rodrigues offered a revealing snapshot. He estimated the presence of over fifty Sateré-Mawé settlements scattered throughout the forest, placing the total population between seven hundred and one thousand.[175] Following a narrow, densely lined forest trail, Barbosa Rodrigues walked half a day before reaching a village of eighty. Its residents cultivated guaraná and had acquired clothes, yet both men and women walked around "almost naked." They cultivated corn, manioc, cashews, and cotton, which they used to sew their hammocks. Palm trees of açaí, tucumã, pupunha, and bacaba in the surrounding forest provided additional nutritional balance. Others had taken to tapping rubber. Barbosa Rodrigues also learned more about Indigenous therapeutics, such as the vine used to prepare paricá, which the Indians used for "constipation or malaise," and a healing practice involving the *putuipe* instrument. In a second village, the botanist observed the preparation and daylong consumption of the ritual guaraná beverage, *çapó* (noted in chapter 1). Of Sateré-Mawé lifeways, the scientist noted: "Loving their independence, they did not want to take the advice of the missionaries that traveled there, congregating the dispersed population to form a center for catechism for the Mundurucus of the plains."[176] The botanist's description highlights the limitations of labor recruitment, capital investment, and profit seeking for the "rationalization" of the trade. It also points to the geographic knowledge and spatial logic of the Indigenous population in claiming the interfluves of the Tapajós-Madeira region, whose smaller rivers and inland territories were relative terra incognita for whites.[177]

In his crusade against rural poverty and geographic isolation, Silva Coutinho dedicated his professional life to science, engineering, and public policy reform. In 1889, while attending the Universal Exposition in Paris, crowned by the inauguration of the Eiffel Tower, he undoubtedly marveled at the technological breakthroughs that promised greater progress for his own country one day. Slavery had been abolished in Brazil the previous year, the last hold-out in the Western Hemisphere, and the enfeebled emperor would be overthrown the following November by adherents of republicanism. The expansion of railroads, steamships, and telegraphs had expedited transportation and communication, albeit quite unevenly, across Brazilian territory. But the intrepid Amazonian traveler, survivor of white-knuckled jungle adventures, took ill with fever in the French capital. He died there on October 11, 1889, at the age of fifty-nine.[178] Others, however, remained on guaraná's trail. Scientists, physicians, and pharmaceutical firms had further investigated the plant, and consumer demand was rising in the Northern Hemisphere.

CHAPTER FOUR

Drug Prospects

Guaraná's Anglo-American Boom and Bust

Guaraná was one of many plant-based drugs that formed the foundation of nineteenth-century medicine. In the days before spices migrated to the supermarket, and herbs to the health food store, druggists and their apprentices knew the distinctive aromas and hues of the plant materials that they pounded, sifted, mixed, or folded into pills, tinctures, syrups, emulsions, and ointments, or that they dispensed in powdered form or liquid extracts supplied by larger drug manufacturers.[1] The *United States Pharmacopoeia* (*USP*) first listed guaraná in 1880, and although the publication carried no legal authority at the time, inclusion as an "officinal" vetted by a committee of elite physicians drawn from state medical societies signaled respectability.[2]

Historians have identified multiple factors to explain the relative success of psychoactive drugs in North American and European markets: scale of production and distribution, pharmacological effect, cultural acceptance, and historical juncture.[3] Guaraná has featured sparingly as a case study.[4] An analysis of the drug's fleeting popularity in nineteenth-century Anglo-American therapeutics, whose documentary base I have accessed over other foreign markets' due to linguistic and logistic facility, can fill this gap, while engaging questions of broader historiographical concern.

In colder climes, nineteenth-century health practitioners and drug promoters claimed guaraná in the pursuit of medical knowledge, pain management, and financial profit. Consonant with then common beliefs that varied medical conditions might be the consequence of the same underlying disturbance, guaraná was recommended for a wide range of ailments—from nose-bleeds, bronchitis, and sciatica to dysentery, gonorrhea, and urinary infections. "Tonic" medicines, such as guaraná, were believed to strengthen organs, muscle fibers, and blood vessels, restoring the bodily synergies and equilibrium necessary for good health.[5]

Guaraná's most consistent indication, however, was for "sick-headache."[6] In 1884, for example, Dr. Francis Brown of Boston touted guaraná and coffee as the most "efficient remedies" for the condition, typically caused by "overwork, which wearies the body while it taxes and worries the mind, and loss of sleep."[7] Gilded Age medical literature also endorsed guaraná for the treatment of neurasthenia, or nervous exhaustion, understood as a somatic condition marked by neural weakness, headache, and an array of debilitating symptoms said to derive from a combination of hereditary disposition and the external stresses of modern life, particularly for the delicate and overly educated.[8] Informed by theories of social Darwinism, physicians assessed nerve weakness as directly proportionate to so-called social progress and racial superiority.[9] Among their remedies and techniques, caregivers proffered guaraná. Like the disease, the cure—a getaway to a spa or a seaside resort, muscular exercise, electrization, or the administration of an "exotic" therapeutic agent—was upheld as fashionable.[10]

Drug companies rushed to meet, or create, the demand for guaraná—or at least claim the substance in their medications. Parke, Davis & Company launched its fluid extract of guaraná (or concentrated preparation in an alcohol solution) in 1874, indicated for use "in sick headache, and pains in the head, and other symptoms, which are caused by a morbid condition of the mucous membrane lining the stomach."[11] It was the first U.S. company to manufacture the drug, although patients could previously acquire a guaraná medicine from the Parisian Grimault firm, which exported the product as far as Australia and New Zealand.[12] Others soon followed. In the 1880s, John Wyeth and Brothers pitched its Elixir Guaraná as a tonic for headache, neuralgia, diarrhea, and gastralgia.[13] The De Forest W. Saxe Company offered guaraná for carbonated soft drinks in 1893 (years before the emergence of Brazil's "national" soda), hawking its Phospho-Guaraná with Celery flavor to drugstores as "excellent for Nervous or Sick Headache."[14] And Keasbey & Mattison's Bromo-Caffeine, purportedly combining guaraná with hydrobromic acid, promised "brain workers" and women (classified as two separate entities) relief from nervous headaches resulting from "overtaxed mental energy or excitement, acute attacks of indigestion, the depression following alcoholic excesses, the suprasensitiveness of chloral, morphia, and opium habitués, and with ladies the headache and backache of neurasthenia, hysteria, dysmenorrhea, and kindred disorders."[15] Thus it was that Dr. Seabury W. Bowen plied his patient and neighbor with Bromo-Caffeine upon his grisly discovery of her father and stepmother's bludgeoned bodies in the family's Fall River, Massachusetts, home in 1892, as the physician subsequently testified at her criminal trial. That would make Lizzie Borden not only the defendant in one of the most sensational murders in U.S. history but probably guaraná's most notorious nineteenth-century consumer.[16]

For customers in the Global North, guaraná was expensive. Among Parke-Davis's potpourri of medicines and nearly five hundred botanical fluid

Parke, Davis & Co.
guaraná fluid extract,
late nineteenth century.
Courtesy of Bert
Easterbrook and
The Herb Museum,
Vancouver.

extracts, the remedy stood out for its cost. In 1878, the firm's fluid extract of guaraná sold for $10 per pound, while that of coca leaves went for $6.50; damiana (for the treatment of male sexual dysfunction) fetched $4.00; and kava kava from the Sandwich Islands (touted as a remedy for gonorrhea, rheumatism, and gout) sold for $6.00.[17] Likewise, among Cincinnati-based Lloyd Brothers' dozens of "Specific Medicine" (or highly concentrated unofficial tinctures of plants extracted by maceration or percolation), its guaraná preparation was one of the costliest.[18]

Correspondence of the Wyeth Company with Lanman & Kemp, a New York–based patent medicine company with extensive commercial outlets and suppliers throughout Latin America, reveals U.S. pharmaceutical firms' difficulties in obtaining the drug. In 1877, Lanman & Kemp sent Wyeth shipments of guaraná from at least two drug traders in Belém, but Wyeth complained of an ongoing shortfall of its monthly target of one hundred pounds.[19] As a British pharmaceutical journal would note, "The consumption in Brazil is known to be very large, and, apart from the paste which is brought into commerce by the Indians of the Amazon territory, the guaraná is cultivated to some extent in the districts of Maués, Villa Bella, and Imperatrix [sic] only."[20] A general labor "shortage" crimped Amazonian drug supply chains: the difficulty of procuring ipecacuanha, for example, stemmed not only from the health hazards of the emetic's acrid juice and pungent dust to workers but from bosses' reluctance to reassign indebted rubber tappers to uproot the plant.[21] At the height of foreign demand for guaraná, Anglo-American government and private interests contemplated or undertook transplantation schemes from South America, albeit without lasting commercial success.

Although guaraná's fame in the Northern Hemisphere radiated during the fin de siècle, its star dimmed in a matter of decades: it was officially dropped from the *United States Pharmacopoeia* of 1920. The drug's high cost and disputed efficacy had roused foreign detractors from the get-go. As a physician attending the USP convention pointed out, prescriptions of guaraná had dwindled, for its sole value as a "nervine and stimulant derived from its caffeine content, which if unassayed was untrustworthy, and which could be more convenient and economically obtained from other sources."[22]

A TROPICAL DRUG'S FAD in wealthier nations might be approached from multiple historiographical perspectives. Economic historians of Latin America will recognize guaraná's late nineteenth-century blip in world markets as another tale of primary export-led growth volatility. From the 1870s to the 1930s, Latin America's integration into the global economy boosted commodity exports and direct foreign investment, yet commercial supply and product substitution consistently affected market value. In Latin America's "commodity lottery," guaraná would not prove a long-term winner in the turn-of-the-century markets above the equator.[23] With coffee and tea promising cheaper jolts amid well-established food practices and social conventions, European and North American markets confined guaraná to the pharmaceutical sector, the clearinghouse whence its caffeine-carrying cohort had long since exited to cash in on the mass beverage market. Their emerging soft drink industries too bypassed guaraná for flavoring, opting for other stimulants, such as coca or kola nuts. Tellingly, unlike at the London International Exhibition of 1862, where Brazil's delegation pitched guaraná as a drink and a medicine, a decade later in Philadelphia it was apparently displayed solely as a pharmaceutical product, alongside other therapeutic plants, such as sarsaparilla, jaborandi, copaiba, ipecacuanha, and guaco.[24] Trickling from North American and European medicine cabinets rather than overflowing their cafés, teahouses, or soda fountains, guaraná would transit in the shadows: in the privacy of the doctor's office, in the patient's consultation with her pharmacist, in the notoriously unregulated nineteenth-century drug markets, in the gray areas where the anguish of physical pain and the light of hope commingle. Even there, guaraná sputtered due to cheaper caffeinated substitutes and the subsequent rise of synthetic medicines. Guaraná's history, in this sense, exemplifies the legendary boom-bust cycles of Brazil's export economy.

Historians of medicine in the United States might situate guaraná's debut instead in the context of soaring, unregulated postbellum drug consumption. Nineteenth-century legislation viewed drugs as an unrestricted good, enabling customers without professional credentials or medical expertise to purchase or receive shipments.[25] High rates of disease and poor diets fueled drug demand, the expansion of railroads facilitated distribution, and the tumult of urbanization fostered multiple ills, both real and perceived. Wounded Civil War infantrymen downed medicines often laden with high percentages of alcohol, opium, or morphine; the plying of psychoactive drugs to soldiers and veterans is a not-so-secret weapon and casualty of war.[26] Sales of patent medicines mushroomed with secret ingredients (suspected by historians of medicine to have been tonics, cathartics, or emetics, many with high levels of alcohol and fortified with opium or cocaine) promising relief from countless maladies.[27] Whereas in 1859 the nostrum industry netted $3.5 million, by 1900 sales were estimated at $59 million, a sevenfold increase in per capita expenditure.[28] Indigenous medicines held distinctive appeal; faith in the "simple" cures of peoples seen as closer to nature had deep colonial roots in North America.[29] In this competitive market, guaraná became a provisional, albeit ultimately unsuccessful, contender.

Historians of science might view guaraná's intercontinental dissemination in the context of colonial botanizing and knowledge transfers. Of course, colonial botany, or "the study, naming, cultivation, and marketing of plants in colonial contexts," stretched back farther, to early modern European mercantilist trade and scientific investigation.[30] As noted, Portugal's empire had allowed for a vast appropriation of medicinal plants, and the global spread and commercialization of pharmacological knowledge.[31] Yet European and North American botanizing expanded overseas in the late nineteenth century with the conquest or exploration of tropical regions.[32] With advances in biochemistry, bacteriology, and epidemiology facilitating military deployment and settler colonialism, and justifying the "benevolence" of such ventures, Western scientific investigation of "new" plants or commercial transplant of old ones buoyed imperial capabilities and ideologies.[33] University of Pennsylvania professor John Harshberger, who coined the term *ethno-botany* in 1896 to incentivize the study of "new uses of plants" for manufacture (particularly those of Native Americans), claimed that the "discovery" of new plants would elucidate "the cultural position of the tribes who used the plants for food, shelter or clothing." He noted that "the well-known classification of men into savage, pastoral, agricultural and civilized, will roughly serve our purpose."[34] Harshberger was correct on one front: approximately three-fourths of biologically active plant-derived compounds have been shown by current scientific research to confirm their folk or ethnomedical application, underscoring the threat posed by the destruction of tropical forests and Indigenous lifeways.[35]

Through Linnaean taxonomy and chemical analysis, guaraná was reclassified. Since the eighteenth century, Western science came to be organized according to disciplines based on specialized procedures and systems whose so-called universal method claimed to ensure the transposability of knowledge and the improvement of society. Quantification allowed things to be "objectively" compared and ordered—at least by those who mastered these techniques and whose selectivity in categorization was mediated by social structures and political resources.[36] Scientists silenced or disparaged Indigenous understandings, although the market appeal of Native American botanicals might favor flashing guaraná's Amazonian origins.

This chapter interweaves these varied historiographical strands, exploring nineteenth-century Western scientists' acquisition and dissemination of knowledge of guaraná and its interface with commercial health care, cultural practices, and epistemologies.[37] Particularly useful is Charles Rosenberg's conceptualization of science as a form of historically specific knowledge and techniques that define and legitimize the discipline; provide its peers (those who see themselves as scientists or prospective scientists) with a shared set of values to motivate and justify behavior; and uphold tenets of selflessness and truth in explaining problems such as illness, social difference, and the vagaries of the life cycle.[38] Beyond therapeutic agents, anthropologists further note, medicines are social objects whose exchange relies on discrete actors and forms of communication.[39] Social attitudes and practices define appropriate standards and settings for drug consumption, while the absence of relevant cultural frameworks muddles the significance and even potential benefits of drug taking.[40] In these manifestations, Western medicine bears fundamental resemblance to traditional Indigenous healing practices. Tracking guaraná's transition to an Anglo-American pharmaceutical, I focus on the historical processes of transmission and adaptation surrounding cross-cultural therapeutic transfers. Nineteenth-century scientists, pharmaceutical firms, and health practitioners who promoted guaraná in the Northern Hemisphere, detaching the plant from its Indigenous cosmologies, relied on elaborate processes of mediation and reassignment to bind together researchers, providers, and patients in new codes and rituals.[41] As this chapter argues, scientists' reinvention of guaraná streamlined the drug's adaptation to wealthier foreign markets, where interest spiked but proved unsustainable.

OVER THE COURSE of the nineteenth century, scientists reclassified guaraná according to the "universal" standards of botany and chemistry. As Europeans voyaging outside their continent encountered many new fruits, vegetables, plants, and medicines—with the six thousand plant species recorded by Caspar Bauhin in 1623 increasing to fifty thousand by Georges Cuvier in 1800—botanists, pharmacists, doctors, and collectors sought to systematize the classification of flora.[42] On the basis of morphological comparison, Karl Linnaeus (1707–88) rationalized the placement of plants within a universal taxonomic system, thereby facilitating the global exchange of knowledge and goods. The establishment of chemistry as a modern science under the influence of Antoine Lavoisier (1743–94) reshaped the practice of pharmacy, while the development of physiology and pharmacology allowed for significant contributions in the field of drug development. Analysis of plant substances—particularly by French and German pharmacists due to their knowledge of chemistry, specialized equipment, and institutional support—led to the discovery in 1817 of alkaloids, a class of organic compounds composed of carbon, hydrogen, nitrogen, and usually oxygen that often possess both poisonous and curative properties. The isolation of the chemical composition of drug molecules and their relationship to physiological activity allowed for the development of new therapeutic agents gleaned from the expansion in European scientific voyages and global trade.[43] Parsing living organisms according to objective properties and quantifiable standards allowed for greater commensurability in scientific knowledge and global interconnection, as well as social hierarchization.[44]

Spearheading the nineteenth-century scientific reclassification of guaraná were the Bavarian brothers Karl and Theodor von Martius. During his three-year voyage to Brazil from 1817 to 1820, botanist Karl von Martius collected thousands of fauna and flora, among which were ninety-two native medicinal

84.

PAULLINIA Cupana.

Paullinia cupana botanical line drawing in *Flora Brasiliensis* (1874–1900). Although illustrations of plants are ancient, Linnaean-style drawings aimed to depict the discrete parts of a plant for the purpose of comparison and botanical classification. Such images facilitated the exchange of knowledge of guaraná in scientific networks. Peter H. Raven Library/Missouri Botanical Garden.

species from the Amazon, belonging to thirty-eight families and offering one hundred different therapeutic uses. First published in 1843, and in Portuguese translation in 1854 (with subsidies from Dom Pedro II), Karl von Martius's *Systema de materia medica vegetal brasileira* described the therapeutic value of 730 species; his fifteen-volume *Flora brasiliensis*, containing information on 22,267 plant species, took over sixty years to complete.[45] Accompanying drawings were produced over decades, some at the time of the journey by the naturalists or artists, and others in Europe based on collected materials. Proliferating in the nineteenth century with advances in printing, botanical illustrations represented the diagnostic characteristics of species and their internal and external morphological characteristics for the purpose of scientific classification.[46]

Guaraná was one of the Amazonian plants that Karl von Martius sought to reclaim. In a lecture at the Royal Bavarian Academy of Sciences in 1829, he related popular use of the plant as a "stomachal, febrifuge and aphrodisiac," though he confessed his uncertainty regarding the bitter drug's "dominant character."[47] For the naturalist, Brazil's Indigenous peoples may have been well-versed in botanical therapies but could offer little systematized knowledge for the advancement of Western science or Christian morality.[48] As "relics of an erstwhile cultured and flourishing race," Indigenous peoples' medical knowledge represented nothing more than "a miserable fragment of ancient science accommodated to nature" and a gross deviation from European understandings of the sick body. Through the "enlightened experimentation" of "competent persons"—namely, Europeans who occupied a "more advanced stage of social life"—the chemical components of Brazilian plants and their physiological effects could be ascertained, instead of prospective users being subjected to "mere domestic traditions, or the hoaxes of ignorant men."[49] It is worth noting that the Bavarian basher of shamanism himself believed in animal magnetism and embraced a romantic view of tropical nature influenced by Alexander von Humboldt and Johann Wolfgang von Goethe.[50] Alongside Indigenous peoples' purported failure to improve their lands (*terra nullius*), disparagement of their knowledge systems sustained racial hierarchies and colonial-era dispossessions.[51]

Based on a sample that he gathered in 1819, Martius reclassified guaraná according to the Linnaean system. The plant's scientific name, *Paullinia sorbilis*, whose genus honored a seventeenth-century Danish botanist, was ironic: Simon Paulli's *Commentarius de abusu tabaci Americanorum veteri, et herbæ thee Asiaticorum in Europe novo* (1661) inveighed against the foreign stimulants then overtaking Europe. *Sorbilis*, deriving from the Latin "to suck in," referenced the species' consumption as a beverage. Guaraná became another type of flowering shrub and liana in the Sapindaceae, or soapberry, family (today with approximately 140 genera and 2,000 species, almost entirely restricted to tropical and subtropical America).[52]

Much has been written on the history and geopolitics of the practice of binomial nomenclature advocated by Linnaeus, a Swedish university professor and practicing physician with an interest in the therapeutic and commercial value of plants and apprehension of the divine in nature. In the name of science, Linnaeus urged standardized classification as a solution to the "Babel" and "barbarism" governing their naming. Once identified, a specimen would represent similar plant types based on component parts regardless of ecological or historical-cultural context. Linnaeus's linguistic limitations as a monolingual Swede may have prompted insistence on Latin as the lingua franca of botany, the language of educated men and one that few women could read. Linnaeus also called for the naming of genera to honor botanists, rewarding their heroic pursuit of science with "immortal renown." Scientists from other fields, such as chemistry, anatomy, and medicine, might also be paid tribute, alongside explorers, monarchs, and patrons. Linnaeus thus reinforced the principle that science is created by great European men. He also championed the notion of priority as a fundamental scientific ideal: that an individual who first published a name and exact description of a plant is considered to have established its identity. To be sure, other Europeans opposed Linnaeus's classification, which was only officially accepted in 1905, not to mention the alternative botanical taxonomies of traditional and Indigenous peoples that have persisted to this day.[53]

Guaraná's renaming by Martius illustrates that botanical nomenclature reflects not only plant morphology but the cultural exchanges that produce colonial knowledge and hierarchies.[54] Indigenous peoples' purported absence of systematic scientific classification served to impugn their mental capacity.[55] In place of a model of collective Indigenous knowledge production stood one that prized individualized authorship and transformative application—the ideological roots of Western patent laws that continue to prejudice traditional knowledge in the marketplace of "individual" ideas and corporate profits.[56]

Indeed, based on the principle of priority, Martius's authorial right to *Paullinia sorbilis* proved contentious. Martius's *Reise in Brasilien*, published between 1823 and 1831, detailed the plant that he had encountered in the Maués region.[57] Prussian geographer Alexander von Humboldt and French botanist Aimé Bonpland, however, had collected a sample of guaraná from Venezuela's upper Orinoco on an earlier journey to South America between 1799 and 1804. It had been classified in 1821 as *Paullinia cupana* in *Nova genera et species plantarum*, part of a seven-volume series edited by German botanist Karl Sigismund Kunth, based on the expedition's collection of some sixty thousand plant specimens. *Cupana* referenced its local Indigenous name. Guaraná would be referred to by both scientific names until 1897, when *Paullinia cupana* was retained due to Kunth's priority in naming the species. Only in 1937, after Brazilian botanist Adolpho Ducke gathered samples of *cupana* from the upper Rio Negro, would Martius's identification of a new species variety be recognized, based on significant morphological differences in the Maués plants from those in upriver locations. The scientific name of guaraná from the lower Amazon region is the mouthful *Paullinia cupana* Kunth var. *sorbilis* (Mart.) Ducke, the only variety that is commercially used.[58]

Karl von Martius's pharmacological assessment of guaraná reflected the continued primacy of humoral theory in early nineteenth-century European notions of etiology. For more than a millennium, a basic tenet of Western medical therapeutics upheld that good health required stabilizing the balance among the four liquid humors of the body: blood, associated with heat and moisture; phlegm, with moisture and cold; black bile, with cold and dryness; and yellow bile, with dryness and heat. An increase or decrease in the quality or quantity of any of these humors destabilized the body's system, producing correlating symptoms.[59] In *Systema de materia medica vegetal brasileira*, von Martius claimed of guaraná:

> It prevents the excessive sensitivity of the intestinal plexus, thus reducing febrile attacks, supports the stomach and intestines, and mainly prevents the excessive evacuation of mucus, somewhat excites the movements of the heart and arteries and increases diaphoresis. It is therefore regarded as a noble remedy: in fevers, or a state of sensibility, increasing as a result of cooling or heat stroke, excessive agitation of the body, sufferings in the soul, prolonged vigils, and sometimes in cramps, flatulence, anorexia (fasting), nervous migraine, skin dryness. It is contraindicated for the state of fullness of the abdominal viscera, saburra, and the disposition of blood to the head. It excites the venereal appetite, but is said to decrease sperm fecundity.[60]

From a sample of guaraná provided by von Martius, his brother Theodor—a professor of pharmacy at Erlangen—went on to name the drug's active principle in 1826, which he called guaranine.[61] The alkaloid's structure, however, was later shown to be a tetramethylxanthine nearly identical to caffeine, which German physician Friedlieb Ferdinand Runge had identified seven years earlier.[62] European scientists conducted additional phytochemical research over the ensuing decades.[63] In 1851, naturalist Richard Spruce noted of the specimens he shipped to the Royal Botanic Gardens: "The essential principle of this substance is said to be identical with Theine and Caffeine, which I can well believe, for the immoderate use of Guaraná relaxes the stomach and causes sleeplessness; precisely the effect which results from the abuse of tea and coffee."[64] In Brazil, extensive chemical analysis of guaraná was conducted by Theodor Peckolt, a Prussian pharmacist who arrived in 1847 at the suggestion of Karl von Martius to study native flora and remit samples to Europe, and who also served as the official drug purveyor for the Brazilian royal family. From his Rio de Janeiro laboratory and pharmacy, Peckolt would analyze thousands of Brazilian plants, publishing several books and more than four hundred scientific works in national and international journals on the nation's materia medica.[65] In 1868, the American Pharmaceutical Association reported that Peckolt "has analyzed the seeds of this plant, which yield the guaraná, and finds them to contain caffeine, yellow fixed oil, brown-green soft resin, red resin, resinous matter, nitrogenous extractive, red coloring matter, amorphous bitter principle, guaranic acid, saponin, gallic acid, iron-greening tannic acid, albuminous matter, starch, glucose, dextrin, pectin, mucilage, malic acid and cellulose."[66]

Through a universal language, scientists rendered guaraná commensurable with better-known stimulants.[67] Shorn of Indigenous understandings, the plant's principles were itemized and ranked. Historians have noted that the delinking of food and drug arose in the context of the Industrial Revolution, when societies obtained the capacity to manufacture chemically refined products, and in expanding economies within which these products might circulate, whether legally or illegally, as commodities.[68] The process, Stephen Hugh-Jones notes, was tied to the formation of specialized medical and pharmacological professions and an established judiciary and police force.[69] Through the publication and dissemination of specialized journals, scientists buttressed global networks and frameworks of knowledge in which guaraná was reinvented as a botanical species and pharmaceutical.

ANGLO-AMERICAN COMMERCIAL INTEREST in guaraná surged following the endorsement by Samuel Wilks of Guy's Hospital in London. In an article in the *British Medical Journal* and the *Lancet* in 1872, the esteemed physician touted guaraná as "a most valuable remedy in sick-headache." Wilks reported only "doubtful effect" on his own migraine—he preferred cannabis—but called for an extended trial in light of his patients' "encouraging" results. As one patient relayed, "I have every reason to believe them a complete preventive of headache, as on the least symptoms I have taken a powder, sometimes a second, in two hours of a time, and in no case have they failed as an effectual cure. I have not had a bad headache since I saw you."[70]

Guaraná had made its way to Wilks's desk circuitously. According to nineteenth-century medical and pharmaceutical journals, Dr. M. Gavrelle, a physician to Brazil's Emperor Pedro I, brought guaraná back to his native France, where he trumpeted the drug's efficacy before the Society of Medicine in 1840 in combating diarrhea and "tedious convalescence."[71] By the 1860s, the Grimault company of Paris prepared various guaraná medicines under the direction of Dr. M. Leconte, a professor of medicine and pharmaceutical chemist.[72] From France, it seems that guaraná traveled to Montreal, where one Mr. Wood experimented with the drug and sent samples to Wilks.[73] The physician's endorsement ricocheted across Anglo-American medical and pharmaceutical journals. Two years later, Parke-Davis launched its guaraná product in the United States, and competitors followed.

With increased foreign interest in guaraná, proposals for transplanting emerged. The Royal Botanic Gardens at Kew, which oversaw the successful transfer of cinchona and rubber to European colonies in Asia, spearheaded the initiative, with François Marie Glaziou, the general director of forests and gardens for Brazil's imperial family, serving as an early intermediary. Glaziou discussed guaraná in eleven letters to Kew between 1878 and 1892, part of a broader arrangement to exchange native seeds and clippings for exotic landscape flora, but ultimately failed to pass along "fresh seeds of this precious plant."[74] Kew then enlisted British diplomats and merchants in Manaus, eventually obtaining twenty seedlings of guaraná in September 1893 for "propagation and ultimate distribution of the plant to India and elsewhere."[75] The following year, Henry Trimen, director of the Royal Botanic Gardens in Peradeniya, Ceylon, reported that the plant was in full bloom.

Trimen's correspondence also suggests guaraná's limitations as a commercial crop in South Asia. "There is little of interest now that the colony is concerned only with advertising Ceylon tea," he noted.[76] Neither would guaraná take off in Trinidad, notwithstanding local naturalists' enthusiasm in 1896 that the Caribbean island's "luxuriance" would ensure success, while commanding $1.00 a pound in New York.[77] Nor had a Lisbon journal's proposal to transport guaraná seeds in sealed jars to Portugal's Atlantic islands and African colonies panned out either—though planters did strike gold by bringing Brazilian cacao to São Tomé.[78] Transplants by North American interests met a similar commercial dead end. Between 1918 and 1922, David Fairchild, the botanist in charge of the U.S. Office of Foreign Seed and Plant Introduction, received guaraná seeds from Brazil through the mediation of the U.S. embassy's commercial attaché. While over the course of his career Fairchild sent home cuttings and seeds of over 200,000 kinds of fruits, vegetables, and grains to diversify U.S. agriculture and cuisine, domestic cultivation of guaraná— unlike his introduction of the avocado, mango, and Medjool date—never got off the ground.[79] And in 1928 and 1939, schemes for guaraná transplantation to Florida or the Caribbean involving botanist and popular nature writer Norman Taylor, which envisioned a caffeine substitute for Coca-Cola in the face of potential wartime disruptions, fell through as well.[80] As environmental historians have noted, aside from some noteworthy cases, price incentives per se rarely cause innovation in cash crop expansion, as opposed to demographic pressure or the erosion of older agrarian systems. The success of crop transfers is also determined by adaptation of technology and knowledge and food preferences.[81]

For Anglo-American pharmaceutical companies, the marketing of a "new" drug entailed a different set of challenges. Parke-Davis's efforts to promote guaraná among health providers and patients in the United States required transforming an Amazonian botanical into a commercially competitive and culturally meaningful regimen of care.

ESTABLISHED IN DETROIT IN 1866, Parke, Davis & Company faced fierce competition, not only from established East Coast pharmaceutical firms but from countless patent medicine companies. "The amount of medicine prescribed in a large city is prodigious, the estimate being that in New York alone at least a million and a half prescriptions are compounded annually," a British medical gazette wrote in 1872. "How much of this is wasted on imaginary ills, no statistics will ever inform us."[82] In launching "new" drugs from "exotic" regions, Parke-Davis sought to upstage more reputable rivals, urging physicians to resist condemning a new remedy until they had tried the firm's products. By the mid-1880s, Parke-Davis had introduced over forty-five preparations, mainly as fluid extracts and plants gathered from company-sponsored collecting expeditions to Latin America and the Caribbean, the Pacific Northwest, and Fiji.[83] Aside from guaraná, the firm took credit for bringing *Eucalyptus globulus*, *Grindelia robusta*, yerba santa, and boldo to the U.S. public.[84]

Concomitantly, the company condemned the shadiness of the patent medicine industry. Like a number of so-called ethical firms, Parke-Davis committed to listing the contents of their medications, as denominated in the *United States Pharmacopoeia*, and to promoting their drug preparations only to physicians, thus renouncing direct-to-consumer advertising, as the practice of the U.S. pharmaceutical industry is known today.[85] Touting product reliability, Parke-Davis asserted: "The claim that a remedy was obtained from an obscure tribe of negroes in Central Africa, or from some 'Celebrated Medicine Man' among the Indians—parties regarded by intelligent people of not more than average scientific attainments in anything but therapeutics—is often sufficient to give a proprietary medicine popular favor and extensive sale."[86] In its in-house publication, *Pharmacology of the Newer Materia Medica*, Parke-Davis further sketched out the racial and gender hierarchies of pharmacological knowledge: "The first knowledge of nearly every medicinal plant official in the pharmacopoeia was obtained from Indian medicine-men, ignorant natives, quacks, and old women." Although information from "unscientific" sources mattered, data gathered from the profession at large held greater value, and even higher on the scale were the results of hospital practice based on "careful observation."[87] In sum, ethical firms boasted a medley of scientific expertise, transparency, altruism, and racial superiority as their calling card.

Parke-Davis's sponsorship of an 1885 scientific expedition by Henry Hurd Rusby, a recent medical school graduate, to the forests of Colombia, Ecuador, Peru, Chile, Bolivia, and Brazil to locate new drugs and improved supply sources for existing pharmaceutical products illustrates well the company's marketing strategies for guaraná.[88] The trip had originated in a proposal by physician and pharmacist Francis E. Stewart to the Smithsonian to fund scientific expeditions to collect materia medica from around the globe, beginning with the Amazon basin. Stewart had faced the stigma of commercialism from medical professionals for his efforts to advertise desiccated bullocks' blood and rectal gelatin capsules as therapeutic products. The Amazonian initiative was hailed as a means to advance knowledge of economic botany, progress in science, and cooperation between physicians and pharmacists. When the Smithsonian proved unresponsive, Stewart convinced Parke-Davis to adopt the plan, suggesting that the company even plant an article in *Popular Science* on the exploration of materia medica in the Amazon basin.[89]

In promoting Rusby's South American voyage, Parke-Davis eyed rising demand for cocaine, whose anesthetic value for surgical use had been detailed by Viennese ophthalmologist Karl Köller in 1884.[90] The firm sought as well the antimalarial cinchona bark and the medicinal shrub "chekan" (*Eugenia chequan*), used to remedy catarrh.[91] The medium was also the message: a botanical expedition, while out of step with European advances in laboratory science, was associated in the public's mind with classic notions of scientific discovery (such as Agassiz's voyage), conferring legitimacy on U.S. firms before the rise of laboratory-developed drugs.[92] As Parke-Davis affirmed in 1892, its pharmaceutical and therapeutic knowledge of the "newer materia medica" had been accumulated from clinical reports and physiological research, as well as "reports from special botanists traveling in the habitats of many of the more important of the newer drugs."[93] Rusby's venture also reinforced the gendered cliché of science: a lone man's crusade against popular ignorance and despair, even at the cost of personal health and safety.[94]

Rusby's two-year journey was certainly eventful. At his hotel in La Paz, Bolivia, an experiment to refine a crude alkaloid of cocaine from coca leaves exploded in flames, leading a panicky, singed Rusby to hurl the fiery still to the cobblestone patio below lest it burn down the inn and, he feared, perhaps the entire city. His shipment of twenty thousand pounds of coca leaves with an estimated value of $250,000 was lost en route across the isthmus of Panama due to the outbreak of revolution.[95] Yet lured by the commercial opportunities of Amazonian exploration and the "publicity possibilities of such an accomplishment," Rusby soldiered on, embarking on a transcontinental journey through the jungle to procure new plant species.[96] Remarkably, he collected forty-five thousand botanical specimens on his South American odyssey, distributed to herbariums around the world. Among those commercially marketed by Parke-Davis were cocillana, a Bolivian tree bark with expectorant qualities used for the treatment of bronchitis (and whose scientific name, *Guarea rusbyi*, honored the "discoverer" who had mined Indigenous knowledge). Rusby's trip received ample media coverage, kicking off an illustrious career. In 1889, he was appointed professor of botany and materia medica at the College of Pharmacy at Columbia University, and subsequently as dean of faculty. In 1891, he was named the honorary curator of the New York Botanical Garden's Museum of Economic Botany, packing its hundreds of glass cases over the next three decades with nearly ten thousand specimens, including guaraná, arranged according to use and "correct nomenclature."[97]

Upon Rusby's return from his maiden voyage to South America, Parke-Davis sponsored a lecture tour across the northeastern United States to promote the therapeutic promises of coca, cinchona, and guaraná.[98] Of the latter, he regaled an audience at the Philadelphia College of Pharmacy in 1887 with tales of his Madeira River journey: "Once you get to an installment of the forest proper, instead of having bright butterflies and singing birds, you

Henry Rusby in the Amazon, c. 1886. Henry Rusby Collection, Archives of
The New York Botanical Garden.

reach a region which is more like a region of death," replete with "prowling
jaguars" and "enormous anacondas." Fortunately, he noted, such was the environment of wild guaraná, with which "we have nothing to do." Pointing to a
map of the lower Madeira, Rusby described how guaraná was planted just as
in a vineyard; how its seeds were washed and roasted upon ripening, pounded
with clubs, and kneaded into a doughy mass; and how it was consumed regionally as a cold beverage. He also vouched for the drug's purity—one marketed by his corporate sponsor. Parke-Davis likewise noted of guaraná's
origins that "contrary to the general belief, no adulteration or substitution of
any kind is resorted to, these Indians vying with one another in the manufacture of the best product."[99] As for guaraná's reputed benefits, Rusby offered
a terse assessment: "Its effects are very refreshing, but its excessive use is del-
eterious. It contains two or three times the quantity of caffeine that coffee
does, producing a happy effect on the nervous system, but if used in excess
bringing on trembling and a palsied condition of the limbs."[100]

In a crowded therapeutic marketplace, ethical firms staked additional
claims to their drugs' efficacy. Parke-Davis was one of the first U.S. companies

to establish standards for alkaloidal drugs and their fluid extracts. Since nineteenth-century medicinal extracts varied considerably from ineffective to toxic, drug manufacturers had typically sought weaker formulas to avoid mishaps, while most doctors preferred compounding the drugs themselves or referring patients to a trusted pharmacist. By 1883, Parke-Davis had introduced twenty chemically assayed fluid extracts of botanical drugs, including guaraná. Other firms, like Eli Lilly and G.D. Searle, followed suit in the 1880s.[101]

In selling guaraná to the U.S. public, Parke-Davis deployed the language of nineteenth-century science to establish its bona fides. The product's label read:

Guaraná

Paullinia sorbilis, Mart; synonyms Brazilian cocoa, pasta guaraná P.G.; part employed, a preparation made from the seeds; natural order, Sapindaceae; habitat, Brazil

Preparation—Fluid extract of a preparation of the seeds, U.S.P.; dose, 5 to 30 minims (0.3 to 2 C. c)

Properties—The physiological effects of Paullinia are chiefly due to its alkaloid; and, as this is identical with caffeine, the therapeutic indications for the remedy are the same as those for caffeine. The special use of paullinia is in the treatment of sick headache or migraine. It is adapted to the so-called nervous form of sick headache, and is less efficient when the attacks are due to stomachal troubles. As it possesses, directly or indirectly, restorative powers, it may be employed to promote constructive metamorphosis. Administered with this view, it may be given with advantage in the convalescence from acute maladies, incipient phthisis, and in wasting diseases generally. From its astringency the remedy is useful also in chronic diarrheas, particularly in the diarrhea of phthisis. Literature supplied upon application.[102]

From a historical perspective, a native Brazilian cultivar had been recategorized according to binomial nomenclature, chemical composition and class of compound, and application through standardized dosage; in essence, a *"droga do sertão"* had become a pharmaceutical. The ingredient in a popular South American beverage had been indicated for a condition—"nervous form of sick headache"—that some physicians deemed exclusive to the overburdened brains of more "advanced" populations. And the contributions of one of its promoters, Henry Hurd Rusby, would be hailed as "new to science"—an honorific denied to Indigenous healers, whom he maligned as "evil of [the] ignorance of faulty appliance, and want of experience, judgment and skill which was inseparable from an art so grossly unspecialized," and from whom Parke-Davis's "new" botanico-medical knowledge was obtained.[103]

Historians of medicine have noted that scientists' appropriation of medicinal plants has involved an elaborate process of laboratory experimentation, record-keeping, and product management. Whereas Indigenous science relied on "oral records for plant recipes, ongoing experiments on patients and animals, metaphysical explanations, traditional herbal products, and harvests from gardens and forests," scientific appropriation entailed "written documentation of medicinal plants, testing of plants with isolated chemicals, esoteric language to explain experiments, expensive techniques for turning plants into pharmaceuticals, and strict control over plant harvests."[104] Yet as Jonathan Liebenau argues, early efforts to develop new drugs and production processes in the United States were based not on innovative methods of scientific research but rather on the recombination of conventional remedies into new products. In the 1800s, most drugs were made through crude processes: mortars were used to powder drugs by hand, and alcohol or other chemicals were used to extract soluble substances. Even in the late nineteenth century, the medical industry in the United States did not immediately produce drugs based on bacteriological theory, since patients and physicians themselves were just coming to accept the idea. And among the larger pharmaceutical firms that had established laboratories by the 1890s, the work focused on measurement of existing drugs in the official or traditional pharmacopoeia and the standardization of the drugs' ingredients. In other words, the ethical firms used a "scientific veneer" to promote their pharmaceutical products but retained older models.[105] In fact, Parke-Davis's marketing of guaraná, spotlighting the Indigenous Amazonian source of the drug, underscores the ways in which "modern" medicine smuggled the "traditional" and the "exotic" into its promotional strategies.[106] It also suggests that given that Indigenous peoples' botanical and medical knowledge has formed a basis of pharmaceutical "discovery" and development, they should be recognized as colleagues rather than "informants" of Western scientists—and entitled to the same intellectual property rights.[107]

THERAPEUTICS—THE PRODUCT of particular understandings of bodily function, varying medical knowledge, and the emotional interaction between healers and patients—is a social process embedded within specific historical periods and cultural contexts.[108] In 1874, after Dr. Finley B. Pugh of Illinois prescribed Parke-Davis's guaraná preparations for treating headaches and "stomach derangements," he lauded the drug's ability "to arrest the waste of the tissues of the body," presumably by "reducing the proportion of phos-phoric acid and urea excreted from the kidneys," and "to keep the body from falling away so rapidly, and thus to enable the less energetic powers of diges-tion still to supply as much as needed to repair the wear and tear of the solid tissues." Dr. O. C. Joslyn of St. Johns, Michigan, not only claimed that Parke-Davis's fluid extract guaraná served to "confine sick headache in its premoni-tory stage" but also indicated the drug for dysentery, diarrhea, and indigestion.[109] The objective here is not to ascertain the exactitude of nineteenth-century medical science regarding guaraná, since practitioners and patients evaluated therapeutics on the basis of knowledge of that era. Rather, it is to understand how disparate social groups in the markets of the North Atlantic incorporated guaraná into existing understandings of biomedical knowledge to favor partic-ular ends.[110] The history of nineteenth-century "Western" health care, into which guaraná was assimilated, is approached through the competing claims and meanings ascribed to science in medicine, as well as the realm of racial and colonial ideologies.[111]

In the early nineteenth century, as Rosenberg notes, Americans believed that health and disease derived from an interaction between the individual's constitutional makeup and environmental settings that required constant at-tention to maintain the body's balance. Since local and systemic ills were viewed as interlinked, physicians relied on regulating secretions to restore the equilibrium of the body and its interrelated parts. Drug actions that produced sweating, diarrhea, salivation, and vomit, resembling the body's responses to disease, seemingly offered assurance to patients of the medication's potency, if not efficacy. For this reason, early nineteenth-century physicians used dif-ferent drugs to treat the same condition: the drug's legitimacy owed to its desired physiological outcome, which also reflected the distinct composition of each patient.[112] This holistic cognitive framework also explains why a doc-tor might treat a wounded patient not only with a salve but with a stimulant as well.[113] To be sure, orthodox physicians faced constant competition from "sectarian" and alternative caregivers, as patients turned to other treatments to restore balance or merely alleviate their distress.[114] These included so-called Indian doctors (white physicians who practiced "medicine according to Indian theory"), whose patients viewed Native Americans as healthier than whites or their medicines as less toxic.[115] Patients might also disregard altogether the physician's advice, alter a prescribed medication or dosage, by-pass the doctor for the pharmacist, self-medicate, let an illness run its course, or attribute their affliction and salvation to God.[116]

While Western medical thinking evolved considerably over the course of the nineteenth century, with advances in European clinical research and professional specialization in universities and teaching hospitals expanding empirical understanding of disease specificity, many orthodox physicians in the United States continued to affirm that disease derived from holistic, constitutional, or humoral imbalance.[117] Physicians still spoke of regulating internal equilibrium and the importance of the body's "vital power"—the sum of its parts—in facilitating recovery. While curtailing traditional depleting practices of bleeding and purging, they retained others, such as diuretics and cathartics, and between the 1850s and 1870s increasingly emphasized the importance of stimulants.[118] Physiology did not appear as a distinct component of the medical curriculum in the United States until the 1880s, and some physicians feared that laboratory research would undermine clinical competence.[119] Driven by traditional ideas as much as patient expectations and competition from sectarian practitioners, physicians retained their commitment to modifying physical symptoms, expediting paths to recovery through the proper combination of drugs and regimen, and alleviating pain.[120] Despite numerous innovations in nineteenth-century medical science, U.S. medical practice—fractured by cross-cutting philosophical, economic, and regional dimensions—continued to embrace traditional therapeutics.

Orthodox physicians tending to headache sufferers, therefore, might prescribe a range of treatments, since their objective was to eliminate the cause of the pain rather than the pain itself.[121] As Jan McTavish notes, when the physician diagnosed the headache's origins in the digestive system, particularly constipation, the antidote might entail cathartics (substances that accelerate defecation) or emetics (inducers of vomiting) and other regulators of the digestive process. Harsh mineral drugs, such as calomel and antimony, or potent doses of botanicals that produced bodily secretions, even leaving patients writhing in pain, ostensibly demonstrated their efficacy. For a headache attributed to an imbalance in the nervous system, the care might include bloodletting, sedatives such as bromides or cannabis, or stimulants such as caffeine.[122] Other remedies included champagne; leeches inserted into patients' nostrils; blistering lotions applied to their shaved heads; jets of hot air blown up their noses; or wide-mouthed, glass-stoppered bottles, half-filled with cotton or fine sponge and laced with two or three drams of bisulphide of carbon, applied up to several times a day for three to five minutes or longer to the temple or as near possible to the seat of pain to prevent the escape of volatile vapors.[123] For headaches deriving from "nervous exhaustion," practitioners of electrotherapeutics might prescribe electricity, administered through battery-operated belts, rings, brushes, and corsets to correct neural disorders deemed physical in origin; one such product, Dr. Scott's Electric Hair-Brush, promised relief from "Nervous Headache in 5 minutes," recharging and soothing "the weary brain," with the bonus of providing "hope for the bald."[124] In other words, patients such as M.N., a thirty-four-year-old woman who suffered from frequent bouts of "sick-headache," generally ending in vomiting, had likely been subjected to a panoply of treatments for a lifelong condition until guaraná appeared "to act like a charm," leaving her feeling "like another woman" in just twenty minutes.[125] And which therapies had Dr. John Stewart of Maine, driven to study medicine for the sole purpose of alleviating his lifelong "sick headaches," endured before he was purportedly "cured" with teaspoonful doses of Parke-Davis guaraná powder administered every fifteen minutes for two years?[126] Or the professional singer, freed by powdered guaraná of crippling headaches that had endangered his career?[127] Or the sixty-year-old Indiana female with a "nervous headache of several years' standing" who experienced a "permanent cure" after taking fluid extract of guaraná in half-teaspoonful doses several times daily for a few weeks?[128]

In the history of medicine, patients' experiences are overshadowed in historical sources by the feats of professional health-care providers.[129] Indeed, the aforementioned patients' testimonies were registered because Parke-Davis leaned on the endorsement of orthodox physicians to promote their products.[130] The company sent drug representatives to doctors' offices, feted medical professionals at its headquarters, gave samples to physicians, and launched several widely distributed in-house publications that described drug products and publicized medical endorsements.[131] This was the context in which two physicians attributed particularly remarkable recoveries to guaraná. In 1892, U.S. army doctor J. Frazer praised the drug's success in treating a soldier hospitalized for months with a condition of "dysenteric character" that had been largely unresponsive to nearly all vegetable and mineral astringents. That same year, Dr. E. Spencer of Evansville, Indiana, hailed guaraná for treating a "respectable married lady" in her late twenties, who for two years was "on the decline with uterine and vaginal problems," which the physician claimed owed to leucorrhoea and vesicular vaginitis. Spencer cleansed the patient with castile soap and warm water, then prescribed guaraná internally and as a local application, and also included salicylic acid and glycerin. After a few weeks, "in a happy mood," the patient informed Spencer that "she was well, her health being better than she had known for a long time before."[132]

Did guaraná cure these patients? Did the physicians stretch the truth to burnish their reputations, and Parke-Davis to sell its guaraná products? Was the reported recovery merely the result of a self-limited condition? Or did symptoms return, never to be reported to the physician or to Parke-Davis? Given the absence of current standards of drug evaluations based on statistical analysis of a large randomized number of patients and double-blind clinical trials, it is impossible to ascertain. I choose instead to focus on how guaraná was marketed by pharmaceutical firms through particular rituals of drug consumption, with distinct communication codes, specialized objects, texts, and practitioners.[133] As medical anthropologists note, taking medicine is both a medical and a social act involving relationships of authority, trust, and concern.[134] The doctor's comforting word, materialized through the writing of a prescription (in abbreviated Latin and ancient symbols in the nineteenth century), reassures both physician and patient that something has been done about an ailment, even when science and technology cannot eliminate uncertainty about health and illness.[135] As an 1880 essay in Parke-Davis's *Therapeutic Gazette* on the firm's "new remedies" stated, since many patients got well without medicine, with drugs merely alleviating suffering and hastening recovery, doctors' "hope and joyful anticipation served to stimulate healthful activity, while sadness and despondency depress the vital energies."[136] The practice lives on: in 1989, research among 141 physicians in the United States found that for almost half, patient demand was the most common reason to prescribe medicine, and 24 percent affirmed that their prescription relied on the intentional use of the placebo effect.[137] Contemporary studies of placebos also show that the prescriber's concern enhances the drug's reception and the patient's chance of recovery, analogous to the "healing hand" or "good word" of traditional healers.[138] Not for nothing did the Greek term *pharmakon* mean "remedy," "poison," and "magical charm."[139]

NEW DRUGS OFTEN generate skepticism as well. Some nineteenth-century physicians preferred to stick to "old-fashioned remedies" rather than experiment with guaraná.[140] Others slammed the drug as impure, ineffective, and costly. An early critic, likely due to rivalry with Parke-Davis, was naval surgeon Edward Robinson Squibb, head of the eponymous New York–based drug firm established in 1858. In Squibb's words, guaraná was "at best a crude preparation of uncertain composition; the secret of its manufacture is jealously guarded by the half-savage Guaranis [*sic*]," and was unworthy of inclusion in the *USP* of 1880.[141] He cited coffee and teas as cheaper and safer substitutes given the reputable quality of their respective caffeine, which he claimed was analogous to guaraná based on physiological tests.[142] Following his death, the Squibb company apparently changed course: its 1906 handbook "for the physician and pharmacist" advertised "Elixir Guarana" for $6.00 a gallon as a sedative and "antineuralgic, mainly in nervous headache," as well as other guaraná preparations. The company touted its powder derivation as "consisting chiefly of crushed seeds of *Paullinia Cupana*, a Brazilian plant," yielding not less than 3.5 percent of its alkaloidal principles as "assayed by official process."[143]

Another detractor was pharmacist James Pemberton, whose 1887 "Essay on Guaraná, Caffeine, and Coca" detailed guaraná's preparation by an "Indian tribe by the name of the Guaraeves [*sic*], whence its name." Pemberton too questioned the drug's purity and efficacy, adding that "thanks to the science of chemistry," guaraná had been entirely "superseded by the use of Caffeine." Conversely, he upheld the kola nut's caffeine as superior to that of tea and coffee, while praising coca for improving physical and mental function and calling for its transplantation to Florida and South Texas.[144] Kola nuts, traded along the Upper Guinea coast for centuries (where they were chewed rather than consumed in a beverage), increasingly entered global markets in the mid-nineteenth century with the shift in transoceanic West African commerce from the Atlantic slave trade to vegetable products. With rising demand from the pharmaceutical and soft drink industries and expansion of steamship transport, the export volume of kola reached 378 tons by 1879 and an estimated 1,000 tons by 1910.[145] Due to challenges with labor, transportation, and overwhelming demand within Brazil, guaraná could not compete with kola nuts on the international market. Pemberton's endorsement of kola over guaraná also harbored a significant dose of economic self-interest. A year earlier, the Georgia pharmacist, Civil War veteran, and morphine addict had launched his patent medicine, Coca-Cola.[146] His repudiation of guaraná ensured kola nuts' primacy in the soft drink's (early) flavoring and the African plant's ultimate brand-name recognition in the United States and worldwide.

In the U.S. pharmaceutical market, guaraná proved unable to triumph over cheaper and purportedly more efficacious forms of caffeine.[147] In a lecture before the American Pharmaceutical Association in 1920, A. Richard Bliss Jr., from the School of Medicine at Emory University, proposed the removal of guaraná along with thirty other vegetable drugs from the *USP* that were "of minor importance, questionable utility and doubtful reliability," based on a questionnaire mailed to all 513 practicing physicians in Atlanta regarding the proposed retention of over 120 vegetable drugs.[148] The elimination of guaraná from the tenth edition of the *USP* in 1920 did not proscribe the drug from pharmaceutical use; as W. A. Bastedo, vice president of the U.S. Pharmacopoeial Convention of 1920, noted, substances dropped from the book could still find a place in the *National Formulary* (revised and issued by the American Pharmaceutical Association), where they would be available in standardized form for practitioners. Yet Bastedo, who recommended the omission of guaraná as one of the drugs or preparations that failed to combine "both worth and extensive employment," had ratified its reduced presence in U.S. therapeutic practice.[149]

Critically, headache sufferers had turned to cheaper synthetic analgesics readily available at drugstores across the nation. Around the turn of the twentieth century, advances in pharmaceutical chemistry led to the introduction of drugs such as aspirin, launched by the Bayer company in 1899, which followed on the heels of other synthetic antipyretics developed by the German organic chemical industry. Pitched initially as antirheumatics and febrifuges, the synthetics' largely unanticipated quality as painkillers, including for treatment of headaches, soon earned them a broad popular following. Although the new drugs did not elucidate the pathology of headache, their effectiveness as non-habit-forming analgesics elevated a prescribing doctor's status or allowed sufferers to circumvent medical authority altogether with successful self-treatment readily available at the corner drugstore. In the 1920s, the discovery that ergot—a fungus with vasoconstricting properties—served to alleviate migraines turned ergotamine tartrate into a standard treatment for the condition.[150]

As synthetics entered the drug market, pharmaceutical chemistry was applied to laboratory-produced compounds, and pharmacognosy to the study of drugs of natural origin. Over the first half of the twentieth century, the latter discipline came under attack by practitioners and researchers whose work examined the taxonomy, anatomy, and morphology of the plant that produced the active constituent rather than focusing on its biochemistry, pharmacology, and therapeutics. Plant-derived medicines, of course, remain vital in the Western pharmaceutical industry. A 1997 study, for example, reported that some 25 percent of prescription drugs are derived from plants, and nearly all the major synthetic medicines are based on prototypes of natural origin. In addition, herbal products in the United States, officially classified as dietary supplements rather than drugs or conventional foods under FDA regulations, reached a volume of $1.5 billion by the late twentieth century.[151] In the developing world, more than 3.5 billion people rely on plants as components of their primary health care.[152]

Nevertheless, many botanicals would never command the prominence in Anglo-American pharmacy that they enjoyed a century earlier—and guaraná is one. The Amazonian plant retreated into relative pharmaceutical obscurity above the equator, another export commodity from Latin America that collapsed under the onslaught of synthetics and "the tentacles of progress" of industrial science.[153] Western pharmaceutical companies, contending with legal and financial risks, would come to focus their research and development on single-activity drugs, or "magic bullets" that affected only one node on a biochemical pathway, while nearly three-fourths of all pharmaceutical research spending in the United States by the late twentieth century was allocated to treatments for cancer, cardiovascular disease, neurological disorders, and microbial disease. Indigenous plant remedies, on the other hand, tend to be more focused on gastrointestinal problems, skin ailments, and gynecological matters due to the more detectable and pressing nature of these conditions and owing to lifestyles or life spans less likely to be afflicted with cancer or heart disease.[154]

Analysis of Google Books Ngram Viewer quantifies the drop in English-language printed references to guaraná: from an all-time high between 1872 and 1886, its frequency dropped to less than one-third that level between 1920 and 1940 and for much of the final half of the twentieth century.[155] But just around the time that Anglo-American pharmacy turned its back on guaraná, the Brazilian soft drink industry had begun to launch its own "real thing."

CHAPTER FIVE

From Guarani to Guaraná

Forging a National Industry

João Coelho de Miranda Leão was not the first to plot guaraná's journey from the winding rivers of northern Brazil to booming metropolises. When the Amazonian physician penned his article in 1919 in the Amazonas Trade Association's journal, however, demand for soft drinks was mounting due to rising urbanization. "Above all, the chemical industry," he wrote, "has to perfect the usual preparations of guaraná to be eagerly received, as a vehicle for a fortifying and stimulating substance, a true *national cola* [italics in original], originating in Brazil."[1]

Miranda Leão was born in Maués in 1869, the grandson of an army colonel who arrived in town in 1839 to quash the Cabanagem rebels and decades later established the Amazonas Trade Association. As a public health inspector in Manaus, a founder of the Sociedade Amazonense de Agricultura, and a member of the local eugenics society, Miranda Leão emblematized regional modernizers' commitment to agricultural rationalization and public health reform.[2] His inspiration for a guaraná-based soft drink most likely originated close to home. A Manaus-based company founded by A. R. de Andrade had been offering its guaraná soda since 1908.[3] It was not the first in Brazil: immigrant German chemists had launched Cyrilla Guaraná in Rio Grande do Sul in 1906.[4] Subsequently, the Fratelli Vita company, founded in Salvador by Italian immigrants (who later opened another factory in Recife), introduced its guaraná-flavored "gazosas" in 1910.[5] Guaraná Antarctica, Brazil's leading flavored brand today, dates to 1921, while Brahma's soda, its main competitor for decades prior to the companies' merger, appeared in 1927.

Miranda Leão never saw his dream come fully to fruition. In 1920, he shot himself, tormented by leprosy contracted in his medical practice, according to his biographer.[6] Yet the Amazonian champion of guaraná's application to the rising Brazilian soft drink industry was not too far off in his prognostication. In his clever Carnival samba of 1934, "Do guarani ao guaraná" (From Guarani to guaraná), Lamartine Babo mused at a land once dominated by Indigenous peoples, now marked by expanding mass consumption of one of their foods. Five years later, a U.S. visitor described guaraná soda as a "refreshing, fatigue-dispelling soft drink" that could be found in bars and soft drink counters throughout Brazil.[7] And in 1954, Cesar Ladeira and Haroldo Barbosa's futuristic play, *O Brasil no ano tres mil*, envisioned that their nation would be "exporting plans for saving the world from a United States in decline, which would be seeking as well to obtain cars, refrigerators, and guaraná manufactured here."[8]

Speculating why cultures adopt new foods, anthropologist Sidney Mintz pithily suggested, "When much else is changing, food habits may change, too."[9] Miranda Leão had the same hunch. Amid the expansion of domestic industry, middle-class consumption, and mass media giving rise to "modern" Brazil, guaraná soft drinks bobbed as symbols of self-fulfillment and social progress. By the latter part of the century, guaraná's principal markets would indeed shift from the sparsely populated central-western and northern regions of Brazil to its urban industrial and consumer cores.

Soft drinks are sweetened water-based beverages, typically with a balancing acidity and carbonation that enhance sensory characteristics. Flavored and often colored and chemically preserved, their primary function is hydration, with sweeteners (usually carbohydrates) and other contents providing energy in a highly assimilable form as well as minor essential nutrients. With water typically making up between 85 and 95 percent of the product and subjected to added chemical treatments by manufacturers, soda's hydration value rises in places where water is avoided due to poor taste or contamination.[10] Many soft drink flavors elaborate on popularly consumed fruit juices and fruit-based beverages, reflective of the customary "substitutions and annexations" in the integration of new foods into existing gastronomies.[11]

Sodas were products and producers of the Industrial Revolution. In 1773, the Royal Society honored British theologian and chemist Joseph Priestley for his "invention" of soda water, which infused water with carbon dioxide by placing it over a fermenting mash. Subsequently, German-born Johann Jacob Schweppe created artificially carbonated water through a pressure pump that allowed a greater volume of gas to be absorbed, later setting up business in London in 1792. In the United States, Benjamin Silliman of New Haven initiated manufacture in 1807, becoming the first patent holder for artificial mineral water.[12] In 1832, John Matthews, a British émigré to the United States, created a machine to artificially carbonate water in larger quantities, using a mixture of sulfuric acid and powdered marble (calcium carbonate) to produce carbon dioxide. His invention, wildly popular in U.S. drugstores and later in Europe, earned him a sobriquet—and a fortune—as "the Soda Fountain King."[13]

While the celebrated therapeutic properties of natural mineral water facilitated the popularization of artificially carbonated drinks, carbon dioxide's
antimicrobial effects guarded against the yeast, bacteria, and mold that dis-
posed fruit-based beverages to spoilage. Fermented drinks such as wine, ci-
der, and beer also enjoy a longer shelf life, but advances in industrial chemistry
enabled the stabilization of beverages without reliance on alcohol.[14] (Given
the penchant for wine and beer among European aristocrats and commoners,
respectively, many on the continent historically passed their days in varied
states of inebriation.)[15] As technology and understanding of spoilage advanced, manufacturers introduced preservatives (such as benzoic acid, sorbic
acid, and sulfuric dioxide) and artificial flavors and colors—undoubtedly cul-
minating in many misfortunes: the term "Codd's wallop" derived from the
dubious concoctions in the early carbonated drink bottles designed and patented by Englishman Hiram Codd in 1870.[16] But it was also the manufacture
of containers and closures capable of containing the gas (such as Codd's
bottle with a round glass "marble" stopper in the neck) that ensured the commercial success of carbonated beverages. And it was European and North
American beverage companies that promoted overseas marketing of their
products as well as the dissemination of techniques of manufacture and
bottling.[17]

Like beer, carbonated beverages were relative latecomers to Brazilian
tables. They arrived alongside other nineteenth- and early twentieth-century
luxury imports, such as patent medicines, perfumes, English butter, mustard,
watches, pianos, saddles, raincoats, sewing scissors, and bicycles. Many of
these items pleasured affluent expatriates, but wealthier Brazilians took a
shine as well.[18] Diets of the well-heeled in Brazil were expanding from largely
homemade foods to those prepared in factories or small cottage industries.
Chic new establishments, such as hotels, cafés, restaurants, and confectioneries, served up beer, soda, ice cream, and other chilled indulgences.[19] By the
turn of the twentieth century, a proliferation of breweries, ice factories, and
flour mills dotted Brazil's largest urban centers, offering novel gustatory experiences and forms of sociability, and reinscribing cities' historical roles as sites
of culinary innovation and privilege.[20] In the city of São Paulo, food products
were the commodity most sold by commercial establishments during the republican era (1889–1930).[21]

Domestic production of soft drinks and beer owed to changes wrought by
immigration, urbanization, and industrialization and their cultural expressions and repercussions. Linked to the coffee export boom and the expansion
of railroads and power stations, Brazil's early industrial wave centered on

nondurable consumer goods to satisfy the demand for cheaper commodities and locally produced spare parts. Textiles, clothing, shoes, and foodstuffs accounted for more than half of industrial output in 1907 and nearly three-quarters in 1919. Manufacturing machinery was imported, while the raw materials typically consisted of low-value products and domestic agricultural inputs—cotton, leather, cereals, sugar, and nonmetallic minerals, such as clay or sand.[22]

Local production rose steadily over the early twentieth century. Imports of food products dropped from an annual average of 19.4 percent for the decade 1901–10 (as part of the overall import structure) to 8.9 percent for 1921–29, while beverages fell from 6 percent to 2.1 percent.[23] By the end of the 1930s, Brazil was close to self-sufficient in consumer goods and supplied over 80 percent of its intermediate goods and over 50 percent of its investment goods.[24] The food and beverage industry also provided thousands of jobs: in 1920, there were over 41,000 men and 3,000 women working in the food and beverage industries, and by 1940, over 156,000 men and 31,000 women.[25]

The proliferation of guaraná soft drinks reflected advances in domestic industrial production. Although a detailed discussion of the origins and evolution of manufacturing technologies of the soft drink is beyond the scope of this book, methods of extracting guaraná for soda manufacture have entailed grinding up the dried seeds and husks and using hot water or hydroalcoholic solutions as solvents.[26] According to a more recent report, one company's patent to produce extracts from guaraná seeds has involved pulping and drying the seeds under controlled heat until they contain 8–10 percent humidity; grinding them to no more than six millimeters in diameter, followed by extraction with 40–60 percent ethanol in a ratio of 1:4 (weight/volume) at 50–70 degrees centigrade; then combining and concentrating the extract and washing solutions under reduced pressure. In a precipitation tank, the concentrated solution receives neutral ethanol to adjust to a minimum of 40 percent and contains a minimum of 1.6 percent caffeine. After cooling at 2–5 degrees Celsius for one to three days, the extract is filtered and adjusted to legal and commercial specifications.[27]

In less technical terms, we might say that the Brazilian beverage industry developed methods to leech guaraná's mix of caffeine, theobromine, and tannins directly from its dried seeds to produce an extract, thereby bypassing the traditional labor-intensive process of pounding, molding, and smoking. Through pasteurization and preservatives, manufacturers inoculated the beverage from the microbes that traditionally tainted urban water supplies and caused countless premature deaths. Through carbonation, sweeteners, fragrance, and additives, the soda companies reinvented the sensory experience of guaraná, replicating a historical pattern of elite assimilation of humbler foods through modification.[28] To be sure, for decades, many manufacturers dispensed with the ingredient altogether in the eponymous product, irking Amazonian merchants and food safety regulators. And through advertisements, the companies signified guaraná consumption as a medium for physical rejuvenation and enhanced leisure.

This chapter focuses first on two noteworthy protagonists in guaraná's transition to mass-produced flavored drink: Luís Pereira Barreto (1840–1923) and Jesus Gomes (1891–1963). A physician and a pharmacist, respectively, each played an important role in the formulation and commercialization of the soft drink. Through reconstruction of their biographies and regional milieux, the broader scientific and social worlds that gave rise to an industrial beverage emerge. As medicinal plants fell under their professional purview— and, more broadly, the human body's relationship to the natural world and to society—their credentialing was important for guaraná's popularization as a soft drink flavor.[29] In the chapter's latter section, I examine Amazonian elites' efforts to expand production, diversify markets, and defend their product from falsification or slander. Guaraná traveled down many different paths to become the namesake of Brazil's national soda. The soft drink's early history illuminates what social scientists have termed "developmental nationalism" in Latin America, or what urban residents experienced or understood as being modern.

IN A SMALL PLAZA in São Paulo stands a ten-meter-high bronze statue of Luís Pereira Barreto. Commissioned by the city's Sociedade de Medicina e Cirurgia as part of an international competition, the monument was installed in 1929, six years after his death. Barreto wears a doctor's gown, flanked on one side by Hygeia, the Greek and Roman goddess of health, and on another by Ceres, the Roman goddess of agriculture and fertility, signaling his contributions to the fields of medicine and agriculture.[30] Paulistanos scurrying across the square in a city of some fifteen million people probably pay scant attention to the towering figure. Yet it was Barreto who extracted the syrup from guaraná for industrial use by Companhia Antarctica Paulista, though the actual formula for the company's guaraná soda was created by Minas Gerais chemist and pharmacist Pedro Baptista de Andrade in 1921.

Profit motives aside, Barreto's investment in the industrial application of guaraná reflected his commitment to the expansion of medical, agricultural, and manufacturing science in Brazil. The physician's belief that "poorly nourished populations could not obviously dedicate themselves to extended and difficult intellectual work" further fired his enthusiasm for the stimulant.[31] For Barreto, guaraná offered Brazilians the promise of physical and economic well-being, his lifelong political goal.

Guaraná Antarctica's manufacturing formula may remain coded, compartmentalized in vaults (reportedly requiring seven different keys), and entrusted to select "guardians" over the last century, but we do know a bit more about the biography and political thought of one of its technologists.[32] Born in Resende, Rio de Janeiro, in 1840 to an elite landowning family, Barreto received his degrees in medicine and the natural sciences from the University of Brussels. Upon returning to Brazil in 1865, he became a successful surgeon in Jacareí before moving his practice to the city of São Paulo in 1883. As a plantation owner, Barreto introduced Bourbon coffee seeds to his fazenda near Ribeirão Preto, yielding a hardier variety of the plant that propelled western São Paulo's boom in the waning years of slavery.[33] An early adherent of the Republican movement that toppled the emperor in 1889, he served as a delegate to the São Paulo state constituent assembly in 1891.

The Republican federalist constitution blessed coffee-producing states with control of export revenues, and Barreto brought further distinction to his adopted home. Aside from directing a yellow fever prevention campaign in Campinas, he founded the Sociedade de Medicina e Cirurgia de São Paulo in 1895, pioneering surgical techniques in Brazil based on the scientific advances of Pasteur and Lister.[34] He also was a member of the patrician Instituto Histórico e Geográfico of São Paulo and the Academia Paulista de Letras, wrote several books, and contributed a regular column to the *Estado de São Paulo*. If Barreto wielded both surgical knife and pen, it was because he sought to tend as much to his compatriots' bodies as to their souls.

As a medical student in Europe, Barreto had converted to positivism. Auguste Comte's "religion of humanity" upheld a hierarchical paradigm in which the human spirit would pass successively through three states: theological, metaphysical, and positivist. For Barreto and his Brazilian coreligionists, positivism's social science offered a political plan of action for the nation's historical development.[35] Trapped in the metaphysical stage of human development, Brazilians required technical and scientific instruction to achieve the "grand industrial evolution" of modern nations.[36] Through state tutelage and nonviolent integration, Indigenous peoples would embark as well on this evolutionary journey from their current "fetishistic" mental state.[37] Neither race nor climate explained Brazil's "colonial character" as a giant coffee plantation dependent on the importation of basic goods but rather, in his words, the nation's "social and moral ills."[38]

For Barreto, applied science would promote agricultural modernization while public health campaigns would ensure immigration and labor productivity.[39] His ideals—adherence to standardized scientific language, transparency of method, utilitarian approach to nature, and abhorrence of abstraction—reflected the professional self-fashioning of turn-of-the-century scientists in Brazil.[40] Or as he chided, apprehension of "the most elementary notions of physics and chemistry make the simple citizen a superior man to the most brilliant literati."[41] That only a technocratic cadre could be entrusted with shepherding Brazilians on this voyage to "modern times"—the positivist ideal of the strong tending to the weak—was never in question. Wary of democracy, Barreto noted in 1918: "For an unprepared people, voting can constitute a fatal agent of retrogression: instead of order and progress [the positivist motto emblazoned on Brazil's flag] we will have disorder and regression."[42]

For Barreto, import substitution represented Brazil's freedom charter. Prior to experimenting with the extraction of guaraná, he planted vineyards on his estate with grapes acquired from the School of Viticulture in Lyon. Barreto aimed not only to apply Pasteurian notions of fermentation to agronomy and attract European smallholders to Brazil but also to turn every vineyard in the subtropical climate into an "avenger against all of the calumnies hurled against our nation."[43]

In this nationalist spirit, Barreto also boasted of developing Brazil's lager beer industry. Beer drinking had expanded in the latter part of the nineteenth century with the influx of German immigrants, who served as brewers and consumers, and due to overall urban growth. Many of the large breweries and beverage companies, including Antarctica, Brahma, and Fratelli Vita, were founded by Europeans, millions of whom flocked to Brazil in the aftermath of abolition and immigration policies favoring the "whitening" of the population. The mass production of low-fermentation beers, however, required cooler temperatures, necessitating a complex system of warehousing and industrial refrigeration that delayed domestic Brazilian manufacture until the 1880s.[44] Barreto claimed he had convinced Companhia Antarctica Paulista to repurpose an ice-making machine from its failed meat factory into a brewery.[45] By the turn of the twentieth century, Antarctica, flush with new business partners, loans, and imported Linde machinery, employed three hundred workers and produced close to fifty thousand

Antarctica trucks in front of São Paulo factory, 1930s. Courtesy of Acervo Histórico, São Paulo Antiga.

hectoliters of beer. Its six-thousand-square-meter factory in the Mooca neighborhood of São Paulo boasted artesian wells of more than one hundred meters in depth, six industrial cauldrons, three ice-making machines, and pasteurized production. Indeed, with high tariffs slapped on imported beer, breweries proliferated in Brazil. By 1911, São Paulo alone had fifty-two, producing millions of bottles of beer annually as well as carbonated water and soda, whose consumption taxes fattened state coffers over ensuing decades.[46]

As the product of European technologies adapted to domestic industrial manufacture, beer often evaded Brazilian prohibitionists' disapprobation, likelier to condemn cachaça due to its higher alcohol content and consumption by people of color. The large breweries also declaimed beer's putative nutritional and restorative value.[47] Barreto admonished that skeptics once doubted Brazil's potential to produce lager beer in warmer temperatures, but its manufacture merely required understanding of microbiology and access to refrigeration. A multimillion-dollar domestic business had blossomed, stanching capital outflows on beverage imports. Brazil's climate had not

changed but something else had, Barreto boasted: "From impotent and dependent on the foreigner we became powerful and emancipated from all foreign tutelage."[48]

Or perhaps Brazil's climate was changing. Previously, only Brazil's elite had
savored chilled beverages: earlier in the nineteenth century, ice chopped by
empresario Frederic Tudor from frozen lakes near Boston had been imported and stored in deep pits.[49] The cookbook *Doceiro nacional* (1883) later
described chemical methods for obtaining ice using sulfuric acid and pressur-
izing machines, but the latter's high cost lent itself only to larger-scale manufacture.[50] The larger breweries in Brazil fueled the popularization of cold
drinks. In the early decades, the companies furnished bars with ice from their
factories or sold chunks door to door, with the premium on cold redounding
to their products' benefit.[51] (Even in the 1930s, only the wealthiest Brazilian
households could purchase imported Frigidaires.) And while folklorist Luís
da Câmara Cascudo noted an initial wariness among the popular classes
toward "coldness" (*frieza*), fearful that ice would burn them, chilled beverages were growing markers of cosmopolitanism and leisure in Brazil, even
shaping soda flavor selection.[52] Manufacturers likely eschewed a coffee soda,
for example, because consumers traditionally drank that beverage hot. Dicafé
Vita, the first coffee-flavored soft drink in Brazil, was introduced in 1972. It
flopped.[53]

Barreto's experimentation with guaraná, then, reflected the positivist physician's broader commitment to modernization.[54] His successful extraction
of the syrup for use in the beverage industry inspired Antarctica to undertake
the development of a guaraná-flavored soft drink in 1909, although the company's calibration of astringency, aroma, and coloration delayed the launch of
Guaraná Champagne for more than a decade.[55] Globally, the soft drink industry relies on the synergy among the sensory responses of sight, smell, and
taste: a mixture of aromatic substances and flavoring aims to please the consumer's sensory receptors, while color adjustment offsets natural variation in
tone, thereby shaping consumers' understanding of well-being and their reception of the drink.[56] Barreto's endorsement of the stimulant's therapeutic
value, first published in the *Jornal de Santos* in April 1905, also served to market the soda.[57]

GUARANÁ SOFT DRINKS further pleased Barreto and other Brazilian physicians as alternatives to alcohol. Although Brazil's temperance movement never
rivaled that of the United States and Europe, organizations such as the Sociedade Anti-Alcoolica do Brasil, the Liga Nacional contra o Alcoolismo, the

Liga Brasileira de Higiene Mental, the União Brasileira Pró-Temperança, and the Brazilian Pharmaceutical Association's Secção Permanente de Anti-Alcoolismo crusaded against alcohol. Bills proposed in the 1910s and 1920s sought to triple taxes on wine, cachaça, and beer, and ban consumption on Sundays and holidays. The stigmatization of alcohol owed to the increased intervention of medical authorities, social scientists, and state and religious officials in the private realm to promote values of hard work and hygiene necessary for a new industrial order. Influenced by eugenic and racist beliefs, early twentieth-century medical authorities and social reformers in Brazil blamed alcohol abuse for the physical and mental degeneration of the national stock. Black and Indigenous populations bore the brunt of anti-vice campaigns. For elite and middle-class women, temperance reform offered entry into formal politics prior to suffrage in 1932 (leveraging their "traditional" role as restrainers of male misconduct), not to mention potential protection from abuse by inebriated partners.[58]

While Barreto sanctioned moderate wine consumption (to "sensitize" the soul), and his admiration for the beer industry suggests measured tolerance, he blamed alcoholism for destroying "the intelligence and talents of youth" and claiming more lives in the Amazon forest than epidemic disease.[59] He lauded São Paulo residents who had "instinctively" swapped alcohol for coffee, tea, maté, and guaraná, "beverages that were more or less tonic and intellectualizing, inciters of cerebral energy."[60] Indeed, medical endorsement of the soft drink was critical to early marketing. The label of Guaraná Espumante bore Barreto's signature and recommendation of the beverage as "Aperitive, Diuretic, Neuro-Muscular, Strengthening and Regularizing the Heart for its Indispensable Functions in the Good Functioning of the Intestines. Rejuvenates the Elderly." The brand's advertisements from the 1920s also featured physicians Estrellita Luz, Plinio Gomilde, and Eduardo Rabello, who promoted the beverage's tonic properties over alcohol. In launching Guaraná Champagne in 1921, Companhia Antarctica Paulista likewise proclaimed the drink as "the last word in non-alcoholic beverages, merging an enjoyable taste with medicinal properties." (The "champagne" in the beverage's title signaled the product's European sophistication and bubbly, amber composition rather than its alcoholic content.)[61]

In 1921, an octogenarian Barreto wrote: "Old age is an unmerited humiliation and death a tragic injustice."[62] Alongside contemplations of his own mortality, the physician's insistence on guaraná's capacity to extend life through the prevention of arteriosclerosis and protection of the gastrointestinal tract derived from his professional ambition amid contemporaneous

Formula do eminente Sabio **Dr. L. P. Barreto**

Bebida agradabilissima ▭ Previne a arteria - esclerose ▭ Fortalece o
Coração ▭ Neuro - muscular ▭ Combate a neurasthenia

Zanotta Lorenzi & C. ● Rua Gusmões, 70 — S. PAULO

Guaraná Espumante ad, São Paulo, 1920. Therapeutic claims and medical endorsements accompanied the early marketing of soft drinks in Brazil. Zanotta, Lorenzi & Cia.'s "extremely agreeable" beverage, touted as a formula of the "eminent sage" Dr. Luís Pereira Barreto, promised to strengthen the heart, prevent atherosclerosis, and combat neurasthenia. Featuring a bare-breasted Indigenous woman as its logo, Espumante also sought to link the product in consumers' mind to the exotic and the erotic. *A Cigarra* 142 (1920): 60. Hemeroteca Digital, Biblioteca Nacional, Rio de Janeiro. Courtesy of Arquivo O Cruzeiro/EM/D.A Press.

Western sociomedical understandings of disease pathology and the aging process.[63] Awarded the Nobel Prize in Physiology or Medicine in 1908 for his research on phagocytosis, Russian biologist Élie Metchnikoff had posited that autointoxication induced by external factors, in particular the putrefactive bacteria in the digestive tract, was a preventable cause of old age and premature death. Metchnikoff, who coined the term *gerontology*, trumpeted the life-prolonging effects of lactic acid bacteria on intestinal antisepsis, purportedly evinced by the longevity of Bulgarian peasants with yogurt-rich diets.[64] Barreto sought the final word for Brazilian science. The nation's Indigenous population, he affirmed, had solved the problem of "intestinal antisepsis" centuries ago with the discovery of guaraná, a "disinfectant" and regulator of "intestinal functions," and one far easier on "civilized stomachs" than yogurt.[65]

In 1923, at the age of eighty-three, Barreto became another "tragic injustice." The elixir of long life could not enable him to cheat death, although he did live a decade longer than Metchnikoff, and close to three times the average life expectancy in Brazil in 1920, at just 31.4 years for men and 32.5 for women.[66] Guaraná's mass consumption in Brazil in the form of a soft drink, however, remains an enduring legacy of the positivist physician's commitment to his nation's industrial development.

WHILE FEW PAULISTAS today may know of Luís Pereira Barreto's innovation, nearly all the residents of the northeastern state of Maranhão know that Jesus saves—that is, Guaraná Jesus, the home-grown soft drink launched in the state capital, São Luís, in 1927 by pharmacist Jesus Norberto Gomes, an atheist. As with Coca-Cola, Pepsi-Cola, and Dr Pepper, Guaraná Jesus originated as a pharmacist's patent medicine. The rise of Guaraná Jesus, predominant in Maranhão for decades due to the regionalization of economic markets, can be analyzed as well in the context of Brazilian pharmacists' broader professional interest in native flora and national industry.

Born in 1891 in Vitória do Mearim and one of eight children, Jesus Gomes lost his father at the age of twelve. Two years later, he moved to São Luís, earning a meager salary as a pharmacist's assistant. After several years washing glass bottles, packaging powders, and delivering medicines to patients' homes, Gomes learned the art of compounding drugs, compiling nearly thirty pages of formulas frequently prescribed by physicians. By twenty, he was able to purchase his own pharmacy through savings and family assistance.[67] Small-town pharmacies in early twentieth-century Brazil served as more than sites for the fabrication and sale of medications. They offered diverse products (just as medicines were sold at other establishments) in a respectable gathering venue for men and often boasted the latest para-phernalia, such as typewriters, cash registers, calculators, carillon clocks, and kerosene-run refrigerators for storing medications.[68]

In a city that lacked physicians, Gomes earned customers' confidence and gratitude, bearing witness, day and night, to the torments of human suffering and social injustice. Deep-seated inequalities and corruption in Brazil pervaded medical care as well, where wealthier clients enjoyed greater access to industrial and commercial pharmaceuticals, while the poor relied on home-made remedies and traditional healers.[69] Jesus Gomes's caregiving to the forlorn of São Luís may have nurtured his leftist sympathies. When he died in April 1963, he lamented his inability as a member of the "petit-bourgeoisie" to fully embrace communism, but insisted that expenses spared on a simple funeral be donated to the Communist Party to help eliminate "physical and moral misery."[70]

During the 1920s, Brazilian pharmacists commonly compounded or manufactured their own medicines.[71] This was the age of the local pharmacological entrepreneur, when the corner druggist knew as much as the researchers employed by the larger domestic pharmaceutical firm and could produce nostrums just as handily "in the business of selling hope."[72] Jesus Gomes launched a number of products: Gomegaya Jesus, an injectable medication for muscular pain; analgesics such as Antigripal Jesus; cough syrups such as Peitoral Jesus, and Jesulina toothpaste. As noted in the *Album gráfico do Estado do Maranhão* of 1923, Gomes's Sanitária pharmacy carried the latest in "pharmaceutical specialties and special items . . . national and foreign."[73]

It was Gomes's effort to replicate the popular medication Magnésia Fluída Granado that led serendipitously to the invention of Maranhão's beloved soda. Gomes had acquired a German-made gas-making machine to manufacture the product (and bottles with the Granado imprint to sell the medicine) but soon faced charges of patent infringement. Stuck with an idle carbonator, he drew inspiration from the Bahia-based Fratelli Vita company, researching the soda manufacturing process and experimenting with various flavors.

Guaraná would have been known to the pharmacist, given the drug's long-standing reputation in Brazil's orthodox and popular health care. As mentioned in chapter 4, pharmacist Theodor Peckolt had extensively researched and published on guaraná in the nineteenth century, but he was far from alone. In 1851, the president of the Sociedade Pharmacêutica Brasileira, Ezequiel Correa dos Santos, reported on the drug's chemical composition and its qualities as a "febrifuge, tonic, aphrodisiac, anti-diarrheal, and coolant."[74] Nineteenth-century formularies consulted by pharmacists, rural estate owners, and folk healers also profiled the drug.[75] These publications included The-odor Langgaard's *Dicionário de medicina doméstica e popular* (published in 1865 and 1873) and Pedro Luis Napoleão Chernoviz's best-selling *Formulário ou guia médico* (1841), which classified indigenous plants such as guaraná accord-ing to therapeutic use and officinal preparation.[76] Physician Alfredo Augusto da Matta's *Flora médica brasiliense* (1912), which described 327 species of Ama-zonian medicinal plants, highlighted guaraná's caffeine content, posology, and efficacy for neuralgia.[77] In the 1920s, the Laboratório Nutrotherápico Dr. Raul Leite & Cia. sold tonics such as Guaranil and Guaraína, and the ingredient already headlined other soft drink manufactures.[78]

Gomes's initial bitter concoction was not a hit among his guinea pigs—his family and friends. During the colonial period, foul-tasting medicines were considered more efficacious, but sugar's prevalence in Brazilian diets also nurtured many a sweet tooth.[79] Gomes continued to tinker, adding cin-namon and clove to please the nose, pink coloring to dazzle the eye, and sugar to reward the brain. In 1927, Kola Guaraná Jesus was formally approved for consumption by the Laboratório Bromatólogico of the Departamento Nacional de Saúde Pública, the food safety agency established in 1920. Guar-aná Jesus's earliest labels claimed that the product was manufactured with rigorously sterilized ozonated water, "an excellent soda to combat physical exhaustion and efficacious treatment of depressions caused by alcoholic beverages."[80]

In the first decades of the twentieth century, advertisements for patent medicines blanketed Brazilian newspapers and magazines (medicaments be-ing their primary source of ad revenue in the 1920s) and pharmacy alma-nacs.[81] The Elixir de Inhame Goulart, for example, guaranteed users "more muscular force, resistance to fatigue and easy breathing," while Neurobiol Brain Tonic promised to combat "cerebral weakness, nervous dyspepsia, neurasthenia, memory loss, and lack of appetite." Pharmacist Cândido Fon-toura's Biotônico Fontoura claimed to "regenerate the blood, the muscles and fortify the nerves." Ratifying the body's social function for hard work, prod-uct marketers echoed the language of medical authorities and sanitarians promoting physical fitness and hygiene as national imperatives.[82]

DURING THE FIRST PRESIDENCY of Getúlio Vargas (1930–45), Brazilian pharmacists had professional and patriotic motives to champion native me-dicinal plants. The inaugural October 1934 edition of *Revista da Flora Me-dicinal* vowed to "show the capitalist our sources of gold, provide the industrialist with primary materials, show the foreigner our wonders, and awaken patriotic love in the Brazilian."[83] With the economy staggering from the Great Depression, imported drugs skewed the balance of payments.[84] Other authors noted that guaraná, indispensable for "today's man" plagued by overwork and fatigue, "was in place to exercise a social function of the highest value."[85] Guaraná had become another input for Vargas's developmentalist project, while exclusive commercial cultivation and overriding consumption in Brazil, in contrast to coffee, conferred special nationalistic cachet to the drug (and its professional connoisseurs). Native plants' protection from foreign usurpers, an old refrain in Brazilian economic botany, particularly following the loss of Amazonian rubber to British agents, provided another patriotic rallying cry.[86]

Behind some pharmacists' promotion of guaraná lurked the dread of professional competition and obsolescence. Indigenous and folk healers long vied with pharmacists and physicians as purveyors of hope.[87] While the penal code of 1890 had criminalized *curandeirismo*, defined as administering or prescribing substances "of any of the kingdoms of nature" as "a curative method for internal or external use," folk healing thrived in Brazil, often linked to religious heterodoxy.[88] Historical research suggests an uptick in prosecutions of witchcraft in Rio de Janeiro and other urban areas in the 1920s and 1930s.[89] Pharmaceutical journals exhorted laboratories to analyze national flora rather than "await the Indians to appear in the market, offering us unknown plants."[90] Authors did not favor the guaraná marked by "primitive use among the Indians" but rather the "medicinal drink or simple soda" made possible by "modern studies and research."[91]

Alternatively, pharmacists' challenge stemmed from the depredation of flora, as Jayme Pecegueiro Gomes da Cruz, representative of the Brazilian Pharmaceutical Association to the Conferência Brasileira de Proteção à Natureza in 1934, railed.[92] His call for "rational" use of natural resources embodied the goals of Brazil's early conservationist movement, led by scientists, for the creation of national parks, reforestation campaigns, arbors and truck farms, botanical gardens, and pharmaceutical research laboratories.[93] Like guaraná, countless Brazilian plants held economic promise, awaiting pharmaceutical study and industrial development.[94] As the *Gazeta da Farmácia* noted in 1946: "Few plants are as known and used in Brazil as guaraná, principally due to the much appreciated and healthful 'carbonated guaranás' that today enjoy nationwide diffusion."[95] In this sense, guaraná served as a "charismatic" plant, a term used by contemporary conservation biologists for those species (typically larger mammals) commanding human empathy due to aesthetic, corporeal, or ecological appeal, or cultural and historical association, and which often headline environmental campaigns to protect larger ecosystems and their inhabitants.[96]

Promotion of guaraná and other botanicals also shored up professional credentials threatened by the influx of synthetic medicines and the substitution of university chairs in materia medica with professorships in pharmacology. With the "rapid invasion" of synthetic drugs in Brazil, native plants risked pharmaceutical oblivion, or at least "the abandonment of their study and industrial usage," pharmacist Virgilio Lucas decried at the Academia Nacional de Medicina in 1937.[97] By the early 1950s, in fact, pharmaceutical exports to Brazil exceeded $37 million, with leading North American drug companies undertaking installation or expansion of factories for in-country production. As one trade journal noted in 1953, Brazilians had a "veritable mania for antibiotics." Lax regulations facilitated self-medication, with patients opting for a penicillin injection at the first sign of a cold.[98]

JESUS GOMES'S FORTUNES REFLECTED shifting trends in Brazil's consumer markets. His soft drinks had originated in the 1920s as homemade remedies claiming therapeutic benefits, with the guaraná flavor enjoying broad endorsement from his professional colleagues. With rising beverage sales, Gomes delinked the Sanitário pharmacy in 1943 from his soda business, renamed Indústria Jesus Ltda. Within a decade, he relocated manufacture to another building, where new bottling machinery ramped up production that passersby could admire through the factory's large picture window. As motor vehicle ownership expanded in Brazil in the 1960s with the rise of a domestic automobile industry, distribution of Guaraná Jesus and other flavors stretched beyond the capital. Among his assortment of homemade patent medicines, only Jesus's line of soft drinks would endure.

Over the postwar decades, multinational drug companies absorbed or eliminated many plant-based pharmaceutical industries in Brazil, furthering the nation's lag in drug research and development.[99] Of course, consumers unable to afford industrial pharmaceuticals or in search of alternative treatments continued to procure guaraná and other medicinal plants. Research carried out at the Mercado Municipal Adolpho Lisboa in Manaus in the late 1990s, for example, found that guaraná was one of the most popular of the nearly 150 medicinal plants sold to urban dwellers, which were typically recommended by friends, neighbors, herbalists, religious healers, or television programs, but never by a doctor.[100] And by the early 2000s, over one hundred laboratories in Brazil marketed sixty-seven types of natural medicines for fifty-three therapeutic uses, most commonly as laxatives, sedatives, vasodilators, expectorants, and amebicides. Nevertheless, in 2011, phytomedicines generated $1.1 billion of a total $43 billion in national pharmaceutical sales in Brazil.[101] Visitors today to a corner pharmacy in Brazil would be less likely to find guaraná for sale as a medicinal than as an ingredient in an over-the-counter energy drink. Then again, they would be likelier to see a woman as their pharmacist: among the nation's 195,000 pharmacists in 2015, 64 percent were women.[102]

After Gomes's death, his children sold off the soda company.[103] The one-time small-time pharmacist may have held communist sympathies, but in 2001, Guaraná Jesus was acquired by the Coca-Cola Company for an undisclosed price. The product has retained its name, along with its dreamy pink color and bubble gum aroma.

IN THE AFTERMATH of João Coelho de Miranda Leão's death, other Amazonian elites took up the promotion and defense of guaraná in the soft drink industry.[104] During the 1930s, Amazonian merchants sought to standardize the pricing of guaraná sticks and roasted seeds—the latter, of poorer quality, sold to soda manufacturers. Founded in Maués in 1934, the Consórcio de Guaraná, encompassing larger producers and merchants, successfully lobbied the government of Amazonas to institute a minimum price for roasted seeds (*guaraná em rama*) sold in Manaus.[105] Immigrant and first-generation entrepreneurs were prominent in the early twentieth-century guaraná trade, though the former represented just 2.25 percent of Amazonas's population in 1920. Among the founding officers of the Guaraná Consortium were president and treasurer Jorge Elias de Almeida, a naturalized Brazilian of Syrian origin (born Salum Hauad); Vice President Salomão Levy, a Moroccan Jew who had arrived in Maués in 1906 at the age of twelve; and Secretaries Pedro (Pietro) Cardelli and Carlos Esteves, born in Italy and Portugal, respectively. Pedro Negreiros, the other secretary, was a member of a prominent clan that emigrated to Maués in the 1870s from Ceará during the great northeastern drought.[106] Italian-born residents of Amazonas and Pará, numbering merely 1,840 in 1920, appear to have played an outsized role.[107] One notable was José (Giuseppe) Faraco, who emigrated from Acquafredda to Maués in 1902; became a prominent guaraná planter, manufacturer, and merchant (according to his grandson, financing cultivation of as many as 50,000 plants); featured his processing facilities in Silvino Santos's promotional film, *No paiz das amazonas* (1921); and was even crowned the King of Guaraná at the National Exposition in Rio de Janeiro in 1922.[108] Henrique Magnani, who arrived from Lucca to Maués in the early 1900s, invented a mechanical grinder for guaraná, which he patented.[109] Japanese immigrants' initial experimentation with commercial guaraná cultivation in the 1930s foundered; they would find greater success with jute in the Parintins region and black pepper at the Tomé-Açu colony in postwar Pará.[110]

Over the 1930s and 1940s, the Amazonas Trade Association aimed to diversify guaraná's markets. According to a 1928 report, smoked sticks (*bastões*) dominated a highly regionalized trade: over 68,458 sticks, or 90 percent of the state's guaraná exports, headed for Mato Grosso, where the stimulant remained a staple of daily life and regional identity.[111] As an essayist noted in 1928 of the capital city's early morning soundscape: "At that hour, inside the house of a true Cuiabano, the type that gets headaches when they don't drink guaraná, one hears the distinct sound of the scraping of guaraná."[112] Newspapers published stories, true or fanciful, of onetime governors of Mato Grosso who dropped everything each day at 4 P.M. because "it was guaraná time"; of a well-heeled female steamboat passenger who roused a German traveler in the wee hours with the clickety-clack of guaraná scraping; of a visitor who, owing to wartime shortages of the drug, encountered kerchief-clad, headache-suffering residents in Livramento lamenting merchant Benedito Leite de Figueiredo's failed transplant of guaraná to Cuiabá three decades earlier, when colder weather on the River Plate killed thousands of seedlings.[113] Whereas Johann Sebastian Bach composed his coffee cantata, and Lu Tung his odes to tea, Dom Francisco de Aquino Correia—a Mato Grosso politician, cleric, and man of letters—rhapsodized about his "beloved drink" in the 1944 poem "O guaraná."[114]

In 1932, the Amazonas Trade Association unveiled a decade-long campaign to supply drugstores, chemical industries, and soda manufacturers in southern Brazil and Europe with thousands of free samples of roasted guaraná seeds, sticks, and extracts for use in pharmaceuticals, beverages, and even chewing gum.[115] The state of Amazonas also launched a public competition to improve the substance's industrial application to carbonated drinks.[116] With scientific identification of caffeine as guaraná's active principle, Amazonians emphasized its exotic origins and supposed advantage over coffee to re-enchant and add value to the commodity.[117] The Amazonas Trade Association, for example, touted guaraná as a prophylactic against "intestinal intoxification" caused by "the pollution of food and modern lifestyles," while reassuring consumers that its "tonifying-cardiac action" was no worse than coffee's.[118] Benjamin Lira, a Rio-based journalist born in Pará, offered a particularly creative marketing pitch.[119] Following a 1939 soccer match between Brazil and Argentina marked by the rival team's consumption of coffee during halftime, Lira exhorted: "We Brazilians, however, have a drink even better than coffee to proclaim as a way for 'footballers' and athletes in general to obtain the beneficial reaction, indispensable in the midst of competitions, for the Victory to which they aspire." Guaraná's analeptic qualities, discovered "in the Brazilian jungle by some poor *bugres* [a pejorative term for Indigenous peoples from the French *bougre*, or 'bugger']," should be "the secret to invincibility of our [team] colors."[120]

Amazonian business leaders and politicians conjured a new El Dorado where guaraná might one day match coffee consumption in Brazil and even conquer the U.S. soda market.[121] Celebrating the imminent launch of a guaraná soda by the Polar Beverages of Worcester, Massachusetts—which had test-marketed the product in several thousand local households and even selected a brand name, Rio Rico—the Amazonas Trade Association crowed in 1952 of "conquering the land of Coca-Cola."[122] That conquest never ensued.

In fact, guaraná faced considerable obstacles for application to Brazil's domestic soda industry as well.[123] Throughout the first half of the century, extractivism continued to dominate Amazonia's economy, while labor scarcity further crimped market expansion and diversification.[124] Production techniques of guaraná remained rudimentary. According to a report from the late 1940s, only one planter in Maués, Henrique Magnani, employed row planting and mechanical mortars—an invention with the capacity to replace thirty workers.[125] Unlike sugar or coffee, whose large producers wielded political power in Brazil, guaraná did not acquire a specialized federal institute to promote research and development during the Vargas era.[126] Some 350 kilometers by river from Manaus (and 1,000 kilometers from the ocean), Maués benefited only twice monthly from regular boat service to the state capital in the late 1930s, although airline service had been recently inaugurated.[127] By 1953, Mato Grosso still consumed some 60 to 80 percent of commercialized guaraná.[128]

IN 1938, the Laboratório de Chimica Bromatológica of Rio de Janeiro's Public Health Department reached a startling conclusion. More than one-quarter of the 234 guaraná sodas, syrups, and powders tested by the public health agency did not contain the ingredient.[129] During World War II, Brazil's Conselho do Comércio Exterior likewise determined that few namesake sodas actually used guaraná.[130] The adulteration of food and drugs was no novelty or secret in Brazil. According to the *Gazeta da Farmácia*, in 1932, of more than nine hundred pharmacies, laboratories, druggists, and herb markets in Rio de Janeiro that sold medicinal plants, all plied doctored products, which the author attributed to the dishonesty of the "legendary woodsmen" who served as suppliers of botanicals.[131] In his 1946 study of guaraná, Dr. Othon Machado denounced "unscrupulous" soda manufacturers who used additives and substitutes.[132] Chemists and pharmacists committed to food and drug safety likewise condemned the falsification of guaraná products; if France authenticated its Champagne, why couldn't Brazil's government ensure beverage integrity?[133] Adulteration contributed to the "demoralization of this very useful trade."[134] None hollered louder than Amazonians, outraged by the gentian-flavored, artificially colored, and otherwise caffeinated soft drinks that evoked nothing of guaraná's "peculiar and lightly bitter taste."[135] Sodas with the "fantasy name of guaraná" sold by the millions nationwide by the mid-1940s, depriving their region of untold profits.[136] A traditional flavor of the Amazon steeped in Indigenous myth and customary usage fronted a hoax of consummate proportions among Brazilians unaware of guaraná's true taste.

According to Manaus-based chemist, pharmacist, and beverage manufacturer Eugene Aubert, adulteration of guaraná soft drinks derived not only from companies' cost cutting and supply bottlenecks.[137] Since the drug had been introduced to carbonated drinks in the early 1900s, he pointed out, manufacturers had struggled to lessen the solution's turbidity.[138] Guaraná's seeds have a high content of fats, oils, and resins, which make the substance less soluble in water than tea or coffee. Visible particles of guaraná appear in the prepared artisanal drink and as sediment at the bottom of the receptacle.[139] Aubert claimed that manufacturers reduced the concentration of the plant's tannins to diminish cloudiness and embellish the drink's appearance. To enhance flavor, they added bitter substances that were more soluble and less turbid, such as gentian, as well as flavorings such as vanilla or tonka beans.[140] In sum, guaraná soft drink manufacturers had compelling reasons to falsify the star ingredient of their popular product, and even more so when limited government capability hobbled the enforcement of food and drug safety.[141] Food manufacturers might send the Instituto Bromatológico an authentic sample for testing but continue to sell adulterated products.[142] In the case of guaraná, the use of caffeinated substitutes bedeviled simple detection through chemical testing. Those companies that labeled their guaraná beverage "artificial" or "imitation" might dispense with the ingredient altogether—a loophole for all drinks, aside from coffee, maté, and milk, where the use of artificial ingredients as substitutes was proscribed.[143]

Tensions between Amazonian traders and beverage companies erupted at the Primeiro Congresso Brasileiro de Bromatologia in 1946. Under Decree-Law no. 7.669 of June 2, 1945, the federal government had established a minimum of 0.3 grams of guaraná for 100 cubic centimeters of liquid in all commercial carbonated and non-carbonated beverages that claimed the ingredient in labels and advertisements. The regulation amended a decree-law from 1944 mandating a minimum of a half gram of guaraná, which the Sindicato da Indústria de Cerveja e Bebidas em Geral in São Paulo had opposed. The new law also required syrups, concentrates, medicines, and other pharmaceutical products to quantify guaraná content in their formulas.[144]

At the food science congress, manufacturers continued to oppose federally regulated guaraná minimums. The industry insisted that women and children, the drinks' biggest consumers, craved a "refreshment and not a medicine" that might pose risks to the latter's "fragile" nervous systems. Fans would jump ship, wrecking an important national industry, composed of many small manufacturers, with "grave effects for the Nation."[145] In another nationalistic salvo, industrialists questioned why producers of this "typically Brazilian soda" should be held to a higher standard of authentication than Coca-Cola.[146] Ultimately, they charged, planters had invited adulteration by failing to meet rising consumer demand.[147] The political implication was clear: the beverage industries, heavily located in the nation's South, acted in the service of Brazil, unlike the Amazonian slackers. In 1950, the soft drink manufacturers would band together to form the Associação Brasileira das Indústrias de Refrigerantes e de Bebidas não Alcoólicas (ABIR), which remains the sector's primary trade association.[148]

Manuel Bastos Lira, the sole Amazonian representative at the congress, deplored that "Brazilians would become fraudsters with their own botany." Guaraná was no "bonbon," he charged; its faint vegetable odor came nowhere near the "perfumeries" of the aromatized sodas, and the industrial beverage's hue could never be as naturally vibrant as that of the traditional smoked stick. Furthermore, manufacturers' concern with guaraná's toxicity for children was alarmist, not to mention hypocritical, given their generous recourse to alternative caffeinated substances. "As a specific fruit of Brazilian flora" that was "one-hundred percent national," Lira asserted, guaraná deserved full state protection from cheap knock-offs.[149] In other words, Lira offered an alternative narrative in which nature trumped culture as emblematic of Brazilian identity. Which, after all, was the quintessential nationalist symbol in a late industrializing tropical country: the jungle plant or the manufacturing plant?

The Amazonians' dispute with beverage manufacturers embodied broader political tensions between Brazil's southern economic core and its periphery. As federal congressman Cosme Ferreira Filho decried in 1948: "Effervescent guaraná became a national drink. In the meantime, the source of all these profits remains abandoned and forgotten. . . . Just as abandoned and forgotten, stricken by illnesses and punished by the contingency of their irremediable poverty, are the inhabitants of the region that produce guaraná, in the municipality of Maués."[150] Bemoaning their "colonial" status, Amazonian elites looked to the federal government to level the playing field. Ferreira Filho unsuccessfully proposed that the Ministry of Agriculture create a research station in Maués to study the agroecology, genetics, and processing of the plant, with funding from an added tax on guaraná sodas.[151]

The Amazonian campaign to enforce guaraná minimums in soft drinks lasted decades. According to a 1960 report, few companies used the ingredient in namesake sodas; manufacturers even claimed that "guaraná" had been genericized to signify any sweetened, carbonated, non-alcoholic beverage.[152] Brazilians could choose from some one thousand brands of "guaraná" soda, though many contained not one milligram of the ingredient.[153] These included *tubaínas*, a cheaper, highly sweetened soda, said to be made of guaraná, citrus, or tutti-frutti flavors.[154] Industrial food systems had begun to deliver Brazilians more varied offerings, but at the cost of compositional integrity. "Everything that is natural in Amazonia ends up losing the privilege of really being so due to the mundane counterfeiting of profiteers," bemoaned Manaus-born historian and folklorist Mario Ypiranga Monteiro in 1965. "Guaraná is included in the order of those copied and fraudulent things."[155] Resentment of outsiders' appropriation of regional resources emerged anew, a defensiveness bred by historical marginalization.

Following the Brazilian military coup of 1964, the battle over guaraná minimums in the beverage industry underwent another legislative round. Law 5.823 of November 14, 1972, popularly known as the Lei dos Sucos (or "Juice Law," part of the National Beverage Code), mandated a minimum of fruit content for industrial juices and sodas, including a minimum 0.2 percent of guaraná in namesake beverages, or 200 grams of seeds to every 100 liters of soft drink. The law also capped the maximum percentage for guaraná sodas at 2 percent.[156] This time, growers in the Amazon found backing from Brazil's agribusiness and food industry. The bill had been proposed by São Paulo congressional representatives to favor expanded markets for their region's citrus growers, offsetting the higher manufacturing costs associated with pasteurization of fresh fruit by granting juice companies a 50 percent reduction in their industrial income tax. With a factory installed in Maués in 1962 to manufacture guaraná extract, Companhia Antarctica backed the legislation to obtain the tax break and to disadvantage competitors using ersatz ingredients.[157]

In 1998, a chemical analysis of forty-two guaraná soft drinks and syrups in Brazil found that most carbonated beverages did show caffeine levels consistent with legally mandated minimums.[158]

Through their dogged efforts, Amazonians had promoted consumer demand and brand protection for guaraná. True, their victory owed to the political authority and deal making of the more influential sectors of Brazil's agroindustry and political class. Moreover, after the guaraná consortium in Maués was dissolved in 1966—hastened by the recent arrival of Antarctica's processing plant amid the military-era push for extra-regional capital investment in Amazonia—small planters went from the clutches of a price-fixing merchant clique to those of an industrial capital oligopoly.[159] Still, Amazonians' tenacity had ensured that the guaraná soft drink now adored by tens of millions in Brazil contains traces of the ingredient, albeit not much of its natural taste.

BRIDGING ANTHROPOLOGICAL DIVIDES that have parsed the biophysical significance, political economy, or semiotics of food, this chapter has placed the production of a Brazilian soft drink in the context of food science, entrepreneurship, import-substitution industrialization, and sectoral divisions in Latin American economies.[160] By 1958, Brazil counted 724 different manufacturers of "sodas and soft drinks," although beer commanded 70 percent of total beverage production.[161] (Among larger companies such as Antarctica and Brahma, beer distribution networks facilitated the marketing of soda.)[162] Rising postwar industrial output enabled the production of more uniform food products, canned foods, and semi-processed meals.[163] Furthermore, the expansion of appliance and refrigerator ownership in the 1950s, propelled by domestic manufactures, encouraged greater food purchases during a decade marked by the opening of the nation's first supermarkets.[164] In this context, the products promoted by Luís Pereira Barreto, Jesus Gomes, and Amazonian commercial interests found growing consumer markets.

Food systems, however, are shaped not only by modes of production and distribution but by ideologies.[165] Mass consumption of guaraná sodas ultimately depended on drinkers willing to ingest the beverage. This begs larger historical questions posed by anthropologists and food studies scholars: How do people apprehend or come to know foods, including processed foods and brands? By what means do those who make and sell food influence consumption patterns?[166] Guaraná sodas didn't just seduce Brazilians with their bubbly, sugary, caffeinated perks. The "fantasy" of guaraná also fueled the beverages' widespread appeal.

CHAPTER SIX

Message in a Bottle

Selling Guaraná

In 1980, seventy-nine-year-old Anilda Antonio do Nascimento reminisced how a dose of guaraná soda and serendipity enabled a long-ago romantic encounter with soon-to-be radio singer Francisco Alves. As a fourteen-year-old domestic servant in Rio de Janeiro, at a time when men still wore "shiny top hats," Nascimento went one hot Saturday afternoon for a guaraná soda at a neighborhood bar. A young man approached, coyly asking to share the drink. Anilda obliged. Afterward, the two strolled through the downtown. According to Nascimento, a courtship ensued, then a marriage, which dissolved when Alves's career as a radio crooner blossomed.[1] How the soda abetted countless other romances in Brazil is as unrecoverable for historians as indelible for their protagonists.

Handwritten notes suggest that Alves did have contact with Nascimento, yet none of his biographers recount this marriage. What interests me here is not the veracity of this account but an elderly woman's gloss on a teenage dalliance. In the narrative, the choice of beverage blunts the young woman's coquettishness, just as it seemingly provides cover for her entry into the bar. After all, in the 1920s, ads for Antarctica "Malt" Beer still had to vouch that the beverage was "appropriate for ladies," while the philanthropic League of Catholic Women in São Paulo pushed for the establishment of a women's restaurant where female workers could enjoy a respectable repast.[2] When Rio's earliest department stores opened in the 1930s, men could drink cocktails at the bar, while women were shuttled off to the tearoom.[3] The story further suggests another source of the soft drinks' enduring appeal: the intimate links between food and affective memory, particularly those associated with one's youth. It is a fitting opening vignette, then, for a chapter concerned with analyzing the popularization of an Amazonian stimulant as a refreshment in Brazil and an icon of national identity.

Dietary habits contain multistranded histories that defy neat unraveling. Like other cultural practices of everyday life, food consumption is sedimented and structured in myriad ways: from the conditions of historical time, climate, and geographic space to the social expectations associated with foods and beverages; from the intergenerational transmission of knowledge to the innovations and novelties often based on substitutional mechanisms or the transfer of functions from one product to another; from attributions of collective belonging to the peculiarities of individuals.[4] A fuller explanation of how Anilda Nascimento and countless other Brazilians of her generation came to savor a drink unfamiliar to their grandparents requires a wide-angle lens to examine a society in transition. It necessitates analysis of the function of soft drinks in popular adaptations of norms of social behavior to shifting historical circumstances.

The rapid industrial and demographic growth of Brazil's urban centers multiplied possibilities for social interaction. Mass media and consumer culture promoted novel forms of self-expression. A growing number of "experts" in health, nutrition, fashion, and etiquette influenced the lifestyles of readers, listeners, and viewers. And state officials expatiated on citizens' rights and responsibilities. Guaraná soda took the field in Brazil during this moment of flux, buoyed by consumers' pursuit of self-improvement and affirmations of social belonging. Nationalist slogans bolstered product marketing. Food's potential to transform the anguish of nutritional privation into momentary pleasure is, of course, also pertinent.[5]

While the correlation of culinary practices to social distinction has been a primary contribution of the interdisciplinary field of food studies, the Brazilian literature has been heavily dominated by the social sciences and health sciences.[6] This chapter explores mediations of race, class, gender, age, and region that endowed Brazilians with disparate stakes, resources, and outcomes in product use. It pays particular attention to the beverages' early appeal to upper- and middle-class women and children in light of normative social roles and dietary customs. Sodas were equal-opportunity enticers, but commercial success relied heavily on women as protagonists and go-betweens. In the beverage factories, they served on the assembly lines. In households, they served up the sweetened formulas that promised familial satisfaction and self-validation. Handlers of choleric youngsters awarded booty to combatants for bodily autonomy.[7] In public arenas, women latched onto a drink that signaled fashionableness and self-possession.

Rising soft drink consumption in Brazil accompanied the growth of the commercial advertising industry, transformed since the late 1920s by the opening of branch offices of U.S. agencies and the expansion of national firms and market research.[8] By the 1930s, many erstwhile luxury items were pitched to the middle class, the sector that spent the largest ratio of their earnings on mass-marketed goods.[9] Brazilian admen linked modern lifestyles to cleanliness, comfort, speed, health, leisure, and technological sophistication; freedom entailed the minimization of risk and the optimization of quality of life.[10] Notions of race, class, gender, and generation informed marketers' campaigns. The spread of radio, tied to state projects of institution building and popular forms of entertainment, gifted advertisers with sound and music to reach broad audiences.[11]

The scripting of guaraná sodas by Brazilian companies and consumers reflects everyday aspirations to make profit, sense, or light of that grand scheme of twentieth-century political and social engineering: modernization. Urbanization and industrial development reshaped traditional practices and beliefs in Brazil. Yet the marketing and consumption of guaraná soft drinks reveal the replication of social hierarchies, the romance with nature, and the allure of magic for the modern subject. The beverages' massification also demonstrates that "economies of regard"—promoting sharing and sociability in day-to-day personal relations and expressed through pleasantries and gift exchanges—are central to both traditional and modern societies.[12]

ALTHOUGH MANY BRAZILIANS relished sodas, women were more in their thrall due to the conventions of food consumption and gender norms. Aside from somatic and sensory gratification, drinking is linked to social sensitivity.[13] Multinational research reveals consistent gender differences, for example, in alcohol consumption: frequent and heavier drinking occurs among men, while longer-term or lifetime abstention is more common among women. A mix of biological and cultural explanations has been posited. Due to the greater amount of lipids and the smaller amount of water in women's bodies, the same amount of alcohol per body weight, consumed in the same length of time, leads to higher blood-alcohol levels for women than it does for men.[14] Critically, men's license to get drunk in public in certain cultural settings can signal superiority to women in status and authority, while female inebriation may trigger fears of sexual assertiveness or vulnerability, or incompatibility with domestic roles.[15] Moral prescription rarely abides fully in social practice, but neither are the burdens of stigma and self-doubt illusory.

Public consumption of alcohol—providing comfort, cheer, and calories—had long been a source of masculine privilege in Brazil. The tavern (*botequim*) facilitated working-class male sociability, coupled with the drinking of cachaça—lovingly ascribed many feminine nicknames, including Our Lady's Water (*Água-de-nossa-senhora*) and Blonde Virgin (*Virgem loira*), and marked by elaborate toasting ceremonies and songs.[16] As a marker of identity and inclusion, the drinking of alcohol is patterned by social expectations (including violent actions), ritualization of behaviors (weaving webs of reciprocity), and

Casa Lopes e Fernandes Cia, Rio de Janeiro, early twentieth century. Augusto Malta Collection, Fundação Museu da Imagem e do Som, Rio de Janeiro.

situational transitions (such as work to leisure).[17] In a memoir of his youth in turn-of-the-twentieth-century Rio de Janeiro, Luiz Edmundo [de Melo Pereira da Costa] recounted men's tipsy nocturnal revelries. After work, throngs of clerks and salesmen crowded the music halls, theaters, bars, cafés, street corners, and public squares to drink. Cachaça, beer, and Portuguese wines were favorites.[18] Indeed, nearly thirty-six hundred establishments in Rio sold alcohol in 1911.[19] "Respectable" women, according to the memoirist, confined to home at nighttime, the poorer ones cramped in summer in sweatboxes lacking electricity, armed with a straw fan, and a bed net for the mosquitoes. An older Luiz Edmundo blanched at former excesses, insisting that family men in Brazil, like those in any other "advanced and progressive country," now spent evenings at home with their wives and children.[20] A 2015 government study, however, found that women in Brazil still had a lower probability of drinking alcohol than men.[21] Sociological research on gender and alcohol consumption in Brazil has also revealed that where women were more educated, worked outside the home, and earned a good income—in other words, where their social roles became similar to those of men—their pattern of drinking alcohol at lower levels also resembled that of men.[22]

It was not random, then, that Anilda Nascimento selected guaraná as her beverage of choice, while Luiz Edmundo drenched his youthful escapades in alcohol—or at least that they opted to portray their younger days with those particular reminiscences. Nor was it random that the anonymous author of a letter to a São Paulo women's magazine in the 1920s, divulging her romantic crush, signed it "Guaraná Espumante," not Ypioca Cachaça.[23] Nor that a radio advertisement from the 1930s featured a man asking a waiter to "bring a soda for my love," to which she dutifully responded, "I want a Guaraná Fratelli Vita!"[24] Nor that an actual waiter at Rio's Parque Recreio restaurant recalled how men would linger over draft beers (*chopes*) while "the women drank guaraná and left earlier."[25] Non-alcoholic and sugary fruit beverages had a customary clientele among women and children in Brazil, just as female sociability traditionally centered around (overseeing) the production and delivery of sweets. Brazil's culture of sweetness and power, as Gilberto Freyre noted, was another legacy of the colonial sugar plantation and its patriarchal mores.[26]

In the nineteenth century, Brazilians referred to fruit juices by a number of names: *refresco, garapa, garapada, gelada, limonada,* and *ponche*. According to the recipe book *Doceiro nacional,* homemade limonadas were made with fruit juice (not exclusively limes), sugar, and water, and favored for their taste and aroma.[27] *Ponche,* a French and Portuguese adaptation of English punch, which had been consumed hot in Europe, came to refer to a cold non-alcoholic beverage in Brazil. *Aluá,* another nineteenth-century alcohol-free drink popular among the poor, was made from an infusion of pineapple rinds, corn, or rice with brown sugar, and sold often by Black female street vendors. Still another late nineteenth-century non-alcoholic quencher was ginger beer (*jinjibirra*), first imported from England and later locally produced (often without ginger) and plied at religious celebrations and country fairs.[28] Like *caramuru,* a beverage made of ground corn, ginger, lemon rind, and water, *jinjibirra* was a favorite among children.[29] At commercial establishments, elite women also savored *sorvetes,* which initially referred to iced drinks made of fruit syrup or cream and vigorously mixed (like a slushy).[30]

Men in Brazil traditionally enjoyed sweetened beverages and juices as well. Dom Pedro II downed sugary water to hydrate in the Rio de Janeiro heat, although the emperor's sweet tooth most likely contributed to his diabetic condition.[31] Conversely, elite nineteenth-century women drank after-dinner liqueurs, particularly those made from fruit, just as in the 1950s they enjoyed cocktails at home.[32] Men, however, could afford to be more unrestrained in their beverage consumption, while women's choices and venues were circumscribed by social practice and locale. "Honorable" women in the nineteenth and early twentieth century had to know the proper codes for drinking in public: when to arrive, what to order, when to vanish.[33] In this sense, sodas represented a form of cultural bricolage in Brazil's culinary tradition: industrial formulas improvised on sweetened alcohol-free and fruit-based beverages rooted in the nation's patriarchal past.

AS INDUSTRIAL BEVERAGES, however, soft drinks significantly differed from homemade *limonadas* in their sociohistorical context. Food systems in Brazilian cities were being affected by industrial growth, linked worldwide to transformations in urban women's labor and household food preparation.[34] Between 1890 and 1940, São Paulo's population skyrocketed from 65,000 to 1,326,000, and Rio de Janeiro's from 523,000 to 1,764,000. The growth in manufacturing and financial and public services expanded the ranks of the white-collar professions and the industrial working class. While industry undercut women's roles as domestic producers, and the professionalization of medicine diminished their importance as caregivers, opportunities for education, employment, and consumerism increased, as did the forums for discussing gender norms.[35] The number of journals in Brazil doubled to nearly three thousand between 1910 and 1930, with many featuring articles on love, marriage, family, homemaking, and personal improvement, and replete with advertisements for food, apparel, and health and beauty products. In the 1920s, radio brought the outside world into the home, and commercial advertising via the airwaves arrived the following decade. The proliferation of cinemas exposed viewers to the modern flapper, the independent working girl, and the "American way of life," while moviegoing extended the nighttime hours for women's public leisure and occasions for commercial repast.[36]

Changes to street and home marked new times. Although enslaved and poor women had traditionally circulated in urban arenas as food vendors, laundresses, domestics, wet nurses, and prostitutes, improvements in infrastructure and transportation allowed wealthier women to venture more comfortably far from home, while a crackdown on street commerce and vice aimed at sanitizing public space.[37] In more affluent homes, the arrival of the gas stove, electricity, and domestic appliances transformed the kitchen, viewed as a "laboratory" by doctors and sanitarians for the modern household.[38]

Technological innovations enabled greater distribution and conservation of food, diets loosened their ties to seasonal patterns, and standardization of mealtimes was linked to work and transport schedules.[39] While domestic chores remained the responsibility of servants in wealthier families, the adoption of new products and appliances and the supervision of tasks enlisted the female head of household's oversight. More broadly, urbanization and market expansion upended traditional patriarchal norms as larger elite kin networks gave away to the nuclear family, courtship constraints were relaxed, and marriage initiatives less dictated by parental will.[40]

Food adaptations—products of historical opportunity or material shortage—often engender social aspirations and anxieties.[41] For conservative commentators such as folklorist and gastronomic historian Luís da Câmara Cascudo, industrial foods violated hallowed traditions. Like the modern world they sustained, processed foods sacrificed sophistication for speed, character for consistency, craft for capacity, and distinctiveness for diffusion. Eating had been reduced to canned goods, and mastery in the kitchen to opening them without cutting one's fingers.[42] Similarly, for Gilberto Freyre, the rise of chilled confections signaled the demise of the "patriarchal dessert" prepared by "the Black women in the kitchen" in plantation households. Fruits once dowsed in sugar for conserves and compotes or warm puddings had found their way into "*sorvetes* and chilled desserts" of European confectioners. Elaborate domestic teatime ceremonies in his native Pernambuco, showcasing elite women's homemaking finesse, had given way to ice cream parlors, confectioneries, and cafés.[43] Cold was the climate of the new industrial order, of cities and their more impersonal relations and cosmopolitan ethos, which Freyre abhorred.[44] That industrial foods sinned by desecrating a traditionally feminine and nonwhite preserve implicitly pervaded such harangues. In historian Rachel Laudan's memorable terminology, "culinary Luddites" often gloss over moral problems intrinsic to the labor of producing and preparing food: that women have other options than working in the kitchen where industrial foods become available, that men have greater opportunities than labor in the fields, and that all have benefited from longer life expectancies.[45] In any event, Freyre and Câmara Cascudo exaggerated the demise of patriarchalism—and of good food—in twentieth-century Brazil. As the scions of the large landowners resettled in urban villas or luxury apartments outfitted with servant quarters, the sex and race of those in the kitchen changed little.

Food, however, did offer options for modern women's self-fashioning. And in magazines, cookbooks, and etiquette manuals, there was guaraná

Guaraná Espumante ad, 1921. *A Cigarra* 165 (1921): 56. Hemeroteca Digital, Biblioteca Nacional, Rio de Janeiro. Courtesy of Arquivo O Cruzeiro/ EM/D.A Press.

soda, touted by columnists and advertisers as the key to homemaking, throwing a party, romancing, living an active lifestyle, and emulating the rich and famous.[46] For example, a 1920s ad for Guaraná Espumante picturing a stargazing female in fashionable dress was dedicated to "sentimental young women," contemplators of starlit nights.[47] Likewise, a poem published in *O Cruzeiro* in 1945, accompanied by a drawing of two swimsuit-clad woman, evoked changing times: "A swimming pool of twenty meters / Girls even shorter / In bathing suits even smaller / tanning their *bodies* [English in original] . . . Coca-Cola, guaraná have crazy lives / their bottles' poor, simple necks / kiss the sexiest mouths."[48] Perhaps writer Rachel de Queiroz best captured soft drinks' liberating potential for women in a 1946 magazine column. Contrasting the traditional celebration of the São João festivities in her northeastern state of Ceará with the goings-on in Rio de Janeiro, she quipped: "Women in Rio want guaraná and the men want beer. There's no green corn to roast in the bonfire; they don't play games with a basin or with egg whites to discover which girl will get married. Girls in 1946 don't believe anymore in these idiocies and don't wait at home to get married. They are the ones that go out finding a husband and they are only happy when they can stand up for themselves."[49] Queiroz's observation about urbanites hankering for industrial beverages was statistically borne out: during World War II, hundreds of millions of bottles of beer and tens of millions of sodas had been filled annually in Brazil, while postwar manufacturers bemoaned product shortages stemming from rising demand, dilapidated machinery, scarce water supply, and legally mandated restrictions on factory work hours.[50]

Nevertheless, salutes to feminine progress in Brazil jostled with calls for restraint. The feared libertinage of the "modern girl" triggered social anxieties amid persistent cross-class double standards regarding sexual behavior.[51] Representing just 15.4 percent of the paid work force in 1940, largely in low-status and "helping" occupations, Brazilian women's normative social roles remained that of wives and mothers whose domestic responsibilities had changed rather than their overall burden.[52] In this context, soft drinks were props as much as quenchers for the modern woman. The romantic stargazer may have been chicly attired, but her supplicant pose and mental drifting signaled social subordination (a transnational staple of gendered advertisement), as did her sanctioned mood-altering beverage.[53] Queiroz may have balked at customary prepping in the kitchen for São João but still upheld soft drinks as women's calling card in contradistinction to men's beer. Likewise, chef Helena Sangirardi affirmed in her domestic column in 1948: "Many of my female friends and acquaintances think it strange that I don't smoke and don't venture past my innocent guaraná in terms of drinks. I know that many of them think I'm 'outmoded,' entirely *old fashioned* [English in original] for this reason." Yet, she defensively added, smoking and drinking harmed women more than they did men due to their "constitution and hormones."[54] In other words, these scripts recycled the social philosophy positing the stronger male body as a principle of the division of foods between the sexes and the rationale for ingestion of stronger substances.[55] In inscribing gender difference in alcohol use, they reinforced a critical way in which societies symbolize and regulate gender roles and the allocation of power.[56]

Brazilian men also consumed soft drinks, of course, whether to slake their thirst, boost their energy, or solidify their upstanding reputation. In 1945, presidential hopeful Eurico Gaspar Dutra, trailed by reporters, made sure to stop at his friend's house to drink "a cold guaraná" on his way to the polling booth.[57] The beverage selection affirmed not only his patriotism but his decorousness. Likewise, socialite Jorge Jabour, profiled in 1953 as one of Rio de Janeiro's most eligible bachelors, preened that in late-night carousing with his buddies, he preferred guaraná.[58] In early soda advertisements, athletic men signaled the product's energizing qualities, endorsed by male physicians and voice-overs. The modern father, less authoritarian or aloof than his forebears, also featured in ad copy: "Do you want to guess a child's wish? Offer them Guaraná Champagne. Nothing will please them more than a good soda."[59]

Soda ads pitched toward men, however, were distinctive in rechanneling cultural tropes of masculine virility and violence, the product of historically conditioned behaviors.[60] In this vein, eroticized imagery of Indigenous women (discussed later in this chapter) and Carnivalesque abandon likely targeted the masculine gaze, capitalizing on guaraná's popular reputation in Brazil as an aphrodisiac. Similarly, a 1970 Guaraná Brahma ad featuring a cocked, foam-spewing bottleneck dared the drinker to "Set free the forces of nature. . . . This is authentic. It still has the savage in its soul. Pure and faithful to its origins. In other words a savage."[61] That same year, Guaraná Champagne Antarctica proclaimed: "If you can hammer your finger and smiling keep it a secret; if you can steal the bride-to-be of the weight lifter, ride a motorcycle so quickly you can't be photographed; Guaraná is your drink to order with your head high."[62] Another ad, presenting a gun-toting bruiser in a Western saloon clasping a glass of guaraná, exhorted: "There comes a time when you have to know: you have to be strong, not your drink." His reward? "The kisses poured forth from the women: one kiss, two, three."[63] These soda ads not only referenced the prerogatives of heavy alcohol consumption, sexual conquest, and impetuousness for Brazilian men but also committed their product to upholding toughness as the measure of a man's worth.

BRAZILIAN AD AGENCIES scrutinized the consumption habits and product preferences of elite and middle-class women, endorsing campaigns sensitive to their tastes and materials written by or about them.[64] According to a 1950 report, the audiences for Brazil's three hundred radio stations were predominantly female. Radio ownership rose from 2.5 million in 1952 to 4.7 million in 1962, while permissible airtime for advertisements increased to 20 percent of daily programming. Beverage companies served as sponsors, with their product jingles and spots (scripts with texts accompanied or unaccompanied by music) etched into listeners' memories.[65]

A 1952 article from *Publicidade & Negócios* on the "psychological foundations" of consumption sheds light on how Brazilian ad agents viewed their repertoire. Human needs, the author noted, could be boiled down to basic necessities or impulses: ambition, appetite, physical activity, beauty, curiosity, social approval, psychological evasion, sexual attraction, safety, health, comfort, economy, conformism, cultural refinement, and self-affirmation.[66] As Erving Goffman has noted, advertisers by and large do not create the ritualized expressions they use; rather, "they seem to draw upon the same corpus of displays, the same ritual idiom, that is the resource of all of us who participate in social situations, and to the same end: the rendering of glimpsed action readable."[67] When it came to the home, Brazilian advertisers aimed to operationalize the prevalent social discourses yoking modern womanhood to traditional roles of caregiving. Homemakers were coaxed to find their fix in food and domestic products.

As modern caregivers, mothers turned to guaraná soft drinks—the wealthier, with greater facility. According to the 1950 census, Brazilian women had on average over six children, one of the highest crude birth rates in the world.[68] Between 1940 and 1950, the nation's population growth rate was roughly 2.8 percent per year.[69] With the expansion of the professional fields of pediatrics and nutrition, often informed by eugenics, directives for scientific caregiving commingled with popular lore.[70] Health professionals emphasized the importance of nutritional intake and balance, physical exercise, and outdoor activities.[71] Between 1934 and 1941, for example, fifty publications related to nutritional science appeared in Brazil. Many articles were published in the *Boletim do Ministério do Trabalho, Indústria e Comércio*, reflective of government efforts to incentivize labor productivity for national development.[72]

A nutritional approach to social ills paroled a nation condemned by theories of racial and climatic determinism.[73] On Brazilian mothers, it placed the onus of ensuring children's proper diets, or supervising servants in food preparation.

Modern nutritional science, it has been observed, relinquishes moral values of wisdom, purity, and asceticism in favor of those of energy, speed, and power.[74] In *Valor social da alimentação* (1937), Ruy Coutinho revealingly assailed malnutrition for "diminishing the energy capacity of human groups, turning competent and active peoples apathetic and indifferent."[75] Improvement in pediatric diets, he argued, would ensure better physical development and hence "greater capacity for physical and intellectual labor."[76] Likewise, Silva Mello's *A alimentação no Brasil: problemas e sugestões* (1946) stated that "children should receive sufficiently nutritious foods capable of meeting their energy needs."[77]

As noted in chapter 5, advertisers routinely pitched physician endorsements of guaraná soft drinks' "energizing" qualities. As early as the 1920s, soda companies sponsored sports tournaments and Carnival celebrations to associate their product with stamina.[78] Guaraná further evoked natural diets and open-air lifestyles of Indigenous populations, now bottled up under stringent sanitary conditions.[79] A 1953 ad for Guaraná Brahma showing five children sharing the soda bottles read: "Give your child the healthiest guaraná. Guaraná Brahma—because it contains the true natural guaraná!" Its "stimulating properties and its purity" ensured a great soft drink for both adults and children.[80] Two years later, a company ad showing a mother with two young daughters boasted of authentic guaraná from the "Amazonian jungles" that was "much healthier for your children!"[81] Indeed, well into the 1980s, guaraná soft drink advertisements alluded to the health benefits of their product.[82]

In 1951, a popular Brazilian journal precociously warned of the dangers of replacing milk and juice in children's diets with beverages laced with caffeine, sugar, benzoic acid, and artificial coloring. Assailing the soft drink industry's deceptive marketing, the exposé also made sure to lambaste women for the "regrettable lack of sense and incredible carelessness of those with the sacred duty to look after the lives of their children."[83] Since the 1930s, Brazilian government policy had pushed for expanded consumption of fresh milk based on foreign studies of its nutritional value and purported fortification of populations of wealthier nations.[84] Health officials more broadly decried "subnutrition," or the lack of quality and balance said to characterize the diets of the affluent.[85] Yet healthier options eluded many. Fresh milk exceeded the budget

Guaraná Brahma ad, 1953. The beverage company urged consumers to drink and give their children the "healthiest guaraná," whose "stimulating properties" and "purity" (symbolized by the Amazonian plant's framing of the tableau) made for an "excellent" soda. Linking children's health and happiness to soda consumption, the advertisement sought to define the entitlements of youth and the responsibilities of modern motherhood. *O Cruzeiro* 3 (October 31, 1953): 41. Hemeroteca Digital, Biblioteca Nacional, Rio de Janeiro. Courtesy of Arquivo O Cruzeiro/EM/D.A Press.

of most urban dwellers in the 1930s and 1940s and was often rancid or even deadly due to the dearth of pasteurizers and refrigerated tanks.[86] Front-page headlines of a Rio daily in August 1941 reported on bacterial contamination of drinking water both at the source and in the bottling process.[87] In larger cities, reductions in forested areas and private gardens pushed up the price of fresh fruit: by the early 1960s, only 29.8 percent of the wealthiest residents of Recife and 10.3 percent of the poorest ate fresh fruit for breakfast.[88] Food preparation may be one way in which women show love, but social and natural resources, calendrical cycles, and notions of family, health, and body image pave the way to the heart—and the stomach.[89] In any event, riven by the choice of what is good and what is healthy, food consumption regularly pits desire against reason.[90] Not to mention the fact that the hesitant homemaker confronted an advertising offensive and the disapprobation of family and friends.

Consumption can entail both coercion and emancipation, subjugation and power.[91] An entrée for "respectable" women into the expanding public sphere, soft drinks made their way as well into their homes. Fantasies of romance and recreation soaked up from soda advertisements might alleviate the tedium of work or marriage. Time saved with a ready-to-drink beverage could be spent elsewhere. Engendering strong affective ties, culinary activities also provided many women a source of happiness, just as men's participation in housework might have been a source of dishonor.[92] Indeed, a materialist analysis would underscore the female protagonist engaging in "food-as-gift" as reproducing a historical dualism in which preparation and distribution of victuals create bonds of care and solidarity while sustaining broader capitalist relations of exploitation and competition.[93]

In the process, a new generation of soft drink consumers emerged in a nation in which between 1950 and 1970, 40 percent of the population was under the age of fourteen and over half were under twenty.[94] The nature of child-rearing and childhood in Brazil was also changing. A traditional source of labor and income in poorer families, children were less financially important for the expanding urban middle classes, albeit emotionally priceless.[95] As Antonio Candido noted, by the early 1950s, corporal punishment of children had become uncommon among this sector, and parental bonds tinged with greater intimacy. Children made use of the more familiar "você" rather than "o senhor" in addressing their fathers, while the kiss replaced the traditional paternal blessing or was combined with it. He also noted the long-standing "tradition of indulgence" in Brazilian families, particularly in ceding to children's desires in both food and play.[96]

In 1950, Helena Sangirardi wrote: "Nowadays, children are used to asking things from their nanny when they go out to the street, mainly ice cream, popcorn, and guaraná."[97] If taste is a collective cultural experience transmitted from birth, along with other values of society, soda manufacturers had more than "guessed a child's wish."[98] The companies had conventionalized soft drink use and venues for consumption. Fratelli Vita of Recife distributed prizes and trophies at youth sports tournaments, sponsored charitable institutions for children and religious festivities, and welcomed school visits to its factory in the 1920s. Likewise, Orlando de Araújo, who headed the soft drink division of Companhia Antarctica in 1954, recalled the outreach to younger consumers. The launching several years earlier of Guaraná Caçula—a smaller, individualized bottle (whose name in Portuguese signifies a family's youngest child)—was just the beginning of the "assault on the young ones," to use Araújo's words. Based on mail-ins from children, the company's public relations department sent birthday wishes and even paid house visits. "That leaves a mark on children, a positive message," Araújo reminisced, in reference to the pipeline secured for future buyers.[99] With like-minded martial metaphor, the Denison Propaganda ad agency was reported as launching "an offensive to conquer a larger share of young consumers."[100] And with similar designs, advertising executive José Leite Machado furnished Jesus Gomes's sugary pink concoction with a new slogan in the 1950s: "Cola Guaraná Jesus, a child's rosy dream." From a purported cure for "physical exhaustion," "alcohol-induced depression," and "excitation of the cerebral functions," Guaraná Jesus had become life through children's rose-colored glasses. Nutritional studies indicate children's predisposition for foods high in sugar, salt, and fat, which trigger the brain's reward system and extend conditioning beyond an energy balance or fleeting high.[101] Eating sates not only craving for food but also hunger for memory; the comfort of certain foods reaches beyond physiological response to the recollections of childhood care.[102]

As food studies scholar Marion Nestle notes, people do not need soft drinks for their health or safety. After all, why would "liquid candy" be considered acceptable for children and adults as a go-to beverage?[103] We might temper such criticism in noting sodas' utility where water supplies are unsanitary. Yet a fuller explanation recognizes advertisers' power to conjure an imaginary world for beverage consumers. If magic in traditional societies tends to the unaccountable, the adverse, or the coincidental, as Malinowski noted, in modern societies advertisers channel feelings of anxiety and fantasy, firing the imagination through particular formulas and rites and inducing transformations to overcome uncertainty and perceived risk.[104] In their campaigns to promote guaraná soft drinks, the art directors and copywriters of advertising agencies in Brazil were magicians. And alongside advertising's promise of security and enchantment came the "lies, seductions, [and] cynicisms that are the price of these civilizing processes."[105]

THAT MODERNITY HAD A COLOR in Brazil beamed from the sodas' advertisements as well.[106] For the period between the 1920s and the 1940s, I found one Black figure in a guaraná ad: a young man serving the drink. Another soft drink ad from 1927 featuring a black silhouette read, "I am black, but I only like the good things. Guaraná Fratelli Vita is really good" (although a prominent Recife journalist condemned the material as racist).[107] These marketing decisions reflected agencies' presumption of their audiences' racial and class profile, as well as the social makeup and bias of the agents themselves. Advertising was historically a white male profession in Brazil that attracted journalists, artists, and recent university graduates; by 1967, still fewer than 1 percent of ad agency executives were Afro-descendants.[108] Even in the late 1980s, an executive at McCann Erickson in São Paulo claimed that U.S.-style advertisements that presented Afro-Brazilians driving cars or drinking Coke would rankle white consumers. Blacks continued to be portrayed as low-level employees—drivers, gardeners, cooks—linked to products associated with physical labor.[109] Testimonials using famous Black singers and soccer players were considered safe in representing the domains of sports, music, and dance. Ads for day-to-day products such as refrigerators, cars, soft drinks, and toothpaste pictured white and middle-class beneficiaries.

Brazil's midcentury population was predominantly white, totaling 62 percent, at least according to the 1950 census.[110] The nation's history of slavery and systemic racism resulted in lower levels of education, income, health care, nutrition, and life expectancy for Blacks than whites. Yet Brazilian advertisers' equating of whiteness with progress perpetuated racial inequalities and exclusions, and was not lost on contemporary social critics. In a 1951 advertising journal, the well-known Black actor Grande Otelo denounced, "You never see in a Brazilian ad a black woman opening a refrigerator, drinking a soda, or dressed in a beautiful bathing suit. Or a black man and his children in a beautiful automobile. . . . Doesn't the black have the right to have a house, buy furniture?" Black consumers wanted the same things as whites, he charged, and bristled at their exclusion from commercial advertising.[111] In a follow-up letter to the editor, one reader deemed Grande Otelo's suggestion as "nice but unrealistic," because "the minute a talcum powder, soda, or automobile ad showed black consumers, they would be branded 'products for blacks' and boycotted."[112] Notions of progress in Brazil, shaded as white and housed as female, cued advertisers. In so doing, advertisements revealed and imputed different values associated with racial and ethnic groups, shaping popular imaginaries and contemporary identities.[113]

Guaraná's marketing of white middle-class lifestyles should not imply the absence of Black consumers. As Bryan McCann notes, in the 1940s, Afro-Brazilians formed a growing percentage of radio listeners as well as consumers of advertised products.[114] Black Brazilians appeared in photographs of Carnival-themed parades sponsored by Guaraná Antarctica. Guaraná even found its way into Afro-Brazilian religious worship; an article about Umbanda noted that among the offerings to the goddess Yemanjá strewn along the seashore, one might find "mirrors, guaraná bottles, combs, and many other objects."[115] The tactics of consumers in everyday life in resisting or adapting to power relations in society through individualized practice and unprogrammed use have been amply explored.[116] What Grande Otelo's protest underscored was the advertising industry's reinforcement of stereotypes about race and social value. In the mid-1990s, with Black activists and entertainers pushing back against media exclusion and typecasting, sales pitches featured more diverse Afro-Brazilians, yet advertisements still tended to focus on their physical strength, sexual appeal, or maternal disposition. An ad for Brahma Guaraná during the World Cup of 1998, for example, paired Ronaldo, a Black soccer player, with his then girlfriend, Susana Werner, a white model with blond hair. In other words, a Black man could emblematize Brazil and promote a soda as long as he excelled on the soccer field, while the paradigmatic Brazilian woman was white and preferably blond.[117]

Indigenous stereotyping likewise characterized soft drink marketing. Images of stolid Native Brazilian men and sexually alluring Native women embellished soda logos and print ads, particularly between the 1920s and the 1940s. The label of Guaraná Fratelli Vita, for example, sported an Indigenous man in North American style headdress, and Guaraná Espumante's featured a bare-breasted woman.[118] The Belém-based Guaraná Simões even claimed product superiority owing to its factory employing "many real-life Indians."[119] These were old colonial tropes in the Americas adapted to new times: whether the native flora and Indigenous chic in interwar Brazilian design, art, and literature; the Vargas regime's embrace of *indigenismo*; or national industries' search for market distinction.[120] Guarany Dyes, Aymoré Biscuits, Marajoara Perfumes, the Guarany Brewery, and the Tupi radio station were other members of the tribe.

Largely confined to rural subsistence or peonage, Indigenous peoples were not, of course, the soda ads' targeted customers. Marketing reflected ad agencies' imaginaries and their intended urban clientele. Black feminist theorist bell hooks has noted that in commodity cultures, "ethnicity becomes spice, seasoning that can liven up the dull dish that is mainstream white culture."[121] For a few cruzeiros, soda drinkers were promised a boost of energy, freedom, libido, or patriotism. Early advertising copy, for example, depicted sexualized encounters of Indigenous women with white men, evoking the legendary prowess of the colonial-era *bandeirantes*.[122] The 1921 Carnival ad for Zanotta, Lorenzi & Companhia's product read: "He Doesn't Suffer nor Sniffle / the Carnivalesque Pierrot / Ever Since He Ran Away / And Abandoned Columbine / And Lives at Ease / with the Beautiful Representative / of Guaraná Espumante / Who is a *bugre* from Amazonia." Another from 1924 featured St. Paul (São Paulo) tempted by two figures bearing Zanotta products—a bare-chested Indigenous woman proffering guaraná, and a chicly dressed white woman holding a Lacta chocolate bar. The differential feminine garb, signaling greater sexual license toward the former, may have been designed to encourage soda consumption by men.[123] Since the 1910s, the beer industry had assigned racist and sexist names to its products, such as Mulatinha and Negrita, and eroticized images for marketing.[124]

As Jackson Lears notes, the advertising industry's "fables of abundance" have drawn on the traditional allure of Carnivalesque indulgence.[125] In early modern Europe, commerce in the new stimulants used exotica to showcase the Native American roots of chocolate and tobacco, the Chinese origin of tea, and the Muslim introduction of coffee to the continent.[126] Indigenous imagery in guaraná marketing likewise fetishized the Other while signaling the soft drink's Brazilian bona fides. In the verse of a Guaraná Espumante ad, for example, a seminude Indigenous woman offered up her product to a distinguished European gentleman: "I come to offer you, sir, as a souvenir, / a fine, delicious beverage dear, / which has even [Brazilian statesman] Ruy Barbosa entranced. / Drunk in Brazil, better, much better / than the vermouths of Italy and the cognacs of France. / Remember, dear *touriste*, by heart its name, / spread it among the elegant people of your country and exclaim: / Guaraná! Guaraná! Guaraná Espumante!"[127] Companhia Antarctica's November 1944 magazine ad, headlined "Acquire the Vitality of an Indian," presented a stoic, feathered Native man.[128]

Ethnographic realism is rarely at hand when outsiders are "playing Indian."[129] Whether inspiring consumer confidence or whimsy, Indigenous images in soft drink advertising aimed to fire city dwellers' imaginations. Amid

Guaraná Antarctica ad, 1944. Conjuring for urbanites the "natural" lifestyle of Indigenous peoples, Companhia Antarctica Paulista affirmed: "The reason for the fortitude of the Indians is in their food, above all the insuperable attributes of guaraná, source of health, energy and vigor, at the reach of all in this delicious drink." *A Cigarra* 128 (November 1944): 124. Hemeroteca Digital, Biblioteca Nacional, Rio de Janeiro. Courtesy of Arquivo O Cruzeiro/EM/D.A Press.

Guaraná
BRAHMA
é o **mais saudável** porque
contém o **verdadeiro guaraná natural**

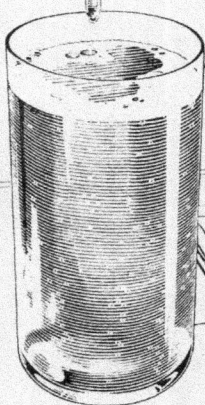

Quando desejar um refrigerante para matar a sêde, não
peça qualquer um... prefira um refrigerante mais saudável.
Exija o Guaraná Brahma! Porque o Guaraná Brahma prova, realmente,
que contém guaraná natural pelo seu sabor característico
e pelas propriedades tônicas que possui. Prefira
também o Guaraná Brahma. É deliciosíssimo!

Guaraná
BRAHMA

PRODUTO DA CIA. CERVEJARIA BRAHMA

Uma garrafa
= 2 copos

O CRUZEIRO, 21 de novembro de 1953

42

Guaraná Brahma ad, 1953. Ads for soft drinks typically depicted beverage consumers as white, reinscribing the social hierarchies in Brazil that linked notions of comfort, health, beauty, leisure, and progress to whiteness. *O Cruzeiro 6* (November 21, 1953): 42. Hemeroteca Digital, Biblioteca Nacional, Rio de Janeiro. Courtesy of Arquivo O Cruzeiro /EM/D.A Press.

the shifting tempos of urban life, guaraná soda represented a product rooted in Brazilian soil and tradition. Amid the impersonality of the public sphere came an assertion of individualism and belonging.[130] In place of the old magic that modernity had purportedly expunged was a new one nostalgically reclaimed or creatively reworked.[131]

During the postwar period, the Indigenous presence in guaraná soft drink advertisements waned, as the product profile shifted from health care to sport and leisure. Marketers discarded the fabled "Indian healer," while eroticized white women became more commonplace in the Brazilian media. Advertisers found trendier images to ply their messages of youthful vigor, pleasure, sex appeal, and escapism. Lounging in bathing suits, playing tennis, or surfing, elegant and athletic white figures urged consumers to "be yourself": the bourgeois ideal of making one's body "a sign of its own ease."[132] Still, the Indigenous foil or fool remained an occasional go-to for advertisers. In a 2007 television commercial for Guaraná Antarctica Ice, an overwrought rain dance by Amazonian warriors produces snowfall in the rain forest.[133] In this sense, the advertising industry retained the bourgeois tendency to reduce the Other to object and spectacle.[134]

GUARANÁ'S POPULARIZATION ALSO REFLECTS postwar transformations in pricing, distribution, and advertising in the Brazilian soft drink market. Coca-Cola blazed the trail, according to a 1950 advertising journal.[135] The domestic soft drink companies' rival offered a business model to emulate.

Coca-Cola began bottling in Brazil in 1942, the same year that Kibon Ice Cream and *Reader's Digest* (launched as *Seleções*) debuted—all celebrating the American way of life.[136] As an important ally against the Axis powers, Brazil profited from credit extended by the Export-Import Bank during World War II—most notably for financing the nation's first steel mill in 1940—but the wartime pact also expanded opportunities for U.S. corporations, including tax deductions for foreign advertising.[137] Coca-Cola had pledged to furnish the soda for five cents to U.S. servicemembers worldwide, including those stationed in northeastern Brazil. Bottling was initiated in Recife near the U.S. military base, soon followed by the opening of a plant in Rio de Janeiro. By 1950, Coke had sixteen bottling plants in Brazil.[138] Throughout Latin America, U.S. direct investment increased from $3 million to $8.3 billion between 1940 and 1960.[139]

In the United States, the company's advertisements showcased Americana; recruited Hollywood celebrities; favored images of women in their mid-twenties (deemed attractive to men, inspiring for women and youths, and nostalgic for elders); featured active and attractive people, often in wholesome settings; promoted notions of pleasure, sociability, and leisure; and offered memorabilia and collectibles to extend its household presence. Coke conducted market research and psychological studies on drinking habits, expending $700 million in advertising in the United States over the course of a century.[140] In Brazil, Coca-Cola worked with McCann Erickson to adapt its message of leisure refreshment for the masses to a newfound South American home. The company took to the airwaves, sponsoring music programs on Radio Nacional, such as *Um milhão de melodias.* Its red signs became commonplace at bars, restaurants, and street kiosks.[141] Its radio jingles, Hollywood-themed posters, print media ads, and bottle-cap sweepstake prizes of watches, bicycles, and sewing machines wooed Brazilian consumers.[142]

According to the advertising trade journal *Publicidade & Negócios* prior to Coke's arrival, Brazilians consumed tonic waters, sodas, and other nonalcoholic beverages more out of custom than effective sales promotion. Guaraná soft drink manufacturers merely "dabbled in advertising," the journal noted.[143] Advertisements from the 1920s referencing European harlequins, champagne, vermouth, and *touristes* bespeak the product's intended elite clientele. Guaraná Espumante's early ads, designed by the well-known illustrator Voltolino, featured caricatured drawings of São Paulo high society because they were the targeted consumers.[144] The product's high-brow profile resonated in endorsements by Pietro Mascagni (who visited the soda factory during the South American premiere of his opera), radio jingles containing verses composed by poet Guilherme de Almeida, and music by classical composer Heitor Villa-Lobos.[145] Soda drinking had also been largely done on special occasions, such as birthdays, holidays, graduations, weddings, and parties, and served at restaurants, clubs, bars, sweet shops, bakeries, and theaters. By the late 1940s, however, Coca-Cola signaled the success of a new marketing model in Brazil: reduced pricing, improved distribution, aggressive advertising, giveaways, and novel cultural messaging. Among the latter was license to chug directly from the bottle, which scandalized some Brazilians but also facilitated the company's efforts to popularize consumption anytime or anywhere.[146]

From the get-go, Coca-Cola had detractors and admirers in Brazil. Domestic soda brands had their loyal fans and nationalistic cachet, and a foreign tar-colored beverage with secret ingredients raised suspicions about health risks and more figurative forms of contamination: in the wartime Northeast, locals maligned Brazilian women who socialized with U.S. infantrymen as

"Coca-Cola girls."[147] Some consumers disliked Coke's "weird flavor" and carbonation, while well-heeled residents of Belo Horizonte in 1950 balked at
preferring a drink "based on the chance of finding in the cap a little piece of
paper announcing a prize."[148] And political conservatives and radicals in Brazil railed at the unremitting symbol of American consumerism. In 1957, Pas-
coal Melantônio published a best seller in Brazil, *Geração Coca-Cola*, which
slammed the influx of North American products and practices that led "devi-
ant youth" to be "headed to complete dissolution and ruin."[149]

In a 1948 essay, however, Auricélio Penteado lauded Coca-Cola's "democratizing" impact on Brazilian culture. The beverage of the common man in
shirtsleeves, the U.S. brand represented "renovation, progress, youth, cleanliness, efficiency, the symbol of a generation." It signaled hope for a future Brazil free of pretention and disrepute—or, in Penteado's literary spin, of "Your
Excellency," bare feet, yellow fever, vice-ridden taverns, bureaucracy, and old
railroads. He contrasted Coke's straightforward message and simple bottle
("it only states the most that modesty permits: it's refreshing") with the puff-
ery of Brazilian soft drink manufacturers and, more broadly, the "decadent
generation of clowns who promise everything and deliver nothing."[150]

The middle-aged Penteado certainly had qualms about Brazil's "Coca-
Cola generation." Brazil's postwar youth, he lamented, no longer devoted
themselves to their studies, composed sonnets, respected their parents, or
spoke proper Portuguese. Gender norms had been shaken, evinced by a for-
wardness toward the opposite sex bred of exaggerated self-confidence. Nevertheless, he conceded, Coca-Cola represented progress, "the diffusion of
comfort throughout Brazil.[151] Although justifiably reluctant to establish cause
and effect between Coke consumption and youthful iconoclasm, Penteado
insisted on a certain commensurability.

Penteado's homage to Coca-Cola is particularly significant for two reasons: the article appeared in *Publicidade & Negócios* and Penteado was no
ordinary writer. A radio station owner, Penteado had founded in 1942 the Instituto Brasileiro de Opinião Pública e Estatística (IBOPE), a media and
market research firm modeled after the Gallup poll in the United States.[152]
IBOPE provided hourly and daily audience breakdowns for prime-time radio
slots, and its monthly reports were scrutinized by broadcasters and advertising agencies.[153] As such, Penteado's essay offers an inkling of advertisers' understanding of guaraná sodas' prospective marketing for the masses.[154] In
fact, two years later, *Publicidade & Negócios* took to Coke's defense amid
mounting debate in Brazil about the impact of foreign capital on national development. In a thinly veiled swipe at Companhia Antarctica Paulista, the

advertising journal slammed the "foolishness of some Brazilians" whose abortive efforts at legal injunctions and political pressures aimed to handicap the U.S.-based company. Coke had benefited glass manufacturers, sugar growers, the transportation sector, and factory workers in Brazil, the article noted—and advertising agencies as well, although unstated by the author. Since mass media advertising disseminates consumerist values, spurring greater demand for goods, the writer insisted, the Brazilian soft drink industry would fare better in emulating Coca-Cola's marketing practices.[155]

In fact, Brazilian beverage companies had begun to do so. Over the course of 1949, aside from launching the less pricey Guaraná Caçula, Companhia Antarctica embarked on one of the most expensive ad campaigns for its time in Brazil. These included radio publicity, magazine spreads, giveaways, and extravaganzas.[156] In March, the company helped crown Marlene, muse of the popular live radio auditorium programs, as "Queen of the Radio," a feat celebrated by Rio's samba schools on Holy Saturday in a downtown parade of over 200,000 people (many transported in trucks by Antarctica) and broadcast by more than one hundred radio stations.[157] Press coverage showed banners and placards declaring, "Long live soda."[158] To commemorate Independence Day, Antarctica organized a Carnival on Ice, featuring one hundred skaters at Rio's Coliseu Metropolitano in a spectacle attended by representatives of the armed forces from Brazil and the Southern Cone.[159] And on the occasion of President Eurico Dutra's visit to Washington, D.C., the company staged guaraná's "democratic" takeover of the United States in a lavish enactment in *O Cruzeiro*, a weekly magazine covering celebrities and patriotic endeavors that reached half a million households in Brazil by the 1950s. In a symbolic inversion of Coca-Cola's trajectory, the American guaraná drinkers photographed included an air force captain, a white woman and a child in front of the Lincoln Memorial, a Black couple in front of the Capitol, four baseball players, and two members of a Tennessee police force.[160]

For brand distinction, guaraná soda manufacturers harnessed a potent force in postwar Brazil: nationalism. A feature article in *O Cruzeiro* marking the arrival of Guaraná Caçula, adorned with images of the assembly lines and carbonation systems in Antarctica's newly opened Rio de Janeiro factory, is emblematic. In the essay, émigré photojournalist Jean Manzon asserted that most Brazilians had not thought of guaraná as a refreshment prior to the 1920s; only a handful of connoisseurs knew of the beverage's traditional preparation, while few could "do like the Indian" in consuming the bitter-tasting drink. Thanks to the soda manufacturer's commissioning of Luís Pereira Barreto and Pedro Baptista de Andrade to create an extract and formula, a "delicious and healthy" drink now hydrated Brazilians battling "the rigors of our climate." One day, the publication predicted, the soft drink would be consumed nationwide, from the wealthiest to the humblest households. Antarctica was "the greatest defender of the national soda industry, the bulwark against foreign competitors who sought to dominate the Brazilian consumer market."[161]

For postwar consumers beholding rapid urban change, including the influx of U.S. goods, Manzon repackaged narratives of national exceptionalism.[162] This was the tale of Indigenous peoples and flora "improved" by science dear to European colonialism and Latin American nationalism.[163] This was the celebration of Brazil's racial-cultural fusion; of Native flavors diluted, recolored, and rebranded as "champagne." This was the triumph of southern factory over northern jungle; of the masculinist logic of industrial science and the naturalized realm of female consumption. This was a story of transformation rooted in tradition; of magic as modernity's foil and filament.[164] This was a parable of national development in Brazil that confirmed reader bias and boosted sales for a corporate sponsor.

Notwithstanding the transnational roots of soft drink production and marketing in Brazil, guaraná sodas were fictionalized as a purely homegrown endeavor. Amid the leveling promise of a "genuinely Brazilian" beverage, the soft drink's authenticity owed as much to its Amazonian heritage as to its reliance on and replication of social hierarchies. And behind a modern product lay the yearning for a genie in a bottle. Soft drinks owe their success not only to low prices enabled by the cost of basic ingredients and maximum distribution, but to the promotion of an image.[165] In 2008, Antarctica's parent company was the third largest advertiser in Brazil, accounting for $136.2 million in sales per year.[166]

MIDCENTURY HERALDING OF SOFT DRINKS' democratizing prospects in Brazil was premature. In 1950, the majority of the nation's population of fifty-two million lived in rural areas, and just over a third lived in towns. Agriculture accounted for three-quarters of the male labor force, whose diets of largely local foods—determined by climate, biology, and political economy—resembled the traditional precarious fare of the global poor.[167] Over half the population above the age of fifteen was illiterate. The average life expectancy of men was 49.1 years, and for women, 52.8. The death rate of children under five was 190 per thousand live births.[168] While a 1952 advertising journal noted that "the habit of drinking Antarctica is taking hold of consumers of all ages," those consumers did not hail regularly from the working class and the poor.[169]

In his 1935 nutritional survey of five hundred working-class households in Recife, Josué de Castro found that a manual laborer with a basic wage of 3$700 réis per day supporting a family with an average of five people spent 72 percent of earnings on food, 12 percent on housing, 9 percent on water and electricity, and 7 percent on miscellaneous expenses. (At that time, U.S. workers earning minimum wage spent 55 percent of their salary on food.) Among surveyed households, all consumed beans, manioc flour, jerky, coffee, and sugar, while 84 percent purchased bread; these six items accounted for 2$760 réis of a daily budget. Analysis of the chemical composition of these foods for a family of five revealed an intake of 1,646 calories per day, far below the average of 3,000 to 4,000 needed for a manual laborer. Consequently, Castro remarked, poor people spoke of "fooling hunger," although deaths linked to malnutrition suggested the limitations of improvisation: the mortality rate in 1935 per one thousand people was 19.45 in Recife, 18.8 in Rio, and 15.3 in São Paulo (also 11.8 in London and 17.1 in New York).[170] Research in 1938 by the Serviço de Higiene Escolar of São Paulo likewise found that 60 percent of kindergarten children suffered from malnutrition. In 1958, working-class families in São Paulo spent 64.3 percent of their income on food. And a quarter century later, 26.7 percent of Paulistano families surveyed suffered from undernutrition.[171] Food insecurity is linked to adverse health outcomes among infants and children.[172]

Soft drinks, however, were steadily amassing devotees among the working class as well, whether to "fool hunger," to evade contaminated water, or as a momentary pleasure. In a study of soda consumption in Rio de Janeiro in May 1950, for example, market researchers visited 120 bars, divided evenly in four different neighborhoods, two of which constituted the working-class areas of Central Brasil and Leopoldina. In the latter neighborhood, they recorded 147 twelve-packs of Guaraná Antarctica sold in one day, and 101 twelve-packs of Coca-Cola. In the tonier beachfront Rio neighborhoods, the bars sold 116 twelve-packs of Antarctica and 133 twelve-packs of Coca-Cola, suggestive of relative interclass parity—except that sodas were also offered at hotels, clubs, gas stations, and stores, and by beach peddlers in Ipanema and Copacabana.[173] The broader social diffusion of soft drink sales is borne out by other surveys. In a March 1953 poll of one thousand housewives in Rio de Janeiro, for example, IBOPE found that 72 percent of respondents from Class A (wealthy), 66 percent from Class B (middle class), and 54.4 percent from Class C (poor) had guaraná soda in their home. Although 40.8 percent of the poorer households had no soda of any kind, the percentage was lower than those without canned beef, canned sausage, tomato extract, canned milk, cooking oil, packaged pudding, or fruit juice.[174]

In 1953, Rachel de Queiroz reported on working-class lunch diets at a typical *botequim* in the industrial area of Rio de Janeiro. Noting the similarity in workers' fare, whether home-cooked or ordered at the establishment (typically rice, beans, and meat stew), she was surprised by their routine purchase of drinks at the restaurant—"guaraná, mineral water, wine, but usually beer"— though beer, at five cruzeiros, was equivalent to the cost of an entire meal. Queiroz decried that state-run cafeterias operated by the Serviço de Alimentação da Previdência Social, created under Vargas in 1940, were too remote from work sites; water was generally lacking for drinking or even washing; park benches were nonexistent; and, in her informants' words, "only dogs eat in the street." Since the eateries only begrudgingly offered water gratis, workers preferred to buy their refreshments and to enjoy the privilege of eating at a table. An earlier study by the São Paulo mayor's office among factory workers in twenty-two neighborhoods quantified Queiroz's observations: while 80 percent of those employed ate close to the workplace, none of the industries had restaurants, kitchens, or lunchrooms.[175] As such, workers frequented nearby restaurants or ate open air in deplorable hygienic conditions lacking access to clean water. Queiroz proposed building additional cafeterias as well as more public benches, spigots, and bathrooms to spare workers the unnecessary expenses to gain "access to a liquid."[176]

Queiroz's identification of the unreliability of public water supplies highlights the practical appeal of industrial beverages. In the 1920s, for example, Luís Pereira Barreto had bemoaned that fecal matter from animals and humans tainted reservoirs and water tanks in São Paulo; a report on the city's waterworks by G. H. de Paula Souza likewise noted contamination of primitive wells and cesspools and water shortages during the dry season. Better-off families purchased mineral water, while those of modest means relied on boiling, since filters were seen as unsafe.[177]

Magazine columnist Lasinha Luís Carlos, however, advanced a different explanation for working-class consumption patterns: "How often does a young man who buys a bottle of guaraná feel happier than when he eats a plate of rice and beans?" Relatedly, why should poor people spend their money on medicines if they suffered from chronic illnesses? Or buy new clothes if they could not wash them?[178] While Carlos did not define the source of guaraná drinkers' "happiness," it surely entailed the sugared energy boost that enabled the reproduction of labor power while fooling hunger as well as the joy of refreshment in the tropical heat. The beverage also offered a break from the ordinary, a token of care, a form of social belonging, a way of being Brazilian. At a working-class *botequim*, the consumption of a bottled beverage signaled refusal to eat in the street "like a dog" or to grovel for a proprietor's favor. On a special occasion for a child, a glass of guaraná glistened as a parent's affirmation of love. In other words, working-class consumption of soft drinks in the 1950s entailed a type of sacrifice or devotion. It represented the fruit of hard work and hardship, displayed through the acquisition of a valued good rather than a "basic" one, or what social scientists distinguish between need and symbol in the choice and use of an object.[179] Still, it would take several decades before all Brazilian consumers could enjoy their guaraná soft drink chilled at home: according to a 1953 IBOPE poll, all wealthy households in Rio de Janeiro owned an electric refrigerator, as did 72 percent of the middle class, but only 14 percent of the poor.[180] Class status in Brazil determined who was cooler.

IN HIS GLOBAL HISTORY of the twentieth century, Eric Hobsbawm reflects on the impact of mass entertainment and consumption on residents of wealthier nations and the urban centers of the developing world since the 1960s. As he writes, "The words which dominated Western consumer societies were no longer the words of holy books, let alone of secular writers, but the brand-names of goods or whatever else could be bought. They were printed on T-shirts, attached to other garments like magical charms by means of which the wearer acquired the spiritual merit of the (generally youthful) life-style which these names symbolized and promised. The images that became the icons of such societies were those of mass entertainment and mass consumption: stars and cans."[181] In fact, Brazil's first aluminum beverage can factory opened in 1989, enabled by multinational investment in domestic manufacture and the advent of self-sufficiency in aluminum production; by 2003, over ten billion cans were being manufactured per year.[182] By 2013, Brazil had become the world's third largest soda manufacturer, directly employing over 300,000 people and supplying sixty-nine liters annually per person.[183] Guaraná sodas accounted for over a quarter of Brazil's annual $43 billion carbonated beverage sales.[184] Along with soccer and samba, the soft drink forms part of Brazilian nationalist iconography.

Employing the analytical lenses of gender, race, class, and generation, this chapter has traced the popularization of guaraná soft drinks in Brazil. Amid urban market expansion and household change, an Amazonian berry reinvented as an industrial flavor became a marker of modern lifestyles and nationalist pride. The beverage's taste, utility, and symbolism favored assimilation into the "common sense world of everyday life," or the familiar scenes of daily existence.[185] The advertising industry, incarnating dominant cultural values, sold an image as much as a product.

As Anthony Giddens notes, routinization is critical to the psychological mechanisms that sustain trust, or "ontological security," in the day-to-day activities of social life. It is linked to "practical consciousness," or the knowledge of rules and tactics, including the positioning of the body in social encounters through which daily life is constituted and remade across time and space.[186] While curbing anxieties and unconscious tensions, mundane conventions of social life critically serve to reproduce the structural qualities of larger collectivities (even if intentional actions have unintended consequences and may lack discursive articulation).[187] Whether the average beverage consumer's concern for self-fulfillment reflected despair at exclusion from the arenas of power or the creative appropriation of the market influences that increasingly shaped everyday life in Brazil, the transformations bred by industrial society were manifest.[188]

With massification of the soft drink, what countless Brazilians have instinctively come to know as "guaraná" bears slight resemblance to the "real" thing. Or does it? Surely, nobody would confuse the flavor or the mode of consumption of the Sateré-Mawé *çapó* with guaraná soda. Yet, as I have argued, the dominant society in Brazil likewise vested a stimulating beverage with the imposition of order, the mediation of social contradictions and paradoxes, and magical powers of transformation. Consider a 1971 ad headlined "A Soda Free from the World's Evils" that reassured consumers: "In a world as artificial as this one, it's incredible that there still is a soda this natural. Preserve what's authentic in you. Drink Guaraná Brahma. The child of the jungles."[189] Consider that thrill-seeking adventure, romance, body enhancement, and bliss was said to await drinkers. Or consider that from the underside of bottle caps materialized refrigerators, bicycles, radios, and cars for a lucky winner.[190] Heeding Lévi-Strauss's claim that the "civilized" and "savage" mind share the same basic structures of thought and classificatory disposition, we can be further swayed by Latour's insight: the "moderns" in Brazil have merely had more specialists, resources, platforms, and networks to adapt and disseminate their guaraná product and its shape-shifting stories.[191] Indeed, it was this institutional power and social organization that the military government weaponized in the development of the Amazon, reconfiguring Sateré-Mawé communities, their renowned crop, and patterns of soft drink consumption in Brazil.

CHAPTER SEVEN

Growing the Pie

Transformations in Brazilian Agriculture and Diet

In the early twentieth century, Brazil's beverage industry transformed the processing of guaraná. Pulverization of the seed and chemical extraction of the syrup overtook the traditional labor-intensive method of molding and smoking the sticks. In the latter half of the century, scientists transformed the plant itself and its biogeography through selective breeding and transplant. Output expanded significantly. Whereas in 1973 the estimated total production of guaraná stood at about 360 metric tons, overwhelmingly from the Maués region, Brazil's annual yield rose to 3,600 metric tons by 2013, led by the northeastern state of Bahia, and valued at roughly US$15 million.[1] Enhanced production of guaraná surpassed the overall increase of 150 percent in Brazilian agricultural output between the 1980s and 2010 which contributed to lower food prices and a national reduction in undernutrition.[2]

Increased guaraná yields largely served the soft drink industry. By the early 1980s, 66 percent of commercial guaraná went to soda manufacture. At the time, two nationwide companies, Antarctica and Brahma, accounted for 84 percent of guaraná soda sales, although smaller regional companies abounded.[3] Home consumption of guaraná soda per capita more than sextupled between 1975 and 2003, a figure that excludes away-from-home eating, an important source of soft drink consumption.[4] By 2004, Brazilians reportedly drank more than seventeen million bottles of guaraná soda per day and purchased an average of eighty-five liters of soft drinks per person per year by 2012.[5] The increased consumption of soft drinks, along with high-fat processed foods, contributed to overnutrition in Brazil, with changes in body composition, stature, and morbidity patterns. In the 1970s, less than 3 percent of men and 8 percent of women in Brazil were considered obese. By the mid-2010s, the Ministry of Health reported 18 percent of adults as obese and more than half overweight.[6] Levels in Brazil of overweight and obesity (defined as a body mass index over 30) were roughly comparable to those in the United States despite a GNP that was nearly seven times lower.[7] Globally, the "nutrition transition" in postwar urban-industrial societies—from diets rich in carbohydrates and proteins to those heavy in fats and sugars, linked to ultra-processed foods controlled by multinational corporations—shaped the trend, compounded by lower levels of physical activity.[8]

Brazil's demographic profile also changed rapidly over the last decades of the twentieth century. The nation's population increased from 93 million to 170 million between 1970 and 2000, although total fertility rates diminished.[9] By 2000, more than 81.2 percent of the nation's total lived in cities. The service sector accounted for 55 percent of Brazil's workforce, while agriculture declined to 25 percent.[10] Over 2 million motor vehicles, 7.8 million television sets, and 3.7 million refrigerators were manufactured. Electricity reached 96 percent of households, 74.6 percent had a refrigerator, and 81 percent had a television set.[11] Women made up 39.6 percent of the economically active population in the early 1990s, nearly triple the level forty years earlier. Their expanded workforce presence increased demand for processed foods and the spread of supermarkets facilitating one-stop shopping, since women still predominantly undertook or oversaw the purchase of groceries and the preparation of household meals.[12] Processed, preservable, and fast industrial foods come with more affordable prices.[13] Between 1970 and 2000, the interpersonal and interregional concentration of wealth in Brazil, however, also remained steady. In 1999, the richest 10 percent of the population had an average income fifteen to twenty times higher than the poorest 40 percent. Only 34 percent of the nation's lower-income households were served by a sewage system and sanitation services.[14]

Guaraná's massification under Brazilian military rule and democratically elected neoliberal governments since the 1990s reflects the evolution of the nation's food system. As an amalgam of food-related activities and their socioeconomic, political, natural, and metabolic environments, food systems comprise a set of linked elements and interdependent processes, as Per Pinstrup-Andersen and Derrill D. Watson II note. Agents include farmers and farm laborers, traders, processors, manufacturers, scientists, policymakers, and consumers. Elements range from market systems, government organizations, technological applications, and agroecological conditions, to transportation and distribution networks and zoonotic diseases. Processes encompass demographic, biophysical, socioeconomic, environmental, epidemiological, and political change. The multidisciplinary nature of food systems renders them as complex for policymaking solutions as for historical analysis: agriculturists focus on output, the commercial food sector on market share, governments on regulation, health professionals on nutrition, environmentalists on ecological impact, consumers on taste and diet.[15] In this chapter, I heed David Goodman and Michael Redclift's call for moving beyond phenomenological approaches to analyze the processes of economic and technological change in the food system through which food has become an industrially produced good.[16]

In the advanced industrial nations, postwar expansion of the food system rested on the incorporation of new markets for commodities and the application of science and technology to agriculture for mass production.[17] Cheap prices for grains and livestock sought to furnish the working class with animal-based proteins (the so-called Fordist diet) while fueling domestic market expansion.[18] As manufacturing and service industries increasingly procured primary commodities for consumers, agriculture became more reliant on mechanization, chemical fertilizers, and other inputs.[19] In 1957, Harvard Business School professors Ray Goldberg and John Davis coined a term to refer to "the sum of all operations involved in manufacture and distribution of farm supplies, production operations on the farm, and the storage, processing and distribution of farm commodities." They called it "agribusiness." The concept understood agriculture as part of a network of agents that operate in interconnected industries, rather than as an isolated sector.[20]

The success of the modern food system in the United States relied on public agricultural research that promoted the collection and dissemination of germplasm and the institutionalization of plant genetic research. The capacity of biogenetics to modify basic characteristics of commercial crops, mitigating the inherent instability of biological processes, in tandem with increased privatization of plant breeding research, created an industrial seed. In the early 1970s, commercial application of new molecular genetic knowledge was tied to expansion in university research centers and biotechnologies concentrated in multinational corporations, while state subsidies augmented market demand for seeds, farm equipment, and agro-industrial inputs.[21] The internationalization of the U.S. food system, rooted in the expansion of the grain-livestock complex and the Fordist model, represented an important lever and legacy of Cold War politics. The Green Revolution, a term coined by United States Agency for International Development (USAID) official William Gaud in 1968, stood in contrast to the Red Revolution of the Soviets.[22]

In Latin America, technology transfers relied on government aid and multilateral loans for the coordination and development of agricultural research. Social stability in the countryside, secured through state repression and political co-optation, further ensured productivity increases.[23] Embraced by Brazil and other developing nations confronting the challenges of rapid demographic and urban growth (amid a vastly different global context for their food systems), this policy model solidified an industrial food order under

U.S. hegemony and sustained the profit strategies of its transnational agri-businesses.[24] In military Brazil, the productivist model pushed by industry and advanced by state planners resulted in agricultural modernization and the appropriation of geographically remote land alongside the reproduction of vast inequalities and social dislocations in the countryside.[25] Increased agricultural productivity and caloric intake also ensued. From the mid-1970s to the early 2000s, undernutrition in children witnessed a cumulative decline of 72 percent, while prevalence among adults was roughly halved.[26] Yet calorie elevation linked to the agricultural productivity of the Green Revolution has also been slow to lessen micronutrient deficiencies and to forestall overnutrition in Brazil and worldwide.[27] According to Brazil's National Survey on Demography and Health of Women and Children (2006–2007), 37.5 percent of sampled households in Brazil suffered from mild or severe food insecurity due to financial constraints, with the former defined by compromises in the quality or variety of food to maintain an intake deemed adequate by household members, and the latter by both the compromised quality and reduced quantity of meals for all family members.[28]

This chapter links the expansion of guaraná crop production in Brazil to state-sponsored and corporate research in plant genetics and biotechnology amid the military government's larger geopolitical project for agricultural and frontier development. As a 1985 Brazilian government report bemoaned, the standard form of non-Indigenous propagation of guaraná by seed enabled genetic variability in terms of the yield per seed per plant, the size and disposition of the fruit and leaves, and resistance to disease. Government scientists emphasized the "need to obtain homogeneity in the plantings, taking advantage of the good characteristics of the species" by preventing pollination of undesirable traits and seeking reproduction through cloning of genetically superior germplasms.[29] An authoritarian state committed to enhancing agro-industrial output and geopolitical advantage sped the transformation of rural landscapes and communities in the name of progress.

Although food has long been a commodity, its transition from a household production and object of exchange value in smaller-scale societies to an industrially produced and consumed good has altered the perception and management of the natural environment.[30] Focused on the modernization of guaraná crop production amid rising soda consumption and overnutrition, technoscientific interventions, and gaping rural inequalities, this chapter explores transformations in agriculture and diet in Brazil over the last half century. Through historical processes that are temporally varied, geographically far-ranging, invariably complex, and often unpredictable in consequence, humans affect food systems and are transformed by them.[31]

INSTITUTIONALIZED AGRICULTURAL RESEARCH in Brazil preceded the military era. The Agronomic Institute of Campinas in São Paulo (founded in 1887), the Luiz de Queiroz Superior School of Agriculture in São Paulo (1901), the Lavras School of Agriculture in Minas Gerais (1908), and the Veterinary School of Viçosa in Minas Gerais (1926) were important teaching and research centers in the twentieth century, although both the absence of a national infrastructure and the difficulty of adapting agricultural know-how from other countries to local conditions limited the diffusion of knowledge.[32] During the first Vargas regime, a succession of agronomic research centers within the Ministry of Agriculture oversaw scientific research by entities such as the Instituto de Química Agrícola, the Instituto de Ecologia e de Experimentação Agrícola, and the Instituto de Óleos. Yet as Herbert Klein and Francisco Vidal Luna argue, these earlier initiatives approached agriculture as a self-sufficient sector rather than as an integral part of an agro-industrial complex in which agriculture served as the consumer of industrial products as well as the supplier of their raw materials.[33]

Prior to military rule, institutional scientific research on guaraná reflected such patchiness. As noted, Silva Coutinho had published on guaraná in the journal of the Imperial Instituto Fluminense de Agricultura and sent botanical samples to Rio's Botanical Garden. A 1912 article by Edgard Roquette-Pinto in a publication of the Sociedade Nacional de Agricultura called for broader commercial cultivation of "a natural resource of Brazil awaiting the industrial development consonant with its practical importance."[34] A somewhat contemporary report by João Alberto Masô, a functionary of the Ministry of Agriculture, surveyed guaraná production in the Maués region, then averaging just twenty to twenty-five tons annually.[35] At Rio's Botanical Garden, scientists celebrated the fruiting of guaraná seedlings in 1936 as proof of the possibility of extra-regional cultivation.[36] Guaraná was also studied at the Instituto Agronômico do Norte (IAN), the first federal agency to conduct agronomic research in the Amazon; botanist João Murça Pires, entrusted in 1945 with the creation of a botanical section and herbarium at IAN (in collaboration with William Andrew Archer, an officer of the USDA's Office of Foreign Agriculture), sought to improve productivity through the selection and introduction of new plant varieties and agricultural technologies.[37] By the early 1950s, IAN had fifty thousand plantings of guaraná at Belterra, site of Henry Ford's onetime grandiose project for rubber cultivation.[38] A number of publications by the Instituto de Pesquisas Agropecuárias do Norte, which succeeded IAN in 1962, focused on guaraná.[39] Yet until the 1950s, public and private agricultural research in Brazil in general was limited, and coordination scant among universities, research centers, and extension services.[40]

Reports from the late 1940s and early 1950s criticized smallholders' haphazard spacing of guaraná seedlings and their manual cultivation and harvesting of the plant.[41] As former Antarctica executive Orlando de Araújo recalled of his site visit in the 1950s: "In the region of Maués, people scattered their guaraná plants throughout the forest without any idea of an orderly plantation."[42] Labor, too, was in short supply. A 1965 study found that an average yield of two arrobas, or thirty kilos of guaraná, required the muscle power of an entire family. Farmers earned a pittance compared to beverage industry profits, but the trade did allow families to acquire finer clothing.[43] Following the harvest, men returned to fishing or hunting, while women planted manioc, sweet potato, coffee, or tobacco, pursuing time-tested mixed subsistence strategies. Rural livelihoods in Maués resembled that of millions living on Brazil's vast frontier or in the shadows of the landed estates, where labor-intensive family production and the barter of goods reflected the limited influence of a market economy.[44] Swidden agriculture, the use of simple tools, the absence of weeding (aside from manioc cultivation), and the exhaustion of soil reflected the repertoire, and resilience, of Brazilian smallholders.

By the early 1960s, Brazil's inequitable system of land distribution and lagging production had elevated the agrarian question to national prominence. Less than 2 percent of rural establishments controlled approximately half of agricultural lands, while coffee overwhelmingly dominated export crops.[45] The agricultural sector, historically reliant on geographic expansion and cheap labor, struggled to match the population and per capita income increases accompanying urban, industrial growth, necessitating systematic importation of foodstuffs.[46] Diets remained limited and precarious for many. Rice, beans, and cereal grains accounted for 45 percent of average calorie intake per person; roots and tubers for 13 percent; and meat, fish, and eggs for just 8 percent. Fats and oils represented 13 percent of total calorie consumption, and sugar, 12 percent. Over half of Brazil's urban population in 1960, or 45 percent of the nation's total, fell below the minimum reference standard for calorie intake, with marked regional variations. In the Northeast, 75 percent of the population did not meet the standard.[47]

In the context of the Cold War, proponents of structural reform through land redistribution sparred with free marketeers advocating transfers of capital and technology. On March 13, 1964, President João Goulart decreed the

Harvesting guaraná, Amazonas, undated. Courtesy of Museu de Imagem e do Som, Manaus.

expropriation of all properties within ten kilometers of federal highways, railways, and water projects. His left-of-center government also sought to advance rural workers' rights and to restrict the repatriation of multinational corporations' profits.[48] Two weeks later, the military removed Goulart, ushering in twenty-one years of authoritarian rule. Through agricultural modernization rather than agrarian reform, the dictatorship aimed to boost export revenues, lower food prices for urban consumers, and reduce the cost of industrial inputs. In traditional areas of commercial cultivation, the military promoted expanded output through subsidized credit, research support, and applied agricultural science.[49] The incorporation of "unproductive" areas of the Cerrado and the Amazon rain forest through public investment and subsidized financing constituted another strategy for agricultural growth.[50]

As Brazil pivoted definitively toward the U.S. model of development, the military eased the increased insertion of transnational firms linked to agricultural machinery, fertilizers, and agrichemicals, as well as downstream sectors such as food distribution, processing, and manufacturing.[51] The modernization of the agricultural sector and the food distribution and commercialization systems featured prominently in the First National Development Plan (1972–74).[52] By 1974, the annual value of low-interest rural loans, tied to the adoption of agricultural equipment, fertilizers, pesticides, and insecticides, reached almost US$16 billion and remained above US$20 billion from 1975 to 1982.[53] Multilateral lending institutions extended loans for the manufacture of industrial inputs as well as the promotion of livestock production for the export sector.[54]

More broadly, the military regime expanded a model of citizenship premised on the mass consumption of goods rather than the exercise of political freedoms. During the dictatorship's "leaden years" (1969–74), which left thousands of political opponents imprisoned and tortured and scores disappeared, Brazil's economic "miracle" sustained double-digit growth rates, much of which was bankrolled by foreign credit. Jingoistic pronouncements aired by government propaganda outlets, the media and advertising industries, and large companies heralded an imminent superpower and consumer emporium.[55] Economic planners in Brazil spoke of wealth generation through a rising GDP as "growing the pie" that would mitigate the nation's historic inequalities. For many Brazilians, change appeared literally right around the corner: between 1967 and 1972, the number of supermarkets more than tripled, from 1,052 stores to 3,500, and by 1978 there were almost 9,000 self-service food stores.[56]

THE DEVELOPMENT OF AGRIBUSINESS in Brazil linked to increased guaraná yields also required the generation or transfer of scientific knowledge and technologies. Over the course of the 1960s, USAID provided over $100 million to train Brazilian agricultural scientists, conduct production surveys, and carry out long-term development planning.[57] A subsequent agreement between the Ministry of Agriculture and USAID financed the graduate study of over a hundred Brazilian researchers in the United States in fields related to agricultural science.[58] Moreover, between 1963 and 1978, under the Special Program for Agricultural Research, USAID played a significant role in funding the establishment of agricultural research departments at Brazilian universities, studying areas such as agricultural economics, soil science, and plant genetics.[59] By the mid-1980s, Brazil boasted more than one hundred graduate programs in agricultural sciences, having granted thirty-six hundred master's degrees and some two hundred doctorates over the previous two decades, as the military government strove to expand higher education and training in science and technology.[60] By 1980, women accounted for

27.8 percent of the postgraduate degrees in biological and health sciences and 11.3 percent in agricultural science, reflecting broader growth in higher education (overall undergraduate enrollment had increased nearly tenfold over the previous twenty-five years) as well as enrollees' determination to reverse historic gender inequalities.[61]

On December 7, 1972, Law 5851 established the Empresa Brasileira de Pesquisa Agropecuária (Brazilian Agricultural Research Corporation, or Embrapa), a public corporation and research arm of the Ministry of Agriculture dedicated to the advancement of agronomic and livestock research and development. Embrapa enjoyed institutional flexibility in coordinating agricultural research among federal and state research units, universities, the private sector, and overseas partners.[62] Federally funded, Embrapa invested heavily in human capital and international collaboration and research.[63] Over the next decades, hundreds of the agency's researchers trained in agricultural colleges and universities in Brazil and abroad, primarily in the United States. Whereas in the early 1970s, only 93 of the 851 researchers in the Ministry of Agriculture's research division held postgraduate degrees, of the 2,444 researchers employed by Embrapa in 2016, 1,829 held doctorates, 330 had master's degrees, and 285 had postdoctoral training.[64] By the late 1980s, 15.5 percent of Embrapa's 1,904 researchers were women, with nearly three-quarters holding advanced degrees.[65]

Productivity gains owed further to Embrapa's organizational model, consisting of a decentralized research network focused on producing knowledge, technologies, and crop varieties suited to Brazil and on products and geographic areas of importance to national development.[66] Grain production increased from eight million tons to over forty-eight million tons from 1970 to 2006, and soy from an area of just under one million hectares to over twenty-three million.[67] Sugarcane output also nearly tripled between 1990 and 2016—from 263 million tons to 749 million tons—reflective of rising demand for ethanol as an engine fuel.[68] The boom in Brazilian production of sugar, soybeans, and corn, particularly since the 1990s—part of a global trend of increasing yields per capita of sweeteners and vegetable oils—supplied numerous industrial food products linked to multinational corporations.[69]

Over the course of nearly five decades, Embrapa helped transform Brazil from a food importer into the breadbasket of the world. From 1975 to 2012, agriculture doubled from approximately 15 percent of Brazil's GDP to 30 percent.[70] By 2018, Brazil had become the world's largest net food exporter, including the world's biggest producer of coffee, sugar, soybeans, and orange juice, and the global leader in beef and poultry exports.[71] Small producers, shunning monocropping, dominated the nation's production of staple foodstuffs.[72]

UNDER MILITARY RULE, guaraná became primed for integrated scientific research and government support. Rising soft drink consumption augured increased demand. During the 1960s, per capita income of Brazilian consumers grew at roughly 3 percent, and the urban population surpassed over half of the nation's total. The expansion of primary education facilitated consumer market access for soft drink manufacturers, which targeted schools in order to reduce distribution costs. Guaraná sodas represented 44 percent of total soft drink sales between 1960 and 1972, with nearly three-quarters consumed in the wealthier southeastern region of the country. Demand was expected to double from 1960 to 1980.[73]

According to a 1973 study, the soda industry acquired 60 percent of annual commercial production of 231 tons of dried roasted seeds.[74] With the Lei dos Sucos (Juice Law) of 1974 requiring minimum fruit content in soft drinks, juices, and syrups, production of 2,050 tons was estimated to meet domestic demand.[75] The rising price of the seed further incentivized the soda companies to expand crop production.[76] Following the law's passage, the two largest guaraná soft drink manufacturers, Antarctica and Brahma, aimed for greater vertical integration. The Superintendência do Desenvolvimento da Amazônia (SUDAM), a federal agency promoting Amazonian development through corporate tax incentives, low-interest credit, and fiscal exemptions, approved Antarctica's project to cultivate 200,000 guaraná plants on 460 hectares at the firm's Fazenda Santa Helena in Maués in 1974.[77] The Banco da Amazônia provided ample credit to larger guaraná growers in Amazonas as well as in Pará.[78]

Antarctica's property housed a large nursery of seedlings and a laboratory, where the firm had earlier conducted scientific experimentation on the crop. In partnership with Embrapa, company agronomists pursued methods to improve yields, from selecting more productive and disease-resistant plants to experimenting with spacing and depth of planting and fertilizing.[79] At Santa Helena, machinery also pulped and washed the seeds prior to dispatch to the company's nearby factory for roasting and extract production.[80] According to a 1982 newspaper article, Antarctica transferred the barreled extract on rafts to Manaus and then downriver to Belém, where it was transported by truck to São Paulo for beverage manufacture and bottling.[81] By 1996, Antarctica's processing plant in Maués was shipping twenty-four thousand liters of the extract monthly to the company's manufacturing complex in São Paulo and ten thousand liters to the Indústria de Bebidas da Amazônia in Manaus.[82] Coca-Cola launched its guaraná soda, Kuat, in 1997, planting four hundred hectares in Presidente Figueiredo, near Manaus.[83]

Brahma opted for crop production outside the Amazon. Agronomists had successfully introduced guaraná to Bahia in 1961, but commercial cultivation began a decade later in the southeastern region of Camamu.[84] By 1983, there were over 1,200 hectares of guaraná planted in southeast Bahia. Fazenda Agro-Brahma, a large property developed by the beverage company in 1975, contained 312 hectares of guaraná by the early 1980s. Smallholders in the region cultivated the remainder with seeds and seedlings distributed by the Comissão Executiva do Plano da Lavoura Cacaueira, a federal agency that historically promoted research and development of cacao. Most of the smallholders' guaraná was bought by Agro-Brahma or sold to merchants in Rio de Janeiro and São Paulo.[85]

Technological and genetic engineering augment profit in modern food systems.[86] Since 1976, Embrapa Western Amazonia had initiated evaluation and breeding of more productive and disease-resistant guaraná plants. Phenotypic selection of superior parent plants began at the Maués experimental site, with thirty-six genitors initially identified in a population originating from over three thousand plants.[87] The scientists sought to create a genetically identical plant through asexual propagation, typically through the removal and planting of a cutting from branches of the healthiest and most productive plants; neither seeds nor genetic modifications are used in the process. For guaraná to be propagated asexually, the procedure required extensive and protracted experimentation with phytohormones to get the cuttings to root. Following the success in rooting cuttings by the end of the 1970s, Embrapa Western Amazonia began selecting parent plants in progeny tests and in traditional production areas.[88] The agency aimed to breed guaraná "clones" with yields greater than 1.5 kilograms of seeds per plant, wide adaptability, resistance to the main diseases (anthracnose and supersprouting fungus disease), improved fruit quality (higher caffeine content), and more uniform maturation.[89] (Embrapa no longer uses the term *clone* due to its ascription by environmentalists and food activists as a form of genetic modification.)[90] The reduction in genetic variety due to selective breeding also increases crop species' vulnerability to biotic and antibiotic stresses.[91]

In October 1983, Embrapa Western Amazonia sponsored the first national symposium on guaraná. The previous year's commercial production of 930 tons, overwhelmingly from the Maués region, represented less than half of internal annual demand.[92] The five-day meeting brought together over two

Percentage of guaraná products in the Brazilian market, 1960–1980

Year	Soda	Stick	Powder	Syrup
1960	40.9	51.9	5.99	1.59
1965	50.1	40.0	8.37	1.5
1970	57.2	30.3	11.11	1.39
1975	62.7	22.4	13.65	1.25
1980	66.8	16.1	16.12	0.98

Source: Sônia Milagres Teixeira, "Estudo do mercado do guaraná," 170.

hundred scientists, technicians, industrialists, politicians, and agriculturists to improve the production and marketing of guaraná. More than forty technical and scientific papers addressed topics such as agronomic research and quality control of seeds and seedlings; technical assistance, rural extension, and credit; data on regional cultivation, agro-industrial demand and output; and strategies for commercialization.[93] The symposium reflected the approach favored generally by Embrapa: research comprising interdisciplinary unit projects geared toward regions and products, and partnering with private and public entities, both national and foreign.[94]

Embrapa agronomic engineer and plant geneticist Afonso Celso Candeira Valois reported on efforts to boost guaraná yields across Brazil and through plant breeding. In addition to cultivation at Maués, 5,500 hectares had been planted in Amazonas, 3,000 in Acre, 2,500 in Bahia, 2,000 in Pará, 1,500 in Rondônia, and 1,500 in Mato Grosso. Moreover, he noted, Embrapa had funded thirteen research projects on guaraná, prioritizing genetic research, fertilization, phytopathology, entomology, harvesting, and socioeconomics.[95] Embrapa had previously compiled an annotated sixty-page bibliography on guaraná's botanical, historical, commercial, phytosanitary, and phytotechnological aspects.[96]

Conferees described Indigenous agroecological knowledge as foundational but obsolete. "We inherited from the indigenous, among various cultural aspects, guaraná, which they domesticated, cultivated, and utilized in various forms and functions. The [agri]cultural practices, as well as the mechanisms of exchange surrounding the product, did not evolve much since then," affirmed Sônia Milagres Teixeira, a rural economist at Embrapa. As historian Nancy Leys Stepan notes, the use of metaphor and analogy is rarely arbitrary in science.[97] That agricultural technicians traced Western acquisition of knowledge about guaraná to an Indigenous "bequest" unburdened by colonialism was one such metaphor, congruent with dominant cultural constructions of interracial harmony in Brazil. Condemnation of contemporary forms of cultivation as analogous to traditional Indigenous methods relatedly served to relegate these communities to an earlier stage of history.[98]

Through plant breeding, Embrapa propagated higher-yielding crop varieties. From the agency's guaraná germplasm bank, accessed about three hundred times by the early 2000s, scientists would select thirty-two elite specimens along with nineteen new cultivars, which were evaluated for at least ten years in the field and transferred to producers between 1999 and 2015.[99] Embrapa also experimented with various insecticides to reduce damage to the plant caused by thrips.[100] By 2015, Brazil's fifteen thousand hectares of planted guaraná achieved an annual production of 3,600 metric tons of dry seed. Embrapa also initiated a functional and genetic genome project for guaraná to obtain knowledge of the evolution and manipulation of genes of agronomic interest.[101]

In Amazonas, annual commercial yields of guaraná increased significantly: between 1990 and 2000, for example, production rose from 446 tons to 899 tons. Yet with output in Bahia nearly quadrupling to 2,770 tons over this same period, and average yields per plant 2.5 times higher than Amazonas's, the latter state's share of national production dropped from 66 percent to 38 percent. Plants in Bahia were typically younger and spared from anthracnose, a disease caused by the *Colletotrichum guaranicola* fungus, while 80 percent of the sexually propagated guaraná plants in Amazonas suffered from medium to severe infestations, requiring the pruning and burning of affected branches and the application of fungicides. Bahian production levels of 1.2 kilograms per plant could only be achieved in Amazonas with improved breeds. The price of guaraná from Maués, however, remained up to five times higher than that from Bahia, due to greater caffeine content resulting from climatic differences.[102]

In 2013, Bahia continued to top guaraná output in Brazil, with 60 percent of domestic production, or roughly 2,500 metric tons per year, followed by Amazonas (24 percent) and Mato Grosso (12 percent).[103] The availability of new lands, introduction of novel farming techniques, collapse in production in established regions, and preparation of new soils have prompted the dissemination of varied crops over the last century in Brazil.[104] Sugar production, dominant in the Northeast during the colonial period and through the nineteenth century, is now centered in the state of São Paulo. And an iconic plant from the Amazon region is now principally cultivated elsewhere in Brazil.

GUARANÁ PRODUCTION OVER the previous half century mirrors inequalities in the nation's agricultural sector. Large landowners across Brazil benefited from crop improvements, mechanization, fertilization, low-interest credit, subsidies, and ties to processors and distributors. From 1969 to 1990, establishments of fifty hectares or more represented only 18 percent of the country's total farms but received 76 percent of available credit.[105] The disinherited swelled the ranks of the landless, migrated to the frontier, or fled to the cities. Between 1960 and 1990, the proportion of Brazil's urban population jumped from 40 percent to 75 percent of the national total—a comparable demographic shift that occurred over the course of nine decades in the United States.[106] By 2016, fewer than 1 percent of the farms in Brazil produced over 50 percent of the gross income in agriculture, while nearly three million farms (66 percent of the total) generated just 3.27 percent.[107] By the end of the decade, the top 1.5 percent of rural landowners occupied 53 percent of all agricultural land.[108]

In the state of Amazonas, large guaraná plantations ranged from eighty to five hundred hectares. The most prominent, Antarctica's Fazenda Santa Helena, had approximately 208,000 plants under cultivation by 2007, producing twenty tons of dry seed annually, roughly 10–15 percent of the company's consumption. Whereas the Antarctica plantation initially generated about eighty grams of guaraná per dried seed, by the early 2000s bred plants were producing 1–1.5 kilos and fruiting in two rather than four or five years.[109] Mechanized clearing of forest also removed the humus and ashes that serve as natural compost and prevent erosion and excessive leaching of the soil.[110]

For some sixteen hundred families cultivating guaraná in the Maués region, accounting for 35 percent of the crop's statewide commercial production in the early 2000s, landholdings averaged three hectares, with an annual yield of thirty kilos.[111] An output of five hundred grams of dried seed per plant was considered good.[112] Fewer than one-third received financing from the Banco da Amazônia, which conditioned loans to cultivation of the bred plant.[113] The higher-yielding guaraná, even when distributed free by Antarctica and public agricultural extension services, locked participating farmers into a crop management system dictated by state research agencies and agro-industrial capital.[114] Smaller producers also complained that bred plants required extensive fertilization, with the attendant risk of overuse and higher expenses.[115] Once beholden to a local merchants' consortium, small producers sold dried seeds at harvesttime primarily to the soda companies or their intermediaries, who dictated prices.[116] Between 1994 and 2000, for example, the price for the crop dropped by nearly half.[117] More than three-quarters of commercial guaraná seed production serves the food industries, with the majority of small farmers tied to this processing chain.[118]

Guaraná had represented a pipe dream of physiocrats and reformers to modernize Amazonian society. Cultivation by smallholders would wean the rural population from extractivism and steady the region's integration into national markets. As late as the 1960s, military-era government officials promoted the upland terra firme crop as a method to plug the region's demographic "voids."[119] Yet guaraná never achieved dominance in the Amazon in the nineteenth or twentieth century. From 1850 to 1950, rubber reigned, and the economy has remained heavily dependent on other forms of extractivism, such as mining and timber, into the twenty-first century. Even within the agricultural sector, the region's eight most important products between 1976 and 2001 were bananas, beans, cassava, coffee, maize, rice, soybeans, and cattle. Small farmers grew most of the staple crops (with shifting cultivation and comparatively low yields); maize and rice occupied an intermediate position; and soybeans and cattle were commercially raised on large farms, which held considerable political sway.[120] In Brazil's northern states, holdings with 1,000 hectares or more represented 2 percent of the farms but controlled 48 percent of the land by the early 2000s; those between 100 and 999 hectares, or 18 percent of properties, held 34 percent. Alongside the northeastern region, the nine Amazonian states, containing the largest percentage of nonwhite populations in Brazil, struggled with the nation's highest rates of poverty and illiteracy.[121]

Like other facets of the Green Revolution, guaraná production since the 1970s was marked by inequalities in the reduction of poverty. Skewed land distribution, insecure ownership, restricted access to inputs and credit, scale bias in agricultural extension, and discrimination against smallholders all served to blunt modern science's promises of equal opportunity.[122] As researchers have noted, some farmers and farmworkers experienced real setbacks from the Green Revolution—or, more specifically, from the policies surrounding its implementation—particularly those who suffered losses in income due to price declines and negligible productivity gains.[123] In more personal terms, one small guaraná planter in Maués bewailed: "After the Revolution [military coup] of 1964, guaraná was planted in other states. Certainly, as a result of this, the price dropped, because some counties have much greater productivity than Maués. That's how we ended up where we are today. We are not going to stop growing guaraná, but we need support, and someone who will pay a fair price for our product."[124]

AS GOODMAN AND REDCLIFT NOTE, the rise of agribusiness and the food industries not only reordered the relationship between humans and the natural environment but also led to the refashioning of ourselves.[125] The greater use of caloric sweeteners, vegetable oils, and animal-source foods, which tracks increases in GNP, urbanization, and foreign investment in fast-food restaurants and Western-style supermarkets, has contributed to the global rise of overweight and obesity.[126] A government report from 2019 found over 25 percent of Brazilian adults to be obese (more than double since the previous nutritional study of 2002–3) and over 60 percent to be overweight.[127] And while the middle-class and wealthier sectors in Brazil accounted for the greatest prevalence of obesity in nutritional surveys of tens of thousands of households from 1975 and 2003, increases were relatively higher among individuals in lower-income groups.[128] In tandem, an epidemiological shift has occurred, marked by the prevalence of morbidity and mortality from chronic and degenerative diseases over infectious diseases linked to poor environmental sanitation and undernutrition.[129] In 2007, 72 percent of the nation's deaths were attributed to non-communicable diseases, especially stroke, cardiovascular disease, and cancer.[130]

Among Indigenous peoples, morbidity levels due to infectious and parasitic diseases remain much higher than those of the general Brazilian population, as does infant mortality and lower life expectancy at birth. Nutritional deficiencies also afflict Indigenous peoples at far greater rates. Unlike among the non-Indigenous population, diarrhea remains a common cause of hospitalization for Indigenous children. Yet health and nutritional studies have also identified the concomitant emergence of obesity, hypertension, and diabetes in a growing number of Indigenous communities across Brazil. In 2008–9, 30.3 percent of nonpregnant Indigenous women were overweight, and 15.8 percent were obese. Dietary changes linked to environmental degradation, increased participation in the market economy, salaried work, reduction of physical activity, and acquisition of purchased food items have fueled such patterns.[131]

The nutrition transition in Brazil and other developing countries has been tied to the rise of ultra-processed foods, characterized by excess simple carbohydrates, sodium, saturated fats, and trans fats, and low dietary fiber and nutrient density. Habit-forming and aggressively marketed, they can overpower humans' innate appetite-control mechanisms, while their inexpensive ingredients (a mere 5 to 10 percent of the retail price) ensure profitability.[132] Since the 1980s, market deregulation allowed for increased penetration of foreign and multinational food corporations into the developing world, with sales increasing 48 percent between 2000 and 2013 by volume in Latin America, compared with 2.3 percent in North America.[133] Eating away from home has also been linked to higher intake of fat and sugars.

In Latin America overall, the sales value in carbonated soft drinks doubled between 2000 and 2013 to $81 billion, surpassing the United States and Canada.[134] The soft drink industry in Brazil is represented by powerful trade groups, such as the Associação Brasileira das Indústrias de Refrigerantes e de Bebidas não Alcoólicas (ABIR) and the Associação Brasileira da Indústria de Alimentos, and is linked to the Alliance of Food and Beverage Associations in Latin America and the U.S.-based Consumer Brands Association (previously the Grocery Manufacturers Association).[135] In 2020, ABIR represented sixty-eight companies, covering 85 percent of the nonalcoholic beverage market in Brazil, with annual production of thirty-one billion liters. Soft drinks and other nonalcoholic beverages accounted for 1.13 percent of Brazil's gross domestic product and generated nearly two million jobs.[136]

The impact of foods on health depends on numerous factors, including their relative importance within diets.[137] Nutritional studies indicate that the caloric delivery from the high-added sugar content of soft drinks, uncompensated by an equivalent reduction in food consumption, has contributed to the rise of overweight and obesity in Brazil.[138] Beverages (excluding alcohol, milk, and milk-based drinks) delivered almost half the sugar in the Brazilian diet, and 17.1 percent of total energy consumption among those surveyed in 2015, or nearly double the World Health Organization's recommendation.[139] In 2018, the country ranked fourth globally in sugar intake, and each year, 300,000 Brazilians are diagnosed with type 2 diabetes.[140] While the Brazilian diet has always consisted of high salt and sugar content, the intake of green vegetables and fruit has decreased by 20 percent over recent decades.[141] Urban diets also witnessed a decline in basic staples over the last quarter of the twentieth century, as the consumption of rice and beans dropped 23 percent and 30 percent, respectively.[142] Concomitantly, increases of up to 400 percent occurred in the consumption of processed food items, such as cookies and soft drinks, and in total fat and saturated fat content in the diet.[143] In a National Dietary Survey from 2008 to 2009 involving 13,569 households, soft drinks ranked ninth (23 percent) in the prevalence of foods consumed on the first day of the study. Consumption varied by age and income level, from 14.4 percent in the lowest income quartile to 31.1 percent in the highest group. Women showed a slightly higher consumption of soft drinks (24.8 percent) to men (21.2 percent), while prevalence was greatest among adolescents (28 percent).[144]

The rise in overweight and obesity is also linked to increased sedentariness. The ubiquity of television sets in the nation's households suggests such leisured patterns, as well as greater exposure to the commercial advertising of processed foods.[145] The threat of street violence provided further incentive to keep youths cooped up inside.[146] According to an IBOPE poll from 2005, Brazilian children watched an average of nearly five hours of television per day.[147] Another study found that food products make up 50 percent of all advertisements to children, the majority of which were considered unhealthy.[148] Several studies in the United States have linked greater likelihood of soda consumption among children to increased television watching and exposure to commercials.[149] As food anthropologist Jeremy MacClancy pithily stated of the contemporary overload of processed foods, commercial advertising, and grab-and-go convenience, "You are what you are made to eat."[150]

MORPHOLOGY IS SOCIOLOGY, notes Marshall Sahlins.[151] Obesity encompasses a combination of material, cultural, and symbolic elements. For centuries, Western cultures idealized fat as a sign of opulence and well-being.[152] In Brazil, where the specter of undernutrition and hunger long stalked the masses, corpulence indicated privilege. Plumpness in Brazilian men historically signaled their prosperity, and for women, fertility as well. As a condition of the wealthy until the mid-twentieth century, obesity might have been impugned as a sign of gluttony or sloth rather than an aesthetic deficit, or a curiosity of bodily form rather than a measure of psychological health. For nationalist thinkers such as novelist Monteiro Lobato and physician Josué de Castro, undernutrition represented the greatest challenge to human development, as countless Brazilian patent medicines promising kilograms to the undersized proclaimed.[153]

Since the 1930s, however, evolving cultural ideals of the body have overtaken dominant sectors of Brazilian society. The industrial emphasis on speed and efficiency—the body as a "lean machine"—supplanted the aestheticization of fat. Medical studies of cardiovascular disease pathologized obesity, insurance agencies monetized ideal weight in actuarial investigations of mortality, and mass media and advertising glamorized svelte women as standards of feminine beauty. The greater availability of scales enabled the constant measurement of weight, while Ancel Keys's 1972 model of body mass index (rebranding nineteenth-century anthropometric methods to calculate relative weight) offered the World Health Organization a standardized metric to quantify overweight and obesity. In this sense, the popularization of weight-loss diets and physical exercise regimens in Brazil since the 1970s represented responses to new perceptions of risk.[154]

As markers of identity, foods often reflect anxieties of social status. With change in diets linked to the industrialization of agriculture and the spread of ultra-processed foods, fat no longer offered an incontrovertible sign of privilege. Poverty and girth were compatible: the historical prerogatives of the wealthy had been democratized in the waistline, if not the wallet. Elites who once prized excess food consumption upheld new dietetic and therapeutic regimens for the body as formulas for beauty and personal achievement.[155] A 2005 study of residents of the Rocinha shantytown in Rio de Janeiro, however, found that while Brazilian working-class populations were influenced by body images in the media, they also associated thinness with deprivation and illness. Overweight symbolized strength and health, the prerequisites for the body's capacity for physical labor. Among overweight poorer populations, the relative cost of fruits and vegetables also made healthier foods less accessible, while the double burden of working-class women of employment and homemaking left little time for preparing food from scratch. For the poor, the consumption of soft drinks promised cheap calories as well as freedom of choice and sensorial delight. Overweight was not only a mark of greater societal abundance in Brazil. It was also a manifestation of food insecurity promoting dependency on inexpensive, habit-forming, energy-dense foods.[156]

Amid shifting bodily aesthetics, guaraná in its unsweetened, powdered form appealed to better-off urbanites as an energy booster and weight loss supplement, endorsed by the fit and famous. Actresses such as Tônia Carrero and Dina Sfat revealed to magazine readers the secrets of their enduring comeliness: practicing yoga and regular consumption of powdered guaraná. Champion swimmer Silvio Fiolo described his go-to power-up beverage as containing blended powdered milk, brewer's yeast, brown sugar, wheat germ, Brazil nuts, and powdered guaraná. [157] The manufacture of powdered guaraná was reportedly pioneered by Amazonas politician and businessman Cosme Ferreira Filho in 1958, substituting demand for the handcrafted smoked stick.[158] One of the product's leading makers and distributors was the Tibiriçá company, founded in Cuiabá in 1971.[159]

More broadly, the powdered guaraná fad reflected the worldwide health food and counterculture movement.[160] A trailblazer in Brazil was Caio Miranda, who opened the Yoga Institute of Rio de Janeiro in the upscale Ipanema neighborhood in 1958 (the first of several such centers he would operate in the city) and authored several books on healthy living.[161] A retired army general and former director of the physical education division of the Ministry of Education, Miranda touted powdered guaraná as part of a healthy diet. Premature aging and death, he wrote in a 1960 article on tips for living 150 years, occurred because individuals failed to understand "the subtle laws that govern the Universe."[162] (On a subsequent visit to Brazil, world-renowned gerontologist Ana

Aslan dubbed guaraná the "Brazilian Gerovital," a reference to the Romanian doctor's antiaging, procaine-based dietary supplement.)[163] A chain smoker from the age of twelve, Miranda fell far short of his dream: he died in 1969 at the age of sixty. But the lifestyle he promoted—physical fitness, yoga, meditation, and natural foods—gained greater purchase in ensuing decades among Brazilians discomfited by technoscience and industrial foods. And in the context of the sexual revolution, natural guaraná's popular reputation as an aphrodisiac undoubtedly attracted additional explorers. On more than one occasion, advice columnists sought to dissuade readers from taking guaraná or catuaba for lackluster libidos, recommending instead greater spontaneity in the bedroom or a visit to the urologist.[164]

Natural guaraná is also far less affordable than the soft drink: amid the urban craze for the supplement in the early 1980s, the media reported a price per kilogram equivalent to a monthly salary at the minimum wage.[165] Although, as noted in chapter 5, in poorer Brazilian households, naturopathic remedies of all sorts substituted for industrial pharmaceuticals.[166] These were important but less traveled commercial paths for guaraná. While the soft drink and energy drink industries accounted for 70 percent of the guaraná market in 2013, the remainder consisted of guaraná powder for direct consumption in capsules or dilution in water (10 percent) or raw materials for pharmaceutical and cosmetic industries (20 percent).[167]

FOOD SYSTEMS ENTAIL A CONVERGENCE of agroecological changes, technical capacities, social roles, and ideologies.[168] The history of guaraná since the 1960s reflects an Amazonian plant transformed by agricultural modernization, the consolidation of industrial food systems, the impact of mass media, and changes in Brazilian lifestyles and diets. The plant's primary repurposing as an industrial input encapsulated the modern Brazil that statesmen, scientists, and cultural elites propounded since independence—whether in the factory, the field, or the home. Here was the fruit of rationalized agriculture cheered by Silva Coutinho; the colonization of frontiers and assimilation of Indigenous cultures spearheaded by Couto de Magalhães; the economic diversification promoted by Luís Pereira Barreto. In daily regimens, the soda's omnipresence signaled the reign of the citizen-consumer championed by Penteado; the freedom for women from traditional labor-intensive domestic burdens embraced by Queiroz and Sangirardi; the folk nationalism celebrated by Freyre and Câmara Cascudo; the energy boosts urged by nutritionists such as Pelegrino; the new rites of membership in a mass society observed and reenacted by countless Brazilians. The commodity's social life encompasses the interlinked realms of countryside and city, agribusiness and industrial food production, corporate concentration and consumer choice, and transformations in plant and human morphology.

As sociologist Renato Ortiz has asserted, over two decades of Brazilian military rule, mass media and consumerism forged bonds and rituals that consolidated a sense of national community.[169] Guaraná's massification bears witness to this "modern tradition," to use Ortiz's memorable term. The boom in consumption of the sodas and other sugar-sweetened beverages signaled the sweep of market-driven processes of identity formation and group belonging.[170] It also suggests that a key to capitalism's success has been its direct line to the brain's limbic system.[171] By 2014, Brazil was the third largest market in the world for carbonated soft drinks, after the United States and Mexico, with sales of liquid refreshments totaling nearly US$43 billion and volumes over 11.3 billion gallons. The nation ranked tenth globally in highest per-person daily calories from sugar-sweetened beverages.[172]

From the margins, however, emerged a concomitant trend tied to the plant's history: an Indigenous people striving to render tradition modern. Engaging with anthropologists, environmentalists, missionaries, and health food and food justice advocates, Sateré-Mawé communities harnessed guaraná for alternative forms of development. Indigenous leaders did not disavow modernization's promise of improvement so much as challenge its excesses and exclusions.

CHAPTER EIGHT

Fast Times, Slow Food
Indigenizing Modernity

In an exchange with Brazilian anthropologists in 1980, Sateré-Mawé Chief Manoelzinho quipped: "The [Sateré-]Mawé are only around because the *civilizado* needs the Mawé to satisfy his vice for guaraná. If not we'd all be gone."[1] Perhaps such existential musing was inevitable for survivors of genocide. While anthropologist Darcy Ribeiro's landmark study a decade earlier also linked the respective plight of Brazil's Indigenous populations to outsiders' varied forms of resource extraction, Chief Manoelzinho's account of interethnic friction offered a historic twist. In this case, the "vice" of the non-Indigenous spared his people from extinction. Guaraná did grant the Sateré-Mawé a certain political cachet: although Brazil's Indigenous peoples' constitutional right to land derives from prior occupation, a government report of 1986 supporting the homologation of Sateré-Mawé territory, for example, upheld their nationalistic importance as "'introducers of the culture of guaraná."[2] Chief Manoelzinho's comment, however, might be understood less as a literalist rendering of Sateré-Mawé history than as recognition of guaraná's embodiment of the cultural exchanges and boundaries that shaped it. Sateré-Mawé survival owed to strategic alliances and selective adaptations of Indigenous sociocultural norms to external influences, processes in which guaraná featured.

Guaraná long operated at different registers in Sateré-Mawé communal life. The product of a primordial being's dismemberment, the plant's mythic origins signify a source of knowledge, the dialectic of predation and transformation of life common to Tupi ontologies, the conflictive relations among affines, and aspirations for transcendence through consensus and *sehay wakuat* (good words). The latter, fundamental to a chief's persuasive power, is believed to be directly linked to the consumption of guaraná; in bygone times, the chief's recitation of the good words inscribed in the sacred *porantim* that inspired communal work projects or conflict resolution was accompanied by ritual drinking of the beverage. More commonly, in formal drinking ceremonies, the consumption of *çapó* is marked by solemnity, concentration, and the contemplation of common values.[3] As also noted, guaraná granted the Sateré-Mawé access to coveted Western goods since the colonial period. Non-Western peoples have long managed foreign arrivals without existential paralysis.[4]

In this chapter's series of snapshots, guaraná emerges as a vessel for ethnic affirmation and adaptation. In the first set of tableaus from the earlier part of the twentieth century, guaraná's importance as a medium of Indigenous social cohesion and interethnic exchange resonates in accounts by missionaries, government officials, and ethnographers. In the latter decades, when military-era and post-authoritarian transformations in Amazonia intensified the political mobilization of Indigenous communities, Sateré-Mawé leaders increasingly wielded guaraná as their "culture" in order to lay claim to legal protections and market distinction.[5]

Indigenous peoples worldwide became modern subjects through bureaucratic norms, market processes, and cultural representations, but they reworked the subordinative logic of states and capital through their own understandings of personhood and history.[6] Marshall Sahlins has dubbed the historical processes whereby Indigenous adaptations have diversified a world unified by capitalism over recent centuries the "indigenization of modernity."[7] It has likewise been marked by reinventions and contradictions, as local communities are more historically contingent, heterogeneous, and divided than commonly portrayed.[8] So, too, the notion of "traditional ecological knowledge," suggestive of hidebound domains, obscures hybrid features and extra-local linkages, or the immanence of traditional knowledge in the procedures through which authority is validated rather than antiquity per se.[9] Through the adaptation of hegemonic norms of capitalist development to Indigenous structures and worldviews lay the reproduction of distinctive ethnic identities.[10] Or put another way: where urban consumers embraced a soft drink redolent of the contradictions of contemporary life—individualism and standardization, escapism and routine, efficiency and waste—guaraná offered the Sateré-Mawé alternative ways to be modern.

"THEY HAD NEVER SEEN ICE before we arrived," Leo Halliwell wrote of the Sateré-Mawé on the Andirá River in the 1930s in his memoir. "The refrigerator on the *Luzeiro* was a source of wonder and delight to them."[11] Halliwell and his wife, Jessie—an electrical engineer and a nurse by training, respectively—would spend over two decades in the Amazon. That the Nebraskans persevered in a world of "wild animals, snakes, and insects" owed to their determination as Seventh-day Adventist missionaries to bring hope and vision to "a home of poverty, sickness, suffering, superstition, and too often death."[12] Their armory, however, included not only the Bible; the missionaries' boat, the *Luzeiro*, remodeled in 1937 to accommodate the aforementioned refrigerator, contained a small infirmary stocked with medications and vaccines dispensed free of charge to stricken river dwellers. (Locals did offer their tithes, where "money was so scarce," through manioc, guaraná, and other foodstuffs.)[13] The vessel also delivered diversion via a generator, a Victrola, and a film projector, the latter drawing hundreds of canoe-bound "natives and nationals" from miles around to see color motion pictures on the life of Christ. Sometimes it was just to behold the glow of a lightbulb.[14] The Halliwells had brought about "light in the jungle" in more ways than one. And then there was the ice, with the Sateré-Mawé clambering aboard the *Luzeiro*, passing chunks from hand to hand, then racing home to share their ephemera with loved ones.[15]

The Adventists' appearance in Sateré-Mawé communities had been facilitated by local power brokers. The first convert in the Amazon was José Batista Michiles, with holdings of more than nine hundred head of cattle, Brazil nuts and other crops, and family influence in the Maués region dating far back: a Michiles had accompanied Louis Agassiz and the Thayer expedition on the voyage from Manaus in 1865. Conversion offered Michiles leverage against political rivals allied with the Catholic hierarchy, and his kin and dependents may have followed him into the Adventist church.[16] It was Michiles who dispatched the Halliwells to preach to the Sateré-Mawé, over whom he also presumably exerted ties as patron and broker.

Halliwell's account of the Sateré-Mawé communities' early contacts with the Adventist mission is peppered with travelogue standards of Native populations as naïfs or ne'er-do-wells.[17] Among the former feature an adolescent who saunters in to an Adventist religious service stark naked (and is then quietly reprimanded by the chief), an Indigenous leader who demands to see the head of the singer that he presumed to be stuffed into the music box of Halliwell's booming Victrola, and a chief who learns that a recently acquired alarm clock requires winding to keep time. Among the latter are "hostile" communities whose "devil dance" keeps Halliwell on edge at night with incessant drumming; Natives who purportedly commit infanticide of those born with defects; and a "local witch doctor" who tormented Honorino Tavares, a Brazilian Adventist missionary who had arrived in Ponta Alegre in 1934 to build a village school and whose livestock was killed and family banished to a rain-drenched lean-to. There is also reference to the mobilization of "hundreds of braves" with poisoned arrows to destroy an encroaching distillery engaged in the extraction of rosewood oil for perfume manufacture. Overall, notwithstanding "very high" morals that distinguished the Sateré-Mawé from the "wild Indians" of the Amazon, Halliwell insisted that they retained "many primitive rites and customs and attitudes." As might be expected in the missionary's memoirs, salvation triumphs despite, or because of, such trials: A converted chief boasts of no longer eating monkey meat. Honorino Tavares's persecutor confesses several years later to a lifetime of sin, seeking out Jesus.[18] Indigenous communities welcome mission schools, where students (both adults and children) work for at least two hours a day to help defray the expenses of their education and to "train them for work" (although according to another account, three years passed before they declared themselves "followers of Christ"). And Halliwell defuses the attack on the distillery by urging the chiefs to appeal to the authorities, with their emissary, upon his return from Manaus, crowing of the governor's support.[19]

Sateré-Mawé villagers, captivated by gadgets, goodwill, and the gospel, figure only faintly in Halliwell's account as initiators or mediators of cultural change. Of course, we need not overstate Indigenous agency in view of structural exploitation and precarity. According to a 1940 Adventist periodical, three thousand residents of the Maués district, or 20 percent of the population, died from malaria over the course of several months that year.[20] Another article reported that the community at Ponta Alegre had embraced the Halliwells' vaccines and faith after members had been ravaged by smallpox.[21] Yet Amazonian Indigenous societies had also long incorporated outside goods and ideas as sources of cultural prestige and renewal.[22] More broadly, notes anthropologist Jonathan Friedman, "in colonial situations there is a tendency among certain forms of hierarchical, kinship-organized societies to identify with the source of 'life-force' that appears to come from the dominant power, and which elevates the status of those closest to such source."[23] That outsiders bearing novel gifts, medicines, and messages of salvation might be welcomed by members of the Sateré-Mawé community does not strain credulity. Halliwell's account of Indigenous response, oscillating between puerile thrill and primitivist threat, offers glimpses, however, of subtler and more sustained patterns of intercultural engagement. Through the stuff and the stories that they chose to share with outsiders and with one another, Sateré-Mawé communities sought to embrace modernity on their own terms.

Halliwell's description of his first meeting with a Sateré-Mawé community, in 1930, illustrates such deliberation. After ordering assembled villagers to silence the din from the tin whistles distributed by the missionary, the "old chief" regaled his visitor with "legends of the river and of Brazil." The first was guaraná. Most likely, amid such ceremony, the chief offered Halliwell a sip of çapó too, although his memoirs do not record such an exchange. For his readers, the missionary did detail the plant's physical appearance, processing, commercial demand, and pharmacological qualities, albeit with predictable bias given Adventist disapprobation of caffeine. "Taken this way it becomes a terrible habit and one very difficult to break," Halliwell noted of guaraná, although he added, "Who knows—maybe, as the old chief insisted, it cures something, if only drowsiness." In relating the plant's myth of origin, Halliwell recast the young child's murderous uncle as a jealous "witch doctor."[24] Of more immediate interest here, however, is the Sateré-Mawé community's showcasing of guaraná in this intercultural exchange as a form of engagement and ethnic affirmation.

Suggestive, too, is the community's initial response to proselytization. That evening, with fifty villagers crowded into the chief's house, Halliwell turned to tell stories of his people. During a sermon on Christ's redemption of sin, Halliwell puzzled at the Indigenous translator's repetitive phrasing. He learned that the interpreter, disavowing the preacher's message, had been prefacing each sentence with "The white man says."[25] While Halliwell boasted that the attendees all yearned "to know more about the life of our Lord," such knowledge would be filtered through Indigenous lenses. Tellingly, to the Adventists' dismay, the riverine population remained highly skeptical of what the "white man" had to say about dietary restrictions. As the church reported in 1938, "The real test with these people on the rivers is not the Sabbath question, because they can keep the Sabbath at will, but it is the health reform and eating question. They have been used to eating freely what forest and water produces, as well as to drinking coffee and guaraná. This becomes a real test to most of them."[26]

Sateré-Mawé communities managed change through historical memory, strategic alliance, and social innovation. After more than a century of inclusion in the Brazilian polity, did Sateré-Mawé leaders really require the missionary's insight "to use moderation" and the art of petitioning to advance their political objectives? Or did they merely seek his backing? In his travel account on the Tapajós River from 1895 to 1896, for example, Henri Coudreau recounted an exchange with Manoel Lourenço da Silva, a Sateré-Mawé aspirant to the "general chiefdom" of his people, who asked the French geographer to vouch for his competence with the governor of Pará.[27] And while we do not know from Halliwell's account the fate of the rosewood distillery (others were certainly present in the Maués region in the 1950s), we do see Sateré-Mawé communities' adaptation of external instruments to navigate the currents of change. Among such interethnic encounters, ice cubes—the enchantment of urban beverage consumers—found their way back to guaraná's inventors. But unlike in wealthier Brazilian urban homes and commercial establishments, the two elements did not mix: the Sateré-Mawé had their own ideas about progress and feeling cool.

BASED ON HIS 1957–1958 FIELDWORK, anthropologist Seth Leacock attributed Sateré-Mawé "political autonomy" to their economic independence and geographic isolation.[28] According to the 1960 census, the population of the county of Maués, larger in physical size than Belgium, numbered just over twenty thousand.[29] Dispersed over two broad geographic areas between the Tapajós and Madeira, one Sateré-Mawé population cluster of approximately six hundred lived along the Andirá in ten villages, most with fewer than fifty people; the other, with some eight hundred people, was distributed along the Marau and Urupadi Rivers. Many Sateré-Mawé did not live in a village at all but in scattered homesteads, just as nineteenth-century observers had noted.[30]

Leacock only visited the communities near the Andirá River, the location of the Indian Protection Service's post at Ponta Alegre, founded in 1921. The Indian Protection Service (SPI) was established in 1910 by Cândido Rondon, an army colonel, Amazonian explorer, and avowed positivist, at the behest of the Ministry of Agriculture.[31] Under Brazil's Civil Code of 1916, Indigenous peoples were defined as "relatively incompetent" in civil matters and subject to state guardianship (*tutela*), ostensibly to prevent abuse. The SPI preached patience and oversight toward Indigenous peoples on their drawn-out journey from "fetishistic" subsistence dwellers to profit-motivated, civic-minded workers. In his 1924 report, regional inspector Bento de Lemos celebrated the Sateré-Mawé and Mundurucu served by the government post as "almost adapted to the customs of civilization." Through hard work and education, the Indigenous were "becoming useful to the State and to the Family," as evinced purportedly by SPI photographs showcasing their Western dress and decorum.[32]

According to Leacock, the Sateré-Mawé resembled in many ways their non-Indigenous neighbors. In addition to similar attire, most Indigenous families had steel tools, aluminum kettles, cloth, soap, salt, and hammocks. Some possessed shotguns, combs, mirrors, and suitcases, and a few owned perfume, hair oil, flashlights, patent medicines, and shoes. Household diets consisted of fish and game, corn, manioc, squash, yams, and watermelon—the latter reflecting the adaptation of foreign cultigens to Amazonian agroforestry. Indigenous religious beliefs incorporated elements of Catholic faith, including the saints, life after death, and the system of godparentage. Many

Aldeiamento do Ariahú - Tres chefes da tribu Maués com
suas respectivas esposas - Rio Anderá.
- 1922 -

Sateré-Mawé leaders and their wives from the Ariaú village on the Andirá River, 1922.
Arquivo Nacional.

men spoke some Portuguese to communicate with outsiders.[33] Between the
1930s and the 1950s, Sateré-Mawé communities, particularly those at Ponta
Alegre and Molongotuba, absorbed a number of migrants from northeastern
Brazil, along with knowledge of their artisanal crafts.[34]

Leacock noted the Indigenous acquisition of outside goods through the exchange of agricultural and extractive products. Manioc flour (*farinha*) was the
principal item traded on the Andirá, while guaraná, grown near the house or
the village, was second in importance. Only a few families cultivated a large
number of guaraná plantations, Leacock noted, though production in the
Maués-Açu region by Indigenous and non-Indigenous agriculturists was
more extensive. Men who partook in work parties to fell rosewood might obtain more expensive items, such as canoes or shotguns. Most families remained in debt to traders and intermediaries, including the SPI post. As

Leacock noted, the government agent at Ponta Alegre conducted business with only a few "creditworthy" Sateré-Mawé men, who had become traders in their own right. Manoel, the "richest" resident of the village of Vila Nova (having received ample merchandise advances from the post over the course of a year), traded in various goods produced by his family or his "customers." In return, he sported a canoe, shotgun, flashlight, several pairs of clothing, and shoes—though Manoel, too, would end the year in the red.[35] In a 1957 study, which revealed an 80 percent drop in Brazil's Indigenous population over the previous half century to under 200,000, including the physical disappearance of 87 Native groups, then-SPI ethnologist Darcy Ribeiro placed the Sateré-Mawé at the penultimate stage in the government's acculturation model (prior to "extinct"): "integrated."[36]

Yet beyond external appearance or sociological label, Sateré-Mawé communities maintained distinctive forms of social organization and cultural practice, Leacock observed. The Indigenous may have sung the "Ladainha de Nossa Senhora" in Latin, but they embraced animistic beliefs in forest spirits and shamanic curing ceremonies. Shotguns felled game, but dream omens and special plants ensured the hunter's success. Key moments in the life cycle, such as menarche and childbirth, remained marked by strict dietary restrictions and social isolation. The Sateré-Mawé consumed çapó frequently during the day, believed to have a "variety of special effects, both physiological and magical."[37] Indeed, the shaman's traditional role in manipulating cosmological domains, often ritually accessorizing guaraná, surfaces in more recent Sateré-Mawé oral histories. One narrator told of his father-in-law, a shaman (*paini*) who had danced with a gourd of çapó, shaking his rattle and singing, as he invoked the protective figures of various animals to lure game to Sateré-Mawé hunters. In another story, a legendary shaman, Chicu Pucu, drinks a thick guaraná prepared by his daughter, blesses it with cigar smoke, invites the assembled villagers to share in the beverage, then prophesizes an imminent bounty of toucans, tinamous, and peccaries for the community, alongside protection from violent thunderstorms.[38]

Leacock also noted that marriage among the Sateré-Mawé revolved around clan exogamy among over twenty nonlocalized clans, typically named for animals and plants (including guaraná), but lacking in external identifying symbols or prerogatives in status, land, or ceremony. Extended families often fractured upon the death of the elder male, whose sons then established their own households or villages with the aspiration of serving as *tuxaua*, although a chief's directives for communal works required consultation with family heads. And while some households more than others prized consumer goods, the value of the trade lay in the excitement of the exchange as much as its use.[39]

Leacock's study, informed by theories of diffusionism and cultural ecology, offered scant sociopolitical context. In legal and institutional standing, the Sateré-Mawé differed notably from their neighbors—although the state's tenuous presence in the backlands compromised its tutelary mission. Among Indigenous groups with long-standing intercultural contact, ethnic distinctions owed to phenotypical and linguistic difference from surrounding populations, difficulties in obtaining official work papers, SPI intervention, and systemic racism.[40] Still, in highlighting the persistence of Sateré-Mawé tradition amid Western novelties, Leacock's research upended fundamentals of evolutionary anthropology and its twentieth-century corollary, modernization theory. Instead, he revealed members of a clan-based society adapting to external vectors, undertaking varied strategies of settlement, subsistence, and trade to uphold community dynamics and autonomy. As an organizational medium for Sateré-Mawé communities and intercultural exchange, guaraná embodied this balance.

The world of the Sateré-Mawé that Leacock left behind was soon convulsed by rapid change. From the 1950s through the 1970s, Brazil's yearly economic growth rate averaged over 7 percent.[41] Fulfilling his campaign promise of "fifty years of progress in five," President Juscelino Kubitschek unveiled the new capital of Brasília in April 1960 in the central-western plateau, a gateway to Amazonian colonization. The thousands of bottles of Guaraná Antarctica supplied by the company for Brasília's inauguration (with some lined up and photographed near the iconic buildings of the National Congress) incarnated Kubitschek's developmentalist strategy, driven by import-substitution industrialization and expanded consumerism.[42] Operation Amazonia, a military government initiative unveiled in 1966 to attract extra-regional investors, hastened the expansion of extractivism and transportation infrastructure.

The Brazilian state historically viewed indigeneity as a deficit, curiosity, or inconvenience. During two decades of authoritarian rule, Brazil's Indigenous communities were besieged in the name of national security and development. Frontier expansion marked an aspiring superpower's battle plan, one in which Cold War geopolitics bulldozed deliberative democracy and local concerns. The model relied heavily on technocratic planning, state and private investment, repression of dissent, and government mediation of social conflict. Territorialization remained central to the state logic of Indigenous elimination.[43]

For Sateré-Mawé communities, resource degradation and the monetization of social value intensified following the 1964 military coup. Reworking legal codes, market logic, and social labels, Indigenous leaders mobilized in defense of land and livelihoods. Sporadic interactions with missionaries, ethnographers, and post officials morphed into sustained strategic alliances with anthropologists and Indigenous rights advocacy networks, environmental nongovernmental organizations (NGOs), and food activists since the 1980s. Once more, guaraná offered the Sateré-Mawé alternative paths to modernity.

IN 1978, AURÉLIO MICHILES, an Amazonian documentarian, arrived in Chief Emilio Tiburcio's village to shoot an ethnographic film. *Guaraná, olho de gente* would showcase the plant's cultural significance for the Sateré-Mawé.[44] With production still underway, however, different crews descended by helicopter on the Indigenous Andirá region in August 1981: the Societé Nationale Elf Aquitaine and Petrobras—the respective state oil companies of France and Brazil—had signed a risk service contract for seismic exploration. Workers cleared some two hundred kilometers of trail and dozens of helicopter pads, undertaking roughly twenty detonations, or seismic shots, each day.[45] The base camp, located two kilometers from the village of Ponta Alegre, became a vector for alcohol abuse and prostitution.[46] Faced with Indigenous and public protest and unpromising test results, Elf initially withdrew. Yet crews returned in September 1982, opening 144 kilometers of trail and 82 clearings and detonating underground charges across vast expanses.[47] In the early 1980s, Elf Aquitaine was the largest company in France in terms of assets, with reported revenues of $14 billion.[48] Brazil's dependency on petroleum imports had slowed economic growth and increased foreign debt since the OPEC crisis, spurring foreign partnerships for domestic exploration.[49]

The Brazilian Constitution of 1967 granted Indigenous peoples permanent possession of their lands, designated as federal territory. Law 6.001 of December 19, 1973 (more commonly known as the Estatuto do Índio) further recognized Indigenous peoples' rights to a "habitat" adequate for their self-sustenance and the maintenance of "custom and tribal conditions" and codified the state's obligation to execute, whenever possible, "programs and projects tending to benefit the native communities."[50] The Estatuto do Índio, however, allowed intervention in Indigenous lands "to work valuable subsoil deposits of outstanding interest for national security and development," pursuant to presidential decree, although third-party authorization for mineral prospecting required "prior understandings" with the National Indian Foundation (FUNAI), the newly renamed Indigenous bureau.[51] By the early 1970s, more than fifty multinational corporations as well as the Brazilian

Companhia Vale do Rio Doce were engaged in mining ventures in the Amazon, benefiting from site identifications of the airborne radar imaging program of the military government's Project RADAM, the loosened restrictions on foreign investment, and the implantation of processing and transport infrastructure.[52] The Estatuto do Índio also retained the system of guardianship and its assimilationist agenda and sanctioned the relocation of Indigenous communities in the interest of national development. Sateré-Mawé leaders decried their communities' fate. As the *tuxaua geral* of the Andirá, Donato Lopes da Paz, exclaimed: "So, how is someone going to enter our land without speaking to us, without our consent?" Raimundo "Dico" Ferreira da Silva, the region's *capitão geral*, bemoaned, "Then the land is no longer ours." And *tuxaua* Emilio of the Marau area protested: "We, none of us want to take out this petroleum. The land is like anything that has life, if you take out the blood, it dies."[53]

Like other military-era policies in the Amazon, the seismic studies carried out by Elf Aquitaine's Brazilian subsidiary, Braselfa, and its principal, Companhia Brasileira de Geofísica, were riddled with procedural irregularities. The project lacked authorization from President João Figueiredo, as required by law; it counted instead on support from the FUNAI delegate in Manaus, who reputedly conferred with Petrobras. Colonel João Nobre da Veiga, a FUNAI director notorious for his anti-Indigenous stance, had been recently booted from office on corruption charges.[54] Sateré-Mawé leaders further accused the oil company of bribing a post official and another Indigenous chief.[55]

State violence in military Brazil is typically associated with clandestine detention centers, where political dissidents suffered unspeakable horrors. Yet the military's targets—opponents or obstructors of authoritarian capitalism—were multiple, with fates varying according to the state's "necropolitics."[56] For Indigenous communities, terror struck more often in the construction of roads, flooding from hydroelectric dams, the burning of forests, invasion of cattle, contamination from mining, and epidemics. Exile was characterized by loss of traditional lands, physical confinement to reduced territory, and assault by the "slow violence" of environmental degradation.[57] According to the official report of the Brazilian National Truth Commission, released only in 2014, the dictatorship contributed to the death or disappearance of over eight thousand Indigenous peoples—nearly twenty times the number of non-Indigenous victims.[58] Chief Emilio Tiburcio had his own language to describe the depredations and desperation that his community suffered. Chiding filmmaker Michiles for an overriding focus on Indigenous lore, he asserted: "You want to tell our history, but there's another story going on right now: the thieves are entering through the window of our house."[59]

The reported exchange between Michiles and Tiburcio during the documentary's filming also sheds light on Indigenous mobilization under military rule. While the Sateré-Mawé avidly shared plant stories—as their ancestors had with Silva Coutinho, Nunes Pereira, and Halliwell—Indigenous leaders insisted on resituating guaraná in contemporary struggles against authoritarianism and multinational corporate power. More broadly, they surmised the political capital of their culture and of mass media in shaping public opinion.

Since the dawn of military rule, the state-led offensive against Indigenous communities and Amazonian ecosystems had engendered vociferous opposition.[60] In 1967, Attorney General Jader Figueiredo released an extensive report documenting abuses against Brazil's Indigenous populations. Charges of genocide blanketed foreign newspapers, hastening the establishment of international Indigenous advocacy groups, such as Survival International (1969) and Cultural Survival (1972), as well as fact-finding missions to Brazil by the Red Cross and the Aborigines Protection Society in the early 1970s. In 1972, progressive Catholic clergy in Brazil, jarred by the violent impact of frontier expansion, established the Conselho Indigenista Missionário (Indigenist Missionary Council, or CIMI), endorsing Indigenous peoples' rights to land and self-determination. By 1984, forty-two pan-Indigenous meetings were convened in Brazil, where leaders, including Sateré-Mawé, rallied around a new organizational framework and politicized identity as "Indians" in defense of their communities.[61]

Commitment to the rule of law, social justice, and respect for Indigenous cultural difference mobilized missionaries, ethnographers, environmentalists, legal scholars, journalists, and artists in Brazil and abroad. Anthropology, the most subversive of the social sciences of late in confronting Western cultural normativity, inspired an alternative *indigenismo*. A government proposal to "emancipate" Indigenous groups in 1978 led opponents of the perceived land grab to establish advocacy organizations, including the Associação Nacional de Apoio ao Índio, the Comissão Pro-Índio, and the Centro de Trabalho Indigenista (CTI). The CTI and CIMI worked closely with Sateré-Mawé chiefs to generate support from the media, educators, political leaders, and state officials.[62] Viewed another way, Brazilian anthropologists, whose expertise often underwrote legal recognition of Indigenous territories, approached Native communities in the context of domestic social struggle, while Indigenous peoples proved to be coproducers of academic research and political agendas rather than mere objects of study.[63]

Multinational corporations such as Elf offered softer targets for Indigenous activists than homegrown investors. In the battle for public opinion, they could be tarred as violators of national sovereignty and potentially held more accountable for damages, as the Sateré-Mawé initiative demonstrates.[64] Following the Elf invasion, Chief Donato and *capitão geral* Dico traveled to Brasília to lodge a complaint with the French ambassador.[65] Rebuffed at the embassy, Dico shared his handwritten complaint with the press: "I don't believe Mr. Ambassador that your country being socialist [a reference to President François Mitterand's parliamentary majority] wants to disrespect my people, the Sateré-Maués [and] I want to tell you still mr [*sic*] Ambassador that from now on I will fight for my people and my land through the Constitution of our nation which is Brazil."[66]

The struggle to expel and encumber Elf mobilized an international set of activists. In conjunction with the CTI's legal team, University of São Paulo law professor Dalmo Dallari filed suit on behalf of the Sateré-Mawé in April 1983 for compensatory damages and an injunction against prospecting, thereby defying FUNAI's exclusive legal representation of Indigenous peoples under the terms of the Estatuto do Índio.[67] Withdrawing once more from the region, Elf offered a compensation of 8.6 million cruzeiros (roughly $86,000); as with the payment following the first invasion, the sum represented just 10 percent of the Indigenous claim.[68] To obtain a larger settlement, the Brazilian Association of Anthropology and the CTI invited French anthropologist Simone Dreyfus-Gamelon to the Sateré-Mawé territory in October 1983 to inventory the damage.[69] Her report, released in France to pressure the company on its home turf, called for additional recompense of 320 million cruzeiros.[70] Negotiations between Elf and the Sateré-Mawé yielded an out-of-court settlement of 150 million cruzeiros (approximately $150,000), which the company paid in August 1984.[71]

The petroleum company also left a lethal legacy: over one hundred undetonated explosives. Indigenous women who discovered the powder's utility as a formicide sprinkled it around their homes, and unsuspecting villagers were poisoned.[72] Reluctant to strain relations with France, the Brazilian government never sought charges against Elf.[73] Among those Indigenous victims listed in the National Truth Commission report are four Sateré-Mawé whose deaths were linked to the seismic exploration: Maria Faustina Batista, Calvino Batista, Dacinto Miquiles, and Lauro Freitas. All were under the age of thirty.[74]

Aurélio Michiles did shoot another shorter documentary, whose title was inspired by the Sateré-Mawé leadership's metaphor of blood. *O sangue da terra,* focused on Big Oil's invasion and the Indigenous pursuit of indemnification, was released in 1984. In the film, Dico affirmed that his people would no longer fight outsiders with arrows and clubs but rather "use the white's law." Here, once more, was the determined repurposing of historic instruments of domination: the camera to upend exoticization, the Portuguese language to reach a wider audience, the legal system to defend communal sovereignty. For good measure, the villagers offered the film crew some *çapó* as a sign of friendship.[75]

BY THE EARLY 1980S, Sateré-Mawé society had become increasingly monetized. Communities relocated closer to riverbanks to facilitate access to goods and social services. Some migrants even moved to nearby towns or to Manaus in search of jobs in the service and informal sectors. Villagers sought out novel electronics, alongside foodstuffs, clothes, tools, and munitions.[76] The culture of consumerism promoted by the military government enticed or entangled even the poorest and most geographically remote.

No matter their locale, the Sateré-Mawé experienced considerable hardship. Rural communities spent at least half the year dedicated to agriculture— cultivation of manioc during the dry summer months and of guaraná during the wetter period between January and June. Middlemen conducted trade on highly inequitable terms, and local ranchers exploited Indigenous labor. The Sateré-Mawé population grew by more than 50 percent over the 1980s, and nutritional deficiencies were widespread.[77] In urban areas, migrants suffered crushing poverty and discrimination.[78] Enrico Uggé, an Italian Catholic missionary who arrived in Parintins in 1971, recalled a local judge's response to a plea for health assistance to the Sateré-Mawé: "But are they Brazilian?"[79]

During the early 1980s, FUNAI undertook Indigenous community development projects throughout Brazil. Ethnodevelopment was hailed by many Latin American social scientists as a means to empower Indigenous peoples.[80] Projeto Sateré-Maué, launched in 1981 with an annual budget of $2.5 million cruzeiros (or approximately US$35,000 by March of that year), aimed at circumventing commercial middlemen through direct marketing of guaraná and manioc. The project hinged on the creation of producer cooperatives and commercial canteens to stock supplies. It was coordinated by the São Paulo–based CTI, which was committed to Indigenous self-determination through land demarcation, education, leadership training, and producer cooperatives. Anthropologist Sônia Lorenz, who arrived in Sateré-Mawé territory in 1978 as a member of Aurélio Michiles's film crew and helped found the CTI, served as the project's director.[81] With the price of guaraná rising in the early 1980s, the media boasted that Indigenous yields might spiral up from two to fourteen tons annually.[82] Between 1981 and 1986, five canteens operated on the Marau River, financed to different degrees by the CTI and of varied duration. From the Elf settlement, deposited in the bank account of the lead chiefs, Sateré-Mawé communities purchased three boats.[83]

Sateré-Mawé myths attribute their limited access to industrial goods to the ancestral rebuff of an emperor's invitation (perhaps Dom Pedro II) to leave the forest. The decision purportedly consigned the Indigenous to trading forest products in return for Western commodities. As Emidio de Oliveira of the Vila Nova community told anthropologist Wolfgang Kapfhammer:

> First, the Emperor lived in the paradise *nusoken*. But he wasn't satisfied, because roaches, mosquitoes and mites ate up people. That's why the Emperor said to his people: "Let's go downriver!" He then sent some of them ahead of him. Those who went ahead later became the Indians. As it happened there were a lot of *bacaba*, *patawá* and *inajá* palm trees along the way. They paused and started to gather the fruits. Only two persons stayed with the Emperor, the monkey *kãi asĩg* and the frog *hawura'i*. *Kãi asĩg* became the first White man. With him the Emperor went downriver. Halfway along the trail he met the others. "Why did you stay here, losing so much time?" The Emperor then spoke to them: "If you don't want to leave, you can stay here just as well. From now on you will live right here in the forest! It is true, there are a lot of products here in the forest: Much *pau-d'arco*, *arumá*-cane, *siringa*-rubber, *cipó*-lianas; there's a lot of money here in the forest! These products you can manage here in the forest. One day I will remember you! In order to exchange new sieves, axes, new clothes; I will bring along a lot of merchandise! I will meet you again!" This is how he talked to the Indians. Then, the Emperor left with *kãi asĩg*. He took along only two persons, *hawura'i* also accompanied him. That's why the Indians stayed here in the forest and raised their children.[84]

In less lyrical terms, Samuel Lopes encapsulated his people's history of social marginalization: "What we are lacking is opportunity." In the town of Maués, he lamented, "I've heard people saying that Indians are dirty, lazy, but Indians are very capable of competing with Whites."[85] With the advent of the community development project and payment of the Elf settlement, the Sateré-Mawé villagers arrived in Manaus on their own vessels, marketed hundreds of kilograms of guaraná directly, returned home with cassette players, watches, and clothing, and obtained basic supplies at their own canteens.[86]

As Chief Manoelzinho of the Rio Marau stated to the press in 1983: "The Indians are now planting more. At first, very, very little. Now they know what's good. Money. Now [they] plant to become rich. When I was a boy, [the town of] Maués was small. Just one road in front. Now Maués is getting better. What I like most about Maués is guaraná in a bottle. I tried beer, but I didn't think it was good."[87] As with demonstrations of agricultural productivity, discourses of consumerism buttressed Indigenous claims to territorial rights and social inclusion.

Sateré-Mawé communities, however, fractured as the canteens gave rise to new village power brokers. Community leaders also sparred over the Elf indemnity: some feared a higher payment would signal territorial surrender, while FUNAI officials coddled accommodators. After the financial settlement, some chiefs (and the CTI) advocated spending restrictions to favor long-term growth, while others demanded immediate and equal distribution among village leaders. Divisions festered among Catholics, Adventists, and Pentecostals, the latter including the nondenominational Wycliffe Bible Institute, which arrived in the Amazon in the late 1950s and created nine churches among the Sateré-Mawé over the ensuing decades.[88]

Beset by logistics challenges common to many smallholders in Brazil, the guaraná project never achieved a self-sustaining revenue stream. Lorenz, however, also pointed to nepotism in supply allocation and scarcity induced by chiefs' customary distributional disposition—behavior defying sound business practice.[89] Fundamentally, greater surplus necessitated modifications in Indigenous lifestyles and worldviews. But why should the Sateré-Mawé curtail visits to relatives in distant villages for the sake of increased yields?[90] Why should they abandon their practice of transplanting guaraná seedlings from the forest in favor of seeds or cuttings from Embrapa's high-yielding cultivars? The former augmented time to harvest and labor for weeding; the latter required expensive doses of hormones, fertilizers, and pesticides; and both methods upended the Sateré-Mawé's traditional relationship with the life cycle of the plant—and the cosmos—as "children of guaraná."[91] And with soda companies setting the price for dried seeds, how much could the most industrious farmer earn?[92] In other words, the Sateré-Mawé had translated development's promises to Indigenous frameworks.

Reflecting on the CTI's short-lived commercial guaraná project, Lorenz envisioned an alternative. What if the Sateré-Mawé marketed their crop to foreigners willing to pay more in the name of ethical production and biocultural diversity? Certification, licensing, and marketing would be start-up challenges, but consumers committed to environmentally friendly practices and fair trade might provide a lifeline for Sateré-Mawé guaraná.[93] After all, times were changing with the global expansion of alternative food networks.

INFUSING CONSUMERS' LIVES with moral meanings through an ethics of care, alternative food movements offered a potential niche for Indigenous-produced guaraná.[94] The International Federation of Organic Agriculture, founded in Germany in 1972, encompassed six hundred member organizations in one hundred countries three decades later, as supply chains for off-season fruits and vegetables reached beyond national borders.[95] Imports of organic foods from the Southern Hemisphere to northern markets reached $500 million by the end of the 1990s.[96] The fair trade model, advanced by European aid organizations in the 1970s, aimed to mitigate North-South inequalities through commodity price floors and premiums, long-term trading contracts, shorter supply chains, and smallholder access to credit. Tropical crops—particularly bananas, coffee, and cacao—featured prominently, produced by agricultural cooperatives and often organically grown by design or default due to the poverty of small farmers. By the turn of the century, fair trade linking southern producers with northern consumers represented $400 million in annual market value.[97]

The repudiation of the agroindustrial model likewise fired the Slow Food movement, founded in Italy in 1989 by Carlo Petrini and other intellectuals affiliated with the Communist Party, which opposed the standardization of foods and cultural tastes. Enshrining the "slow" life tied to agroecology, artisanal production, gastronomic tradition, and gustatory delight, the movement pledged to defend food varieties, plant breeds, and customs endangered by industrial agriculture and ultra-processed foods. Through its Ark of Taste project, the Slow Food Foundation for Biodiversity (an entity of Slow Food International) showcases foods produced in limited quantities and linked to the cultural traditions and palates of a community; those particularly threatened by industrial homogenization and environmental damage earn the "Presidium" distinction, with the organization striving to safeguard endangered varieties and breeds. By 2010, the Slow Food movement was working with small farmers in over one hundred countries and had over eighty thousand members worldwide.[98]

Launched in Sateré-Mawé communities in 1995, the Projeto Integrado de Etnodesenvolvimento, better known as Projeto Waraná, adhered to the principles of Fairtrade International and the European Union's organic agriculture regulations barring chemical fertilizers and synthetic pesticides.[99] The Forest Garden Products certification, obtained by the Sateré-Mawé in 1997, recognized the preservation or restoration of original ecosystems according to the principles of analog forestry, a silvicultural method that blends crops into the natural environment, promotes the renewal of vegetation in deforested or degraded lands, and sustains local populations and their traditional practices in their original habitat.[100] In 2004, the Slow Food Foundation for Biodiversity included Mawé guaraná in its pilot project in Brazil, conferring a Presidium label with an aim toward protecting the Native plant and its ecosystems, traditional production practices (including the use of clay ovens rather than iron grill plates), and "the art of its respectful consumption." The program was established in partnership with President Luiz Inácio Lula da Silva's Zero Hunger program, which endorsed small-scale production and cultivation of traditional crops to increase food security, protect biodiversity, and bolster local communities.[101]

Projeto Waraná was one of twelve global case studies featured in the Food and Agriculture Organization of the United Nations' 2018 report on agroecology to facilitate a "transition towards more productive, sustainable and inclusive food systems worldwide by enabling countries to produce healthy and nutritious food while protecting the environment and ensuring social inclusion."[102] By 2019, Projeto Waraná included between three hundred and four hundred families, whose marquee crop was sold to European fair trade organizations at up to ten times the average price on the Brazilian market.[103]

The promotion of Mawé guaraná in alternative food networks involved the translation of endogenous cultural understandings to the worldviews of foreign consumers.[104] For Indigenous communities, the project entailed the integration of concepts of Western science, development economics, and law with local forms of knowledge of the plant.[105] Urban romances with the rain forest jostled with the historically more ambivalent views of Native Amazonians toward nature. As Kapfhammer has noted, while the Mawé invoked protective figures, such as the "mother of animals," to attract game and ensure bounty, and enacted ritualistic dances as part of shamanistic communion with the nonhuman natural world, enchanted natural beings also sowed communal strife, while consumption of or contact with certain "cold" plants and animals relegated the sufferer to the underworld of the Great Snake (*moi'ok*).[106] In other words, adhesion to fair trade, organic, and Slow Food standards necessitated reconciliation of Mawé notions of hierarchy, particularism, and animism with the values and imaginaries of Western consumers.[107] In this context, the Indigenous glossing of guaraná as their "culture"—a shared collective patrimony (even in need of legal protection from outsiders) rather than an anthropological abstraction for internally unequal and contingent forms of knowledge—strove for recognizable forms of claims-making and product branding.[108] As Sérgio Garcia Wara affirmed of Projeto Waraná in a 2019 interview with the Slow Food Foundation for Biodiversity: "This is our culture, our cultural and immaterial heritage, something extremely relevant to us. This is our identity and with no traditions we are nothing. . . . This is our form of resistance: through food."[109] Indeed, the spelling of "waraná," differing from standard orthography in Portuguese, whose alphabet traditionally lacked the letter "W," signified Indigenous reclaiming of the plant.[110]

PROJETO WARANÁ'S EMERGENCE is indissociable from late twentieth-century transformations in Sateré-Mawé society, the political ecology of Amazonia, and global trends in environmental and food politics. The Brazilian Constitution of 1988 disavowed a centuries-long assimilationist policy toward Indigenous peoples. In addition to granting Indigenous populations the inalienable right to permanent possession of "traditionally occupied" lands to ensure their "physical and cultural reproduction," the charter eliminated the system of guardianship, according the right to self-representation in civil disputes, with recourse to the office of the attorney general.[111] The International Labour Organization's Indigenous and Tribal Peoples Convention, 1989 (No. 169), ratified by Brazil in 2002, likewise affirmed Indigenous and tribal populations' right to "exercise control over their own institutions, ways of life and economic development and to maintain and develop their identities, language and religions, within the framework of the State in which they live."[112]

Following the UN Conference on Environment and Development in Rio de Janeiro in 1992, foreign governments and multilateral lending institutions committed to sustainable development in the Amazon hailed Indigenous peoples as environmental stewards.[113] Between 1997 and 2001, with funds from the Pilot Program to Conserve the Brazilian Rain Forest, financed by members of the G7, the European Union, the World Bank, and the government of Brazil, FUNAI demarcated 22.7 million hectares of land as Indigenous territory, which would come to comprise 18 percent of the Legal Amazon region.[114] Nongovernmental organizations could seek funding for sustainable development projects from Brazil's environmental ministry, which allocated PP-G7 funds.[115]

Environmental NGOs in Brazil witnessed 73 percent growth between 1980 and 1990, with 2,562 "environmental and animal protection organizations" registered by 2005.[116] For foreign environmental NGOs active in Brazil, local alliances deflected accusations of imperialist meddling or privileging plants over people, while policy makers in international development encouraged "trade not aid."[117] For private companies tapping the geographic imaginaries of urban consumers alienated from nature in their work and leisure, an Amazonian Eden offered venues for profit and do-good publicity.[118] By 2000, for example, business partnerships had been struck between the Yanawana and the Aveda Corporation for a supply of annatto and andiroba oil, between the Kayapó and Body Shop cosmetics, and between the Baniwa and the Tok & Stok Brazilian home furnishing store.[119]

With the return to democratic rule, Indigenous organizations proliferated across Brazil. In the Amazon region, their number increased from 10 in 1988 to 180 by 2000. Among them was the Conselho Geral da Tribo Sateré-Mawé (CGTSM), founded in 1991 to represent the group's collective interests.[120] The CGTSM existed under the umbrella of the pan-Indigenous Coordenação dos Povos Indígenas da Amâzonia Brasileira (COIAB), established in 1989 with the support of the Catholic Church. The growth of Indigenous organizations reflected the acquisition of new constitutional rights, the reduced role of the state under neoliberalism, decentralization in the international development model, and the globalization of environmental politics. Moving beyond land struggles to demand improved access to health care, education, and environmental protection, Indigenous communities sought support for projects from NGOs, municipal and state agencies, foreign lenders, and private companies.[121]

The confluence of rapid population growth, environmental degradation, increased household reliance on purchased foods, and precarious health care and schooling spelled significant challenges for Brazil's Indigenous peoples. According to a 1995 report, for example, 40 percent of Sateré-Mawé children and 35 percent of adults suffered from malnutrition due to the paucity of animal game and fish.[122] A 2003 demographic survey of 1,531 rural Sateré-Mawé households (7,502 residents) revealed a fertility rate of eight children per woman (similar to that of other Indigenous communities in Brazil), with slightly over half of the population under the age of fifteen.[123] Just a small percentage of Indigenous rural dwellers earned salaries as teachers, health agents, and public servants, while subsistence production predominated.[124]

Backed by the CGTSM, Projeto Waraná was the product of an international partnership spearheaded by Obadias Batista Garcia, an Indigenous leader, and Maurizio Fraboni, an Italian development economist who founded the Associação de Consultoria e Pesquisa Indianista da Amazônia (Amazonian Indigenous Consultancy and Research Association, or Acopiama), an NGO promoting the global marketing of goods produced by traditional peoples.[125] Fraboni had read Sônia Lorenz's book detailing the commercial guaraná project in the 1980s when he made the acquaintance of Garcia, then serving as secretary of the pan-Indigenous COIAB organization. Garcia had migrated as a youth with his family to Manaus and later to the town of Bar-reirinha, and his intercultural experience would serve him well as the director of Projeto Waraná, which necessitated attending training seminars, negotiating with financing agencies, and meeting with foreign buyers. In 2000, Garcia was elected to the town council of Barreirinha and subsequently served as president of the CGTSM for twelve years. Like other influential members of the Sateré-Mawé tribal council, Obadias Batista Garcia was an evangelical Protestant.[126]

For Sateré-Mawé producers, the project offered to boost family revenues and the general social welfare and cultural pride of communities. As Sérgio Garcia Wara noted, "My father, Obadias, wanted to create a project within our culture and our reality, which is guaraná."[127] Individual producers sell their guaraná according to varied interest and productivity to an Indigenous syndicate, the Consórcio dos Produtores Sateré-Mawé (CPSM), the auxil-iary body of the tribal council created in 2009, which sets prices annually and negotiates longer-range contracts and market channels with distributors. Ini-tially, revenues from Projeto Waraná were divided evenly: one-third to the producers, one-third to Acopiama, and the remaining third to the tribal council to support social services and forest management.[128] Manufacture of the powder was originally outsourced to a non-Indigenous firm, Agrorisa Produtos Alimentícios Naturais. Since 2020, the Sateré-Mawé have con-trolled the processing and export of powdered guaraná, along with twelve other botanical products, which are shipped to Europe.[129]

Projeto Waraná presents an alternative to Embrapa's technoscientific, pro-ductivist model. Indigenous producers must follow common production protocols in terms of fair trade, agroecology, analog forestry, and access to shared benefits to be part of the consortium.[130] (The common property re-gime does not apply to guaraná fields that are individually owned, whose pro-ducers have the right to market their crop to any buyer, including the soda companies.) To sustain traditional planting practices, the consortium's 2008 protocol mandates Indigenous cultivation of guaraná from seedlings from the forest or those that spontaneously germinate from a planted shrub, thereby rejecting Embrapa's standardized breeding project. Protection of native guaraná species from extinction is promoted through cross-pollination by bees.[131] In this way, the Sateré-Mawé uphold their territory as the true germplasm bank of guaraná, ensuring greater genetic diversity, rather than the homogeneous and stable varieties managed by Embrapa.[132]

The production protocol and common property regime of the Sateré-Mawé guaraná project seek to buttress community identity and market distinction through the very cultural reappropriation of the plant.[133] Although the UN Convention on Biological Diversity of 1992 as well as Brazilian legislation established a system of access to genetic resources and related traditional knowledge and benefit sharing regarding use, guaraná's availability as a raw material prior to the legal regulation foreclosed remuneration to the Sateré-Mawé for domesticating the plant through the consistent use of "wild" forest seedlings.[134] Similarly, the International Convention for the Protection of New Varieties of Plants, adopted in 1978, does not cover landraces (local cultivars improved by traditional agricultural methods) but legally protects cultivars obtained through scientific improvement, such as the seed varieties of guaraná developed by Embrapa.[135] Thus, Geoffroy Filoche notes, the Sateré-Mawé's alternative regulatory framework is rooted in a symbolic recovery of the plant, linked to the cultural distinctiveness and political and economic empowerment of their people.[136]

Sateré-Mawé producers market their guaraná internationally through commercial partnerships with Guayapi Tropical and the CTM Altromercato consortium, European distributors tied to the Fairtrade International network.[137] The Paris-based Guayapi Tropical company, which has worked with the Sateré-Mawé product since 1995 and represented 65 percent of Projeto Waraná's market in 2018, sells Indigenous guaraná to pharmacies and health food stores in France and other European countries.[138] In Italy, the CTM Altromercato, encompassing over one hundred associations and cooperatives, accounted for 20 percent of the market for Indigenous guaraná. The remainder of the Sateré-Mawé guaraná was sold in Brazilian markets under the Nusoken brand, whose name honors the anscestral place of origin.[139]

Commodification of Sateré guaraná through fair trade and Slow Food forums employs time-tested marketing strategies for forest products. The product is touted as a "mythical and mystical plant from the Amazonian forest and a treasure for the Sateré-Mawé people who have been conserving its secrets for thousands of years." Pharmacological tributes to the "physical and cerebral energizer" target "students, athletes, workers, watchmen, artists and intellectuals" in language reminiscent of late nineteenth-century advertisements.[140] Yet consonant with alternative consumption's narrative of "caring from a distance," distributors now stress company commitment "to preserve their [Sateré-Mawé] identity, their culture and their territory."[141] Promotional literature emphasizes the fair price to producers rather than obscuring the social conditions of commodity production.[142] And the forbidding jungle of

Henry Hurd Rusby's account gives way to the sanctity of the rain forest and "reconstitution of the original ecosystems." Indigenous land use, once censured as backward and inefficient, holds the key to sustainable development. In other words, the emphasis on Indigenous guaraná's geographic origins, agroecology, cooperativism, and millennial know-how seeks to convey notions of "quality."[143]

PROJETO WARANÁ has not resolved political conflicts among the Sateré-Mawé or tensions between capitalist logic and kin-based systems of exchange.[144] Disputes over extra-local contacts, revenue sharing, the impact of change, and other divisions besetting marginalized populations have surfaced.[145] In 2008, two Sateré-Mawé leaders—Derli Bastos Batista, who presented himself as the president of the tribal council, and Jecinaldo Barbosa Cabral, who served as the president of COIAB—accused Maurizio Fraboni and Guayapi Tropical of diverting funds from Projeto Waraná and unauthorized commercialization of Indigenous cultural patrimony. Obadias Garcia and his contingent were also said to profit at the expense of "the majority of the Sateré-Mawé people and their traditional leaders, who are marginalized in this process of raising foreign money, and do not benefit at all, despite the illicit use of their image." The formal complaint, lodged with the Ministry of Foreign Relations, FUNAI, and the Brazilian police, arose over the disparity between the price offered to guaraná producers and resale prices in foreign markets, as well as the publication of a book in France recounting the plant's cultural significance. "They use our knowledge and our images as marketing in Europe and the United States and this is worth a lot. They steal and take advantage of our wisdom," stated Cabral. Although Batista and Cabral protested in the name of "the majority of the Sateré-Mawé people and their traditional leaders," the recriminations more accurately represented contested paths to change expressed through idioms of traditional authority.[146] For their part, Fraboni and Garcia asserted that Batista had been removed earlier as president of the council due to statutory violations, while the French book merely republished well-known stories about the plant. As to the price difference between the point of purchase and resale, Fraboni retorted, "That's the market."[147]

While Projeto Waraná represents an alternative to agricultural technoscience and the industrial food system, farmers must adhere to the production standards and marketing logic of its certifiers and buyers. For producers spread out over vast territories, river peddlers or in-town merchants provide marketing alternatives to the consortium, although the latter offered roughly

$10 per kilogram in 2017, an amount 50 percent higher than the regional price. Still, Sateré-Mawé growers have collectively commercialized just twenty tons of dried seed annually, while nationwide production exceeds three thousand tons. Indigenous families involved in the project produce between one and twenty kilograms of dried seed per year, with earnings ranging from $5 to $115.[148] Since the project's inception, in fact, only a small segment of the community has engaged in commercial production of guaraná. According to a 2003 demographic survey, just 301 of 4,556 Sateré-Mawé rural dwellers over the age of ten considered guaraná production a prime economic activity for their household, with men three times more likely than women to stress its economic importance. Conversely, among 1,344 interviewees whose households produced manioc, 68 percent reported selling the crop's derivatives to peddlers or in-town markets. Overall, while 566 individuals were dedicated to processing guaraná (the sticks and seeds being the predominant by-products), only 360 sold their seeds to the Indigenous consortium for marketing through the fair-trade system. Most sticks were for domestic consumption, reflective of the overwhelming preponderance of interviewees who grew food for household use (97 percent) compared to those who sold staple crops (14.5 percent) in local markets.[149]

A subsequent report by Slow Food has highlighted the growth of Projeto Waraná—from 8,767 kilograms produced by 200 families in 2006, to 14,373 kilograms from 338 families in 2018—yet overall participation remained low.[150] Retirement pensions and conditional cash transfers under the federal Bolsa Família program (launched in 2003) far outstripped earnings from Projeto Waraná in sustaining households. Sales in the fair-trade initiatives generated only 20 percent of family revenue, compared to 80 percent from social welfare benefits. For a household with two retirees, for example, the income from pensions would be equivalent to the annual production of 540 kilos of guaraná sold at a fair-trade price. Tellingly, Sateré-Mawé informational materials on public assistance translate the word "rights" as *hesaika*, or "vital force," a term traditionally linked to a man's physical strength.[151] The Sateré-Mawé continue to filter the logic of states, faiths, and markets through an Indigenous lens. Amid new political settings and dominant cultural frameworks, the Indigenous trade in guaraná once more comprises a form of selective engagement.

IN 1698, Father João Bettendorff penned the first written description of guaraná. Over the ensuing centuries, outsiders transformed the cultivation, application, and signification of guaraná consonant with their social structures and cultural values. Guaraná's "improvement" embodied narratives of progress in Brazil, historically premised on the "whitening" of society and scientists' objectification and control of the natural world. To be sure, the Indigenous image in Western minds was never unambiguous or unconflicted.[152] Alongside disparagement of Indigenous "primitivism" came tributes to therapeutic know-how. Skeptics of modernity's totalizing systems sought refuge in the perceived holism of Indigenous cultures.[153] And domestic and international laws offered the legal foundations, if not necessarily the enforcement, of formal protections for Indigenous peoples. The cultural survival of the Sateré-Mawé fundamentally owed to adaptations of external vectors to Indigenous ways of being. As a medium of exchange, guaraná served as an ongoing point of contact, as illustrated in this chapter's series of historical vignettes.

Over the course of the twentieth century, the social networks sustaining guaraná's commercial circulation diversified. An artisanal regional beverage became a trace ingredient in a namesake multibillion-dollar soft drink industry owing to the consolidation of agribusiness and the food industries, the standardization of production linked to technoscience and the law, and the impact of mass media and consumerism. Concomitantly, health-conscious and active urbanites sought out the powdered form as a nutritional supplement and an alternative to industrial food systems. With the modernization of Brazilian society and the accelerated development of the Amazon, the kin-based, largely subsistent communities of the Sateré-Mawé became increasingly monetized. Occasional exchanges with missionaries, traders, and Indigenous bureau officials expanded to strategic meetings with representatives of development agencies, nongovernmental organizations, Indigenous rights and food activists, scientists, and academics.[154]

To market guaraná through alternative channels, the Sateré-Mawé producers' consortium deployed new vocabularies in their people's age-old battle for survival. These included catchwords common to the modern world—*citizenship, rights, progress, science, culture, environment,* and *tradition*—which were reworked by the Sateré-Mawé as tools of political and economic empowerment, fusing certain understandings of the past with those offering possibilities for change. Consider the juxtapositions in the Association of Sateré-Mawé Indigenous Women's self-designation in promoting Projeto Waraná: "being the mythical children of Guaraná, the masters who taught the world the cultivation and use of the plant, and the guardians of its natural genetic bank."[155] Or Obadias Batista Garcia's statement of his community's intent to obtain a seal of Appellation of Controlled Origin for Indigenous guaraná from the Instituto Nacional de Propriedade Intelectual certifying the exclusive link between the product and its place origins (and awarded in 2020): "The mythology says that the Sateré are the children of guaraná, but there's nothing on paper. The Appellation of Origin will recognize this juridically."[156] Or Sérgio Garcia Wara's observation: "Our ancestors said that guaraná is the beginning of knowledge. The CPSM was created to forge economic autonomy and policies for our use, for the prospect of a future in our own territory. We work within this ideology."[157]

The historically adaptive processes surrounding Projeto Waraná were neither uniform nor uncontested in clan-based, small-scale communities. Nor was the commercial guaraná undertaking the primary source of income for most Indigenous households. Yet as a rejection of the technoscientific agricultural model and the homogenization of the industrial food system, the project made a bold political statement about an Indigenous people's past and future. As the website of the Sateré-Mawé producer consortium affirms: "Our struggle is to *produce*. So that our People do not fall into the trap of depending on government assistance to turn us once more into children . . . so we are not manipulated, bought off, or blackmailed by anyone . . . so we can maintain and elevate our project in the future towards ecology, cultural renewal, internal democracy, and shared responsibilities towards one another, as envisioned in the Statute of the Sateré-Mawé Tribal Council."[158] Or as Obadias Batista Garcia noted in 2021, "[Projeto Waraná] has given us financial and political autonomy so that we can create our own policies to manage our land." After all, "there would be no Sateré-Mawé without waraná and no waraná without the Sateré-Mawé."[159]

Conclusion
A Brazilian Original

The history of guaraná's transition from Indigenous cultivar to mass-consumed commodity constitutes another chapter in the trade of soft drugs that shaped the modern world. Other facets of this global story are better known. During the eighteenth century, as Europe's population increased by more than 50 percent, consumption of tobacco surged from an estimated 50 million to 125 million pounds; coffee, from 2 million to 120 million; chocolate, from 2 million to 13 million; and tea, from 1 million to 40 million.[1] European demand for stimulants fueled the transatlantic slave trade and the New World plantation complex, state expansion and colonial rule, and the transformation of the natural environment.[2] Europe's so-called age of Enlightenment was also the age of addiction.[3]

The massification of guaraná in Brazil bears similarities to the European incorporation of soft drugs. As with guaraná, early modern physicians' certification eased consumer use of stimulants—though they, too, had their medical detractors.[4] Like guaraná, mass consumption of coffee, tea, tobacco, and chocolate relied on complex rearrangements in modes of use and representation. Similar to guaraná, neither coffee nor tea was served sweetened in their originating cultures, with the fusion of bitter and sweet becoming a powerful symbol of European cuisine and power. Westernization showcased "exotic" origins—the Native American image on tobacco wrappings, the "Turk's Head" for coffeehouses, the Indigenous woman on guaraná soda labels—as a signal of mastery over other cultures and a consumer flight of fancy. Marketers imbued stimulants with novel meanings: the cigarette, a sign of grit; coffee, a fuel for work; tea, a symbol of refinement; chocolate, the language of love; guaraná, a hallmark of modern lifestyles.

Many stimulants prevalent in their cultures of origin, however, struggled to gain a foothold in Europe and North America—whether due to cost-related matters of production, distribution and shelf life, psychoactive effects, or cultural aversion.[5] Coca was rejected by sixteenth-century Spaniards, perhaps due to abhorrence of Indigenous mastication of the leaf or its association with a restive, subjugated population; it only became a major global commodity in the twentieth century in the form of cocaine, an illicit narcotic.[6]

Maté, adored for centuries in Paraguay, Argentina, Uruguay, and southern Brazil (and later in Syria, where it was brought back by former immigrants to South America), remains heavily concentrated in regional consumption, though its reputation as a "healthy" beverage has piqued recent consumer interest elsewhere.[7] Yaupon, a holly bush native to the southeastern United States and North America's only known caffeinated plant, was widely consumed as a tea by Native Americans and colonial settlers, and even traded in Europe at the time of the Revolutionary War. But yaupon faded into obscurity in the United States over the nineteenth century as the beverage became associated with poor rural dwellers unable to afford imported Chinese tea; its scientific name, *Ilex vomitoria*, coined by British botanist William Aiton in 1789, notwithstanding the plant's absence of emetic properties, surely did not help boost sales.[8] Betel nut and khat, stimulants cherished in South Asia and the tropical Pacific, and in the Middle East and Africa, respectively, failed to obtain widespread popularity in the West.

Guaraná, too, never came to headline everyday social interactions in Amsterdam, Paris, London, or New York. Smallholder cultivation and processing in the Amazon bedeviled the large-scale enterprise and control of production and distribution that characterized the more globally extended stimulants. Labor shortages and high transportation expenses elevated production costs, while supply chains favored consumers in the South American heartland. European and North American affinity for coffee and tea also meant that guaraná confronted dietary conservatism.[9] Even in Brazil, due to market disarticulation, guaraná had thrived largely as a regional beverage, repurposed and nationalized only in the twentieth century through soft drink manufacture and distribution. Although guaraná's derivatives circulate today in 170 nations, primarily as an ingredient in energy drinks, the plant's commercial cultivation is restricted to Brazil, where consumption is also predominant.[10] The namesake product accounts for 25 percent of the national soda market, with the Antarctica brand commanding 75 percent of domestic sales, and Coca-Cola's Kuat Guaraná controlling roughly the remainder.[11] Brazilians nowadays consume nearly four hundred million liters of Guaraná Antarctica annually.[12]

Guaraná's origins and industrial application in Brazil have made for compelling nationalist narrative. In a popular Portuguese-language book (2008) listing a hundred words to "better know Brazil," guaraná earned an entry written by the president of the national PEN Club.[13] Likewise, science journalist Marcelo Leite celebrated guaraná, alongside samba, caipirinha, and feijoada, as Brazil's "principal legacy to civilization."[14] While few would argue that multitudes in Brazil adore guaraná soda—surely none of the fourteen million followers on Guaraná Antarctica's Facebook page, which touts the product as a "Brazilian original"—discourses of authenticity can constrict realms of historical inquiry and public debate.[15] Most traditions, including culinary habits, derive from long-standing exchanges and adaptations of goods and ideas rather than pristine forms. They are better seen as social constructions born of power struggles and patchworks, rather than timeless, bounded patterns of human behavior.[16]

Indeed, because exchanges, borrowings, and imitations are universal to humankind and fundamental to the dynamism of pluralistic societies, it is not the appropriation of culture per se that is indefensible; rather, it is a lack of respect accorded to forms of self-expression by marginalized populations, the uncompensated acquisition of Indigenous and subaltern knowledge, and the commercial exploitation of their communities.[17] It is misrecognition of the structural unevenness of exchanges as originators of modernity's multiple forms, or the overstatement or misattribution of cultural distinctions to characterological essences rather than historical processes. Likewise objectionable are discourses of multiculturalism that sugarcoat social inequalities.

Notwithstanding guaraná soft drinks' nationalistic cachet, the leading manufacturers' recent history reflects the global conglomeration of the Brazilian beverage industry under neoliberalism. In 1989, Brazilian financiers Jorge Paulo Lemann, Marcel Herrmann Telles, and Carlos Alberto Sicupira acquired Brahma, Antarctica's archrival, for $50 million. Ten years later, Antarctica and Brahma merged in a stock swap to become Companhia de Bebidas das Américas, or AmBev, with annual sales of approximately $5.8 billion.[18] Subsequent to a merger with the Belgium-based Interbrew, the new firm, InBev, acquired Anheuser-Busch in a $52 billion takeover bid in 2008.[19] In the 2010s, the multinational firm now known as AB InBev paid over $100 billion to acquire Grupo Modelo of Mexico and SABMiller, solidifying its position as the world's largest brewer.[20] In 2015, multibillionaires Lemann, Telles, and Sicupira controlled nearly 23 percent of AB InBev through their private investment firm.[21] Guaraná Antarctica has become one of the two hundred brands marketed by the corporation in 130 countries.[22] The age-old dream of Brazilian modernizers espousing faith in agricultural technology and industrial science to conquer domestic and foreign markets had come true. Perhaps that is the popular soft drink's most authentic tradition.

THIS BOOK HAS SOUGHT to examine outsiders' reformulation of an Indigenous crop for energetic and economic gains. It has explored the knowledge systems, institutions, and itineraries that reframed understandings and uses of guaraná, and the social practices and cultural values that the stimulant has sustained.[23] Guaraná's transition from jungle liana to Sateré-Mawé cultivar and totem, to regional beverage and pharmaceutical, to national soft drink, reflects the legacies of Indigenous forest management, Portuguese colonial frontier occupation, Brazilian agro-industrial development, and postwar mass consumption. The transformation was effectuated through networked actors armed with varied systems of knowledge, influence, and grades of mobility who sought to invest in guaraná cultural meaning and social power. These ranged from the Indigenous people whose rendering of the plant endeavored to shape the natural world, order the cosmos, and chart paths of social integration amid the traumas of colonialism; to the botanists, chemists, pharmacists, and physicians whose globalized scientific principles and networks served to reclassify the plant and sideline traditional forms of knowledge; to the advertisers enticing Brazilian drinkers to the modern-day fountain of youth; to the nationalists procuring iconic symbols. Demand has owed to the millions in Brazil seeking a remedy for thirst or hunger, a boost for fatigue, a food for comfort, an aphrodisiac for inspiration, a respite from routine, an affirmation of social belonging. Together, these patterns reflect how settler colonialism, capitalist expansion, Western science, and nationalism have shaped Brazilian society over time. Guaraná's history also reveals an Indigenous people's lifeways and sustained challenges to varied tactics of elimination.[24]

In a connective approach, this study has assembled ethnographic and historical pieces to reconstruct the making of a plant, a product, and a people. I have sought to underscore the institutional and discursive linkages that structure social inequalities, thereby parting ways with the popular notion of the "two Brazils"—of seemingly compartmentalized regions and economies.[25] What a jungle vine that crept into the homes of millions embodies is the twined Brazils, the co-constitution of the nation's socio-geographic landscapes.

Yet both history and anthropology are implicitly comparative disciplines, concerned with change and continuity over time and similarities and differences among peoples, respectively. Among the Sateré-Mawé, guaraná traditionally reinforced the kinship relations that cemented trust and cosmologies that infused meaning in communal life. Conversely, the popularization of the soda owed to an array of specialized occupations and institutions to effect large-scale changes in human relations with the natural environment and to engender public faith in abstract, impersonal systems.[26] The mass circulation of guaraná soft drinks in Brazil bespeaks social relations that came to revolve primarily around the exchange of goods and services rather than co-operativism and reciprocal duties, as well as new understandings of the self in society that redefined risk control as the protection of the individual, and progress as self-fulfillment and personal comfort.[27] My assessment of guaraná's reinvention as a taste of Brazil has tracked long-term transformations in social knowledge, structure, and behavior, attentive to the historical processes through which objects and ideas removed from cultural context are re-embedded, or translated, according to newfound institutional mediations, material practices, and epistemological frameworks.[28]

Alongside the adaptations and divergences that elevated certain notions of guaraná to national fame in Brazil over others, this study has also suggested cross-cultural commonalities in the plant's history. A starting point has been the human-induced evolution and transcultural distinction of psychoactive plants due to their power to alter states of consciousness and the mind-body connection.[29] Relatedly, nonhuman entities are shown as intrinsic to the making of all human societies, and the divide between nature and culture illusory.[30] A history of guaraná reveals knowledge as a socially situated domain, whose validation and application derive from the interactions of differentially empowered actors and culturally specific criteria.[31] I have also contended that systems of classification, embodied experiences, and the routinization of behaviors surrounding the beverage serve to buttress a social order and sense of security in both Sateré-Mawé communities and in the dominant culture of Brazil.[32]

A social biography of guaraná further elucidates the persistence of "traditional" attitudes in modern societies. Skepticism bred by technoscience's totalizing logic has sparked embrace of natural living and alternative lifestyles. Health, reproduction, mortality, and the power of nature ultimately evade the intentionality or control of all humans, prompting Westerners' assorted recourse to professionals, products, and prayers. Guaraná's mass marketing in Brazil reflects the enduring enchantment of nature and allure of magic for the modern subject. Its consumption evinces moreover the importance of sociability and trust rooted in personal relations in modern societies.[33]

In his landmark text, *The Constitution of Society*, Anthony Giddens defines history as "the structuration of events in time and space through the continual interplay of agency and structure: the interconnection of the mundane nature of day-to-day life with institutional forms stretching over immense spans of time and space." Of fundamental importance, he posits, is analyzing the historical ordering of social practices and the reproduction of the structural components of entities and institutions through individual actors' daily behavior.[34] This study of guaraná, animated by diverse historical agents and settings, has sought to trace patterns of social reproduction and transformation in the constitution of Brazilian society. Linking shaman to scientist, laboratory to laborer, missionary to market, hothouse to household, field to factory, and rain forest to restaurant, the plant's history underscores the exchanges, adaptations, and structuration in the making of a good, an ethnic group, and a nation. On these grounds, we can concur with guaraná's millions of fans: in that gourd, capsule, package, can, or bottle truly lies a wonder.

Notes

Introduction

1. João Martins da Silva Coutinho, "Notícia sobre o uaraná ou guaraná," 12–13. The spelling of Sateré-Mawé and their denomination by outsiders has varied historically. I use the Indigenous endonym and current Portuguese orthography but retain alternative spelling and appellations, such as Maué, Maués, or Mawé, that appear in historical sources and publications.
2. "How Many Are They?"
3. "Sateré Mawé."
4. Marcelo Leite, "Os filhos do guaraná," *Folha de São Paulo*, May 2, 2010.
5. Alvarez, *Satereria*, 18–19.
6. Teixeira and Brasil, "Estudo demográfico dos Sateré-Mawé," 135–54; Teixeira, *Sateré-Mawé*; Linstroth, "Conflict Avoidance among the Sateré-Mawé of Manaus, Brazil," 249–75.
7. "Sateré Mawé."
8. Teixeira, *Sateré-Mawé*, 102, 108–110.
9. Teixeira and Brasil, "Estudo demográfico dos Sateré-Mawé," 144; Uggé, *Sateré-Maué*, 24–29.
10. "Sateré Mawé."
11. Atroch and Nascimento Filho, "Guaraná," 225–36. On the Indigenous presence in the Tapajós-Madeira region, see Menéndez, "Uma contribuição para a etno-história da área Madeira-Tapajós."
12. Uggé, *Mitologia Sateré-Maué*, 13–14.
13. Alvarez, *Satereria*, 144–45; Nunes Pereira, *Os índios Maués*, 12; "Sateré Mawé."
14. See Daniel Belik, "Indigenous Routes"; José Oliver, "Archaeology of Forest Foraging," 51.
15. Atroch and Nascimento Filho, "Guaraná," 225–36.
16. Hopkins, "Modelling the Known and Unknown Plant Biodiversity of the Amazon Basin," 1401; Prance, "Forest Refuges," 137–58.
17. Henman, "Guaraná," 314.
18. Atroch and Nascimento Filho, "Guaraná," 225–36.
19. Filoche and Pinton, "Who Owns Guaraná?," 386.
20. On Indigenous technologies and European colonialism in the early modern Atlantic, see Norton, "Subaltern Technologies and Early Modernity in the Atlantic World."
21. Congretel and Pinton, "Local Knowledge, Know-How and Knowledge Mobilized in a Globalized World"; Schmidt, *O guaraná, sua cultura e indústria*, 12; Schimpl et al., "Guaraná," 15. An earlier work had speculated on the origins of the plant's name based on cognates in Indigenous languages, without coming up with a definitive origin. See Monteiro, *Antropogeografia do guaraná*, 19–20.
22. Sérgio Garcia Wara (president, Consórcio de Produtores Sateré-Mawé, Parintins), interview by author via WhatsApp, December 23, 2021.

23. Wolfe, "Settler Colonialism and the Elimination of the Native"; Clément, "Historical Foundations of Ethnobiology," 161–87. A sweeping history of medicine in Brazil (1977) disparaged Indigenous medical arts as "empirical, mystical, and magical"; see Santos Filho, *História geral da medicina brasileira*, 114. In the Latin Americanist scholarship, see Safier, "Global Knowledge on the Move"; Sanjad, Pataca, and Santos, "Knowledge and Circulation of Plants"; Norton, "Tasting Empire"; Crawford, *Andean Wonder Drug*.

24. On historians, see Friedman, "Myth, History and Political Identity"; Certeau, *Writing of History*, 64–79.

25. See, for example, Schivelbusch, *Tastes of Paradise*; Mintz, *Sweetness and Power*; Norton, *Sacred Gifts, Profane Pleasures*; Jamieson, "Essence of Commodification." On entangled histories in the Atlantic world, see Bauer and Norton, "Introduction: Entangled Trajectories." A recent scholarly article on guaraná as a global commodity is Beaufort, "La mercatique transatlantique d'un végétal psychoactif."

26. See, for example, Foster, *Coca-Globalization*; Elmore, *Citizen Coke*. On energy drinks, see Yoquinto, "Truth about Guaraná."

27. One noteworthy exception would be anthropologist Alba Figueroa's "Guaraná: A máquina do tempo dos Sateré-Mawé," although the synthetic essay approaches the plant's complex history largely from the perspective of Indigenous history.

28. As a renowned Brazilian nutritionist proclaimed in 1951: "Only a people that possesses a language, an architecture, and a cuisine truly possesses a character, a personality, a culture of their own, a national conscience." Peregrino Júnior, *Alimentação e cultura*, 10. See also *Cozinheiro nacional*, 1–2; Belluzzo and Heck, *Doces sabores*, 37; Dória, *A formação da culinária brasileira*; Feliciano, "Literatura e construção de uma brasilidade pela culinária"; Nil Castro da Silva, "Culinária e alimentação em Gilberto Freyre."

29. Fry, *Para inglês ver*, 47–53.

30. See, for example, Courtwright, *Forces of Habit*; Breen, *Age of Intoxication*; Bradburd and Jankowiak, "Drugs, Desire, and European Economic Expansion"; Gootenberg, *Andean Cocaine*; Dawson, *Peyote Effect*. On Brazil, see Carneiro, "Proibição da maconha."

31. Beck, "Caffeine, Alcohol, and Sweeteners," 179.

32. Milanesio, *Workers Go Shopping in Argentina*, 90.

33. See Putnam, "Transnational and the Text-Searchable."

34. Sherratt, introduction, 8; Sherratt, "Alcohol and Its Alternatives," 15.

35. Smail, *On Deep History and the Brain*.

36. See Schmidt, *O guaraná*, 12; Schimpl et al., "Guaraná," 15; Monteiro, *Antropogeografia do guaraná*, 19–20; Henman, "Guaraná," 314.

37. Beck, "Caffeine, Alcohol, and Sweeteners," 173. See also Weinberg and Bealer, *World of Caffeine*; Pollan, *Caffeine*; E. N. Anderson, "Caffeine and Culture."

38. Kewer et al., "Habitual Intake of Guaraná and Metabolic Morbidities."

39. Moustakas et al., "Guaraná Provides Additional Stimulation over Caffeine."

40. Mendes and Carlini, "Brazilian Plants as Possible Adaptogens"; Ângelo et al., "Guaraná." See also a review of the pharmacological studies in Schimpl et al., "Guaraná"; Kewer et al., "Habitual Intake of Guaraná and Metabolic Morbidities"; Lima et al., "Modulatory Effects of Guaraná."

41. Pollan, *Botany of Desire*, 139–40, 164–65.

42. Pollan, *Botany of Desire*, 139–40.
43. Carneiro, "Transformações do significado da palavra 'droga,'" 17.
44. Kopytoff, "Cultural Biography of Things," 67–68.
45. Barthes, "Toward a Psychosociology of Contemporary Food Consumption," 20–27; Cunha, *"Culture" and Culture*, 75; Sahlins, *Culture and Practical Reason*, 100.
46. Latour et al., "Down to Earth Social Movements," 355; Secord, "Knowledge in Transit," 665.
47. Jardine and Spary, "Natures of Cultural History."
48. On Indigenous acquisition and resignification of Western goods, see Hugh-Jones, "Yesterday's Luxuries, Tomorrow's Necessities."
49. Wara, interview.
50. Mintz, "Food and Its Relationship to Concepts of Power"; Cook and Crang, "World on a Plate." For an overview, see Pilcher, "Embodied Imagination in Recent Writings on Food History."
51. Goodman and Redclift, *Refashioning Nature*, 241, 248; Mintz, *Tasting Food, Tasting Freedom*, 5–6, 35, 67; Montanari, *Food Is Culture*, xi–xii.
52. Mintz, *Tasting Food, Tasting Freedom*, 5–6, 13, 35, 67; Montanari, *Food Is Culture*, xi–xii.
53. Cook, Crang, and Thorpe, "Tropics of Consumption"; Kopytoff, "Cultural Biography of Things," 67–78.
54. Marcus, "Ethnography in/of the World System," 101; Cook and Crang, "World on a Plate"; Tsing, *Mushroom at the End of the World*. For related approaches in the Latin Americanist historical literature, see Tinsman, *Buying into the Regime*; Soluri, *Banana Cultures*; Garfield, *In Search of the Amazon*.
55. Latour, *We Have Never Been Modern*, 101–3.
56. Marcus, "Ethnography in/of the World System," 101.
57. Geertz, *Interpretation of Cultures*; Nygren, "Local Knowledge in the Environment-Development Discourse"; Brunk, "Philosophical and Ethical Issues," 161–62.
58. Secord, "Knowledge in Transit," 658–59.
59. See Armitage and Guldi, *History Manifesto*, and the penetrating critique in Megill, "'Big History' Old and New."
60. Giddens, *Constitution of Society*, xxiv, 24. On eating as a patterned activity, see Douglas, "Deciphering a Meal."
61. See Merchant, *Death of Nature*; Mignolo, *Darker Side of Western Modernity*.
62. Benedict Anderson, *Imagined Communities*.

Chapter One

1. Prance, "Seeds of Time," 1–2.
2. Elisabetsky and Shanley, "Ethnopharmacology in the Brazilian Amazon," 201. See also Gottlieb and Mors, "Fitoquímica amazônica."
3. Balick and Cox, *Plants, People, and Culture*, 92, 145–46; Carneiro, "Transformações do significado da palavra 'droga,'" 15.
4. See Hartmann, *A nomenclatura botânica dos Borôro*, 7.

5. Carlyle, *On Heroes, Hero-Worship, and the Heroic in History*.

6. See, for example, Miller, *Plant Kin*.

7. Hartmann, *A nomenclatura botânica dos Borôro*, 12.

8. Stasi et al., *Plantas medicinais na Amazônia*, 23.

9. Balick and Cox, *Plants, People, and Culture*, 183.

10. Latour, *We Have Never Been Modern*.

11. Morelle, "Key Report Makes New Tally for Number of World's Plants"; Warren, "Why Do We Consume Only a Tiny Fraction of the World's Edible Plants?"

12. Saouma, foreword, v; Food and Agriculture Organization, "Staple Foods."

13. Schiebinger, *Plants and Empire*; Balick and Cox, *Plants, People, and Culture*, 2.

14. Soejarto and Farnsworth, "Tropical Rain Forests," 245. See also Mori et al., *Tropical Plant Collecting*, 240–43; Lathrap, "Antiquity and Importance of Long-Distance Trade Relationships," 171.

15. Revilla, *Plantas da Amazônia*.

16. Elisabetsky and Shanley, "Ethnopharmacology in the Brazilian Amazon," 201–14.

17. Lévêque, *A biodiversidade*; Skirycz et al., "Medicinal Bioprospecting of the Amazon Rainforest," 1; Capobianco, *Biodiversidade na Amazônia brasileira*. On failed transfers of Amazonian medicinals to external markets, see Breen, *Age of Intoxication*, 17–18.

18. For a sample, see Nazaré and Figueiredo, *Contribuição ao estudo do guaraná*.

19. Saouma, foreword, v.

20. See Boaventura de Sousa Santos, *Epistemologies of the South*.

21. Prance, "Increased Importance of Ethnobotany and Underexploited Plants," 135.

22. Bermejo and León, preface, xix.

23. Alfaro, Paczka, and León, "Introduction of Flora from the Old World," 27–28.

24. León, "Plant Genetic Resources of the New World," 10; Alfaro, Paczka, and León, "Introduction of Flora from the Old World," 27–28.

25. Clement, "Crops of the Amazon and Orinoco Regions," 198.

26. Petersen, Neves, and Heckenberger, "Gift from the Past"; Neves, *Arqueologia da Amazônia*.

27. Denevan, "Estimating Amazonian Indian Numbers in 1492."

28. Turnbull, "Local Knowledge and Comparative Scientific Tradition," 30; Chambers and Gillespie, "Locality in the History of Science."

29. Safier, "Global Knowledge on the Move," 133–45.

30. Keller, *Amazon and Madeira Rivers*, 131–32.

31. Balick and Cox, *Plants, People, and Culture*, 3; Clément, "Historical Foundations of Ethnobiology"; Breen, *Age of Intoxication*, 22; Sanjad, Pataca, and Santos, "Knowledge and Circulation of Plants."

32. Prance, "Seeds of Time," 1–2.

33. Pollan, *Botany of Desire*; Coccia, *Life of Plants*.

34. Miller, *Plant Kin*, 6; Balick and Cox, *Plants, People, and Culture*, 11; Wohlleben, *Hidden Life of Trees*.

35. Krug et al., "Nocturnal Bee Pollinators." Personal communication with Cristiane Krug, September 23, 2020.

36. Nazaré and Figueiredo, *Contribuição ao estudo do guaraná*, 11.

37. Schimpl et al., "Guaraná," 17; Baumann, Schulthess, and Hänni, "Guaraná Rewards Seed Dispersers."

38. Weinberg and Bealer, *World of Caffeine*, 219–33.

39. Beck, "Caffeine, Alcohol, and Sweeteners," 174–75.

40. Miller, *Plant Kin*, 5.

41. Beck, "Caffeine, Alcohol, and Sweeteners," 173.

42. Levis, Flores, et al., "How People Domesticated Amazonian Forests."

43. Pollan, *Botany of Desire*.

44. José Oliver, "Archaeology of Forest Foraging," 51; Levis Flores, et al., "How People Domesticated Amazonian Forests."

45. Levis, Costa, et al., "Persistent Effects of Pre-Columbian Plant Domestication."

46. Balée, *Cultural Forests of the Amazon*.

47. Clement, "Crops of the Amazon and Orinoco Regions," 196.

48. Prance, "Migration of Plants," 27–28.

49. José Oliver, "Archaeology of Forest Foraging," 55.

50. Crowe, "The Hunter-Gatherers," 50–85.

51. Arroyo-Kalin, "Amazonian Formative," 483.

52. Arroyo-Kalin, "Amazonian Formative," 485.

53. Arroyo-Kalin, "Amazonian Formative," 478.

54. Petersen, Neves, and Heckenberger, "Gift from the Past," 86–105.

55. See Arroyo-Kalin, "Amazonian Formative," 491; Denise Gomes, "Indigenous Societies in Brazil"; Denevan, "Pristine Myth"; Heckenberger and Neves, "Amazonian Archaeology"; Diegues, *O mito moderno da natureza intocada*; Meggers, *Amazonia*.

56. Clement, "1492 and the Loss of Amazonian Crop Genetic Resources," pts. 1 & 2.

57. Clement, "Crops of the Amazon and Orinoco Regions," 196; Levis, Flores, et al., "How People Domesticated Amazonian Forests."

58. Lathrap, "Antiquity and Importance of Long-Distance Trade Relationships," 171; Cunha and Almeida, "Indigenous People, Traditional People, and Conservation in the Amazon."

59. Edith Almeida, *Guaraná*, 5; Schimpl et al., "Guaraná," 16.

60. Clement et al., "Origin and Domestication of Native Amazonian Crops," 88–90.

61. Filoche, "Making the Difference with a Common Plant," 173; Congretel and Pinton, "Local Knowledge, Know-How and Knowledge Mobilized in a Globalized World," 527–43.

62. Congretel and Pinton, "Local Knowledge, Know-How and Knowledge Mobilized in a Globalized World," 531.

63. Cunha, "Antidomestication in the Amazon," 126–36.

64. Laudan, *Cuisine and Empire*.

65. Othon Machado, "Contribuição ao estudo das plantas medicinais do Brasil."

66. Their account from *Personal Narrative of Travels to the Equinoctial Regions of the New Continent, during the Years 1799–1804* is summarized in Spruce, "On Some Remarkable Narcotics of the Amazon Valley and Orinoco," 192–93.

67. Henman, "Guaraná," 335; Henman, *O guaraná*, 13.

68. Henman, "Guaraná," 333. Mathews, *Up the Amazon and Madeira Rivers*, 16–17. For a broader discussion of the importance of Indigenous technologies in the production of knowledge, see Norton, "Subaltern Technologies and Early Modernity in the Atlantic World."

69. Montanari, *Food Is Culture*, 13–21.

70. Lévi-Strauss, *The Raw and the Cooked*.

71. Turner, "Crisis of Late Structuralism," 23–25.

72. Lathrap, "The Antiquity and Importance of Long-Distance Trade Relationships," 170–86. On barter among Indigenous Amazonian populations, see Hugh-Jones, "Yesterday's Luxuries, Tomorrow's Necessities."

73. Menéndez, "Contribuição ao estudo das relações tribais na área Tapajós-Madeira," 271–86.

74. Bernardo Silva, *Viagens no sertão do Amazonas*, 47.

75. Schmidt, *O guaraná*, 9–10.

76. Spruce, *Notes of a Botanist on the Amazon and Andes*, 297–98; Patiño, *Plantas cultivadas y animales domésticos en América equinoccial*, 254.

77. Lorenz, *Sateré-Mawé*, 52–53.

78. Pereira, *Os índios Maués*, 42.

79. Schimpl et al., "Guaraná," 16–17.

80. Atroch and Nascimento Filho, "Guaraná," 225–36.

81. Lorenz, *Sateré-Mawé*, 53.

82. Lorenz, *Sateré-Mawé*, 52–65.

83. Lorenz, *Sateré-Mawé*, 44.

84. João Barbosa Rodrigues, *O Rio Tapajós*, 110–11.

85. Coutinho, "Notícia sobre o uaraná ou guaraná," 7.

86. Henman, "Guaraná," 333; Figueroa, "Guaraná," 63.

87. Henman, *O guaraná*, 26–27.

88. Figueroa, "Guaraná," 63.

89. Alvarez, *Satereria*, 154–55.

90. Pereira, *Os índios Maués*, 67.

91. Alvarez, *Satereria*, 144–53.

92. "Sateré Mawé."

93. Kapfhammer, "Divine Child and Trademark," 221.

94. Figueroa, "Guaraná," 62–65; Alvarez, *Satereria*, 145–48.

95. Nimuendajú, "Maué and Arapium," 247.

96. Lorenz, *Sateré-Mawé*, 39–44; "Sateré Mawé."

97. Henman, *O guaraná*, 26–27.

98. Figueroa, "Guaraná," 65–66.

99. Nimuendajú, "Maué and Arapium," 249; Mario Ypiranga Monteiro, *Antropogeografia do guaraná*, 32–34. See also Martius, *Natureza, doenças, medicina e remédios dos índios brasileiros*, 279.

100. Nimuendajú, "Maué and Arapium," 249–51; Pereira, *Os Índios Maués*, 47.

101. Pereira, *Os índios Maués*, 65–66.

102. Henman, *O guaraná*, 28–29; Monteiro, *Antropogeografia do guaraná*, 32; Nimuendajú, "Maué and Arapium," 245–54.

103. Rodrigues, Ribeiro Neto, Silva, "Saberes indígenas e ressignificação," 217–18.

104. Figueroa, "Guaraná," 56–58; Alvarez, *Satereria*, 146–52; Kapfhammer, "Divine Child and Trademark," 214.

105. Kapfhammer, "Divine Child and Trademark," 221–22; "Sateré Mawé."

106. Figueroa, "Guaraná," 66; Nimuendajú, "Maué and Arapium," 249.

107. Pereira, *Os índios Maués*, 120–26.

108. Santos-Granero, introduction, 4.

109. Kapfhammer, "Divine Child and Trademark," 215.

110. Pereira, *Os índios Maués*, 116.

111. Fausto and Heckenberger, introduction, 14. Or as Eduardo Viveiros de Castro affirmed of Araweté cosmologies, "The person is inherently in transition; human destiny is a process of Other-becoming." Castro, *From the Enemy's Point of View*, 1.

112. Alvarez, *Satereria*, 18–19, 148–49.

113. Kapfhammer, "Divine Child and Trademark," 220–21.

114. Alvarez, *Satereria*, 18–19, 36.

115. Turner, "Ethno-Ethnohistory," 236.

116. Friedman, "Myth, History and Political Identity"; Fausto and Heckenberger, introduction, 14–15; Whitehead, introduction, xviii.

117. Jonathan Hill, introduction, 9.

118. Clement et al., "Origin and Domestication of Native Amazonian Crops," 88–90.

119. Pivetta, "Guaraná DNA."

120. Clement et al., "Origin and Domestication of Native Amazonian Crops," 74. I thank Charles Clement for his clarifications.

121. Pollan, *Botany of Desire*, 196.

122. Chambers and Gillespie, "Locality in the History of Science," 232–37.

123. Cunha, "Antidomestication in the Amazon," 126–36.

124. Chambers and Gillespie, "Locality in the History of Science," 232–37.

125. Mark Harris, "Making of Regional Systems."

126. Richard White, *Middle Ground*.

127. See Carvalho Júnior, "Índios cristãos no cotidiano das colônias do norte (século XVII e XVIII)."

Chapter Two

1. Apolinário, "Plantas nativas, indígenas coloniais," 182; Chauí, *Brasil*.

2. Alves, "Produção de fitoterápicos no Brasil," 456–57; Leite, "Verdes que em vosso tempo se mostrou," 84; Edler, "Plantas nativas do Brasil nas farmacopeias portuguesas e europeias," 104.

3. Ricardo Ferreira Ribeiro, "Tortuosas raízes medicinais," 159–60.

4. Cagle, *Assembling the Tropics*; Holanda, *Visão do paraíso*; Janiga-Perkins, "Pero de Magalhães Gândavo's *História da Província Santa Cruz*."

5. Scarano, "Patrimônio florístico brasileiro," 69.

6. Cagle, *Assembling the Tropics*, 16; Márcia Moisés Ribeiro, *A ciência dos trópicos*, 21–23; Carneiro, "O saber fitoterápico indígena e os naturalistas europeus," 25.

7. Bettendorff, *Crônica da missão dos padres da companhia de Jesus no estado do Maranhão*, 36–37.

8. Nunes Pereira, *Os índios Maués*, 15, 30–31.

9. See Chambouleyron et al., "'Formidável contágio.'"

10. Arenz, "Não Saulos, mas Paulos."

11. Ângela Domingues, *Viagens de exploração geográfica na Amazônia em finais do século XVIII*, 12–13.

12. See Breno Machado dos Santos, "Os Jesuítas no Maranhão e Grão-Pará seiscentista."

13. Walker, "Acquisition and Circulation of Medical Knowledge"; Walker, "Medicines Trade," 412; Steven Harris, "Jesuit Scientific Activity in the Overseas Missions," 194–96.

14. Edler, "Medical Knowledge and Professional Power"; Márcia Moisés Ribeiro, *A ciência dos trópicos*, 94–97.

15. Renn and Hyman, introduction.

16. On the Iberian Atlantic world more generally, see Bleichmar et al., *Science in the Spanish and Portuguese Empires*. For Brazil in particular, see Gesteira, "A América portuguesa e a circulação de plantas"; Furtado, "Tropical Empiricism"; Leite, "Verdes que em vosso tempo se mostrou"; Edler, "Plantas nativas do Brasil nas farmacopeias portuguesas e europeias"; Sanjad, Pataca, and Santos, "Knowledge and Circulation of Plants."

17. Trouillot, *Silencing the Past*; Farge, *Allure of the Archives*.

18. The trend is discussed by various authors, including Crawford, *Andean Wonder Drug*; Furtado, "Topical Empiricism"; Schiebinger, *Plants and Empire*.

19. Quoted in Arenz, "Do Alzette ao Amazonas," 38.

20. See Roller, *Contact Strategies*; Sanjad, Pataca, and Santos, "Knowledge and Circulation of Plants."

21. Jaeckel, "Antônio Vieira e João Felipe Bettendorff."

22. Carvalho Júnior, "A ordem da missão e os jogos da ação," 23–41.

23. Arenz, "Do Alzette ao Amazonas," 25–30.

24. Chambouleyron, "Indian Freedom and Indian Slavery."

25. Quoted in Chambouleyron, "Indian Freedom and Indian Slavery," 55.

26. On the Amazon, see Domingues, "Os conceitos de guerra justa de resgate e os ameríndios do Norte do Brasil"; Sommer, "Colony of the Sertão"; Ibáñez-Bonillo, "Processos de guerra justa en la Amazonía portuguesa."

27. Chambouleyron, "Indian Freedom and Indian Slavery," 54–71. See also Roller, *Contact Strategies*; Alves-Melo, "Portuguese Crown's Policies towards Indians in the 17th and 18th Centuries."

28. João Azevedo Fernandes, *Selvagens bebedeiras*; Eduardo Viveiros de Castro, *A inconstância da alma selvagem*, 226–34.

29. Eduardo Viveiros de Castro, *A inconstância da alma selvagem*, 183–96.

30. Raminelli, *Imagens da colonização*, 141.

31. Carvalho Júnior, "A ordem da missão e os jogos da ação," 25; Eduardo Viveiros de Castro, *A inconstância da alma selvagem*, 190.

32. Castelnau-L'Etoile, "Uses of Shamanism," 616–37.

33. See Raminelli, *Imagens da colonização*.

34. Jaeckel, "Antônio Vieira e João Felipe Bettendorff," 173–74.

35. Chambouleyron, "Indian Freedom and Indian Slavery," 59–63.

36. Jaeckel, "Antônio Vieira e João Felipe Bettendorff"; Carvalho Júnior, "A ordem da missão e os jogos da ação," 27–28.

37. Quoted in Jaeckel, "António Vieira e João Felipe Bettendorff," 174.

38. Souza, *Devil and the Land of the Holy Cross*; Ramos, *Indigenism*; Guzmán, *Native and National in Brazil*.

39. Menéndez, "Uma contribuição para a etno-história da área Madeira-Tapajós."

40. Menéndez, "Uma contribuição para a etno-história da área Madeira-Tapajós"; Camila Loureiro Dias, "Jesuit Maps and Political Discourse"; Arenz, "Do Alzette ao Amazonas," 54–56.

41. Mark Harris, "Making of Regional Systems," 622. See also Daniel Belik, "Indigenous Routes."

42. See Roller, *Amazonian Routes*.

43. Bettendorff, *Crônica da missão dos padres da companhia de Jesus*, 37. Colonial prosetylization is also explored in Uggé, *Sateré-Maué*, 18–25.

44. Quoted in Jaeckel, "Antônio Vieira e João Felipe Bettendorff," 177.

45. Alden, "Some Reflections on Antonio Vieira," 7–16.

46. Arenz, "Do Alzette ao Amazonas," 34–35.

47. Breno Machado dos Santos, "Os Jesuítas no Maranhão e Grão-Pará seiscentista," 154.

48. Arenz, "Do Alzette ao Amazonas," 41–49.

49. Bettendorff, *Crônica da missão dos padres da companhia de Jesus*, 538–39.

50. Bettendorff, *Crônica da missão dos padres da companhia de Jesus*, 539–40. On Bettendorff and the strategy of conciliation, see Mayer, "Jesuítas no estado do Maranhão e Grão-Pará."

51. Arenz, "Do Alzette ao Amazonas," 57; Mark Harris, "Making of Regional Systems," 634.

52. Menéndez, "Uma contribuição para a etno-história da área Madeira-Tapajós," 369.

53. Leacock, "Economic and Social Factors in Maué Persistence," 17.

54. Walker, "Acquisition and Circulation of Medical Knowledge," 247–70; Walker, "Medicines Trade," 408.

55. Edler, *Boticas & pharmácias*, 133.

56. Walker, "Medicines Trade," 416.

57. Gesteira, "A América portuguesa e a circulação de plantas," 14–51; Russell-Wood, *Portuguese Empire*, 148–82.

58. Walker, "Acquisition and Circulation of Medical Knowledge," 247–70.

59. Walker, "Medicines Trade," 427; Vera Regina Beltrão Marques, *Natureza em boiões*, 283; Gesteira, "A América portuguesa e a circulação de plantas," 42–44; Leite, "Verdes que em vosso tempo se mostrou," 54–93; Kury and Sá, "Flora brasileira: Um percurso histórico," 59.

60. Giorgetti, Rossi, and Rodrigues, "Brazilian Plants with Possible Action on the Central Nervous System."

61. See Walker, "Medicines Trade"; Costa and Leitão, "Portuguese Imperial Science, 1450–1800," Russell-Wood, *Portuguese Empire*, 148–82; Breen, *Age of Intoxication*; Edler, "Medical Knowledge and Professional Power"; Cagle, *Assembling the Tropics*.

62. See Carvalho Júnior, "Visão do diabo," 159–94; Lapa, *Livro da visitação do Santo Ofício da Inquisição ao estado do Grão-Pará*, 176. On the competitive therapeutic marketplace in colonial Brazil, see Edler, "Medical Knowledge and Professional Power," 47–54; Apolinário, "Plantas nativas, indígenas coloniais," 182; Edler, "Plantas nativas do Brasil nas farmacopeias portuguesas e europeias," 100; Breen, *Age of Intoxication*. On decontextualization and secularization of Indigenous botanical knowledge, see Furtado, "Tropical Empiricism," 137; Crawford, *Andean Wonder Drug*, 35–39.

63. Edler, "Medical Knowledge and Professional Power," 50; Walker, "Medicines Trade," 406, 419; Kury and Sá, "Flora brasileira: Um percurso histórico," 22; Edler, "Plantas nativas do Brasil nas farmacopeias portuguesas e europeias," 96–137.

64. Walker, "Medicines Trade," 406; Leite, "Verdes que em vosso tempo se mostrou," 54–93.

65. Edler, "Medical Knowledge and Professional Power," 45–65; Leite, "Verdes que em vosso tempo se mostrou," 58; Ricardo Ferreira Ribeiro, "Tortuosas raízes medicinais," 161–63.

66. Leite, "Verdes que em vosso tempo se mostrou," 72.

67. Calainho, "Jesuítas e medicina no Brasil colonial," 65.

68. Edler, "Plantas nativas do Brasil nas farmacopeias portuguesas e europeias," 130.

69. Santos Filho, *História geral da medicina brasileira*, 91; Walker, "Medicines Trade," 403–31.

70. Vera Regina Beltrão Marques, *Natureza em boiões*, 71–82. See also Silva Filho, "Entre as mezinhas lusitanas e plantas brasileiras"; Edler, "Plantas nativas do Brasil nas farmacopeias portuguesas e europeias," 132–34.

71. Silva Filho, "Medicinal Plants of Brazil in the Pharmacopoeia of the Friar João de Jesus Maria," 207–22; Silva Filho, "Entre as mezinhas lusitanas e plantas brasileiras," 255–56.

72. Santos Filho, *História geral da medicina brasileira*, 91; Edler, "Plantas nativas do Brasil nas farmacopeias portuguesas e europeias," 108; Walker, "Medicines Trade," 412; Holanda, *Caminhos e fronteiras*, 74–89.

73. See Walker, "Medicines Trade," 407–8; Furtado, "Tropical Empiricism."

74. Edler, "Plantas nativas do Brasil nas farmacopeias portuguesas e europeias."

75. Daniel, *Tesouro descoberto no Rio Amazonas*, 406.

76. Cagle, *Assembling the Tropics*, 43–45.

77. Ricardo Ferreira Ribeiro, "Tortuosas raízes medicinais," 161–69.

78. Quoted in Carneiro, "O saber fitoterápico indígena e os naturalistas europeus," 23.

79. Edler, "Medical Knowledge and Professional Power," 50; Ricardo Ferreira Ribeiro, "Tortuosas raízes medicinais," 164–65.

80. Furtado, "Tropical Empiricism," 137.

81. Márcia Moisés Ribeiro, *A ciência dos trópicos*, 43–44, 94–100; Edler, "Medical Knowledge and Professional Power," 47–54.

82. Bettendorff, *Crônica da missão dos padres da companhia de Jesus*, 528–29, 563–64.

83. Martius, *Natureza, doenças, medicina e remédios dos índios brasileiros*, 279; Patiño, *Plantas cultivadas y animales domésticos en América equinoccial*, 257.

84. Nimuendajú, "Maué and Arapium," 253; Nunes Pereira, *Os índios Maués*, 75.

85. Nunes Pereira, *Os índios Maués*, 68–72.

86. Edler, *Boticas & pharmácias*, 133.

87. See Domingues, *Viagens de exploração geográfica na Amazônia*, 426.

88. Sanjad, "Portugal e os intercâmbios vegetais no mundo ultramarino"; Braga, *Sabores do Brasil em Portugal*, 91.

89. Domingues, *Viagens de exploração geográfica na Amazônia*, 54.

90. João Pereira Caldas to Martinho de Melo e Castro, Pará, February 11, 1778, Arquivo Histórico Ultramarino (AHU), Conselho Ultramarino, Brasil-Pará, box 79, doc. 6530.

91. Walker, "Medicines Trade," 426.

92. Casal, *Corografia brazílica*, 314; Figueroa, "Guaraná," 68.

93. Herzog, "Dialoguing with Barbarians," 61–88.

94. Castro, *A inconstância da alma selvagem*, 194–95, 206–10, 223–25.

95. Herzog, "Dialoguing with Barbarians."

96. Mark Harris, "Making of Regional Systems," 625.

97. Apolinário, "Plantas nativas, indígenas coloniais," 198; Roller, *Contact Strategies*; Garfield, *Indigenous Struggle at the Heart of Brazil*, 59–61.

98. Francisco Jorge dos Santos, *Além da conquista*, 115–64.

99. Bettendorff, *Crônica da missão dos padres da companhia de Jesus*, 525; Figueroa, "Guaraná," 63–64.

100. Figueroa, "Guaraná," 64; Uggé, *Mitologia Sateré-Maué*, 21.

101. McEwan, "Seats of Power," 176–97.

102. Nunes Pereira, *Os índios Maués*, 34; Nimuendajú, "Maué and Arapium," 251.

103. Queirós, "Viagem e visita do sertão," 100–101.

104. Queirós, "Viagem e visita do sertão," 187.

105. Moreira Neto, *Índios da Amazônia*, 127; Menéndez, "A área Madeira–Tapajós," 290.

106. Noronha, *Roteiro da viagem da cidade do Pará*, 27.

107. Sampaio, *Diário da viagem*, 6.

108. Cunha, *Índios no Brasil*, 74.

109. Francisco Jorge dos Santos, *Além da conquista*.

110. Faraco, *Maués*, 31–36; Menéndez, "A área Madeira-Tapajós," 289.

111. Mark Harris, "Making of Regional Systems," 624–25.

112. Spix and Martius, *Viagem pelo Brasil*, 3:274–75.

113. Leacock, "Economic and Social Factors in Maué Persistence," 83.

114. Roller, *Contact Strategies*, 63, 66, 90.

115. Spix and Martius, *Viagem pelo Brasil*, 3:403; Moreira Neto, *Índios da Amazônia*, 127–32.

116. Spix and Martius, *Viagem pelo Brasil*, 3:409.

117. Roller, *Contact Strategies*, 44.

118. Henrique, "Presente de branco," 206.

119. Spix and Martius, *Viagem pelo Brasil*, 3:115, 274.

120. Moreira Neto, *Índios da Amazônia*, 127–32.

121. On the Cabanagem, see Mark Harris, *Rebellion on the Amazon*.

122. Moreira Neto, *Índios da Amazônia*, 133–37; Menéndez, "A área Madeira-Tapajós," 292. Indigenous heroism in the Cabanagem is still recounted in Satere-Mawé communities. See Alvarez, *Satereria*, 25–26.

123. Viktor, *Brasil: Amazonas-Xingu*, 138.

124. Mark Harris, *Rebellion on the Amazon*.

125. Moreira Neto, *Índios da Amazônia*, 136.

126. Moreira Neto, *Índios da Amazônia*, 136–38.

127. Moreira Neto, *Índios da Amazônia*, 138; Uggé, *Sateré-Maué*, 25.

128. Spruce, "Journal of a Voyage from Santarém," 270–78.

129. Moreira Neto, *Índios da amazônia*.

130. "Sateré Mawé"; Nunes Pereira, *Os índios Maués*, 12–15.

131. Nimuendajú, "Maué and Arapium," 248; Nunes Pereira, *Os índios Maués*, 41.

132. Moreira Neto, *Índios da amazônia*, 138–39.

133. *Relatório que a Assembléa Legislativa Provincial do Amazonas apresentou na abertura da sessão ordinaria em o dia 7 de setembro de 1858*, n.p.

134. Linstroth, "Conflict Avoidance among the Sateré-Mawé," 249–50.

135. John Manuel Monteiro, *Tupis, tapuias e historiadores*, 1. The term originated with historian Karen Spalding (1972).

136. Sampaio, *Diário da viagem*, 4–6; Figueroa, "Guaraná," 68.

137. Henman, *O guaraná*.

138. Borrowing here from Rappaport, *Politics of Memory*, 208.

139. See Nil Castro da Silva, "Culinária e alimentação em Gilberto Freyre"; Fry, *Para inglês ver*, 47–53.

140. Tempass, "O Brasil e a sua culinária indígena," 117–29.

Chapter Three

1. L. Agassiz to Charles Sumner, December 26, 1865, in Elizabeth Agassiz, *Louis Agassiz*, 638; L. Agassiz to his brother-in-law, Thomas G. Cary, March 23, 1863, in Elizabeth Agassiz, *Louis Agassiz*, 582; Brice and M. Figueiroa, "Charles Hartt, Louis Agassiz, and the Controversy over Pleistocene Glaciation in Brazil"; Gregório, "Uma face de Jano," 99–100; Medeiros, *A liberdade da navegação do Amazonas*; Saba, *American Mirror*, 93–104.

2. Bergmann, "Troubled Marriage of Discourses," 85; Croce, *Science and Religion in the Era of William James*, 122; Gerassi-Navarro, "Picturing the Tropics from Humboldt to Darwin," 218–19; Winsor, *Reading the Shape of Nature*, 11–12; Lurie, *Louis Agassiz*.

3. Croce, *Science and Religion in the Era of William James*, 123.

4. Marcou, *Life, Letters, and Works of Louis Agassiz*, 146–49; Antunes, "A rede dos invisíveis." See Joaquim Gonçalves, vigário geral do bispado, to various Amazonian parish priests, Belém, August 19, 1865, Elizabeth Cary Agassiz Papers, Papers Connected with the Brazilian Expedition, A-3, folder 16, p. 10.

5. Kury and Sá, "Flora brasileira," 42–43.

6. See Stepan, *Picturing Tropical Nature*, 31–35; Irmscher, *Louis Agassiz*, 43–44.

7. Kury and Sá, "Flora brasileira," 19.

8. Mark Harris, *Rebellion on the Amazon*, 55–59; Bates, *Naturalist on the River Amazons*, 132.

9. McCook, "'Squares of Tropic Summer.'"

10. Stepan, *Picturing Tropical Nature*, 31–35; Hideraldo Costa, *Cultura, trabalho e luta social na Amazônia*; Rosa Belluzzo, *O Brasil dos viajantes*; Mello-Leitão, *História das expedições científicas no Brasil*; Kury, "Viajantes-naturalistas no Brasil oitocentista"; Hemming, *Naturalists in Paradise*.

11. See Drayton, *Nature's Government*; Brockway, *Science and Colonial Expansion*; Browne, "Biogeography and Empire."

12. Schlothauer, "Munduruku and Apiaká Featherwork."

13. Holway, *Flower of Empire*.

14. Irmscher, *Louis Agassiz*; Gould, *Mismeasure of Man*.

15. Kury, "A sereia amazônica dos Agassiz."

16. Agassiz and Agassiz, *Journey in Brazil*, 292–99.

17. See Irmscher, "Mr. Agassiz's 'Photographic Saloon'"; Stepan, *Picturing Tropical Nature*, 85–112; Maria Helena P. T. Machado, "Nineteenth-Century Scientific Travel and Racial Photography"; Haag, "Secret Photos of Professor Agassiz."

18. Agassiz to Sumner; Jean Louis Rodolphe Agassiz, *Conversações scientíficas*, 52–53; Agassiz and Agassiz, *Journey in Brazil*, 246–47.

19. Haag, "Day on Which Brazil Said 'No' to the United States"; Luz, *A Amazônia para os negros americanos*; Hecht, *Scramble for the Amazon*, 141–54; Maria Helena P. T. Machado, "A ciência norte-americana visita a Amazônia," 68–75.

20. Agassiz and Agassiz, *Journey in Brazil*; Kury, "A sereia amazônica dos Agassiz."

21. Agassiz and Agassiz, *Journey in Brazil*, 301–2; Paton, *Elizabeth Cary Agassiz*, 89–92.

22. Orton, *Andes and the Amazon*, 236.

23. Paton, *Elizabeth Cary Agassiz*, 69–70.

24. Barreiro, *Imaginário e viajantes no Brasil do século XIX*.

25. Agassiz and Agassiz, *Journey in Brazil*, 301–2.

26. Gregório, "Uma face do Jano," 61.

27. See Bates, *Naturalist on the River Amazons*, 211, 309; Fletcher and Kidder, *Brazil and the Brazilians*, 547–48.

28. See Benchimol, *Navegação e transporte na Amazônia*, 13.

29. Agassiz and Agassiz, *Journey in Brazil*, 300.

30. L. Agassiz to George Ticknor, Nahant, October 24, 1863, in Elizabeth Agassiz, *Louis Agassiz*, 585; Marcou, *Life, Letters, and Works of Louis Agassiz*, 148.

31. João Martins da Silva Coutinho, "Exploração do Amazonas," 5.

32. Eduardo José de Moraes, *Navegação interior do Brasil*, 20.

33. Antonio Carlos Robert Moraes, "O sertão."

34. See Lopes, *O Brasil descobre a pesquisa científica*; Dantes, ed., *Espaços da ciência no Brasil*; Heloisa M. Bertol Domingues, "As ciências naturais e a construção da nação brasileira."

35. Cribelli, *Industrial Forests and Mechanical Marvels*; Kury, "Plantas sem fronteiras."

36. Pádua, "Flora e Nação," 124; Nicolau Joaquim Moreira, *Diccionário de plantas medicinais brasileiras*, 65, 139–43.

37. João Martins da Silva Coutinho, "Notícia sobre o uaraná ou guaraná," 9.

38. Agassiz and Agassiz, *Journey in Brazil*, 315–16. See also Losada and Drummond, "Espíritos cheios de bichos"; Slater, *Dance of the Dolphin*; Jean Louis Rodolphe Agassiz, *Conversações scientíficas*, 70.

39. Agassiz and Coutinho, "Sur la geologie de L'Amazone," 685–91; Glick, introduction, 22–23.

40. The theme is explored in Peard, *Race, Place, and Medicine*.

41. Lopes, *O Brasil descobre a pesquisa científica*, 100.

42. Brice and Figueirôa, "Charles Hartt, Louis Agassiz, and the Controversy over Pleistocene Glaciation in Brazil," 170–71.

43. Moreira and Massarani, "Naturalists and the Popularization of Science"; Kern, "'Amazonian Idol,'" 214–21.

44. João Martins da Silva Coutinho, "Rascunho da Carta ao Cônego Siqueira Mendes, Presidente da Província do Pará, solicitado o número de óbitos, batizados e casamentos acontecidos entre os ano de 1848 e 1867," Pará, October 10, 1868, Museu Emilio Goeldi (MEG), Fundo Silva Coutinho (FSC), Active Correspondence (CA) 5, box 1, p. 1.

45. João Martins da Silva Coutinho, "Relatório apresentado ao Ilm. e Exm. Sr. Dr. Manoel Clementino Carneiro da Cunha."

46. Skidmore, *Black into White*.

47. Andermann, *Optic of the State*, 24.

48. Winsor, *Reading the Shape of Nature*, 43–44.

49. On his biography, see Jardim, Fernandes, and Fonseca, "Silva Coutinho"; Reis, *História do Amazonas*, 214.

50. Reis, *História do Amazonas*, 193–95, 211–15; Cardoso, "O Eldorado dos Deserdados."

51. Delson, "Beginnings of Professionalization in the Brazilian Military."

52. See Sousa Neto, *Planos para o Império*.

53. João Martins da Silva Coutinho, "Relatório apresentado ao Ilm. e Exm. Sr. Dr. Manoel Clementino Carneiro da Cunha"; Reis, *História do Amazonas*, 214; Jardim, Fernandes, and Fonseca, "Silva Coutinho," 462; Rebouças, *Apontamentos sobre a via de comunicação do Rio Madeira*, 5.

54. *Vultos da geografia do Brasil*, 89–91.

55. Jardim, Fernandes, and Fonseca, "Silva Coutinho," 457–79.

56. Lopes, *O Brasil descobre a pesquisa científica*, 85, 148.

57. On the IHGB, see Schwarcz, *Spectacle of the Races*.

58. Cribelli, "'These Industrial Forests'"; Dantas, *Espaços da ciência no Brasil*.

59. On the botanical garden, see Nepomuceno, *O jardim de D. João*.

60. Jardim, Fernandes, and Fonseca, "Silva Coutinho," 471–72; Lopes, *O Brasil descobre a pesquisa científica*, 117, 127, 141.

61. "Relatório apresentado à Assembléa Legislativa da província do Amazonas pelo Exm. Senr. Dr. Manoel Clementino Carneiro da Cunha," 16–17; "Relatório sobre os produtos agrícolas do alto Amazonas," appendix D, 4.

62. See Souza Neves, *As vitrines do progresso*; Elkin, "Promoting a New Brazil"; Lankester, "Relatório de E. Lankester," 36–37; Jardim, Fernandes, and Fonseca, "Silva Coutinho," 462–63; Santos and Torres, "O catálogo de produtos naturais e industriais da primeira exposição nacional."

63. For broader discscussion, see Cañizares-Esguerra, "Iberian Science in the Rennaissance"; Cañizares-Esguerra, "How Derivative Was Humboldt?"; Duarte, "Between the National and the Universal."

64. See Cardoso, "O Eldorado dos Deserdados," 139–92; Ishii, "O homem que virou rio," 105–6; Roller, "River Guides, Geographical Informants, and Colonial Field Agents."

65. "Exploração do Amazonas: Offícios do Dr. S. Coutinho"; Silva Coutinho, "Rascunho de Carta sobre a necessidade . . . Mambuahy," Paricatuba, July 16, 1863, MEG, FSC, AC 2, Box 1, 1.r.

66. João Martins da Silva Coutinho, "Officio do engenheiro J. M. da Silva Coutinho sobre o uaraná e outros produtos da província do Amazonas."

67. Bastos, *O vale do Amazonas*, 298–301.

68. João Martins da Silva Coutinho, "Notícia sobre o uaraná ou guaraná," 10–11.

69. Sena, *Entre anarquizadores e pessoas de costumes*; Moutinho, *Notícia sobre a província de Matto Grosso*, 115.

70. Davidson, "How the Brazilian West Was Won," 65–66.

71. Elisabeth Siqueira, *História de Mato Grosso*, 34.

72. Sena, *Entre anarquizadores e pessoas de costumes*, 18, 215.

73. See Menéndez, "Uma contribuição para a etno-história da área Madeira-Tapajós"; Menéndez, "A área Madeira-Tapajós," 288; Francisco José de Lacerda e Almeida, *Diário da*

viagem, 23–24; Mathews, *Up the Amazon and Madeira Rivers*, 16–17; Serra, "Navegação do Rio Tapajós para o Pará," 11–12; Tavares, *O Rio Tapajoz*.

74. Chandless, "Notes on the Rivers Arinos, Juruena, and Tapajós," 278; Sena, *Entre anarquizadores e pessoas de costumes*, 228–31.

75. *Collecção das leis provinciaes de Mato Grosso sancionadas e promulgadas no anno de 1854; Collecção das leis provinciaes de Mato Grosso sancionadas e promulgadas no anno de 1850; Collecção das leis provinciaes de Mato Grosso sancionadas e promulgadas no anno de 1857.*

76. "Correspondência da villa do Diamantino, datada de 16 de junho de 1857," *Noticiador Cuiabano* 9 (June 1857): 3–4.

77. Magalhães, *O selvagem*, 197.

78. Antutérpio Dias Pereira, "O viver escravo em Cuiabá," 79.

79. Moutinho, *Notícia sobre a província de Matto Grosso*, 44, 211.

80. João Martins da Silva Coutinho, "Notícia sobre o uaraná ou guaraná," 12.

81. João Martins da Silva Coutinho, "Notícia sobre o uaraná ou guaraná," 9; Keller, *Amazon and Madeira Rivers*, 110–11. See also Hirsch, "Betelnut 'Bisnis' and Cosmology," 92.

82. Spruce, "Botanical Objects Communicated to the Kew Museum," 174.

83. Antutérpio Dias Pereira, "O viver escravo em Cuiabá," 48, 107.

84. Moutinho, *Notícia sobre a província de Matto Grosso*, 13.

85. João Martins da Silva Coutinho, "Notícia sobre o uaraná ou guaraná," 12; Moutinho, *Notícia sobre a província de Matto Grosso*, 209–10.

86. Chandless, "Visit to the India-Rubber Groves," 190–91.

87. Moutinho, *Notícia sobre a província de Matto Grosso*, 9, 27, 97.

88. Spruce, *Notes of a Botanist on the Amazon and Andes*, 181. Spix and Martius likewise noted that muleteers and backland travelers took guaraná to treat diarrhea. Spix and Martius, *Viagem pelo Brasil*, 1: 248.

89. João Martins da Silva Coutinho, "Notícia sobre o uaraná ou guaraná," 12; Moutinho, *Notícia sobre a província de Matto Grosso*, 209–10.

90. Steinen, *Uma expedição ao Xingu*, 84.

91. Moutinho, *Notícia sobre a província de Matto Grosso*, 13–19.

92. See João Martins da Silva Coutinho, "Notícia sobre o uaraná ou guaraná," 10; Moutinho, *Notícia sobre a província de Matto Grosso*, 209–14; Lévi-Strauss, *Tristes Tropiques*, 249. For a more detailed description, see Daniel Belik, "Indigenous Routes," 121–22.

93. João Martins da Silva Coutinho, "Notícia sobre o uaraná ou guaraná," 7; Spruce, "Botanical Objects Communicated to the Kew Museum," 174; Tavares, *O Rio Tapajoz*, 31.

94. Rodrigues, *O Rio Tapajós*, 108.

95. João Martins da Silva Coutinho, "Notícia sobre o uaraná ou guaraná," 10–11.

96. Hoehne, *Plantas e substâncias vegetais tóxicas e medicinais*, 185–86. Revisionist scholarship has questioned the depiction of the helpless Indigenous at the hands of nineteenth-century traders. See Henrique and Morais, "Estradas líquidas, comércio sólido"; Roller, *Contact Strategies*.

97. João Martins da Silva Coutinho, "Notícia sobre o uaraná ou guaraná," 6.

98. *Relatório apresentado à Assembléa Legislativa da província do Amazonas na sessão ordinária do 1º de Outubro de 1864*, 36.

99. Spix and Martius, *Viagem pelo Brasil*, 3:163.

100. Van Valen, *Indigenous Agency in the Amazon*, 59–60; *Relatório com que o Exm. Snr. Dr. Antônio Epaminondas de Mello, presidente da província do Amazonas, entregou a administração da província do Amazonas*, 344.

101. Orton, *Andes and the Amazon*, 270.

102. Keller, *Amazon and Madeira Rivers*, 110–11. See also Mathews, *Up the Amazon and Madeira Rivers*, 16–17.

103. Agassiz and Agassiz, *Journey in Brazil*, 299–305; Mark Harris, *Rebellion on the Amazon*, 61; Van Valen, *Indigenous Agency in the Amazon*, 59–60; Faraco, *Maués*, 32.

104. João Martins da Silva Coutinho, "Relatório apresentado ao Ilm. e Exm. Sr. Dr. Manoel Clementino Carneiro da Cunha," Appendix G, 13.

105. Ângela Domingues, *Viagens de exploração geográfica na Amazônia*, 33–38.

106. Duarte da Ponte Ribeiro, "Considerações sobre o estado precário da província de Matto Grosso," Rio de Janeiro, October 18, 1859, 1ª Comissão Brasileira Demarcadora dos Limites Archive and Library, Coleção Ponte Ribeiro, A73.

107. Sousa Neto, *Planos para o Império*.

108. Bastos, *O vale do Amazonas*, 298–301. Brazil's suspicion toward neighboring countries is discussed in Luis Claudio Villafane Gomes Santos, *O Brasil entre a América e a Europa*.

109. Moraes, *Navegação interior do Brasil*, 38, 49–50.

110. See Magnoli, *O corpo da pátria*, 111–12; Reis, *História do Amazonas*, 211–15.

111. Kelerson Semerene Costa, "Intervenções humanas na natureza amazônica," 92–93.

112. Chambouleyron, "Cacao, Bark-Clove and Agriculture in the Portuguese Amazon Region"; Mark Harris, *Rebellion on the Amazon*, 133–41.

113. Penna, *Falla dirigida á Assembléa Legislativa Provincial do Amazonas, no dia 1º de outubro de 1853*, 41–43.

114. Amazonas, *Dicionário topográfico, histórico, descritivo*, 32–33, 44; João Martins da Silva Coutinho, "Breve notícia sobre a extracção da salsa e da seringa"; Reis, *História do Amazonas*, 226–27. On food imports, see also Robin L. Anderson, *Colonization as Exploitation in the Amazon Rainforest*.

115. Reis, *História do Amazonas*, 227; *Relatório apresentado ao Exmo. Sr. Dr. Agesilão Pereira da Silva*, 35; José Coelho da Gama e Abreu, *A Amazônia*, 9.

116. See, for example, *Relatório apresentado à Assembléa Legislativa Rovincial* [sic], *pelo excellentíssimo senhor doutor João Pedro Dias Vieira*, 9. For a broader discussion, see Weinstein, *Amazon Rubber Boom*.

117. *Relatório com que o Exm. Sr. Dr. Antônio Epaminondas de Mello, presidente da província do Amazonas, entregou a administração da província do Amazonas*, 320–21. Reis, *História do Amazonas*, 203; João Martins da Silva Coutinho, "Breve notícia sobre a extracção da salsa e da seringa."

118. Amazonas, *Dicionário topográfico, histórico, descritivo*, 32–33.

119. See the description of Serpa [Itacoatiara] from the 1850s in Bates, *Naturalist on the River Amazons*, 182–83; João Martins da Silva Coutinho, "Relatório apresentado ao Ilm. e Exm. Sr. Dr. Manoel Clementino Carneiro da Cunha," Appendix G, 1–2.

120. Coutinho, "Exploração do Amazonas: Offícios do Dr. S. Coutinho," 15.

121. João Martins da Silva Coutinho, "Breve notícia sobre a extracção da salsa e da seringa"; Kelerson Semerene Costa, "Intervenções humanas na natureza amazônica," 90–93;

Jardim, Fernandes, and Fonseca, "Silva Coutinho," 459; Reis, *História do Amazonas*, 226–27. See also Pádua, *Um sopro de destruição*, 204–6.

122. João Martins da Silva Coutinho, "Breve notícia sobre a extracção da salsa e da seringa."

123. João Martins da Silva Coutinho, "Notícia sobre o uaraná ou guaraná," 12.

124. João Martins da Silva Coutinho, "Relatório apresentado ao Ilm. e Exm. Sr. Dr. Manoel Clementino Carneiro da Cunha," Appendix G, 20.

125. João Martins da Silva Coutinho, "Relatório da exploração do Rio Purus," 86.

126. "Exploração do Amazonas: Officios do Dr. S. Coutinho," 5.

127. João Martins da Silva Coutinho, "Notícia sobre o uaraná ou guaraná," 12.

128. Orton, *Andes and the Amazon*, 334.

129. João Martins da Silva Coutinho, "Relatório apresentado ao Ilm. e Exm. Sr. Dr. Manoel Clementino Carneiro da Cunha," Appendix G, 16–21; Nunes, "O 'valor' das terras amazônicas no século XIX."

130. João Martins da Silva Coutinho, "Relatório da exploração do Rio Purus."

131. João Martins da Silva Coutinho, "Notícia sobre o uaraná ou guaraná," 12.

132. Kelerson Semerene Costa, "Intervenções humanas na natureza amazônica," 94.

133. Reis, *História do Amazonas*, 230–32; Agassiz and Agassiz, *Journey in Brazil*, 268–69, 281, 287–91. An earlier description of state coercion is found in Spruce, *Notes of a Botanist on the Amazon and Andes*, 294. On impressment more generally, see Beattie, *Tribute of Blood*.

134. Agassiz and Agassiz, *Journey in Brazil*, 269.

135. Pádua, *Um sopro de destruição*, 204–6; "Dr. João Martins da Silva Coutinho," *Revista do Clube de Engenharia* 14 (1906): 9. On commercial agriculture's links to settler colonialism, see Wolfe, "Settler Colonialism and the Elimination of the Native."

136. On nature and state captures on the frontier, see Andermann, *Optic of the State*, 127.

137. Moraes, *Navegação interior do Brasil*, 35.

138. Kodama, "Os estudos etnográficos no Instituto Histórico e Geográfico Brasileiro"; Moreira, "O ofício do historiador e os índios."

139. Schuster, "'Brazilian Native' on Display."

140. See Kern, "'Amazonian Idol.'"

141. Heloisa M. Bertol Domingues, "As ciências naturais e a construção da nação brasileira," 41–60.

142. See Roller, *Contact Strategies*; Miki, *Frontiers of Citizenship*.

143. Spix and Martius, *Viagem pelo Brasil*, 3:137–38. See also John Manuel Monteiro, "As 'raças' indígenas no pensamento brasileiro do império," 15–22.

144. Cunha, *Índios no Brasil: história, direitos, e cidadania*, 64.

145. Henrique, "Sobre a (in)visibilidade dos índios da Amazônia."

146. Cunha, *Índios no Brasil*, 63–70.

147. *Relatório que a Assembléa Legislativa Provincial do Amazonas apresentou na abertura da sessão ordinária em o dia 7 de Setembro de 1858 Francisco José Furtado*, 22.

148. "Discurso pronunciado pelo Exmo Sr. Deputado Bernardo de Souza Franco na Sessão da Câmara Geral Legislativa de 4 de junho deste ano," reprinted in *Treze de Maio*, November 14, 1840.

149. *Relatório apresentado à Assembléa Legislativa da província do Amazonas na sessão ordinária do 10 de outubro de 1864, pelo Dr. Adolfo de Barros Cavalcanti de Albuquerque Lacerda,* 36.

150. *Relatório com que o Exm. Snr. Dr. Antônio Epaminondas de Mello, presidente da província do Amazonas, entregou a administração da província do Amazonas,* 333.

151. Bastos, *O vale do Amazonas,* 294–95.

152. Tavares, *O Rio Tapajoz,* 35–36.

153. Rodrigues, *O Rio Tapajós,* 110–11; Rodrigues, "Extracto de um livro inédito," 151–52; Mori and Ferreira, "Distinguished Brazilian Botanist," 73–85.

154. Andermann, *Optic of the State,* 58–85.

155. João Martins da Silva Coutinho, "Relatório da exploração do Rio Purus," 80–82.

156. João Martins da Silva Coutinho, "Notícia sobre o uaraná ou guaraná," 7.

157. "Exploração do Amazonas: Offícios do Dr. S. Coutinho," 5.

158. Magalhães, *O selvagem,* 56–57, 75–76; Henrique, "O soldado-civilizador"; Borges, Medina, and Monteiro, "Ciência, imaginário e civilização em Couto de Magalhães."

159. João Martins da Silva Coutinho, "Notícia sobre o uaraná ou guaraná," 12–13.

160. Fausto and Heckenberger, introduction, 1, 13; Jonathan Hill, introduction, 5–7.

161. I am borrowing here from Alfredo Cordiviola's discussion of Andre Rebouças, Euclides da Cunha, Silvio Romero, and Nina Rodrigues in *Richard Burton: A Traveller in Brazil,* 289.

162. "Exploração do Amazonas: Offícios do Dr. S. Coutinho," 5.

163. Marcou, *Life, Letters, and Works of Louis Agassiz,* 150–51.

164. Agassiz and Agassiz, *Journey in Brazil,* 304–5.

165. João Martins da Silva Coutinho, "Notícia sobre o uaraná ou guaraná," 7.

166. João Martins da Silva Coutinho, "Notícia sobre o uaraná ou guaraná."

167. João Martins da Silva Coutinho, *Relatório da Comissão Brasileira apresentado ao Exm. S. Conselheiro Thomas José Coelho de Almeida,* 21–27, 99.

168. Abreu, *A Amazônia,* 60.

169. Chandless, "Visit to the India-Rubber Groves of the Amazons," 219; Van Valen, *Indigenous Agency in the Amazon,* 67–68.

170. Rodrigues, *O Rio Tapajós,* 110.

171. Coudreau, *Viagem ao Tapajós,* 44.

172. Lévi-Strauss, *Tristes Tropiques,* 249–50.

173. Sousa Neto, *Planos para o império.*

174. See Cribelli, *Industrial Forests and Mechanical Marvels.*

175. Rodrigues, *O Rio Tapajós,* 110.

176. Rodrigues, *O Rio Tapajós,* 108–11.

177. Daniel Belik, "Indigenous Routes," 156.

178. *Vultos da geografia do Brasil,* 89–91.

Chapter Four

1. Testimonies of Ernest L. Harris and George A. Seyfarth in Sonnedecker, Cowen, and Higby, *Drugstore Memories,* 119, 137.

2. Gabriel, "Thing Patented Is a Thing Divulged," 141.

3. Courtwright, *Forces of Habit.*

4. The most comprehensive study to date is Beaufort, "La mercatique transatlantique d'un végétal psychoactif."

5. Estes, "Pharmacology of Nineteenth-Century Patent Medicines," 4–5.

6. See Parke, Davis & Company, *Pharmacology of the Newer Materia Medica,* 769.

7. Francis F. Brown, "Sick Headache," *Canada Medical Record* 13, no. 7 (April 1885): 158.

8. See Beard, *American Nervousness,* 96; Greenway, "'Nervous Disease' and Electric Medicine," 56, 70; Gijswijt-Hofstra, introduction, 24; Furst, *Before Freud,* 36.

9. Greenway, "'Nervous Disease' and Electric Medicine," 56; Campbell, *Neurasthenia,* 1.

10. Gijswijt-Hofstra, introduction.

11. "Fluid Extract Guaraná," *Chicago Medical Journal and Examiner* 31, no. 12 (December 1874), n.p.

12. "Sick Headache! Neuralgia! Grimault & Co.'s Guaraná," *Otago Daily Times,* September 22, 1882; "Grimault & Co. Pharmaceutical Chemists," *Northern Territory Times and Gazette,* May 19, 1883.

13. See ads in *Canada Medical Record* 12, no. 12 (1884); *St. Louis Medical and Surgical Journal* 42, no. 6 (1882); Wyeth Laboratories, *Epitome of Therapeutics,* 12.

14. Saxe, *Saxe's New Guide, or Hints to Soda Water Dispensers,* ad preceding index (n.p.).

15. "The Secret of a Clear Head: Bromo-Caffeine for Bain Workers," https://collections.nlm.nih.gov/bookviewer?PID=nlm:nlmuid-101512753-bk.

16. "Testimony of Dr. Seabury W. Bowen in the Trial of Lizzie Borden," Famous Trials, Douglas O. Linde, June 8, 1893, www.famous-trials.com/lizzieborden/1449-bowentestimony.

17. "Publisher's notes," *Therapeutic Gazette* 2, no. 1 (January 1878): 26.

18. "Lloyd Brothers Specific Medicines," *Eclectic Medical Journal* 47, no. 6 (June 1887): 248.

19. See Samuel G. Pond & Cia. to Lanman & Kemp, Pará, September 6, 1877; December 3, 1877; and February 25, 1878, Hagley Museum and Library (HML), Lanman & Kemp Records (LK), box 25; and José Amando Mendes to Lanman & Kemp, Pará, November 27, 1877, HML, LK, box 21; John Wyeth & Brother to Lanman & Kemp, Philadelphia, October 25, 1877, HML, LK, box 38.

20. "Review of the Drug Market," *Chemist and Druggist* 31 (October 1887): 465.

21. "An American Drug-Collector: A Chat with Professor H.H. Rusby, New York," *Chemist and Druggist* 42–43 (July 1893): 12–14.

22. Philemon E. Hommell, "Comments on U.S. Pharmacopoeia and National Formulary Drugs and Preparations," *Practical Druggist* 38 (May 1920): 23–24.

23. Topik and Wells, *Second Conquest of Latin America;* Bulmer-Thomas, *Economic History of Latin America;* Prado Júnior, *História econômica do Brasil.*

24. João Martins da Silva Coutinho, *Relatório da Comissão Brazileira apresentado ao Exm. S. Conselheiro Thomas José Coelho de Almeida,* 99.

25. McTavish, *Pain and Profits,* 28.

26. Sivulka, *Soap, Sex and Cigarettes,* 38; Courtwright, *Forces of Habit.*

27. McTavish, *Pain and Profits,* 38.

28. McTavish, *Pain and Profits,* 34.

29. Breen, *Age of Intoxication,* 83.

30. Schiebinger and Swan, introduction, 2.

31. Walker, "Acquisition and Circulation of Medical Knowledge."

32. Osseo-Asare, *Bitter Roots*, 108–9.

33. Clément, "Historical Foundations of Ethnobiology"; Arnold, introduction, 11–17; Headrick, *Tentacles of Progress*; Hobsbawm, *Age of Empire*; Rodgers, *American Botany*, 314–15; Raby, *American Tropics*.

34. Harshberger, "Purposes of Ethno-Botany," 146–54.

35. Soejarto and Farnsworth, "Tropical Rain Forests," 245.

36. Rottenburg and Merry, "World of Indicators," 5–16.

37. Renn and Hyman, introduction, 24.

38. Rosenberg, *No Other Gods*, 1–4.

39. Van der Geest, Whyte, and Hardon, "Anthropology of Pharmaceuticals," 170–71.

40. Sherratt, introduction, 3–4; Montagne, "Pharmakon Phenomenon," 13; Schivelbusch, *Tastes of Paradise*.

41. Risse, "Road to Twentieth-Century Therapeutics," 51–52.

42. Schiebinger, *Plants and Empire*, 204.

43. Parascandola, "Alkaloids to Arsenicals," 80–81; Lesch, "Conceptual Change in an Empirical Science," 310–15, 324.

44. Hornborg, "Animism, Fetishism, and Objectivism," 21–32; Rottenburg and Merry, "World of Indicators"; Breen, *Age of Intoxication*, 82.

45. Breitbach et al., "Amazonian Medicinal Plants Described by C.F.P. von Martius," 180–89; Martius, *Systema de materia medica vegetal brasileira*.

46. Ormindo, "Imagens para a ciência," 67–76.

47. Karl von Martius, "Sobre algumas drogas brasileiras," translated by Oswaldo Riedel, *Revista da Flora Medicinal* 7 (April 1936): 439–45.

48. Lisboa, *A Nova Atlântida de Spix e Martius*.

49. Martius, *Systema de materia medica vegetal brasileira*, 18–19, 27–31, 36–37.

50. See Lisboa, *A Nova Atlântida de Spix e Martius*; Márcia Moisés Ribeiro, *A ciência dos trópicos*, 135–36.

51. Brunk, "Philosophical and Ethical Issues," 162–66.

52. Schimpl et al., "Guaraná," 15.

53. Schiebinger, *Plants and Empire*, 218–21; Schiebinger and Swan, "Introduction," 2–3.

54. Schiebinger and Swan, introduction, 8; Mukharji, "Vishalyakarani as *Eupatorium ayapana*."

55. Clément, "Historical Foundations of Ethnobiology," 161–87. More broadly, see Adas, *Machines as the Measure of Men*.

56. Jaszi and Woodmansee, "Beyond Authorship."

57. Adolpho Ducke, "Diversidade dos Guaranás," *Rodriguésia* 3, no. 10 (1937): 155–56; Schmidt, *O guaraná*, 7.

58. Ducke, "Diversidade dos Guaranás," 155–56; Pires, "Guaraná e Cupana."

59. Estes, "Therapeutic Crisis of the Eighteenth Century," 31–32; Schiebinger, *Plants and Empire*, 166.

60. Martius, *Systema de materia medica vegetal brasileira*, 132–34.

61. *Yearbook of Pharmacy 1871*, 41–42; Schimpl et al., "Guaraná," 17.

62. Henman, "Guaraná," 315; Weinberg and Bealer, *World of Caffeine*, xvii–xix.

63. See Beaufort, "La mercatique transatlantique d'un vegetal psychoactif."

64. Spruce, "Botanical Objects Communicated to the Kew Museum," 174.

65. Santos, Pinto, and Alencastro, "Theodoro Peckolt," 666–70.

66. "Sapindaceae," *Proceedings of the American Pharmaceutical Association at the Sixteenth Annual Meeting* (Philadelphia: Merrihew & Son, 1869), 181, https://archive.org/stream /proceedingsamero5meetgoog/proceedingsamero5meetgoog_djvu.txt.

67. In contemporary studies, the caffeine-bearing plants are routinely lumped together. See, for example, Weckerle, Timbul, and Blumenshine, "Medicinal, Stimulant, and Ritual Plant Use."

68. Sherratt, introduction, 1.

69. Hugh-Jones, "Coca, Beer, Cigars, and Yagé," 47.

70. Samuel Wilks, "Guaraná: A Remedy for Sick Headache," *British Medical Journal* 1, no. 590 (April 1872): 421; Wilks, *Lectures on Diseases of the Nervous System*, 433; Samuel Wilks, "Guaraná," *Lancet* 100 (October 1872): 507.

71. *Bulletin of the Lloyd Library*, 48. For nineteenth-century scientific investigation and marketing of guaraná in France, see Beaufort, "La mercatique transatlantique d'un vegetal psychoactif."

72. "Grimault & Co. Pharmaceutical Products," *St. Louis Medical Reporter* 4, no. 4 (June 1869).

73. A. H. Kollmyer, "Lecture Read before the Medico-Chirurgical Society of Montreal, June 4, 1875," *Canada Medical Record* 3 (August 1874–July 1875): 555–59.

74. Brito et al., "Exchange of Useful Plants between Brazil and England," 1–10; Glaziou to Thiselton-Dyer, Rio de Janeiro, November 23, 1878, Royal Botanic Gardens, Kew (RBG), Director's Correspondence (DC), 215/92.

75. William T. Thiselton-Dyer to Leister, Royal Gardens Kew, February 13, 1893; Royal Botanical Garden Seebpore, near Calcutta, to Thiselton-Dyer, January 13, 1893; "Proceedings of the Agri. Horti. Society of India, January–March 1893; Edward Grey, October 10, 1893; Hugh Wyndham to Earl of Roseberry, Rio de Janeiro, June 7, 1893; Brocklehurst & Co. to Wyndham, Manaus, September 22, 1893; Royal Kew Garden to Edward Grey, November 25, 1893, RBG, Brazil, Cultural Products etc., 1852–1908.

76. Henry Trimen to Daniel Morris, Peradeniya, Ceylon, April 3, 1894, KG, DC, 163/210.

77. E. D. Ewen, "Some Economic Plants and their Planting Prospects," *Journal of the Trinidad Field Naturalists' Club* 2, no. 12 (February 1896): 294–97.

78. "Guaraná," *O panorama* 1, no. 2 (1842): 178–79; Walker, "Establishing Cacao Plantation Culture in the Atlantic World."

79. U.S. Department of Agriculture, Bureau of Plant Industry, *Inventory of Seeds and Plants Imported by the Office of Foreign Seed and Plant Introduction during the Period from July 1 to September 30, 1922*, 3; U.S. Department of Agriculture, Bureau of Plant Industry, *Inventory of Seeds and Plants Imported by the Office of Foreign Seed and Plant Introduction during the Period from October 1 to December 31, 1918*, 43. On Fairchild, see Gollner, *Fruit-Hunters*.

80. "Agreement between Norman Taylor and Law Voge," October 25, 1928; Taylor to Voge, January 12, 1929; Norman Taylor to George Merck, June 1, 1933; Norman Taylor to Eric [?], October 4, 1939; R. W. de Greeff to Taylor, New York, February 1, 1944, and March 8, 1944; "Guaraná: Report on the Availability, Prices, Production, and Cultivation of Guaraná as found in Brazil," March 1944; Taylor, "Guaraná (*Paullinia cupana*): Preliminary Report," July 24, 1944; and Taylor, "Guaraná: Supplementary Report," August 3, 1944, New York

Botanical Garden (NYBG), Norman Taylor Papers (NTP), File *Paullinia cupana* (Guaraná), 1912–44.

81. Beinart and Middleton, "Plant Transfers in Historical Perspective."

82. Quoted in Liebenau, *Medical Science and Medical Industry*, 11.

83. Liebenau, *Medical Science and Medical Industry*, 45; Hoefle, "Early History of Parke-Davis," 29.

84. Parke, Davis & Company, *Pharmacology of the Newer Materia Medica*, iii.

85. McTavish, *Pain and Profits*, 46–47; Liebenau, *Medical Science and Medical Industry*, 6–8.

86. W. H. Rouse, "New Remedies," *Therapeutic Gazette* 1, no. 1 (1880): 4–6.

87. Parke, Davis & Company, *Pharmacology of the Newer Materia Medica*, iii.

88. Kingsland, *Evolution of American Ecology*, 25; "Professor Rusby's Expedition, and the Introduction of Pichi," *Therapeutic Notes* 1, no. 1 (February 1894): 3.

89. "Dr. F. E. Stewart Made the Following Announcement . . . ," n.d., Wisconsin Historical Society (WHS), Francis Edward Stewart Papers (FESP), box 9, folder 3; F. E. Stewart to Edward Mott Wolley, June 25, 1920, WHS, FESP, box 9, folder 2; Parke-Davis to Francis E. Stewart, Detroit, December 15, 1882, WHS, FESP, box 6, folder 9.

90. Gootenberg, *Andean Cocaine*, 24.

91. Kingsland, *Evolution of American Ecology*, 25.

92. Liebenau, *Medical Science and Medical Industry*, 45.

93. Parke, Davis & Company, *Pharmacology of the Newer Materia Medica*, iii.

94. Oreskes, "Objectivity or Heroism?"

95. Rusby, *Jungle Memories*, 99–100; Williams and Fraser, "Henry Hurd Rusby," 273–79.

96. Rusby, *Jungle Memories*, 101.

97. Williams and Fraser, "Henry Hurd Rusby," 273–79; Bender, "Henry Hurd Rusby," 79; Kingsland, *Evolution of American Ecology*, 26; "Syrup Cocillana Compound," *New England Medical Monthly* 27, 1 (1908): x; "A Chat with Prof. H. H. Rusby," *Bulletin of Pharmacy* 7, no. 1 (January 1893): 465; "Twenty-Five Years a Teacher in a College of Pharmacy," *Druggists Circular* 58 (January 1914): 45; Henry H. Rusby, "An Enumeration of the Plants Collected by Dr. H. H. Rusby in South America, 1886–1886," *Bulletin of the Torrey Botanical Club* 27, no. 1 (January 1900): 22–31.

98. H. H. Rusby, "Abstract of a Lecture on Cinchona, Coca, and Guaraná," *Pharmaceutical Record and Weekly Market Review* 8 (March 1888): 69–70.

99. Parke, Davis & Company, *Pharmacology of the Newer Materia Medica*, 766.

100. H. H. Rusby, "On Guaraná," *American Journal of Pharmacy* 60, no. 5 (May 1888): 266–67.

101. Hoefle, "Early History of Parke-Davis," 30; Liebenau, *Medical Science and Medical Industry*, 43.

102. Parke, Davis & Company, *Epitome of the Newer Materia Medica*, 13.

103. Rusby, "The College of Pharmacy of the City of New York," 93; Rossi-Wilcox, "Henry Hurd Rusby," 3–4; Williams and Fraser, "Henry Hurd Rusby," 273–79. See also Courtwright, *Forces of Habit*, 48.

104. Osseo-Asare, *Bitter Roots*, 17.

105. Liebenau, *Medical Science and Medical Industry*, 1, 12, 41, 142.

106. See also Gabriel, "Indian Secrets, Indian Cures."

107. Balick and Cox, *Plants, People, and Culture*, 60.

108. Risse, "Road to Twentieth-Century Therapeutics," 51–52.

109. Parke, Davis & Company, *Pharmacology of the Newer Materia Medica*, iii.

110. S. E. D. Shortt, "Physicians, Science, and Status," 60.

111. Warner, "Science in Medicine," 37–58.

112. Rosenberg, "Therapeutic Revolution."

113. Liebenau, *Medical Science and Medical Industry*, 13.

114. McTavish, *Pain and Profits*, 13–25.

115. McNamara, "Indian Medicine Show," 431–45.

116. Estes, "Therapeutic Crisis of the Eighteenth Century," 45–46; Rosenberg, "Therapeutic Revolution"; McTavish, *Pain and Profits*, 5; W. MacDowall, "Notes on Guaraná," *Practitioner: A Journal of Therapeutics and Public Health* 11 (July–December 1873): 161–75.

117. McTavish, *Pain and Profits*, 4, 49–50; Shortt, "Physicians, Science, and Status," 53.

118. Rosenberg, "Therapeutic Revolution."

119. Shortt, "Physicians, Science, and Status," 57–58.

120. Rosenberg, "Therapeutic Revolution," 498–99.

121. McTavish, *Pain and Profits*, 4.

122. McTavish, *Pain and Profits*, 15–24. See also Estes, "Pharmacology of Nineteenth-Century Patent Medicines," 4.

123. McTavish, *Pain and Profits*, 24; "Valuable Remedy for Headache."

124. Greenway, "'Nervous Disease' and Electric Medicine," 47–73.

125. MacDowall, "Notes on Guaraná," 161–75.

126. Parke, Davis & Company, *Pharmacology of the Newer Materia Medica*, 768.

127. Kollmyer, "Lecture Read before the Medico-Chirurgical Society of Montreal, June 4, 1875."

128. "Guaraná, Chionanthus," *Therapeutic Gazette*, 2, no. 2 (1878): 85–86.

129. Porter, "Patient's View."

130. McTavish, *Pain and Profits*, 44–45, 56; Liebenau, *Medical Science and Medical Industry*, 14, 44.

131. "Agents," *Therapeutic Gazette*, 2, no. 1 (January 1879): 25–26; McTavish, *Pain and Profits*, 48–50.

132. Parke, Davis & Company, *Pharmacology of the Newer Materia Medica*, 769.

133. Bell, *Ritual Theory, Ritual Practice*, 134, 141, 170, 204–5; Rios and Smith, "Function of Drug Rituals."

134. Van der Geest, Whyte, and Hardon, "Anthropology of Pharmaceuticals," 153–78.

135. Whyte, van der Geest, and Hardon, *Social Lives of Medicines*, 121; McTavish, *Pain and Profits*, 21.

136. Rouse, "New Remedies," 4–6.

137. Whyte, van der Geest, and Hardon, *Social Lives of Medicines*, 128.

138. Whyte, van der Geest, and Hardon, *Social Lives of Medicines*, 124.

139. Montagne, "Pharmakon Phenomenon," 11–13.

140. Editorial, *New Remedies* 7 (1878): 161–62; *Irish Hospital Gazette* 3 (1875): 77.

141. Edward R. Squibb, Edward H. Squibb, and Charles F. Squibb, "Guaraná," *An Ephemeris of Materia Medica, Pharmacy, Therapeutics, and Collateral Information* 2, no. 4 (July 1884): 612–16.

142. "Tea, Coffee, Guaraná, and Caffeine, as Therapeutic Agents," *Therapeutic Gazette*, n.s., 5 (1884): 560.

143. *Squibb's Materia Medica*, 67, 115.

144. J. S. Pemberton, "Essay on Guaraná, Caffeine, and Coca," *Proceedings of the Georgia Pharmaceutical Association* 12 (April 1887): 17–21.

145. Lovejoy, "Kola in the History of West Africa."

146. Pendergrast, *For God, Country, and Coca-Cola*; Elmore, *Citizen Coke*.

147. "Guaraná," *Digest of Comments of the Pharmacopoeia of the United States of America*, 406–7.

148. Bliss, "Proposed Vegetable Drug Deletions."

149. W. A. Bastedo, "The National Formulary, Useful Drugs, and the Coming Revision of the Pharmacopoeia," *Journal of the American Medical Association* 74, no. 12 (March 1920): 18–19.

150. McTavish, *Pain and Profits*, 79–85, 164.

151. Tyler, "Recent History of Pharmacognosy," 161–66.

152. Balick and Cox, *Plants, People, and Culture*, 57–58.

153. Headrick, *Tentacles of Progress*.

154. Balick and Cox, *Plants, People, and Culture*, 56–59.

155. "Guaraná," Google Books Ngram Viewer.

Chapter Five

1. João Coelho de Miranda Leão, "O guaraná," *Revista da Associação Comercial do Amazonas* 151 (November 1927): n.p. According to the trade journal, the article was originally published in 1919.

2. On Miranda Leão's biography, see Bittencourt, *Dicionário amazonense de biografias*, 359–62.

3. "Fábrica de bebidas gazosas," *Revista da Associação Comercial do Amazonas*, January 15, 1939.

4. Marchi, *De duas, uma*, 95–96.

5. Arruda, *A história da Fratelli Vita no Recife*.

6. Bittencourt, *Dicionário amazonense de biografias*, 359–62.

7. Norman Taylor to Eric [?], October 4, 1939, NYBG, NTP, File *Paullinia cupana* (Guaraná), 1912–44.

8. A. Accioly Netto, "Teatro no Rio," *O Cruzeiro*, November 20, 1954, 99.

9. Mintz, *Tasting Food, Tasting Freedom*, 24.

10. Ashurst, introduction, 7–8; Taylor, "Ingredients," 23–29. For a historical overview, see Levin, *Soda and Fizzy Drinks*; Emmins, "Soft Drinks."

11. Ashurst, introduction, 5; Montanari, *Food Is Culture*, 105–13.

12. Emmins, "Soft Drinks," 705–6.

13. O'Neill, "History of the Soda Fountain."

14. Emmins, "Soft Drinks," 703.

15. Courtwright, *Forces of Habit*, 10–14.

16. Taylor, "Ingredients," 16–17.

17. Emmins, "Soft Drinks," 709–11; "Secret Science of Soda"; Lea, "Processing and Packaging"; "Veja como é produzido o refrigerante de guaraná."

18. Graham, *Britain and the Onset of Modernization in Brazil*, 112–24.

19. Monteleone, *Sabores urbanos*, 99–102, 128.

20. Monteleone, *Sabores urbanos*, 18–19; Laudan, "Plea for Culinary Modernism," 39.

21. Deaecto, *Comércio e vida urbana na cidade de São Paulo*, 88.

22. Baer, *Brazilian Economy*, 27–29, 39; Deaecto, *Comércio e vida urbana na cidade de São Paulo*, 70.

23. Baer, *Brazilian Economy*, 35.

24. Baer, *Brazilian Economy*, 40; Walter Belik, *Food Industry in Brazil*, 6.

25. Besse, *Restructuring Patriarchy*, 142–43.

26. Henman, "Guaraná," 325–26.

27. Schimpl et al., "Guaraná," 19.

28. Montanari, *Food Is Culture*, 38.

29. Leopoldo de Lima e Silva, "O guaraná," *Revista da Associação Brasileira de Farmacêuticos* 9 (September 1938): 397–406; Galeno Neno, "Resenha Pharmacêutica: Guaraná," *A Gazeta da Farmácia* 2, no. 17 (September 1933): 7; E.A., "Guaraná Estabilizado," *A Gazeta da Farmácia* 3, no. 31 (November 1934): 1.

30. Nascimento, "Monumento a Luiz Pereira Barreto."

31. Barreto, "A higiene da mesa," 15.

32. Marchi, *De duas, uma*, 98–100.

33. Barros, *A evolução do pensamento de Pereira Barreto*, 97–99; "Médico introduz café Bourbon na região," *Folha de São Paulo Ribeirão*, June 19, 2001.

34. Begliomini, "Luiz Pereira Barreto."

35. Alonso, "O postivismo de Luís Pereira Barreto," 1–14.

36. Quoted in Barros, *A evolução do pensamento de Pereira Barreto*, 175.

37. Barros, *A evolução do pensamento de Pereira Barreto*, 32–33.

38. Barreto, "O século XX sob o ponto de vista brasileiro," 38–42; see also Barros, *A evolução do pensamento de Pereira Barreto*, 54, 188–89.

39. Barros, *A evolução do pensamento de Pereira Barreto*, 97–99.

40. Sá, *A ciência como profissão*, 117–39.

41. Quoted in Barros, *A evolução do pensamento de Pereira Barreto*, 243–44.

42. Quoted in Barros, *A evolução do pensamento de Pereira Barreto*, 248.

43. Barreto, "A vinha e a civilização," 14–23; Begliomini, "Luiz Pereira Barreto." See also Oliver, "Debates científicos e a produção do vinho paulista," 3.

44. See Marques, *A cerveja e a cidade*, 25; Monteleone, *Sabores urbanos*, 175–81; Cascudo, *História da alimentação*, 2: 816–17.

45. Luís Pereira Barreto, "A arte de fabricar o vinho," *O Estado de São Paulo*, November 16, 1899.

46. Carone, *A evolução industrial de São Paulo*, 199–20; Marques, *A cerveja e a cidade*, 100.

47. Marques, *A cerveja e a cidade*, 222–35, 242–44.

48. Barreto, "A arte de fabricar o vinho."

49. See Herold, "Ice in the Tropics," 162–77.

50. *Doceiro nacional*, 287–88.

51. Marques, *A cerveja e a cidade*, 150; Deaecto, *Comércio e vida urbana na cidade de São Paulo*, 87–88; Arruda, *A história da Fratelli Vita*, 22.

52. Cascudo, "Esfriando bebidas," 178–79.

53. Arruda, *A história da Fratelli Vita*, 68.

54. Simão, "Modernização e civilização em debate," 12.

55. Abreu, Araujo Júnior, and Cruz, "Painel," 151.

56. Taylor, "Ingredients," 34–35, 41.

57. "O guaraná," *Revista da Associação Comercial do Amazonas*, July 15, 1939.

58. Carneiro, *Bebida, abstinência e temperança*, 249–50; Marques, *A cerveja e a cidade*, 233–34; E. W., "Direito legítimo contra falso 'direito,'" *Boletim da Associação Brasileira de Pharmacêuticos* 5 (May 1930): 23–24; Soihet, *Condição feminina e formas de violência*; Fernando Sérgio Dumas dos Santos, "Alcoolismo."

59. Barreto, "A vinha e a civilização," 14. Luiz Pereira Barreto, "A Policultura no Pará," *O Estado de São Paulo*, January 17, 1899.

60. Barreto, "A higiene da mesa," 19.

61. See, for example, advertisements in *Fon-Fon*, December 9, 1923; "Guaraná Espumante Zanotta," *A Cigarra*, 1925; Marchi, *De duas, uma: A fusão da mesa*, 90; "A função social do guaraná," *A Gazeta da Farmácia* 6, no. 68 (December 1937): 11.

62. Begliomini, "Luiz Pereira Barreto."

63. See "O guaraná começa a ser exportado," *A Gazeta da Farmácia* 5, no. 50 (June 1936): 4; "O guaraná," *Revista da Associação Comercial do Amazonas*, July 15, 1939. On late nineteenth- and early twentieth-century Brazilian physicians' engagement with global trends in medicine, see Sá, *A ciência como profissão*, 107–42.

64. Morley, "Brief History of Geriatrics," 1133.

65. Masô, "O guaraná," 143–52; "O uso do guaraná," *A Gazeta da Farmácia* 3, no. 30 (October 1934): 15; "Guaraná," *Almanaque brasileiro Garnier para o ano 1912*, 120–21.

66. Ludwig, *Brazil: A Handbook of Historical Statistics*, 85; Cytrynowicz and Cytrynowicz, *Indústria Farmacêutica no Brasil*, 4.

67. See the biography by his son, Elir Jesus Gomes, *Jesus: sua vida, seu sonho*; Scarpin, "Cinema, guaraná e comunista"; Previdelli, "O ateu, com fama de comunista, que inventou o Guaraná Jesus."

68. Guimarães, *Civilizando as artes de curar*, 110.

69. I am borrowing here from Guimarães, *Civilizando as artes de curar*, 109–10, and Figueiredo, "O arranjo das drogas nas boticas e farmácias mineiras."

70. Elir Jesus Gomes, *Jesus*, 46–47.

71. See Edler, *Boticas & pharmácias*, 114.

72. Dietz, *Soda Pop*, 15.

73. Elir Jesus Gomes, *Jesus*, 29.

74. "10ª Sessão Literária em 24 de setembro de 1851," *Revista Pharmacêutica* 1, no. 5 (November 1851): 73–75.

75. Guimarães, *Civilizando as artes de curar*, 28, 59.

76. Chernoviz, *Formulário ou guia médico*, 319. The guide went through nineteen Portuguese-language editions between 1842 and 1924.

77. Matta, *Flora médica brasiliense*, 17, 143–44.

78. See the advertisements in *Jornal da moças*, August 6, 1925.

79. Holanda, *Caminhos e fronteiras*, 110–11.

80. Elir Jesus Gomes, *Jesus*, 32.

81. Ricardo Ramos, "1500–1930," 1–6.

82. See Temporão, *A propaganda de medicamentos e o mito da saúde*; Mario Luiz Gomes, "Vendendo saúde! Revisando os antigos almanaques de farmácia"; Edison Veiga, "O Biotônico Fontoura e o Monteiro Lobato," *Veja São Paulo*, September 18, 2009.

83. "A flora medicinal brasileira," *Revista da Flora Medicinal* 1 (October 1934): 23.

84. "O guaraná e a longevidade" *A Gazeta da Farmácia* 14, no. 165 (January 1946): 15.

85. "A função social do guaraná," 11; Arthur Simon, "Guaraná-Football," *A Gazeta da Farmácia* 7, no. 82 (February 1939): 8.

86. See, for example, F. C. Hoehne, "A necessidade de uma flora brasileira," *Revista Brazilea* 1 (1917): 5–10. I thank Dominichi Miranda de Sá for this reference.

87. For nineteenth-century Brazil, see Sampaio, *Nas trincheiras da cura.*

88. See Roth, *Miscarriage of Justice*, 41.

89. Borges, "Healing and Mischief," 190.

90. R. Freitas, "Rumo à flora brasileira" *A Gazeta da Farmácia* 8, no. 87 (July 1939): 9.

91. "O guaraná e suas propriedades," *A Gazeta da Farmácia* 14, no. 167 (March 1946): 8.

92. Jayme Pecegueiro Gomes da Cruz, "1ª Conferência Brasileira de Proteção à Natureza: proteção às plantas medicinais," *Revista da Flora Medicinal* 1 (October 1934): 4–21.

93. Franco and Drummond, *Proteção à natureza e identidade nacional no Brasil.*

94. "A flora medicinal brasileira," 24; Virgílio Lucas, "Conceito moderno da fitoterapia," *Revista da Associação Brasileira de Farmacêuticos* 18, no. 11 (November 1937): 492. See also Oswaldo de Almeida Costa, "Da necessidade de incrementar-se o estudo e o uso das plantas medicinaes brasileiras" *A Gazeta da Farmácia* 95 (March 1940): 1, 4.

95. "O guaraná e a longevidade," 15.

96. See Crane, "Can We Save the Charismatic Megaflora?"; Hall, James, and Baird, "Forests and Trees as Charismatic Mega-Flora."

97. Lucas, "Conceito moderno da fitoterapia," 490–97.

98. "O brasileiro adora tomar injeções," *Publicidade & Negócios* 13, no. 180 (March 1953): 6–7.

99. Tania Maria Fernandes, "Medicamentos no Brasil," 119–24.

100. Borrás, *Plantas da Amazônia.*

101. Lucio Alves, "Produção de fitoterápicos no Brasil," 452–53, 502; Freitas, *A estrutura do mercado guaraná de fitoterápicos.* See also Fernandes, *Plantas medicinais.*

102. Angelita Cristine Melo, "Pharmacy in Brazil," 381–90.

103. Previdelli, "O ateu, com fama de comunista, que inventou o Guaraná Jesus."

104. See José Lindoso, "Da indústria extrativa na economia amazonense," *Boletim da Associação Comercial do Amazonas* 6, no. 72 (July 1947): 50–52; "O progresso das indústrias amazonenses," *Revista da Associação Comercial do Amazonas* 12, no. 155–56 (April 1928); Eugene Aubert, "O problema do guaraná," *Revista da Associação Comercial do Amazonas* 199 (July 1933).

105. See *Estatutos de Consórcio de Guaraná organizado entre produtores e comerciantes manipuladores*; "Fixação do preço mínimo do guaraná," *Revista da Associação Comercial do Amazonas* 227 (November 1935).

106. *Estatutos de Consórcio de Guaraná*; Silva, "O guaraná," 397–406. On the biographical data, see Faraco, *Maués.*

107. Emmi, "Raízes italianas no desenvolvimento da Amazônia," 53–54, 76.

108. Faraco, *Maués*, 160; Emmi, "Raízes italianas no desenvolvimento da Amazônia," 168–69.

109. Faraco, *Maués*, 180–82; "Problemas da economia amazonense," *Boletim da Associação Comercial do Amazonas* 84 (July 1948): 11.

110. See Yamada, "Japanese Immigrant Agroforestry in the Brazilian Amazon"; Homma, Freitas, and Ferreira, "As concessões de terras para os japoneses na Amazônia na década de 1920," 135–63.

111. José Avelino Menezes Cardoso, "O guaraná," *Revista da Associação Comercial do Amazonas* 12, nos. 155–56 (April 1928).

112. "O amanhecer em Cuiabá," *O Matto-Grosso* 39, no. 2102 (May 1928). See a similar description in Corrêa and Pena, *Dicionário das plantas úteis do Brasil*, 554.

113. "Postaes," *O Matto-Grosso*, March 23, 1930; Firmo Rodrigues, "O guaraná," *A Cruz: Órgão da Liga do Bom Jesus*, July 28, 1940, 2; Firmo Rodrigues, "O guaraná e o sal," *A Cruz: Órgão da Liga do Bom Jesus*, June 6, 1943, 2; Rodrigues, "O guaraná."

114. José de Mesquita, "O guaraná," *A Cruz: Órgão da Liga Catolica da Archidiocese* 35, no. 1650 (October 1944): 1.

115. "A propaganda do guaraná," *Revista da Associação Comercial do Amazonas* 189 (December 1932); "O guaraná," *Revista da Associação Comercial do Amazonas* 195 (March 1933). See the column in *Revista da Associação Comercial do Amazonas* 265 (January 1939), and "Problemas da Amazônia," *Boletim da Associação Comercial do Amazonas* 50 (September 1945): 12–13.

116. "A aplicação do guaraná nas bebidas gazosas," *Revista da Associação Comercial do Amazonas* 235 (July 1936).

117. Cardoso, "O guaraná"; Cook and Crang, "World on a Plate."

118. "O guarana nos desarranjos intestinaes e sua relação com a luta contra a velhice," *Revista da Associação Comercial do Amazonas* 238 (October 1936).

119. See Benjamin Lima's biography in Bittencourt, *Dicionário amazonense de biografias*, 130–34.

120. Simon, "Guaraná-Football," 8.

121. Cosme Ferreira Filho, "O guaraná," *Boletim da Associação Comercial do Amazonas* 7, no. 78 (January 1948): 3–7.

122. "Guaraná vs. Coca-Cola: como vender nos Estados Unidos," *Boletim da Associação Comercial do Amazonas* 132 (July 1952): 43–44.

123. Cardoso, "O guaraná."

124. Lindoso, "Da indústria extrativa na economia amazonense," 50–52.

125. "Problemas da economia amazonense," *Boletim da Associação Comercial do Amazonas* 84 (July 1948): 11.

126. Nunes Pereira, *Panorama da alimentação indígena*, 198–99.

127. "Maués foi incluida no systema de escalas da Panair do Brasil," *Revista da Associação Comercial do Amazonas* 241 (January 1937).

128. Edith Ewerton de Almeida, *Guaraná*, 13.

129. Silva, "O guaraná," 404. See also Albuquerque, *Da chímica bromatológica do guaraná*.

130. M. B. Lira, "Aspectos bromatológicos do guaraná," *Boletim da Associação Comercial do Amazonas* 6, no. 62 (September 1946): 18–21.

131. Jayme P. Gomes da Cruz, "Do commércio e da regulamentação das plantas medicinaes no Brasil," *A Gazeta da Farmácia,* June 1, 1932, 2.

132. Othon Machado, "Contribuição ao estudo das plantas medicinais do Brasil—o guaraná," *Rodriguésia* 10, no. 20 (December 1946).

133. "Guaranás de guarara," *A Gazeta da Farmácia* 13, no. 144 (April 1944): 17; "A função social do guaraná," 11.

134. Jayme Pecegueiro Gomes da Cruz, "1ª Conferência Brasileira de Proteção à Natureza," 14.

135. Amando Mendes, *Amazônia econômica,* 183–89; Lira, "Aspectos bromatológicos do guaraná," 18–21.

136. "A defesa do guaraná," *Revista da Associação Comercial do Amazonas* 198 (June 1933); "Guaraná: Primeiro Congresso Brasileiro de Bromatologia," *Boletim da Associação Comercial do Amazonas* 5, no. 59 (June 1946): 12–15; Ferreira Filho, "O guaraná," 3–7; Batista, *O complexo da Amazônia,* 208–10.

137. See "Indicador da exportação guaraná," *Revista da Associação Comercial do Amazonas* 265 (January 1939); Eugene Aubert, "Guaraná estabilizado," *A Gazeta da Farmácia* 31 (November 1934): 1; "O guaraná como elixir de longa vida," *Revista da Associação Comercial do Amazonas* 229 (January 1936).

138. Eugene Aubert, "A proteção legal de guaraná," *Revista da Associação Comercial do Amazonas* 207 (March 1934).

139. Henman, "Guaraná," 316, 334.

140. Lira, "Aspectos bromatológicos do guaraná," 18–21; Costa, "A indústria do guaraná no Amazonas," 93–103.

141. "O guaraná," *A Gazeta da Farmácia* 13, no. 145 (May 1944): 21.

142. "Guaraná: Primeiro Congresso Brasileiro de Bromatologia," 12–15.

143. Francisco de Albuquerque, "Da chimica bromatológica do guaraná," *Chimica bromatológica, chimica taxicólogica e chimica legal: actas e trabalhos* 6 (1937?): 93–113, reissued by *Revista da Flora Medicinal,* copy located in NYBG, NT, File Paullinia Cupana (Guaraná), 1912–44; Maravalhas, *Estudos sobre o guaraná e outras plantas produtoras de cafeína,* 13–16; "Guaraná rótulo e guaraná de verdade," *Boletim da Associação Comercial do Amazonas* 41 (December 1944); "Guaraná: Primeiro Congresso Brasileiro de Bromatologia," 12–15.

144. Sá Peixoto, "O problema da aplicação do guaraná," *Boletim da Associação Comercial do Amazonas* 7, no. 84 (July 1948): 26–28.

145. "Guaraná: Primeiro Congresso Brasileiro de Bromatologia," 12–15.

146. "Guaraná versus Coca-Cola," *A Gazeta da Farmácia* 17, no. 192 (April 1948): 28.

147. "Guaraná: Primeiro Congresso Brasileiro de Bromatologia," 12–15; Peixoto, "O problema da aplicação do guaraná," 26–28.

148. "Palavra do presidente," *Revista ABIR 2019/2020,* 6, https://abir.org.br/abir/wp-content/uploads/2020/03/revista-abir-2020.pdf.

149. Lira, "Aspectos bromatológicos do guaraná," 18–21; "Guaraná: Primeiro Congresso Brasileiro de Bromatologia," 12–15.

150. Costa, "A indústria do guaraná no Amazonas," 93–103.

151. "Estação experimental da cultura do guaraná," *Boletim da Associação Comerical do Amazonas* 6, no. 69 (April 1947): 10.

152. A. de Miranda Bastos, "Guaraná e guaranás," *Diário de Pernambuco* (July 24, 1960).

153. Toscano, "Yes, nós temos Coca-Cola," 266–67.

154. Roosevelt Garcia, "Dez curiosidades sobre a Tubaína," *Veja São Paulo*, September 26, 2017, https://vejasp.abril.com.br/blog/memoria/dez-curiosidades-sobre-a-tubaina/; Gertner, Gertner, and Guthery, "Coca-Cola's Marketing Challenges in Brazil," 239.

155. Monteiro, *Antropogeografia do guaraná*, 21.

156. Nazaré and Figueiredo, *Contribuição ao estudo do guaraná*.

157. See the testimony by Orlando de Araújo, the former Antarctica executive, in Juliana Almeida, *Saberes e fazeres*, 50; Marchi, *De duas, uma*, 96, 101; Homma, "Guaraná," 307.

158. Meurer-Grimes, Berkov, and Beck, "Theobromine, Theophylline, and Caffeine," 293–301.

159. Costa, "A indústria do guaraná no Amazonas," 93–103.

160. Pilcher, "Embodied Imagination in Recent Writings on Food History."

161. "Indústria nacional de bebidas a procura de novos mercados," *Indústria e Mercados* 6 (May 1961): 2–3.

162. Marchi, *De duas, uma*, 104.

163. Walter Belik, *Food Industry in Brazil*, 6, 30.

164. Cruz, *Fabricação de refrigerantes*, 3; Silva, "Eu vi os supermercados nascerem," 278–85.

165. Goodman and Redclift, *Refashioning Nature*, 44.

166. Mintz, *Tasting Food, Tasting Freedom*, 14, 17.

Chapter Six

1. Orlando Criscuolo, "Anilda, o grande amor de Chico Viola," *O Cruzeiro* 16 (April 15, 1980): 30–33.

2. "Cerveja 'Malte' de Antarctica," *A Cigarra* 12 (1924), n.p.; Suk, "'Only the Fragile Sex Admitted.'"

3. Woodard, *Brazil's Revolution in Commerce*, 74.

4. Certeau, Giard, and Mayol, *Practice of Everyday Life*, 185; Montanari, *Food Is Culture*, 110.

5. Montanari, *Food Is Culture*, 17.

6. Important recent works include Monteleone, *Sabores urbanos*; Toscano, "Yes, nós temos Coca-Cola"; Rosa Belluzzo, *Nem garfo, nem faca*; Macêdo, "A cozinha mestiça"; Teresa Cristina Novaes Marques, *A cerveja e a cidade do Rio de Janeiro*.

7. Adapted from Certeau, *Practice of Everyday Life*, 189–90.

8. Woodard, *Brazil's Revolution in Commerce*, 24–68; McCann, *Hello, Hello Brazil*, 217–22.

9. McCann, *Hello, Hello Brazil*, 224; Owensby, *Intimate Ironies*; Serviço "X," São Paulo, January 1943 IBOPE. Arquivo Edgard Leuenroth (AEL), IBOPE Serviço X (SX), SX 001–015, vol. 1.

10. I am borrowing here from Milanesio, *Workers Go Shopping in Argentina*, 90, and Rose, "Authority and the Genealogy of Subjectivity." See also McCann, *Hello, Hello Brazil*, 222; "Função social da propaganda," *Publicidade & Negócios* 7, no. 72 (April 1947): 12.

11. McCann, *Hello, Hello Brazil*, 217–22.

12. Offer, "Between the Gift and the Market."

13. Booth, "Influences on Human Fluid Consumption," 53–73.

14. Holmila and Raitasalo, "Gender Differences in Drinking," 1763–69.

15. Wilsnack et al., "Gender and Alcohol Consumption," 1487–1500; Kerr-Corrêa et al., "Differences in Drinking Patterns between Men and Women in Brazil," 49–68.

16. Carneiro, *Bebida, abstinência e temperança*, 211–12, 218, 258–59. See also Chalhoub, *Trabalho, lar e botequim*; Matos, *Meu lar é um botequim*, 68; Monteleone, *Sabores urbanos*, 48–65; Cascudo, *História da alimentação no Brasil*, 2:751.

17. Carneiro, *Bebida, abstinência e temperança*, 241.

18. Edmundo, "Bebia-se no Rio de Janeiro de 1900," 107–9.

19. Souza, "Cachaça, vinho, cerveja da colônia ao século XX," 68.

20. Edmundo, "Bebia-se no Rio de Janeiro de 1900," 108.

21. Pereira et al., "Beverages Consumption in Brazil," 1166.

22. Holmila and Raitasalo, "Gender Differences in Drinking," 1763–69.

23. "Perfil de Clovis S. Pinto," *A Cigarra* 22 (1923): n.p.

24. Arruda, *A história da Fratelli Vita no Recife*, 43.

25. Silvia Donato, "Todo mundo chorou quando o Recreio fechou," *Revista da Semana* 57, no. 20 (May 1957): 24.

26. Freyre, *Açúcar*.

27. *Doceiro nacional ou arte de fazer toda a qualidade de doces*, 248.

28. Cascudo, *História da alimentação no Brasil*, 2: 813–819.

29. Monteleone, *Sabores urbanos*, 182.

30. Monteleone, *Sabores urbanos*, 166–70.

31. Vianna, "O que comia o imperador," 147–51.

32. Toscano, "Yes, nós temos Coca-Cola," 241–42.

33. Monteleone, *Sabores urbanos*, 159.

34. Goodman and Redclift, *Refashioning Nature*, 1–46.

35. Besse, *Restructuring Patriarchy*, 16–20.

36. Besse, *Restructuring Patriarchy*, 21–27; Woodard, *Brazil's Revolution in Commerce*, 62–64; Martins, "Da fantasia à História," 65.

37. Besse, *Restructuring Patriarchy*, 16–20; Monteleone, *Sabores urbanos*, 65–71. On the nineteenth century, see Richard Graham, *Feeding the City*; Maria Odila Silva Dias, *Power and Everyday Life*; Sandra Lauderdale Graham, *House and Street*.

38. See João Luiz Máximo da Silva, *Cozinha modelo*; Jurandir Freire Costa, *Órdem médica e norma familiar*.

39. Besse, *Restructuring Patriarchy*, 17.

40. Candido, "Brazilian Family," 307–8.

41. Montanari, *Food Is Culture*, 105–13.

42. Cascudo, *História da alimentação no Brasil*, 1:28–29.

43. Freyre, *Açúcar*, 57–60. On teatime in Brazil, see Carneiro, "O corpo sedento," 154–55.

44. Monteleone, *Sabores urbanos*, 167.

45. Laudan, "Plea for Culinary Modernism," 41–43.

46. Helena B. Sangirardi, "Lar doce lar," *O Cruzeiro* 50 (October 4, 1947): 65.

47. "Guaraná Espumante," *A Cigarra* 8, no. 165 (1921): n.p.

48. "Piscina de vinte metros . . . ," *O Cruzeiro* 2 (November 3, 1945): 22.

49. Rachel de Queiroz, "São João," *O Cruzeiro* 35 (June 22, 1946): 90.

50. "Porque há falta de bebidas," *Publicidade & Negócios* 7, no. 71 (March 1947): 8–10; "Encontrado o sucedâneo para a cortiça, aqui no Brasil," *A Gazeta da Farmácia*, April 1944, 15.

51. Besse, *Restructuring Patriarchy*, 36–37, 80; Caulfield, *In Defense of Honor*; Candido, "Brazilian Family," 309.

52. Besse, *Restructuring Patriarchy*, 81, 119–23; 140–41; Goodman and Redclift, *Refashioning Nature*, 19, 44; Furquim, "O consumidor e os meios de comunicação," 291.

53. Goffman, *Gender Advertisements*.

54. Helena B. Sangirardi, "A mulher e o alcóol," *O Cruzeiro* 49 (September 25, 1948): 96.

55. See Bourdieu, *Distinction*, 192.

56. Holmila and Raitasalo, "Gender Differences in Drinking."

57. David Nasser, "7 milhões votam," *O Cruzeiro* 7 (December 8, 1945): 14.

58. Ibrahim Sued, "Entre os 10 grandes solteiros do Rio," *Manchete* 47 (March 1953): 12.

59. See the Guaraná Antarctica ad "Você quer adivinhar a vontade de qualquer criança?" *O Cruzeiro* 30 (May 19, 1945): 26.

60. Candido, "Brazilian Family," 311.

61. "Liberte as forças da natureza," *O Cruzeiro* 25 (June 16, 1970): 2.

62. "A melhor maneira de pedir guaraná é de cabeça erguida," *O Cruzeiro* 48 (November 24, 1970): 175.

63. "Tem uma idade em que v. sabe: Forte tem que ser você, não a bebida," *A Cigarra* 11 (November 1970): 115.

64. "Quais os assuntos mais lidos pela mulher nos jornais," *Publicidade & Negócios* 7, no. 71 (March 1947): 12; Woodard, *Brazil's Revolution in Commerce*, 43, 106–7.

65. Ortiz, *A moderna tradição brasileira*, 39–47; Woodard, *Brazil's Revolution in Commerce*, 102, 174–75; Marcondes, *Uma história da propaganda brasileira*, 27–28; Arruda, *A história da Fratelli Vita*, 44–46.

66. A. P. Carvalho, "O anúncio como elemento de evasão psicológica," *Publicidade & Negócios* 12, no. 164 (July 1952): 87–88.

67. Goffman, *Gender Advertisements*, 84.

68. Klein and Luna, *Modern Brazil*, 10; Besse, *Restructuring Patriarchy*, 92–93, 144–45.

69. J. Walter Thompson Company, *Latin American Markets, 1956*, 31.

70. Otavo, *Progressive Mothers, Better Babies*; Roth, *Miscarriage of Justice*.

71. Mello, *A alimentação no Brasil*; Jaime Rodrigues, "Alimentação popular em São Paulo (1920 a 1950)."

72. Bezerra, "Educação alimentar e a constituição de trabalhadores fortes." See also Dutra, *O ardil totalitário*.

73. Bezerra, "Educação alimentar e a constituição de trabalhadores fortes."

74. Barthes, "Toward a Psychosociology of Contemporary Food Consumption," 171–72.

75. Ruy Coutinho, *Valor social da alimentação*, 21; see also Mello, *A alimentação no Brasil*, 18.

76. Ruy Coutinho, *Valor social da alimentação*, 335.

77. Mello, *A alimentação no Brasil*, 36.

78. See the material on the match between the soccer teams from Jaú and Bauru, São Paulo, competing for the Guaraná Espumante Cup in *A Cigarra* 8, no. 174 (1921): n.p.; and Arruda, *A história da Fratelli Vita*, 53.

79. Peregrino Júnior, *Alimentação e cultura*, 50–52.

80. "Dê ao seu filho o guaraná mais saudável," *A Cigarra* 237 (December 1953): 1.

81. "Seus filhos, como V. também, 'adoram' o delicioso sabor original do Guaraná Brahma," *Fon-Fon* 2495 (January 29, 1955): 2.

82. See, for example, the advertisement "O Mundo Maravilhoso do Guaraná Antarctica," *Manchete* 1604 (January 1983): 126.

83. "Cuidado com os refrigerantes," *Fon-Fon* 2327 (March 17, 1951): 8–12.

84. Brinkmann, "Leite e modernidade: Ideologia e políticas de alimentação na era Vargas."

85. Coutinho, *Valor social da alimentação*, 14–21.

86. Brinkmann, "Leite e modernidade: ideologia e políticas de alimentação na era Vargas."

87. "Águas minerais que envenenam o povo!" *O Radical*, August 1, 1941; "Grave perigo, as águas minerais!" *O Radical*, July 23, 1941.

88. Toscano, "Yes, nós temos Coca-Cola," 107–8.

89. Parkin, *Food Is Love*.

90. Certeau, Giard, and Mayol, *Practice of Everyday Life*, 187–88.

91. See Schor, "In Defense of Consumer Critique," 16–30; Moya, *Delirious Consumption*, 3–5.

92. Certeau, Giard, and Mayol, *Practice of Everyday Life*, 151; Bourdieu, *Distinction*, 195.

93. Myers, "Logic of the Gift," 406. See also Woortmann, "A comida, a família e a construção do gênero feminino."

94. Yunes, "Population of Brazil," 393–404.

95. Offer, "Between the Gift and the Market."

96. Candido, "Brazilian Family," 308.

97. Helena B. Sangirardi, "O valor do dinheiro," *O Cruzeiro* 2 (October 28, 1950): 128.

98. Montanari, *Food Is Culture*, 62.

99. See the testimony by Orlando de Araújo, "O guaraná de Maués e a Antarctica," on the website of the Museu da Pessoa, February 18, 2008, https://acervo.museudapessoa.org/pt/conteudo/historia/o-guarana-de-maues-e-a-antarctica-44663.

100. "Expressos," *Manchete* 1739 (August 17, 1985): 83.

101. Andrew Hill, "Developmental Issues in Attitudes to Food and Diet," 259–66.

102. Kat Eschner, "Comfort Foods Aren't Magic, but Memory Might Be," *Smithsonian*, December 5, 2016, www.smithsonianmag.com/smart-news/comfort-foods-arent-magic-memory-might-be-180961300; Certeau, Giard, and Mayol, *Practice of Everyday Life*, 183–89.

103. Nestle, *Soda Politics*, 3, 115.

104. I have borrowed here from Raymond Williams, "Advertising: The Magic System"; Moeran and Malefyt, "Performing Magical Capitalism"; Moeran, "Business, Anthropology and Magical Systems."

105. Rose, "Authority and the Genealogy of Subjectivity," 322.

106. Brazilian conflation of whiteness and progress is addressed in Weinstein, *Color of Modernity*; Dávila, *Diploma of Whiteness*.

107. See Arruda, *A história da Fratelli Vita*, 58.

108. McCann, *Hello, Hello Brazil*, 221–25.

109. Rial, "Racial and Ethnic Stereotypes in Brazilian Advertising," unpublished paper, http://navi.ufsc.br/files/2017/11/Race_Ethnic-Stereotypes_Rial.pdf.

110. Klein and Luna, *Modern Brazil*, 15.

111. Grande Otelo, "O negro e a publicidade," *Publicidade & Negócios* 11, no. 131 (February 1951): 15.

112. "O negro e a publicidade," letter to the editor from F. Góes, *Publicidade & Negócios* 11, no. 132 (March 1951): 2.

113. Rial, "Racial and Ethnic Stereotypes in Brazilian Advertising."

114. McCann, *Hello, Hello Brazil*, 225.

115. Ubiratan de Lemos, "Meia-noite em ponto: Vida e morte na encruzilhada," *O Cruzeiro* 32 (May 6, 1967): 24.

116. Certeau, *Practice of Everyday Life*.

117. Rial, "Racial and Ethnic Stereotypes in Brazilian Advertising."

118. Arruda, *A história da Fratelli Vita*, 14.

119. "A bebida dos índios," *Para Todos*, August 18, 1928, 12.

120. Siqueira, "Natural Contrasts: Images of Brazilian Flora from Tropical Exuberance to Rustic Landscape," 157–64; Roiter, "Panorama modernista: influência indígena no art déco brasileiro," 74–89.

121. bell hooks, *Black Looks*, 39.

122. On the myth of the bandeirantes, see Weinstein, *Color of Modernity*.

123. See the ad "A S. Paulo, o grande santo," *A Cigarra* 12, no. 224 (1924): n.p.

124. Teresa Cristina Novaes Marques, *A cerveja e a cidade*, 151.

125. Lears, *Fables of Abundance*, 17–39.

126. Schivelbusch, *Tastes of Paradise*, 20–21, 41, 182.

127. Dalmir Reis Jr., "Guaraná Espumante—1921," Propagandas históricas, www.propagandas historicas.com.br/2014/08/guarana-espumante-1921.html.

128. "Adquira a vitalidade de um índio," *O Cruzeiro* 5 (November 25, 1944): 59.

129. Deloria, *Playing Indian*.

130. McCann, *Hello, Hello Brazil*, 223.

131. Pels, introduction.

132. I have borrowed here from Bourdieu, *Distinction*, 218.

133. "Comercial: Nevou na Amazônia," www.youtube.com/watch?v=uVT6bJAnm8c.

134. Barthes, *Mythologies*, 152–53.

135. "Ainda sobre anúncios de 'public relations,'" *Publicidade & Negócios* 10, no. 111 (April 1950): 9; "Refrigerantes no Distrito Federal," *Publicidade & Negócios* 10, no. 117 (July 1950): 22.

136. See Tota, *Seduction of Brazil*, 33; Woodard, *Brazil's Revolution in Commerce*, 117–27.

137. Woodard, *Brazil's Revolution in Commerce*, 122.

138. Arruda, *A história da Fratelli Vita*, 45, 62–65; Ryan, "Coca-Cola in Brazil."

139. O'Brien, *Century of U.S. Capitalism in Latin America*, 108.

140. Dietz, *Soda Pop*; Pendergrast, *For God, Country, and Coca-Cola*.

141. On Coca-Cola's early advertising in Brazil, see McCann, *Hello, Hello Brazil*, 226; Woodard, *Brazil's Revolution in Commerce*, 115–17.

142. "O fracasso da campanha cocacolizante em Belo Horizonte," *Publicidade & Negócios* 10, no. 109 (March 1950): 12–13. On Coke as a "glocal" product, see Foster, *Coca-Globalization*, 33–73.

143. "Refrigerantes no Distrito Federal," 22.

144. Martins, "Da fantasia à História," 75.

145. "Impressões do maestro P. Mascagni por ocasião da sua visita às Fábricas Lacta e Guaraná Espumante," *A Cigarra* 10, no. 195 (1922): n.p.

146. Arruda, *A história da Fratelli Vita*, 62.

147. Arruda, *A história da Fratelli Vita*, 63; Toscano, "Only Thing Like Coca-Cola Is Coca-Cola Itself."

148. "O fracasso da campanha cocacolizante em Belo Horizonte."

149. Woodard, *Brazil's Revolution in Commerce*, 329–37.

150. Auricélio Penteado, "Coca-Cola e o cangaço: efeitos sociais, econômicos e políticos de refrigerante." *Publicidade & Negócios* 8, no. 88 (September 1948): 20.

151. Penteado, "Coca-Cola e o cangaço," 20.

152. On the foundation of IBOPE, see Woodard, *Brazil's Revolution in Commerce*, 97–102.

153. McCann, *Hello, Hello Brazil*, 22.

154. "Função social da propaganda," 12.

155. "Refrigerantes no Distrito Federal," 22; Moya, *Delirious Consumption*, 16.

156. "Refrigerantes no Distrito Federal," 22. On *O Cruzeiro*, see Woodard, *Brazil's Revolution in Commerce*, 35, 92, 171.

157. Arlindo Silva, "Uma paulista sobe ao trono," *O Cruzeiro* 21 (March 12, 1949): 77–78.

158. Jean Manzon, "Parada extra do samba," *O Cruzeiro* 29 (May 7, 1949): 53.

159. Jean Manzon, "Tire o quépi ao gelo," *O Cruzeiro* 50 (October 1, 1949): 47.

160. John Gallagher, "As aventuras de um rei," *O Cruzeiro* 36 (June 25, 1949): 71–76.

161. Jean Manzon, "O caçula da Antarctica: No império do Guaraná Champagne," *O Cruzeiro* 2 (October 29, 1949): 64–76.

162. Woodard, *Brazil's Revolution in Commerce*, 132–33.

163. Laurelyn Whitt, *Science, Colonialism, and Indigenous Peoples*.

164. Pels, introduction.

165. Nestle, *Soda Politics*, 115–30.

166. Sinclair, "Advertising Industry in Latin America," 42. On the merger, see Marchi, *De duas, uma*, 130–66.

167. Klein and Luna, *Modern Brazil*, 5; Laudan, "Plea for Culinary Modernism," 38.

168. Klein and Luna, *Modern Brazil*, 7.

169. João de La Fontaine, "A copy-clínica do Dr. La Fontaine," *Publicidade & Negócios* 12, no. 158 (April 1952): 39.

170. Castro, *As condições de vida da classe operária no Recife*.

171. Jaime Rodrigues, "Alimentação popular em São Paulo (1920 a 1950)," 221–55.

172. Poblacion et al., "Food Insecurity and the Negative Impact on Brazilian Children's Health," *Food and Nutrition Bulletin* 37, no. 4 (2016): 585–98.

173. "Refrigerantes no Distrito Federal," 22.

174. "Serviço de Pesquisa entre Consumidores, Grupo III—Produtos Alimentícios e Domésticos No. 37," Edição Abril 1953, AEL, IBOPE, Serviço de Pesquisa entre Consumidores (SPC), SPC 003.

175. Jaime Rodrigues, "Alimentação popular em São Paulo (1920 a 1950)," 221–55. See also Weinstein, *For Social Peace in Brazil*, 147–78, on efforts to create "district kitchens."

176. Rachel de Queiroz, "Comida de pobre," *O Cruzeiro* 12 (January 3, 1953): 114.

177. Souza, "Aspectos do problema da água de alimentação em São Paulo," 109–24. See also Deaecto, *Comércio e vida urbana na cidade de São Paulo*, 62; Barreto, "A higiene da mesa."

178. Lasinha Luís Carlos, "A audaz navegadora," *Fon-Fon*, October 30, 1954, 17.

179. Oliven and Pinheiro-Machado, "From 'Country of the Future' to Emergent Country," 53–65.

180. "Serviço de Pesquisa entre Consumidores, Grupo III."

181. Hobsbawm, *Age of Extremes*, 513.

182. "História da lata de alumínio para bebidas," accessed April 16, 2022, www.abralatas .org.br/wp-content/themes/abralatas/docs/historiaConteudo.pdf.

183. Cruz, *Fabricação de refrigerantes*, 3.

184. "Guaraná Antarctica: 10 Million Fans," Ad Age, January 21, 2013. https://adage.com /creativity/work/10-million-fans/30475.

185. Garfinkel, *Studies in Ethnomethodology*, 35–36, 53.

186. Giddens, *Constitution of Society*, xxiii–xxiv, 60, 90.

187. Giddens, *Constitution of Society*, xxiii–xxiv, 8, 25.

188. Giddens, *Constitution of Society*, 14–19.

189. See the ad "Guaraná Brahma, um refrigerante sem as maldades do mundo." *Manchete* 1004 (July 17, 1971): 39.

190. Arruda, *A história da Fratelli Vita*, 54.

191. Lévi-Strauss, *Savage Mind*; Latour, *We Have Never Been Modern*.

Chapter Seven

1. Batista, *O complexo da Amazônia*, 158–60; Atroch and Nascimento Filho, "Guaraná," 228.

2. Klein and Luna, *Feeding the World*, 115; Martha, Contini, and Alves, "Embrapa."

3. Sônia Milagres Teixeira, "Estudo do mercado do guaraná," 170.

4. Vasconcelos, Vasconcelos, and Vasconcelos, "Fome, comida, e bebida na música popular brasileira," 732. See also Mondini and Monteiro, "Mudanças no padrão de alimentação"; Instituto Brasileiro de Geografia e Estatística, *Pesquisa de orçamentos familiares, 2002–2003*; Pereira et al., "Beverages Consumption in Brazil," 1164–72.

5. Beck, "Caffeine, Alcohol, and Sweeteners," 179; Utsumi, "Brazilian Soda Market."

6. Huber, "Slow Food Nation"; Nestle, *Soda Politics*, 202–3.

7. Popkin and Mendez, "Rapid Shifts in Stages of the Nutrition Transition," 75.

8. Levy-Costa et al., "Disponibilidade domiciliar de alimentos no Brasil," 530–40.

9. Carvalho and Wong, "Fertility Transition in Brazil."

10. Monteiro, Conde, and Popkin, "Trends in Under- and Overnutrition in Brazil," 234–37.

11. Baer, *Brazilian Economy*, 3–5.

12. Bruschini, *Mulher e trabalho*, 12; Bruschini, "Work and Gender in Brazil in the Last Ten Years"; Reardon et al., "Rise of Supermarkets in Africa, Asia, and Latin America," 1140–46.

13. Laudan, "Plea for Culinary Modernism," 44.

14. Monteiro, Conde, and Popkin, "Trends in Under- and Overnutrition in Brazil," 235.

15. Pinstrup-Andersen and Watson, *Food Policy for Developing Countries*, 3–12.

16. Goodman and Redclift, *Refashioning Nature*, 242–49.

17. Goodman and Redclift, *Refashioning Nature*, 89.

18. Goodman and Redclift, *Refashioning Nature*, 100, 109.

19. Burbach and Flynn, *Agribusiness in the Americas*, 109; Goodman and Redclift, *Refashioning Nature*, xii.

20. Zylberstajn, "Agribusiness Systems Analysis," 114–17.

21. Goodman and Redclift, *Refashioning Nature*, 98–103, 150–51, 167–73, 185.

22. Patel, "Long Green Revolution," 5.

23. Goodman and Redclift, *Refashioning Nature*, xiv, 152.

24. Goodman and Redclift, *Refashioning Nature*, 112, 134, 230; Burbach and Flynn, *Agribusiness in the Americas*, 15, 132; Motoyama, Queiroz, and Vargas, "1964–1985," 368–70.

25. Hornborg, "Technology as Fetish," 133.

26. Batista Filho and Rissin, "A transição nutricional no Brasil," 181–91. See also Monteiro, Mondini, et al., "Da desnutrição para a obesidade," 248.

27. Pingali, "Green Revolution," 12302–8; Gómez et al., "Post-Green Revolution Food Systems and the Triple Burden of Malnutrition," 17.

28. Poblacion et al., "Food Insecurity and the Negative Impact on Brazilian Children's Health," 586.

29. Superintendência da Amazônia, Departamento de Setores Produtivos, *Guaraná*, 5.

30. Goodman and Redclift, *Refashioning Nature*, 234.

31. Pinstrup-Andersen and Watson, *Food Policy for Developing Countries*, 3–12.

32. Klein and Luna, *Feeding the World*, 156–57.

33. Mengel, "Modernização da agricultura e pesquisa no Brasil," 66–67, 80, 149–50; Klein and Luna, *Feeding the World*, 156.

34. Roquette-Pinto, *O guaraná*, 9.

35. Masô, "O guaraná," 143–52.

36. Porto, "Plantas indígenas e exóticas provenientes da Amazônia," 132–33; Pires, "O guaraná," unpublished manuscript.

37. Prance, "João Murça Pires (1917–1944)," 653–54; Pires, "O guaraná."

38. Edith Ewerton de Almeida, *Guaraná*, 5.

39. Corrêa, Pinto, and Santos, *Guaraná: resumos informativos*.

40. Klein and Luna, *Feeding the World*, 155.

41. Edith Ewerton de Almeida, *Guaraná*, 3.

42. See the testimony in Juliana Almeida, *Saberes e fazeres*.

43. Monteiro, *Antropogeografia do guaraná*, 9, 49.

44. Klein and Luna, *Feeding the World*, 24–25.

45. Klein and Luna, *Feeding the World*, 21–27, 32.

46. Martha, Contini, and Alves, "Embrapa," 205.

47. Instituto Brasileiro de Economia, Centro de Estatística Econômica, *Food Consumption in Brazil*.

48. Burns, *History of Brazil*, 497–500.

49. Mueller and Mueller, "Political Economy of the Brazilian Model of Agricultural Development," 16–20; Klein and Luna, *Feeding the World*, 2.

50. Martha, Contini, and Alves, "Embrapa," 205.

51. Mengel, "Modernização da agricultura e pesquisa no Brasil," 43; Patel, "Long Green Revolution," 16; Goodman and Redclift, *Refashioning Nature*, 145.

52. Mengel, "Modernização da agricultura e pesquisa no Brasil," 38.

53. Goodman and Redclift, *Refashioning Nature*, 145; Mueller and Mueller, "Political Economy of the Brazilian Model of Agricultural Development," 17.

54. Burbach and Flynn, *Agribusiness in the Americas*, 98, 115.

55. Fico, *Reinventando o otimismo*.

56. Woodard, *Brazil's Revolution in Commerce*, 268–69, 385.

57. Nehring, "Yield of Dreams," 211.

58. Mengel, "Modernização da agricultura e pesquisa no Brasil," 12.

59. Nehring, "Yield of Dreams," 213.

60. Velho and Krige, "Publication and Citation Practices of Brazilian Agricultural Scientists," 45–62.

61. See Motta, *As universidades e o regime militar*; Motoyama, Queiroz, and Vargas, "1964–1985"; Rosemberg and Pinto, *A educação da mulher*, 71; Leta, "As mulheres na ciência brasileira."

62. Martha, Contini, and Alves, "Embrapa," 213.

63. Corrêa and Schmidt, "Public Research Organizations and Agricultural Development in Brazil."

64. J. Irineu Cabral, *Sol da manhã*, 161.

65. Ruschel, "Women in Agricultural Science in Brazil," 661–67.

66. Martha, Contini, and Alves, "Embrapa," 212.

67. Nehring, "Yield of Dreams," 206.

68. Klein and Luna, *Feeding the World*, 212.

69. Klein and Luna, *Feeding the World*, 202; Carlos Monteiro, "Nutrition and Health," 729–31; Jacobs and Richtel, "How Big Business Got Brazil Hooked on Junk Food."

70. Nehring, "Yield of Dreams," 212.

71. Klein and Luna, *Feeding the World*, 1, 49, 125.

72. Goodman and Redclift, *Refashioning Nature*, 141.

73. Brandt et al., *Avaliação do mercado brasileiro de guaraná*, 5–10.

74. Nazaré and Figueiredo, *Contribuição ao estudo do guaraná*, 30.

75. Batista, *O guaraná da Amazônia*, 210.

76. Tocchini, "Alguns aspectos sobre o guaraná (*Paullinia cupana* var. *sorbilis* Ducke)," 41–54; Sônia Milagres Teixeira, "Estudo do mercado do guaraná," 164.

77. Juliana Almeida, *Saberes e fazeres*, 50–52.

78. "Guaraná: Uma advertência," *ACA Boletim Mensal* 1 (August 1977): 9.

79. "Antárctica inicia o cultivo racional," *O Estado de São Paulo*, April 18, 1982.

80. Juliana Almeida, *Saberes e fazeres*, 50–52.

81. "Antárctica inicia o cultivo racional."

82. Cláudia Guerra, "Produção de guaraná tem queda de 76.9%," *A Crítica*, June 23, 1996.

83. Néri, "A guerra pelo guaraná da Amazônia."

84. Homma, "Guaraná," 313–14.

85. Sacramento, "A guaranaicultura no estado da Bahia," 129–42.

86. Goodman and Redclift, *Refashioning Nature*, 250.

87. Atroch and Nascimento Filho, "Guaraná," 225–36.

88. Juliana Almeida, *Saberes e fazeres*, 56.

89. Atroch and Nascimento Filho, "Guaraná"; Atroch et al., "Domesticação e melhoramento de guaranazeiro"; Fioravanti, "Luzeia."

90. Filoche and Pinton, "Who Owns Guaraná?," 388n21.

91. Keneni, Bekele, and Imtiaz, "Vulnerability of Modern Crop Cultivars."

92. Valois, "Discurso proferido por Afonso Celso Candeira Valois," 21–25. See also "Antárctica inicia o cultivo racional."

93. Luiz Antelmo Silva Melo, "Apresentação," n.p.

94. Klein and Luna, *Feeding the World*, 159.

95. Valois, "Discurso proferido por Afonso Celso Candeira Valois," 21–25.

96. See Corrêa, Pinto, and Santos, *Guaraná*.

97. Stepan, "Race and Gender."

98. Fabian, *Time and the Other*.

99. Atroch and Nascimento Filho, "Guaraná"; Atroch et al., "Domesticação e melhoramento de guaranazeiro," 333–61; Fioravanti, "Luzeia."

100. Ronaldo José Michiles, "A cadeia produtiva do guaraná: um estudo com o guaraná no município de Maués," 19.

101. Atroch and Nascimento Filho, "Guaraná."

102. Enríquez, Silva, and Cabral, *Biodiversidade da Amazônia*, 98–111; Schimpl et al., "Guaraná," 16; Nascimento Filho, "Interação genótipos X ambientes, adaptabilidade, estabilidade e repetibilidade em clones de guaraná," 1; Fioravanti, "Luzeia"; Néri, "A guerra pelo guaraná da Amazônia."

103. Fioravanti, "Luzeia."

104. Klein and Luna, *Feeding the World*, 202–9.

105. Nehring, "Yield of Dreams," 213.

106. Reardon and Timmer, "Economics of the Food System Revolution."

107. Mueller and Mueller, "Political Economy of the Brazilian Model of Agricultural Development," 16.

108. Gross, "As Brazilian Agribusinesss Booms, Family Farms Feed the Nation."

109. Juliana Almeida, *Saberes e fazeres*, 50–52; Enríquez, da Silva, and Cabral, *Biodiversidade da Amazônia*, 98–111; Abreu, Araújo Júnior, and Cruz, "Agroindústria do guaraná," 151–54.

110. Henman, "Guaraná," 317–19.

111. Atroch et al., "Domesticação e melhoramento de guaranazeiro."

112. Erickson, Corrêa, and Escobar, "Guaraná (*Paullinia cupana*) as a Commercial Crop in Brazilian Amazonia," 273–86.

113. "Embrapa defende a qualidade de seu guaraná modificado," *Gazeta Mercantil*, August 23, 2001.

114. Ronaldo José Michiles, "A cadeia produtiva do guaraná," 55; Goodman and Redclift, *Refashioning Nature*, 104.

115. See José Francisco Marques's testimony in Juliana Almeida, *Saberes e fazeres*, 61.

116. Superintendência da Amazônia, Departamento de Setores Produtivos, *Guaraná*, 18–20; Sônia Milagres Teixeira, "Estudo do mercado do guaraná," 171.

117. Enríquez, Silva, and Cabral, *Biodiversidade da Amazônia*, 98–111.

118. Congretel et al., "Found Again in Translation?," 583.

119. See Corrêa, Pinto, and Santos, *Guaraná*, 39.

120. Simon and Garagorry, "Expansion of Agriculture in the Brazilian Amazon."

121. Klein and Luna, *Feeding the World*, 198–203.

122. Pingali, "Green Revolution."

123. Evenson and Gollin, "Assessing the Impact of the Green Revolution," 758–62. https://science-sciencemag-org.ezproxy.lib.utexas.edu/content/300/5620/758 — corresp-1.

124. See José Francisco Marques's testimony in Juliana Almeida, *Saberes e fazeres*, 65.

125. Goodman and Redclift, *Refashioning Nature*, xviii; see also Hornborg, "Technology as Fetish," 123.

126. Popkin and Mendez, "Rapid Shifts in Stages of the Nutrition Transition," 68–80.

127. Umberlândia Cabral, "Um em cada quatro adultos do país estava obeso em 2019," 9.

128. Monteiro, Conde, and Popkin, "Income-Specific Trends in Obesity in Brazil, 1975–2003," 1808–12. The national surveys were carried out in 1975, 1989, and 2003. See also Batista Filho and Rissin, "A transição nutricional no Brasil," 181–91.

129. Popkin and Mendez, "Rapid Shifts in Stages of the Nutrition Transition," 68–80.

130. Pereira et al., "Beverages Consumption in Brazil," 1164–72.

131. Coimbra et al., "First National Survey of Indigenous People's Health and Nutrition in Brazil."

132. Monteiro et al., "Increasing Consumption of Ultra-Processed Foods and Likely Impact on Human Health," 5–10; Carlos Augusto Monteiro, "Nutrition and Health," 729–31; Pan-American Health Organization, *Ultra-Processed Food and Drink Products in Latin America*; Pan-American Health Organization, "Ultra-Processed Foods Are Driving the Obesity Epidemic in Latin America, Says New PAHO/WHO Report."

133. Pan-American Health Organization, *Ultra-Processed Food and Drink Products in Latin America*; Jacobs and Richtel, "How Big Business Got Brazil Hooked on Junk Food."

134. Pan-American Health Organization, *Ultra-Processed Food and Drink Products in Latin America*, 15–16.

135. Huber, "Slow Food Nation."

136. "Panorama do setor," *Revista ABIR* (2019/2020): 10–13.

137. Carlos Augusto Monteiro, "Nutrition and Health," 729–31.

138. Popkin and Hawkes, "Sweetening of the Global Diet, Particularly Beverages," 174–86.

139. Pereira et al., "Beverages Consumption in Brazil," 1164–72.

140. Locatelli, "Agreement to Reduce Sugar in Brazil Excludes Main Products"; Jacobs and Richtel, "How Big Business Got Brazil Hooked on Junk Food."

141. Rtveladze et al., "Health and Economic Burden of Obesity in Brazil."

142. Vasconcelos, Vasconcelos, and Vasconcelos, "Fome, comida, e bebida na música popular brasileira," 723–41. See also Mondini and Monteiro, "Mudanças no padrão de alimentação," 79–89; Instituto Brasileiro de Geografia e Estatística, *Pesquisa de orçamentos familiares, 2008–2009*; Instituto Brasileiro de Geografia e Estatística, *Pesquisa de orçamentos familiares, 2002–2003*.

143. Levy-Costa et al., "Disponibilidade domiciliar de alimentos no Brasil," 530–40; Sant'Anna, *Gordos, magros e obesos*, 153.

144. Souza et al., "Most Consumed Foods in Brazil."

145. Monteiro, Conde, and Popkin, "Trends in Under- and Overnutrition in Brazil," 234–37.

146. Jacobs and Richtel, "How Big Business Got Brazil Hooked on Junk Food."

147. Morais, "Um cardápio gordo em casa e na TV."

148. Aliança pela Alimentação Adequada e Saudável, "Obesidade infantil: precisamos falar sobre a publicidade de alimentos."

149. Nestle, *Soda Politics*, 135.

150. MacClancy, *Consuming Culture*, 217.

151. Sahlins, "On the Culture of Material Value and the Cosmography of Riches," 168.

152. Montanari, *Food Is Culture*, 118.

153. Sant'Anna, *Gordos, magros e obesos*, 33–39.

154. Sant'Anna, *Gordos, magros e obesos*, 123–68.

155. Sant'Anna, *Gordos, magros e obesos*.

156. Ferreira and Magalhães, "Obesidade e pobreza," 1793. For a comparative discussion, see Laraia, "Food Insecurity and Chronic Disease," 203–12.

157. "Aracy na bronca," *O Cruzeiro* 34 (June 15, 1981): 53.

158. Homma, "Guaraná," 313; Costa, "A indústria do guaraná no Amazonas," 93–103.

159. See the website of Guaraná Tibiriçá, www.guaranatibirica.com.br/a-empresa.

160. Belasco, *Appetite for Change*.

161. "A chama do coração: uma releitura das obras do Caio Miranda."

162. João Martins, "Como viver 150 anos," *O Cruzeiro* 45 (August 20, 1960): 51–53.

163. Homma, "Guaraná," 308.

164. Maria Teresa, "Impotência é sintoma," *O Cruzeiro* 14 (March 15, 1980): 112; Maria Teresa, "Desinteresse sexual," *O Cruzeiro* 2504 (May 30, 1982): 74.

165. "Guaraná, 'o elixir da longa vida,'" *Jornal do Commércio*, September 13–14, 1983.

166. "É a volta às origens," *O Cruzeiro* 31 (April 30, 1981): 48.

167. Schimpl et al., "Guaraná," 17.

168. Goodman and Redclift, *Refashioning Nature*, 5.

169. Ortiz, *A moderna tradição brasileira*. See also Woodard, *Brazil's Revolution in Commerce*.

170. General trends are from Monteiro, Conde, and Popkin, "Trends in Under- and Overnutrition in Brazil," 234–37.

171. Courtwright, *Age of Addiction*.

172. Popkin and Hawkes, "Sweetening of the Global Diet," 174–86; "Coca-Cola in Brazil: Global Events and Energy Drinks Could Drive Growth (Part 1)," *Forbes*, March 12, 2014.

Chapter Eight

1. Quoted in "A proposta do Centro de Trabalho Indigenista—CTI," 1980, Instituto Sociambiental (ISA), Código I4D00045.

2. Parcerer No. 085/86—GT PORT. INTERMINISTERIAL No. 002/83—DECRETO 88.118/83, authored by José Apoena Soares de Meirelles, Renato D'Almeida Leoni, and João Pacheco de Oliveira Filho, Brasília, February 25, 1986. The reference to guaraná also appears in the report to Sarney by Minister of Interior Ronaldo Costa Couto and Minister of Agrarian Reform and Development Dante Martins de Oliveira, E. M. Ministerial No. 131, August 4, 1986, Instituto Socioambiental (ISA).

3. See Alvarez, *Satereria*, 144–56; Kapfhammer, "Divine Child and Trademark," 214–22; Congretel and Pinton, "Local Knowledge, Know-How and Knowledge Mobilized in a Globalized World," 531.

4. Sahlins, "What Is Anthropological Enlightenment?"

5. Cunha, *"Culture" and Culture.*

6. See Hirtz, "It Takes Modern Means to Be Traditional"; Oliveira, *O nascimento do Brasil e outros ensaios,* 267.

7. Sahlins, "What Is Anthropological Enlightenment?"

8. Dove, "Indigenous People and Environmental Politics."

9. See, for example, Nygren, "Local Knowledge in the Environment-Development Discourse," Cunha, *"Culture" and Culture*; Agrawal, "Dismantling the Divide between Indigenous and Scientific Knowledge." For the Sateré-Mawé, see Congretel et al., "Found Again in Translation."

10. See Oliveira, *O nascimento do Brasil,* 268.

11. Halliwell, *Light in the Jungle,* 157.

12. Halliwell, *Light in the Jungle,* 17–18; see also Oliver Montgomery, "Advancement in the Face of Adversity," *Ministry* 6 (June 1933): 13.

13. Hall, *Adventurers for God,* 186; Ronald L. Wearner, "Luzeiro I," *Adventist Heritage* 12, no. 2 (Summer 1988): 43; "East Brazil Notes," *South American Bulletin* 7, no. 8 (August 1931): 6.

14. Leo B. Halliwell, "An Interesting Word from Brazil," *Advent and Sabbath Review Herald* 115, no. 5 (Feburary 1938): 1.

15. Halliwell, *Light in the Jungle,* 27, 156–57.

16. E. H. Wilcox, "Opening up the Amazon," *South American Bulletin* 5, no. 2 (February 1929): 7; Halliwell, *Light in the Jungle,* 91. On conversion to Protestantism among Indigenous peoples of South America, see Brown, "Facing the State, Facing the World," 315.

17. Halliwell, *Light in the Jungle,* 157.

18. The account is also mentioned in Halliwell, "A Marvelous Change," *Advent Review and Sabbath Herald* 115, no. 7 (February 1938): 15.

19. Halliwell, *Light in the Jungle,* 90–91, 156–60, 172–77; Wearner, "Luzeiro I," 46.

20. H. O. Olson, "The Amazon Camp Meeting," *Advent Review and Sabbath Herald* 117, no. 33 (August 1940): 12.

21. Clarence W. Hall, "Medicine Man on the Amazon," *Advent Review and Sabbath Herald* 133, no. 45 (November 1956): 45.

22. On the value of foreign goods, see Sahlins, "On the Culture of Material Value and the Cosmography of Riches," 170.

23. Friedman, "Myth, History and Political Identity," 197.

24. Halliwell, *Light in the Jungle,* 88–89.

25. Halliwell, *Light in the Jungle,* 90.

26. J. L. Brown, "Amazon Meetings," *South American Bulletin* 14, no. 11–12 (November–December 1938): 8.

27. Coudreau, *Viagem ao Tapajós,* 46.

28. Leacock, "Economic Life of the Maué Indians," 28.

29. Monteiro, *Antropogeografia do guaraná,* 7.

30. See Coudreau, *Viagem ao Tapajós,* 44–46. For accounts of village life from the 1980s, see Lorenz, *Sateré-Mawé,* 33–37.

31. Hemming, *Die If You Must,* 16–19.

32. Joaquim Melo, *SPI: a política indigenista no Amazonas,* 169–70.

33. Leacock, "Economic Life of the Maué Indians," 28.

34. Rodrigues, Ribeiro Neto, and Silva, "Saberes indígenas e ressignificação no processo identitário dos Sateré-Mawé/AM," 59–76.

35. Leacock, "Economic Life of the Maué Indians," 22.

36. Darcy Ribeiro, *Línguas e culturas indígenas do Brasil*, 7–21.

37. Leacock, "Economic Life of the Maué Indians," 28.

38. Kapfhammer, "Amazonian Pain," 155–56, 164.

39. Leacock, "Maué Kinship and Omaha Terminology," 59–76.

40. See, for example, Roberto Cardoso de Oliveira, *O índio e o mundo dos brancos*.

41. Baer, *The Brazilian Economy: Growth and Development*, 71–73.

42. "Bebidas, comida e música," *Manchete*, special edition (April 21, 1960): 76–78; see also Woodard, *Brazil's Revolution in Commerce*, 221–22.

43. Wolfe, "Settler Colonialism and the Elimination of the Native."

44. The film *Olho de gente* (1983) has been posted on the Sateré-Mawé website, Portal dos Filhos do Waraná: www.nusoken.com/livre-academia-do-war%C3%A1/i-sec%C3% A7%C3%A3o-patrim%C3%B4nio-hist%C3%B3rico-cultural/a-07-capit%C3%A3o-dico -tuxaua-donato-tuxaua-emilio-tuxaua-evaristo-tuxaua-manoelzinho.

45. See Sônia da Silva Lorenz, "Relato do Processo de Luta dos Sateré-Mawé Contra a Elf-Aquitaine, e do Encaminhamento dado a Indenização Recebida," Centro de Trabalho Indigenista, 1985, Cod. SMD00035, ISA.

46. Centro Ecumênico de Documentação e Informação, "Líder Sateré-Mawé denuncia 'Elf-Equitaine,'[*sic*]" *Aconteceu: Povos indígenas no Brasil*/1981, no. 10 (April 1982): 11.

47. Sylvia Caiuby Novaes, "Os índios vão à justiça," *Folha de São Paulo*, April 22, 1983.

48. John Carson-Parker, "How Elf Works for France," *New York Times*, November 22, 1981.

49. Eurípedes Claiton, "A luta dos Sateré contra o petróleo," *Porantim*, November 1981, 10–11.

50. Brasil, Lei No 6.001, December 19, 1973, www.camara.leg.br/proposicoesWeb/prop _mostrarintegra;jsessionid=0DA671C140AF6BCB4D5D901A5BD51021.proposicoesWeb Externo2?codteor=670971&filename=LegislacaoCitada+-PL+5560/2009.

51. Alcida Rita Ramos, *Indigenism*, 202.

52. Davis, *Victims of the Miracle*, 87–90.

53. Chiefs Dico and Donato quoted in Claiton, "A luta dos Sateré contra o petróleo," *Porantim*, November 1981, 10; Chief Emílio quoted in Lorenz, *Sateré-Mawé*, 98

54. "Corrupção, novo inimigo Sateré," *Porantim* (January–February 1982). On Nobre da Veiga, see Garfield, *Indigenous Struggle at the Heart of Brazil*, 197–202.

55. "Suborno de caciques agita aldeia invadida pela busca de petróleo," *O Dia*, November 13, 1981; "Índios protestam contra invasão da reserva por técnicos de petróleo," *O Liberal*, October 25, 1981; Eurípedes Claiton, "Em Brasília: 'A saída de Kasuto,'" *Aconteceu: Povos indígenas no Brasil*, December 2, 1981, 3.

56. Mbembe, *Necropolitics*.

57. Nixon, *Slow Violence and the Environmentalism of the Poor*.

58. Brasil, Comissão Nacional da Verdade, *Relatório: textos temáticos*, Vol. 2, 203–64.

59. See the testimony by Aurélio Michiles, "Sobre a obra *O sangue da terra*."

60. See Davis, *Victims of the Miracle*; Green, *We Cannot Remain Silent*, 266–67, 281–83.

61. See Garfield, *Indigenous Struggle at the Heart of Brazil*, 178–79; Oliveira, *O nascimento do Brasil*, 276–77.

62. Lorenz, "Relato do Processo"; Uggé, *Sateré-Maué*, 30; Eurípedes Claiton, "A luta dos Sateré contra o petróleo"; III Assembleia Nacional do CIMI: Encontro dos Tuxauas da Zona Indígena do Rio Andirá-Amazonas, Assunto a ser tratado: Estrada Maués-Itaituba," Vila Simão do Rio Andirá, June 28, 1979, ISA; Novaes, "Os índios vão à justiça."

63. Peirano, "Anthropology with No Guilt," 186–98; Dent, "Studying Indigenous Brazil."

64. See Acker, *Volkswagen in the Amazon*.

65. "Embaixada da França não recebe indígenas," *Correio Braziliense*, October 27, 1982.

66. The Sateré-Mawé leaders' visit to Brasília and the content of the letter to the French ambassador are shown in the film *O sangue da terra*, 21:55.

67. Dalmo de Abreu Dallari, "Justiça para o índio," *Folha de São Paulo*, April 23, 1983; Lorenz, *Sateré-Mawé*, 100.

68. "Funai acertará indenização de empresa a tribo," *Folha de São Paulo*, February 27, 1982. See also Lorenz, *Sateré-Mawé*, 97; "Índios recebem 5 milhões por danos a sua reserva," *O Globo*, March 12, 1982.

69. See the document signed by Raimundo Ferreira da Silva and other Indigenous leaders and non-Indigenous activists, "Reinvindicações da Comunidade dos Índios Sateré- Mawé a Cia Estatal Francesa Elf-Aquitaine, Apresentadas por Ocasião da Visita de Simone Dreyfus-Gamelon à Área Sateré-Mawé em Outubro de 1983," Manaus, November 2, 1983, ISA.

70. "Inquérito da FUNAI para apurar mortes," *A Crítica*, November 10, 1983; "Indenização insuficiente," *O Estado de São Paulo*, December 8, 1983; Lorenz, *Sateré-Mawé*, 100–101, 116, 153. See also Sônia da Silva Lorenz and Sylvia Caiuby Novaes, "Fatos e não boatos," *Folha de São Paulo*, May 15, 1984.

71. "Índios aceitam proposta da petrolífera Elf-Aquitaine," *O Globo*, July 28, 1984; "Elf paga aos índios 150 mil dólares," *A Notícia*, August 1, 1984.

72. "Explosivos não detonados provocam a morte de índios da tribo Sateré-Mawé," *Folha da Tarde*, June 16, 1984; "Empresa francesa deixa dinamite em reserva indígena," *Diário Popular*, December 8, 1983; "Sateré confirma morte de índios e exibe dinamite," *A Notícia*, January 25, 1984. See also Dallari's testimony in Juliana Almeida, *Saberes e fazeres*, 18–19.

73. João Pinduca Rodrigues, "Muitos petardos enterrados," *A Crítica*, January 16, 1992.

74. Brasil, Comissão Nacional da Verdade, *Relatório: textos temáticos*, Vol. 2, 236–37.

75. See the Sateré-Mawé leader's testimony in *O sangue da terra*, 27:22.

76. See Lorenz's testimony in Juliana Almeida, *Saberes e fazeres*, 15–17.

77. "Índios maués têm projeto agrícola de Cr\$2,5 milhões para o plantio do guaraná," *Jornal do Brasil*, March 13, 1981; Lorenz, *Sateré-Mawé*, 75–76; Miguel Pacheco, "Luta contra humilhação é meta dos Sateré-Mawé," *A Crítica*, July 4, 1993.

78. Márcio Uchôa, "Preconceito marca relação entre índios e brancos em Manaus," *O Estado de São Paulo*, February 14, 1994.

79. "The Missionary of the Sateré-Mawé," May 29, 2019, www.pimeusa.org/2019/05/the-missionary-of-the-Sateré-Mawé.

80. See Stavenhagen, "Ethnodevelopment."

81. "A proposta do Centro de Trabalho Indigenista—CTI," 1980, COD I4D00045, ISA; Lorenz, *Sateré-Mawé*, 67, 79.

82. "Índios maués têm projeto agrícola de Cr$2,5 milhões."

83. Lorenz, *Sateré-Mawé*, 104, 123–25.

84. See Kapfhammer, "Amazonian Pain," 160–61.

85. See Samuel Lopes's testimony in Juliana Almeida, *Saberes e fazeres*, 21–22.

86. Lorenz, *Sateré-Mawé*, 90, 123–25; "Índios contam com barcos como ajuda," *A Crítica*, December 1, 1992.

87. "Guaraná, 'o elixir da longa vida,'" *Jornal do Commércio*, September 13–14, 1983.

88. Lorenz, *Sateré-Mawé*, 116–20, 128, 173; "Caciques discutem por verbas da indenização," *A Crítica*, May 10, 1983; "Sateré desmente Dico e não quer dinheiro," *A Crítica*, January 20, 1984; Alvarez, *Satereria*, 128, 173.

89. Lorenz, *Sateré-Mawé*, 84, 90, 118–20.

90. Lorenz, *Sateré-Mawé*, 132.

91. Henman, "Guaraná," 317–19; Congretel and Pinton, "Local Knowledge, Know-How and Knowledge Mobilized in a Globalized World."

92. Alvarez, *Satereria*, 158.

93. Lorenz, *Sateré-Mawé*, 140; Raynolds, "Re-embedding Global Agriculture," 297–309.

94. Goodman, "Reading Fair Trade."

95. Allen and Kovach, "The Capitalist Composition of Organic"; Getz and Shreck, "What Organic and Fair Trade Labels Do Not Tell Us."

96. Raynolds, "Re-embedding Global Agriculture."

97. Michael Goodman, "Reading Fair Trade"; Getz and Shreck, "What Organic and Fair Trade Labels Do Not Tell Us"; Raynolds, "Re-embedding Global Agriculture."

98. Lotti, "Commoditization of Products and Taste," 71–83.

99. Food and Agriculture Organization of the United Nations and Institut National de la Recherche Agronomique, *Constructing Markets for Agroecology*, 101–10.

100. Guayapi website, accessed April 16, 2022, www.guayapi.com/en/#our-sectors; Eric Marx, "Going Beyond Organic: Analog Forestry," *Christian Science Monitor*, October 19, 2009, www.csmonitor.com/Business/2009/1019/going-beyond-organic-analog -forestry.

101. "Waranà: A Tale of Indigenous Resistance," February 26, 2019, https://www .fondazioneslowfood.com/en/warana-a-tale-of-indigenous-resistance/; Food and Agriculture Organization of the United Nations and Institut National de la Recherche Agronomique, *Constructing Markets for Agroecology*; Carolina Carmona Dias, "O Movimento Slow Food no Brasil"; Daniel Coelho de Oliveira, "Comida, carisma e prazer"; Donati, "Pleasure of Diversity in Slow Food's Ethics of Taste," 227–42; "Slow Food Brazil on the Front Line in the Fight to Save Biodiversity," December 5, 2016, https://www.fondazioneslowfood.com/en/slow -food-brazil-the-front-line-the-fight-to-save-biodiversity/.

102. Food and Agriculture Organization of the United Nations and Institut National de la Recherche Agronomique, *Constructing Markets for Agroecology*, 101–110.

103. Alvarez, *Satereria*, 131, 161–62; Beaufort, "Le *Waraná* des Indiens Sateré Mawé," 95–121; Ricardo and Ricardo, *Povos indígenas no Brasil, 2001–2005*, 493–94.

104. Goodman, "Reading Fair Trade," 891–915.

105. Alvarez, *Satereria*, 133. The process is well explored in Congretel et al., "Found Again in Translation?"

106. Kapfhammer, "Amazonian Pain," 155–60.

107. Alvarez, *Satereria*, 163–66; Kapfhammer, "Divine Child and Trademark," 221.

108. Cunha, *"Culture" and Culture*, 79; Brown, *Who Owns Native Culture?*, 3.

109. Wara, quoted in "Waranà: A Tale of Indigenous Resistance."

110. Guayapi website.

111. See Garfield, *Indigenous Struggle at the Heart of Brazil*, 211–15.

112. International Labour Organization, Indigenous and Tribal Peoples Convention, 1989 (No. 169).

113. Conklin and Graham, "Shifting Middle Ground," 695–710.

114. Oliveira, *O nascimento do Brasil*, 252, 266, 281, 305.

115. See Barbosa, *Guardians of the Brazilian Rainforest*, 154–55.

116. Barbosa, *Guardians of the Brazilian Rainforest*, 35.

117. Conklin and Graham, "Shifting Middle Ground."

118. Burke, "Cooperatives for 'Fair Globalization'?"; Albert, "Associações indígenas e desenvolvimento sustentável na Amazônia brasileira," 198; Bryant and Goodman, "Consuming Narratives"; Cook and Crang, "World on a Plate."

119. Simone Romero, "Índios da Amazônia aderem à economia global," *Gazeta Mercantil*, June 28, 2000; Maurício Lima, "Capitalismo nas aldeias," *Veja*, January 24, 2001.

120. Alvarez, *Satereria*, 173.

121. Albert, "Associações indígenas e desenvolvimento sustentável na Amazônia brasileira," 197.

122. Ivânia Vieira, "Desnutrição atinge 40% das crianças," *A Crítica*, April 23, 1995; "Líderes Sateré-Mawé reclamam do abandono," *A Crítica*, August 5, 1988. Malnutrition persisted over the course of the decade. See "Fome e miséria entre os índios do grupo Sateré," *A Crítica*, April 20, 1999.

123. See Teixeira and Brasil, "Estudo demográfico dos Sateré-Mawé," 139.

124. Pery Teixeira, *Sateré-Mawé*, 10, 50.

125. See a description in Fraboni, "Waraná: O legítimo guaraná dos Sateré-Mawé," 469–71.

126. Alvarez, *Satereria*, 158–64; Kapfhammer, "De 'Sateré puro' (*Sateré sese*) ao 'novo Sateré' (*Sateré pakup*)."

127. Sérgio Garcia Wara, president of the Consórcio de Produtores Sateré-Mawé, Parintins, interview with author (via WhatsApp), December 23, 2021.

128. See "Os Índios Sateré-Mawé, Filhos do Guaraná," *Almanaque Brasil Socioambiental*, 427; Fraboni, "Waraná," 470; Wright, Kapfhammer, and Wiik, "Clash of Cosmographies," 415.

129. Sérgio Garcia Wara, interview with author.

130. Food and Agriculture Organization of the United Nations and Institut National de la Recherche Agronomique, *Constructing Markets for Agroecology*; Beaufort, "Le Waraná des Indiens Sateré Mawé"; Vignoli, "Manejo de *Paullinia cupana* var. *sorbilis* (Mart.) Ducke."

131. Fraboni, "Waraná," 470; Congretel et al., "Found Again in Translation?," 579–600.

132. Filoche, "Making the Difference with a Common Plant," 181; Congretel et al., "Found Again in Translation?"

133. Filoche, "Making the Difference with a Common Plant," 182; Congretel et al., "Found Again in Translation?"

134. Filoche and Pinton, "Who Owns Guaraná?," 385.

135. Filoche and Pinton, "Who Owns Guaraná?," 390. On Indigenous peoples' disadvantages vis-à-vis intellectual property rights, see Dove, "Center, Periphery and Bio-Diversity"; Brown, "Can Culture be Copyrighted?"

136. Filoche, "Making the Difference with a Common Plant," 173–84.

137. Alvarez, *Satereria*, 132.

138. See Claudie Ravel, "Commerce equitable: A la découverte du guaraná, trésor des Indiens Sateré," interview, *Le Petit Journal*, July 13, 2012, https://lepetitjournal.com/commerce-equitable-la-decouverte-du-guaraná-tresor-des-indiens-Sateré-199545; Alvarez, *Satereria*, 161; "Os Índios Sateré-Mawé, Filhos do Guaraná," *Almanaque Brasil Socioambiental*, 427.

139. Food and Agriculture Organization of the United Nations and Institut National de la Recherche Agronomique, *Constructing Markets for Agroecology*.

140. Guayapi website.

141. Bryant and Goodman, "Consuming Narratives."

142. Guayapi website.

143. Filoche and Pinton, "Who Owns Guaraná?," 392–93.

144. Rodrigues, Ribeiro Neto, and Silva, "Saberes indígenas e ressignificação," 206–29; Ferreira, "Wará: ensaios sobre as interferências do comércio justo na formação política das lideranças Sateré-Mawé."

145. Conklin and Graham, "Shifting Middle Ground."

146. Brown, "Facing the State, Facing the World," 307–26.

147. "CGTSM denuncia ação irregular de ONG e empresa francesa que exploram guaraná." November 10, 2008, www.coiab.com.br; "Acusados no caso do guaraná dos índios Sateré-Mawé respondem à denúncia," November 29, 2008, www.amazonia.org.br; Fraboni and Batista, "Esclarecimento: para que serve uma fortaleza," November 19, 2008, www.terramadre.slowfoodbrasil.com; Prazeres, "Índios denunciam ação illegal de ONG francesa no Amazonas." These articles can be found in the on-line archive of ISA.

148. Congretel et al., "Found Again in Translation?"

149. Pery Teixeira, *Sateré-Mawé*, 131–32. See also Alvarez, *Satereria*, 164.

150. "Waranà: A Tale of Indigenous Resistance."

151. Kapfhammer and Garnelo, "Programas sociais e Agência Indígena entre os Sateré-Mawé."

152. Berkhofer, *White Man's Indian*.

153. Dove, "Indigenous People and Environmental Politics," 191–208.

154. Congretel and Pinton, "Local Knowledge, Know-How and Knowledge Mobilized in a Globalized World," 533.

155. See the pamphlet "AMISM - Associação das Mulheres Indígenas Sateré-Mawé" from the early 2000s in ISA, Código SMD00034.

156. "Projeto GATA apoia a 1ª Feira de Troca de Sementes, Sabores e Saberes na Terra Indígena Andirá-Marau (AM/PA), June 15, 2015"; "Tribo indígena recebe selo de Denominação de Origem Controlada para o guaraná que produz," Rádio Vaticano, April 4, 2012. See also Filoche, "Making the Difference with a Common Plant," 177; Filoche and Pinton, "Who Owns Guaraná?," 394–95; Slow Food, "Brazilian Appellation of Origin Granted to the Sateré-Mawé Indigenous People's Waraná."

157. Sérgio Garcia Wara, interview with author.

158. Emphasis in original. See the webpage of the Consórcio dos Produtores Sateré-Mawé, Portal dos Filhos do Waraná, www.nusoken.com.

159. Quoted in Catherine Balston, "Guaraná: The 'Edible Eyes of the Amazon,'" BBC Travel, April 29, 2021.

Conclusion

1. Jordan Goodman, "Excitania," 126–29.

2. See Schivelbusch, *Tastes of Paradise*; Courtwright, *Forces of Habit*; Breen, *Age of Intoxication*.

3. See Jordan Goodman, "Excitania"; Smail, *On Deep History and the Brain*, 179–87; Breen, *Age of Intoxication*.

4. Schivelbusch, *Tastes of Paradise*, 43.

5. See the discussion in Courtwright, *Forces of Habit*, 53–59.

6. Gootenberg, *Andean Cocaine*, 16–19.

7. Samoggia, Landuzzi, and Vicién, "Market Expansion of Caffeine-Containing Products."

8. Stirn, "Yaupon: The Rebirth of America's Forgotten Tea."

9. See Francisco Ignacio de Carvalho Moreira, *Relatório sobre a Exposição Internacional de 1862*, lxxvi.

10. Beaufort, "Le *Waraná* des Indiens Sateré Mawé"; Atroch et al., "Domesticação e melhoramento de guaranazeiro."

11. Priscila Néri, "A guerra pelo guaraná da Amazônia: Coca-Cola e AmBev investem pesado para alcançar maior produtividade e qualidade," *O Estado de São Paulo*, December 7, 2003.

12. Catherine Balston, "Guaraná: The 'Edible Eyes of the Amazon,'" BBC Travel, April 29, 2021, www.bbc.com/travel/story/20210428-guaran-the-edible-eyes-of-the-amazon?referer =https%3A%2F%2Fwww.bbc.com%2Fnews%2Fworld-latin-america-36028247.

13. Leal, "Guaraná," 165.

14. Marcelo Leite, "Os filhos do guaraná," *Folha de São Paulo*, May 2, 2010.

15. Guaraná Antarctica, Facebook, www.facebook.com/GuaranaAntarctica.

16. Hobsbawm and Ranger, eds., *Invention of Tradition*.

17. Young and Brunk, introduction, 1–10; Brown, *Who Owns Native Culture?*, 4–10, 252.

18. "Brazilian Brewers to Merge in Stock Swap," *Los Angeles Times*, July 13, 1999.

19. Tim Bowler, "Brazilian Recipe for Brewing Success," BBC News, July 14, 2008; "Stella Firm Buys Budweiser Brewer," BBC News, July 14, 2008; David Kesmodel, Dennis K. Berman, and Dana Cimilluca, "Anheuser, Inbev Reach a Deal for $52 Billion," *Wall Street Journal*, July 14, 2008.

20. "A Giant Drinks Merger. Beer Monster." *Economist*, September 19, 2015, 60; Lisa Brown, "A-B InBev Finalizes $100 Billion Acquisition of SAB Miller, Creating World's Largest Beer Company," *Chicago Tribune*, October 11, 2016.

21. Sean Farrell, "The Megabrew Takeover—a Tale of Beers, Billions and Blue Bloods," *Guardian*, October 9, 2015.

22. Bowler, "Brazilian Recipe for Brewing Success."

23. Kopytoff, "Cultural Biography of Things," 67–68; Cook and Crang, "World on a Plate," 148.

24. Wolfe, "Settler Colonialism and the Elimination of the Native."

25. Lambert, *Os dois Brasis*. For a trenchant critique, see Weinstein, *Color of Modernity*.

26. Hornborg, "Animism, Fetishism, and Objectivism," 24; Giddens, *Consequences of Modernity*, 22, 83, 102, 113.

27. Coe and Palmer, "Words of Our Ancestors"; Tansey and Rayner, "Cultural Theory and Risk."

28. Hornborg, "Animism, Fetishism, and Objectivism," 24; Rottenburg, "On Juridico-Political Foundations of Meta-Codes," 484.

29. Courtwright, *Forces of Habit*.

30. Latour, *We Have Never Been Modern*.

31. Nygren, "Local Knowledge in the Environment-Development Discourse," 267–88; Brunk, "Philosophical and Ethical Issues," 161–62.

32. Giddens, *Constitution of Society*, xxiii–xxiv.

33. See Giddens, *Consequences of Modernity*, 102, 114–17; Renn and Hyman, introduction, 17; Sahlins, "On the Culture of Material Value and the Cosmography of Riches," 181.

34. Giddens, *Constitution of Society*, 24, 362–63.

Bibliography

Archives and Libraries

Belém
    Arquivo Público do Estado do Pará
    Banco da Amazônia
    Centro de Documentação e Biblioteca
    Museu Emilio Goeldi
        Arquivo João Martins da Silva Coutinho
        1ª Comissão Brasileira Demarcadora de Limites, Library and Archive
        Coleção Ponte Ribeiro
Bronx, NY
    New York Botanical Garden
        LuEster T. Mertz Library, Archives and Manuscripts
        Norman Taylor Papers
Cambridge, MA
    Harvard University
    Museum of Comparative Zoology, Ernst Mayr Library
        Thayer Expedition Papers
    Schlesinger Library, Radcliffe Institute
        Elizabeth Agassiz Cary Agassiz Papers
Campinas, São Paulo
    Arquivo Edgard Leuenroth
        Fundo Ibope
Detroit, MI
    Detroit Public Library, Burton Historical Collection
        Parke, Davis & Company Records, 1862–1969
Lisbon
    Arquivo Histórico Ultramarino
        Conselho Ultramarino
London
    Royal Botanic Gardens, Kew, Library and Archives
        Director's Correspondence
        Miscellaneous Reports Collection
    Royal Geographical Society
        William Chandless Collection
Madison, WI
    Wisconsin Historical Society
        Francis Edward Stewart Papers, 1866–1938

Manaus
    Associação Comercial do Amazonas
    Museu Amazônico
    Museu Imagem e Som
Rio de Janeiro
    Associação Brasileira dos Farmacêuticos Library
    Biblioteca Nacional
        Hemeroteca Digital
    Instituto Histórico e Geográfico Brasileiro
São Paulo
    Instituto Socioambiental
Wilmington, DE
    Hagley Museum & Library
        Lanman & Kemp Records (1840–1925)

Interviews

Sérgio Garcia Wara, Parintins (via WhatsApp), December 23, 2021

Botanical, Medical, and Pharmaceutical Journals

American Journal of Pharmacy
Boletim da Associação Brasileira de Pharmacêuticos
Botanical Gazette
British Medical Journal
The Bulletin of Pharmacy
Bulletin of the Lloyd Library and Museum of Botany, Pharmacy and Materia Medica
Bulletin of the Torrey Botanical Club
The Canada Medical Record
The Chemist and Druggist
The Chicago Medical Journal and Examiner
The Cincinnati Lancet and Clinic New Series
The Doctor: A Monthly Review of British and Foreign Medical Practice and Literature
The Druggists Circular
The Eclectic Medical Journal
An Ephemeris of Materia Medica, Pharmacy, Therapeutics, and Collateral Information
Gaillard's Medical Journal
A Gazeta da Farmácia
Irish Hospital Gazette
Journal of the American Medical Association
Journal of the American Pharmaceutical Association
Journal of the Trinidad Field Naturalists' Club
The Lancet
New England Medical Monthly
New Remedies

Pharmaceutical Record and Weekly Market Review
The Practical Druggist
The Practitioner: A Journal of Therapeutics and Public Health
Proceedings of the American Pharmaceutical Association
Proceedings of the Georgia Pharmaceutical Association
The Retrospect of Medicine
Revista da Associação Brasileira de Farmacêuticos
Revista da Flora Medicinal
Revista Pharmacêutica
Rodriguésia
The St. Louis Courier of Medicine
St. Louis Medical Reporter
Therapeutic Gazette
Therapeutic Notes
Yearbook of Pharmacy

Periodicals

Aconteceu: Povos indígenas no Brasil
Adventist Heritage
The Advent Review and Sabbath Herald
Almanaque Brasil Socioambiental
Almanaque brasileiro Garnier
Archivos de hygiene e saúde pública
Boletim da Associação Comercial do
    Amazonas
Boletim do Instituto de Tecnologia de
    Alimentos
Bulletin de la Société Géologique de France
The Chicago Tribune
The Christian Science Monitor
A Cigarra
A Crítica
A Cruz: Órgão da Liga Católica da
    Archidiocese
A Cruz: Órgão da Liga do Bom Jesus
O Cruzeiro
O Dia
Diário de Pernambuco
Diário Popular
The Economist
O Estado de São Paulo
Folha da Tarde
Folha de São Paulo
Folha de São Paulo Ribeirão

Fon-Fon
Forbes
Gazeta Mercantil
O Globo
The Guardian
Indústria e Mercados
Jornal do Brasil
Jornal do Commércio
Journal of the Royal Geographical Society
    of London
O Liberal
Los Angeles Times
Manchete
O Matto-Grosso
The Ministry
The New York Times
Northern Territory Times and Gazette
A Notícia
Noticiador Cuiabano
O Panorama
Otago Daily Times
Para Todos
Le Petit Journal
Porantim
Publicidade & Negócios
O Radical
Revista ABIR

Revista Brazilea
Revista da Associação Comercial do
   Amazonas
Revista da Semana
Revista do Club de Engenharia
Revista Espaço Aberto

Revista da Sociedade de Geographia do Rio
   de Janeiro
Smithsonian Magazine
South American Bulletin
Treze de Maio
The Wall Street Journal
Veja

Published Primary Sources

Abreu, José Coelho da Gama e. *A Amazônia: As províncias do Pará e Amazonas e o governo central do Brazil*. Lisbon: Minerva, 1883.

Abreu, Luiz Eduardo Lobão de, João de Souza Araújo Júnior, and Lídia Loureiro de Cruz. "Painel: Agroindústria do guaraná." In *Anais do 1º Simpósio Brasileiro do Guaraná, 24 a 28 de Outubro de 1983, Manaus, AM*, 149–54. Manaus: EMBRAPA and UEPAE, 1984.

Agassiz, Elizabeth Cary, ed. *Louis Agassiz: His Life and Correspondence*. Vol. 2. New York, Houghton, Mifflin, 1893.

Agassiz, Jean Louis Rodolphe. *Conversações scientíficas sobre o Amazonas feitas na sala do externato do collégio de Pedro II durante o mez de Maio de 1866*. Rio de Janeiro: J. Villeneuve, 1866.

Agassiz, Louis, and Elizabeth Cabot Cary Agassiz. *A Journey in Brazil*. Boston: Ticknor and Fields, 1868.

Agassiz, Louis, and João Martins da Silva Coutinho. "Sur le geologie de L'Amazone." *Comptes Rendus de Academie des Sciences* 64 (1868): 1269–71.

Albuquerque, Francisco de. *Da chímica bromatólogica do guaraná*. Rio de Janeiro: Separata da Revista Alimentar, 1937.

Almeida, Edith Ewerton de. *Guaraná*. Rio de Janeiro: Ministério da Agricultura, Serviço de Estatística da Produção, 1953.

Almeida, Francisco José de Lacerda e. *Diário da viagem do Dr. Francisco José de Lacerda e Almeida pelas capitanias do Pará, Rio Negro, Matto Grosso, Cuyabá e São Paulo nos anos de 1780 a 1790*. São Paulo: Typ. de Costa Silveira, 1841.

Amazonas, Lourenço da Silva Araújo e. *Dicionário topográfico, histórico, descritivo da comarca do Alto Amazonas*. Recife: Typografia Commercial de Meira Henriques, 1852.

Barreto, Luiz Pereira. "A higiene da mesa." In *Antologia da alimentação no Brasil*, edited by Luís da Câmara Cascudo, 147–51. Rio de Janeiro: Livros Técnicos e Científicos, 1977.

———. "O século XX sob o ponto de vista brasileiro." In *Plataforma política do positivismo ilustrado*, edited by Antônio Paim, 38–42. Brasília: Editora Universidade de Brasília, 1981.

———. "A vinha e a civilização." In *Plataforma política do positivismo ilustrado*, edited by Antônio Paim, 14–23. Brasília: Editora Universidade de Brasília, 1981.

Bartholow, Roberts. *A Practical Treatise on Materia Medica and Therapeutics*. New York: D. Appleton, 1903.

Bastos, A. C. Tavares. *O vale do Amazonas*. São Paulo: Companhia Editora Nacional, 1937.

Bates, Henry Walter. *The Naturalist on the River Amazons*. London: Electric Book, 2000.

Beard, G. M. *American Nervousness: Its Causes and Consequences*. New York: G. P. Putnam's Sons, 1881.

Bettendorff, João Felipe. *Crônica da missão dos padres da companhia de Jesus no Estado do Maranhão*. Belém: Fundação Cultural do Pará Tancredo Neves; Secretaria de Estado da Cultura, 1990.

Bowen, Seabury W. "Testimony of Dr. Seabury W. Bowden in the Trial of Lizzie Borden." *Famous Trials*, edited by Douglas O. Linder. University of Missouri, Kansas City School of Law: 2016. www.famous-trials.com/lizzieborden/1449-bowentestimony.

Brasil. Comissão Nacional da Verdade. *Relatório: textos temáticos*. Vol. 2. Brasília: CNV, 2014.

Campbell, Hugh. *Neurasthenia: Cerebro-Spinal Exhaustion*. 16th ed. London: Henry Renshaw, 1883.

Casal, Manuel Aires de. *Corografia brazílica* [1817]. Vol. 2. Rio de Janeiro: Imprensa Nacional, 1945–47.

Castro, Josué de. *As condições de vida da classe operária no Recife: Estudo econômico de sua alimentação*. Recife: Editora Massangana, 2015.

Chandless, William. "Notes on the Rivers Arinos, Juruena, and Tapajós." *Journal of the Royal Geographical Society of London* 32 (1862): 268–80.

———. "A Visit to the India-Rubber Groves of the Amazons." In *Illustrated Travels: A Record of Discovery, Geography, and Adventure*, edited by H. W. Bates, 190–91. London: Cassell, Petter, Galpin, 1869.

Chernoviz, Pedro Luiz Napoleão. *Formulário ou guia médico*. 6th ed. Paris: Em Casa do Autor, 1864.

Collecção das leis provinciaes de Mato Grosso sancionadas e promulgadas no anno de 1850. Cuiabá: Typographia do Echo Cuiabano, 1851.

Collecção das leis provinciaes de Mato Grosso sancionadas e promulgadas no anno de 1854. Cuiabá: Typographia do Echo Cuiabano, 1854.

Collecção das leis provinciaes de Mato Grosso sancionadas e promulgadas no anno de 1857. Cuiabá: Typographia do Echo Cuiabano, 1858.

Costa, Flavio Guimarães da. "A indústria do guaraná no Amazonas." In *Anais do 1º Simpósio Brasileiro do Guaraná, 24 a 28 de Outubro de 1983, Manaus, AM*, 93–103. Manaus: EMBRAPA and UEPAE, 1984.

Coudreau, Henri. *Viagem ao Tapajós (28 de Julho de 1895 a 7 de Janeiro de 1896)*. Translated by A. de Miranda Bastos. São Paulo: Companhia Editora Nacional, 1941.

Coutinho, João Martins da Silva. "Breve notícia sobre a extracção da salsa e da seringa: Vantagens de sua cultura." In *Relatório apresentado na abertura da 2ª sessão da Assembleia Legislativa da Provincia do Amazonas pelo Exm. Snr. Dr. Sinval Odorico de Moura, presidente da Mesma Província, em 25 de Março de 1863*, 41–51.

———. "Exploração do Amazonas: Offícios do Dr. S. Coutinho." In Ministério da Agricultura, *Relatório do Anno de 1865 apresentado a Assemblea Geral Legislativa na 4ª Sessão da 12a Legislatura*, Annex C, 1–2. Rio de Janeiro: Typographia Perseverança, 1866.

———. "Notícia sobre o uaraná ou guaraná." *Revista Agrícola do Imperial Instituto Fluminense de Agricultura* 4 (June 1870): 1–13.

———. "Officio do engenheiro J. M. da Silva Coutinho sobre o uaraná e outros produtos da província do Amazonas." In Ministério da Agricultura, *Relatório do Anno de 1865 apresentado a Assemblea Geral Legislativa na 4ª Sessão da 12ª Legislatura,* Annex C, 1–2. Rio de Janeiro: Typographia Perseverança, 1866.

———. "Relatório apresentado ao Ilm. e Exm. Sr. Dr. Manoel Clementino Carneiro da Cunha, presidente da província do Amazonas, por J. M. da Silva Coutinho, encarregado de examinar alguns lugares da província, especialmente o Rio Madeira debaixo do ponto de vista da colonisação e navegação." In *Relatório da Repartição dos Negócios da Agricultura, Commércio e Obras Públicas apresentado à Assemblea Geral Legislativa na segunda sessão na décima primeira legislatura pelo respectivo ministro e secretário de Estado Manoel Felizardo de Souza e Mello,* Appendix G, 1–23. Rio de Janeiro: Typographia Universal de Laemmert, 1862.

———. *Relatório da Comissão Brazileira apresentado ao Exm. S. Conselheiro Thomas José Coelho de Almeida, Ministro e Secretário de Estado dos Negócios e Agricultura, Comércio e Obras Públicas.* Rio de Janeiro: Typographia Nacional, 1878.

———. "Relatório da exploração do Rio Purus apresentado pelo engenheiro João Martins da Silva Coutinho, 1862." In *Relatório apresentado à Assembléa Geral Legislativa na terceira sessão da décima segunda legislatura pelo Ministro e Secretário de Estado dos Negócios de Agricultura, Commércio e Obras Públicas Jesuíno Marcondes de Oliveira e Sá,* Annex O, 1–96. Rio de Janeiro: Typographia Universal de Laemmert, 1865.

Coutinho, Ruy. *Valor social da alimentação.* Rio de Janeiro: Civilização Brasileira, 1937.

Cozinheiro nacional. Rio de Janeiro: B. L. Garnier, 1895.

Daniel, João. *Tesouro descoberto no Rio Amazonas.* Vol. 1. Rio de Janeiro: Anais da Biblioteca Nacional, 1975.

Doceiro nacional ou arte de fazer toda a qualidade de doces. Rio de Janeiro: Typographia Garnier Irmãos, 1895.

Estatutos de Consórcio de Guaraná organizado entre produtores e comerciantes manipuladores. Manaus: Papelaria Velho Lino, 1934.

Fletcher, James C., and D. P. Kidder. *Brazil and the Brazilians.* Boston: Little, Brown, 1867.

Halliwell, Leo. *Light in the Jungle: The Thirty Years' Mission of Leo and Jessie Halliwell along the Amazon.* New York: D. McKay, 1959.

Harshberger, J. W. "The Purposes of Ethno-Botany." *Botanical Gazette* 21, no. 3 (March 1896): 146–54.

Instituto Brasileiro de Geografia e Estatística. *Pesquisa de orçamentos familiares, 2002–2003: Primeiros resultados: Brasil e grandes regiões.* Rio de Janeiro: IBGE, 2004.

———. *Pesquisa de orçamentos familiares, 2008–2009: Despesas, rendimentos e condições de vida.* Rio de Janeiro: IBGE, 2010.

J. Walter Thompson Company. *The Latin American Markets, 1956: A Descriptive and Statistical Survey of 30 Markets Made up of Almost 173 Million People* (New York: McGraw-Hill, 1956).

Keller, Franz. *The Amazon and Madeira Rivers: Sketches and Descriptions from the Note-Book of an Explorer.* Philadelphia: J. B. Lippincott, 1875.

Lankester, E. "Relatório de E. Lankester." In Francisco Ignacio de Carvalho Moreira, *Relatório sobre a Exposição Internacional de 1862 apresentado a S.M. o Imperador,* 36–37. London: Thomas Brettell, 1863.

Lapa, José Roberto do Amaral. *Livro da visitação do Santo Ofício da Inquisição ao Estado do Grão Pará, 1763–1769, texto inédito e apresentação José Roberto do Amaral Lapa*. Petrópolis: Vozes, 1978.

Leacock, Seth. "Economic and Social Factors in Maué Persistence." PhD diss., University of California, Berkeley, 1958.

———. "Economic Life of the Maué Indians." *Boletim do Museu Paraense Emílio Goeldi*, Nova Série, Antropologia, no. 19 (1964): 1–30.

———. "Maué Kinship and Omaha Terminology." *Journal of Anthropological Research* 29, no. 1 (Spring 1973): 59–76.

Magalhães, José Vieira Couto de. *O selvagem*. 3rd ed. São Paulo: Companhia Editora Nacional, 1935.

Maravalhas, Nelson. *Estudos sobre o guaraná e outras plantas produtoras de cafeína*. Manaus: Instituto Nacional de Pesquisas da Amazônia, 1965.

Marcou, Jules. *Life, Letters, and Works of Louis Agassiz*. Vol. 2. New York: Macmillan, 1896.

Martius, Karl Friedrich Philipp von. *Natureza, doenças, medicina e remédios dos índios brasileiros*. Translated by Manoel Agosto Pirajá da Silva. São Paulo: Companhia Editora Nacional, 1939.

———. *Systema de materia medica vegetal brasileira*. Translated by Henrique Velloso d'Oliveira. Rio de Janeiro: Laemmert, 1854.

Masô, João Alberto. "O guaraná." *Revista da Sociedade de Geographia do Rio de Janeiro*. Vols. 9–11, 1906–1908. 143–52. Rio de Janeiro: Imprensa Nacional, 1918.

Mathews, Edward Davis. *Up the Amazon and Madeira Rivers, through Bolivia and Peru*. London: Sampson Low, Marston, Searle & Rivington, 1879.

Matta, Alfredo da. *Flora médica brasiliense*. Manaus: Imprensa Oficial, 1913.

Mello, A. da Silva. *A alimentação no Brasil: problemas e sugestões*. Rio de Janeiro: Edições Cruzeiro, 1946.

Melo, Luiz Antelmo Silva. "Apresentação." In *Anais do 1º Simpósio Brasileiro do Guaraná, 24 a 28 de Outubro de 1983, Manaus, AM*, 8. Manaus: EMBRAPA and UEPAE, 1984.

Mills, Charles K. *The Nervous System and Its Diseases: A Practical Treatise on Neurology for the Use of Physicians and Students*. Philadelphia: J. B. Lippincott, 1898.

Moraes, Eduardo José de. *Navegação interior do Brasil; notícia dos projectos apresentados para a juncção de diversas bacias hydrographicas do Brasil, ou rápido esboço da futura rede geral de suas vias navegáveis*. Rio de Janeiro: Laemmert, 1894.

Moreira, Francisco Ignacio de Carvalho. *Relatório sobre a Exposição Internacional de 1862 apresentado a S.M. o imperador*. London: Thomas Brettell, 1863.

Moreira, Nicolau Joaquim. *Diccionário de plantas medicinais brasileiras*. Rio de Janeiro: Correio Mercantil, 1862.

Moutinho, Joaquim Ferreira. *Notícia sobre a província de Matto Grosso, seguida d'um roteiro da viagem da sua capital a São Paulo*. São Paulo: Typographia de H. Schroeder, 1869.

Murray G. Motter, and Martin I. Wilbert, eds. "Guaraná." In *Digest of Comments on the Pharmacopoeia of the United States of America and on the National Formulary for the Calendar Year Ending December 31, 1909*, 406–7. Washington, DC: Government Printing Office, 1912.

Noronha, José Monteiro de. *Roteiro da viagem da cidade do Pará, até as ultimas colônias do sertão da província, escripto na Villa de Barcellos pelo Vigário Geral do Rio Negro no Anno de 1768*. Pará: Typographia de Santos & Irmãos, 1862.

Orton, James. *The Andes and the Amazon; or, Across the Continent of South America*. New York: Harper and Brothers, 1870.

Parke, Davis & Company. *An Epitome of the Newer Materia Medica, Standard Medicinal Products, and Fine Pharmaceutical Specialties*. 2nd ed. Detroit: Parke, Davis, 1886.

———. *The Pharmacology of the Newer Materia Medica*. Detroit: George S. Davis, 1892.

Penna, Herculano Ferreira. *Falla dirigida à Assembléa Legislativa Provincial do Amazonas, no Dia 1º de Outubro de 1853, em que se Abriu a sua 2ª Sessão Ordinária, pelo Presidente da Província, o Conselheiro Herculano Ferreira Penna*. Amazonas: Typographia de M.S. Ramos, 1853.

Peregrino Júnior, João. *Alimentação e cultura*. Rio de Janeiro: Serviço de Alimentação da Previdência Social, 1951.

Queirós, João de São José de, "Viagem e visita do sertão em o Bispado do Grão-Pará em 1762–1763." *Revista do Instituto Histórico e Geográfico Brasileiro* 9 (1847): 43–107, 179–227, 328–75, 476–527.

Rebouças, Antonio Pereira. *Apontamentos sobre a via de comunicação do Rio Madeira*. Rio de Janeiro: Typographia Nacional, 1870.

Relatório apresentado à Assembléa Legislativa da província do Amazonas na sessão ordinária do 1º de Outubro de 1864, pelo Dr. Adolfo de Barros Cavalcanti de Albuquerque Lacerda, presidente da mesma província. Pernambuco: Typographia de Manoel Figueiroa de Faria & Filho, 1864.

Relatório apresentado à Assembléa Legislativa da província do Amazonas pelo Exm. Senr. Dr. Manoel Clementino Carneiro da Cunha, presidente da Mesma Província, na sessão ordinária de 3 de Maio de 1862. Pará: Typographia de Frederico Carlos Rhossard, 1862.

Relatório apresentado à Assembléa Legislativa Rovincial [sic], pelo excellentíssimo senhor doutor João Pedro Dias Vieira, digníssimo presidente desta província, no Dia 8 de Julho de 1856 por occasião da primeira sessão ordinária da terceira legislatura da mesma assembléa. Barra do Rio Negro: Typographia de F. J. S. Ramos, 1856.

Relatório apresentado ao Exmo. Sr. Dr. Agesilão Pereira da Silva, presidente da província do Amazonas pelo Dr. Domingos Jacy Monteiro, depois de ter entregue a administração da província em 26 de Maio de 1877. Manaus: Typographia do Amazonas de José Carneiro dos Santos, 1878.

Relatório com que o Exm. Snr. Dr. Antônio Epaminondas de Mello, presidente da província do Amazonas, entregou a administração da província do Amazonas ao Exc. Snr. Dr. Gustavo Adolpho Ramos Ferreira vice-presidente da mesma em 24 de junho de 1866. Recife: Typographia do Jornal do Recife, 1866.

Relatório que a Assembléa Legislativa Provincial do Amazonas apresentou na abertura da sessão ordinária em o dia 7 de setembro de 1858 ao Francisco José Furtado, presidente da Mesma Província. Manaus: Typographia de Francisco José da Silva Ramos, 1858.

Relatório sobre os produtos agrícolas do alto Amazonas. In *Relatório apresentado à Assembléa Legislativa da província do Amazonas pelo Exm. Senr. Dr. Manoel Clementino Carneiro da Cunha, presidente da Mesma Província, na sessão ordinária de 3 de Maio de 1862*, Appendix D, 4. Pará: Typographia de Frederico Carlos Rhossard, 1862.

Rodrigues, João Barbosa. "Extracto de um livro inédito." In *Revista da Exposição Anthropologica Brazileira*, edited by Alexandre José de Mello Moraes, 150–52. Rio de Janeiro: Pinheiro & C., 1882.

———. *O Rio Tapajós*. Rio de Janeiro: Typografia Nacional, 1875.

Roquette-Pinto, Edgar. *O guaraná*. Rio de Janeiro: Serviço Nacional de Agricultura, 1912.

Rusby, Henry H. "The College of Pharmacy of the City of New York." *The University Magazine* 11, no. 2 (August 1894): 93–109.

———. *Jungle Memories*. New York: Whittlesey House, 1933.

Sacramento, Célio Kersul do. "A guaranaicultura no estado da Bahia." In *Anais do 1º Simpósio Brasileiro do Guaraná, 24 a 28 de Outubro de 1983, Manaus, AM*, 129–42. Manaus: EMBRAPA and UEPAE, 1984.

Sampaio, Francisco Xavier Ribeiro de. *Diário da viagem que em visita, e correição das povoações da capitania de S. Jozé do Rio Negro fez o ouvidor, e intendente geral da mesma Francisco Xavier Ribeiro de Sampaio, no anno de 1774 e 1775*. Lisbon: Typografia da Academia, 1825.

Saxe, De Forest W. *Saxe's New Guide or Hints to Soda Water Dispensers*. Chicago: Saxe Guide, 1898.

Serra, Ricardo Franco de Almeida, "Navegação do rio Tapajós para o Pará." *Revista do Instituto Histórico e Geográfico* 9 (1847): 1–16.

Silva, Bernardo da Costa e. *Viagens no sertão do Amazonas*. Porto: Arthur Jose de Sousa & Irmão, 1891.

Souza, Francisco Bernardino de. *Curiosidades e lembranças do valle do Amazonas*. Pará: Typographia do Futuro, 1873.

Spix, Johann Baptist von, and Carl Friedrich Philipp von Martius. *Viagem pelo Brasil, 1817–1820*. Translated by Lúcia Furquim Lahmeyer. 3 vols. Belo Horizonte: Itatiaia/ São Paulo: Editora da Universidade de São Paulo, 1981.

Spruce, Richard. "Botanical Objects Communicated to the Kew Museum, from the Amazon or Its Tributaries, in 1853." *Hooker's Journal of Botany and Kew Garden Miscellany* 7 (1855): 245–52.

———. "Journal of a Voyage from Santarém to the Barra do Rio Negro." *Hooker's Journal of Botany and Kew Garden Miscellany* 3 (1851): 270–78.

———. *Notes of a Botanist on the Amazon and Andes*. London: Macmillan, 1908.

———. "On Some Remarkable Narcotics of the Amazon Valley and Orinoco." *Ocean Highways Geographic Review* 1, no. 55 (1873): 184–93.

Squibb's Materia Medica. 1906 ed. New York: E. R. Squibb & Sons, 1906.

Steinen, Karl von den, *Uma expedição ao Xingu*. Brazil: Fundação Projeto Rondon-MINTER; Ministério da Educação-SESU, 1975[?].

Superintendência da Amazônia, Departamento de Setores Produtivos, *Guaraná: aspectos agroeconômicos, região norte*. Belém, 1985.

Tavares. R. L. *O Rio Tapajoz*. Rio de Janeiro: Typographia Nacional, 1876.

Teixeira, Pery. *Sateré-Mawé: Retrato de um povo indígena*. Manaus: UFAM, 2005.

Teixeira, Pery, and Marília Brasil. "Estudo demográfico dos Sateré-Mawé: Um exemplo de censo participativo." In *Demografia dos povos indígenas no Brasil*, edited by Heloísa Pagliaro, Marta Maria Azevedo, and Ricardo Ventura Santos, 135–54. Rio de Janeiro: Editora Fiocruz, 2005.

Teixeira, Sônia Milagres. "Estudo do mercado do guaraná." In *Anais do 1º Simpósio Brasileiro do Guaraná, 24 a 28 de Outubro de 1983, Manaus, AM*, 155–75. Manaus: EMBRAPA and UEPAE, 1984.

U.S. Department of Agriculture, Bureau of Plant Industry. *Inventory of Seeds and Plants Imported by the Office of Foreign Seed and Plant Introduction during the Period from July 1 to September 30, 1922*. Washington, DC: Government Printing Office, 1924.

———. *Inventory of Seeds and Plants Imported by the Office of Foreign Seed and Plant Introduction during the Period from October 1 to December 31, 1918*. Washington, DC: Government Printing Office, 1922.

Valois, Afonso Celso Candeira. "Discurso proferido por Afonso Celso Candeira Valois, representante da Embrapa, por ocasião da abertura do 1º Simpósio Brasileiro do Guaraná." In *Anais do 1º Simpósio Brasileiro do Guaraná, 24 a 28 de Outubro de 1983, Manaus, AM*, 21–25. Manaus: EMBRAPA and UEPAE, 1984.

"A Valuable Remedy for Headache." In *The Cincinnati Lancet and Clinic*, n.s., vol. 16, edited by J. C. Culberston, 170–71. Cincinnati: J. C. Culbertson, 1886.

Viktor, Prince Adalbert Ferdinand Berengar. *Brasil: Amazonas-Xingu*. Translated by Eduardo Lima Castro. Belo Horizonte: Itatiaia, 1977.

Wilks, Samuel. *Lectures on Diseases of the Nervous System*. London: Churchill, 1883.

Wyeth Laboratories. *An Epitome of Therapeutics with Special Reference to the Laboratory of John Wyeth & Brother Incorporated*. Philadelphia: John Wyeth & Brother, 1901.

Secondary Sources

Abreu, João Capistrano de. *Chapters of Brazil's Colonial History, 1500–1800*. Translated by Arthur Brakel. New York: Oxford University Press, 1997.

Acker, Antoine. *Volkswagen in the Amazon: The Tragedy of Global Development in Modern Brazil*. Cambridge: Cambridge University Press, 2017.

Adas, Michael. *Machines as the Measures of Men: Science, Technology, and Ideologies of Western Dominance*. Ithaca, NY: Cornell University Press, 2015.

Agrawal, Arun. "Dismantling the Divide between Indigenous and Scientific Knowledge." *Development and Change* 26, no. 3 (July 1995): 413–39.

Albert, Bruce. "Associações indígenas e desenvolvimento sustentável na Amazônia brasileira." In *Povos indígenas no Brasil, 1996/2000*, edited by Carlos Alberto Ricardo, 197–207. São Paulo: Instituto Socioambiental, 2000.

Alden, Dauril. "Some Reflections on Antonio Vieira: Seventeenth-Century Troubleshooter and Troublemaker." *Luso-Brazilian Review* 40, no. 1 (Summer 2003): 7–16.

Alfaro, M. A. Martínez, R. Ortega Paczka, and A. Cruz León. "Introduction of Flora from the Old World and Causes of Crop Marginalization." In *Neglected Crops: 1492 from a Different Perspective*, edited by J. E. Hernández Bermejo and J. León, 23–31. Rome: Food and Agriculture Organization of the United Nations, 1994.

Aliança pela Alimentação Adequada e Saudável. "Obesidade infantil: precisamos falar sobre a publicidade de alimentos." Huffington Post Brazil. April 12, 2018. https://web .archive.org/web/20200927014512/https://www.huffpostbrasil.com/alianca-pela

-alimentacao-adequada-e-saudavel/obesidade-infantil-precisamos-falar-sobre-a
-publicidade-de-alimentos_a_23409516.

Allen, Patricia, and Martin Kovach. "The Capitalist Composition of Organic: The Potential of Markets in Fulfilling the Promise of Organic Agriculture." *Agriculture and Human Values* 17, no. 3 (2000): 221–32.

Almeida, Juliana. *Saberes e fazeres: o guaraná de Maués*. São Paulo: Museu da Pessoa, 2007.

Alonso, Angela. "O positivismo de Luís Pereira Barreto e pensamento brasileiro no final do século XIX." São Paulo: Instituto de Estudos Avançados da Universidade de São Paulo, 1995. www.iea.usp.br/publicacoes/textos/alonsopositivismo.pdf.

Alvarez, Gabriel O. *Satereria: tradição e política—Sateré-Mawé*. Manaus: Valer; CAPES; Prodoc, 2009.

Alves, Lucio F. "Produção de fitoterápicos no Brasil: história, problemas e perspectivas." *Revista Virtual de Química* 5, no. 3 (May–June 2013): 456–57.

Alves-Melo, Patricia. "The Portuguese Crown's Policies towards Indians in the 17th and 18th Centuries." *Oxford Research Encyclopedia of Latin American History*. https://oxfordre.com/latinamericanhistory/view/10.1093/acrefore/9780199366439.001.0001/acrefore-9780199366439-e-626.

Amazonia.org.br. "Acusados no caso do guaraná dos índios Sateré-Mawé respondem à denúncia," Terras Indígenas no Brasil, November 29, 2008. https://terrasindigenas.org.br/noticia/62577.

Andermann, Jens. *The Optic of the State: Visuality and Power in Argentina and Brazil*. Pittsburgh: University of Pittsburgh Press, 2007.

Anderson, Benedict. *Imagined Communities: Reflections on the Origin and Spread of Nationalism*. 2nd ed. London: Verso, 1991.

Anderson, E. N. "Caffeine and Culture." In *Drugs, Labor, and Colonial Expansion*, edited by William Jankowiak and Daniel Bradburd, 159–76. Tucson: University of Arizona Press, 2003.

Anderson, Robin L. *Colonization as Exploitation in the Amazon Rainforest, 1758–1911*. Gainesville: University Press of Florida, 1999.

Ângelo, Paula C. S., Carlos G. Nunes-Silva, Marcelo M. Brígido, Juliana S. N. Azevedo, Enedina N. Assunção, Alexandra R. B. Sousa, Fernando J. B. Patrício, et al. "Guaraná (*Paullinia cupana* var. *sorbilis*), an Anciently Consumed Stimulant from the Amazon Rain Forest: The Seeded Fruit Transcriptome." *Plant Cell Reports* 27, no. 1 (2008): 117–24.

Antunes, Anderson Pereira. "A rede dos invisíveis: Uma análise dos auxiliares na expedição de Louis Agassiz ao Brasil (1865–1866)." Master's thesis, Fundação Oswaldo Cruz, Casa de Oswaldo Cruz, 2015.

Apolinário, Juciene Ricarte. "Plantas nativas, indígenas coloniais: Usos e apropriações da flora da América portuguesa." In *Usos e circulação de plantas no Brasil, séculos XVI–XIX*, edited by Lorelai Kury, 182–227. Rio de Janeiro: Andrea Jakobsson Estúdio, 2013.

Arenz, Karl Heinz. "Do Alzette ao Amazonas: vida e obra do Padre João Felipe Bettendorff (1625–1698)." *Revista Estudos Amazônicos* 5, no. 1 (2010): 25–30.

———. "Não Saulos, mas Paulos: uma carta do Padre João Felipe Bettendorff da missão do Maranhão (1671)." *Revista de História* 168 (January–June 2013): 271–322.

Armitage, David, and Jo Guldi. *The History Manifesto*. Cambridge: Cambridge University Press, 2017.

Arnold, David, ed. Introduction to *Imperial Medicine and Indigenous Societies*, 1–26. Manchester: Manchester University Press, 1988.

Arroyo-Kalin, Manuel. "The Amazonian Formative: Crop Domestication and Anthropogenic Soils." *Diversity* 2, no. 4 (2010): 473–504.

Arruda, Gustavo. *A história da Fratelli Vita no Recife*. Recife: Self-published, 2014.

Ashurst, Philip R., ed. Introduction to *The Chemistry and Technology of Soft Drinks and Fruit Juices*, 1–14. Sheffield: Sheffield Academic Press, 1998.

Associação Brasileira dos Fabricantes de Latas de Alta Reciclabilidade. "História da lata de alumínio para bebidas." Abralatas. April 6, 2015. www.abralatas.org.br/wp-content /themes/abralatas/docs/historiaConteudo.pdf.

Atroch, André Luiz, and Firmino J. do Nascimento Filho. "Guaraná—*Paullinia cupana* Kunth var. *sorbilis* (Mart.) Ducke." In *Exotic Fruits Reference Guide*, edited by Sueli Rodrigues, Ebenezer de Oliveira Silva, and Edy Sousa de Brito, 225–36. London: Academic Press, 2018.

Atroch, André Luiz, F. J. Nascimento Filho, P. C. S. Angelo, D. V. Freitas, N. R. Sousa, M. D. V. Resende, and C. R. Clement. "Domesticação e melhoramento de guaranazeiro." In *Domesticação e melhoramento: espécies amazônicas*, edited by Aloízio Borém, Maria Tereza G. Lopes and Charles R. Clement, 333–61. Viçosa: Universidade Federal de Viçosa, 2009.

Baer, Werner. *The Brazilian Economy: Growth and Development*. 5th ed. Westport, CT: Praeger, 2001.

Balée, William. *Cultural Forests of the Amazon: A Historical Ecology of People and their Landscapes*. Tuscaloosa: University of Alabama Press, 2013.

Balick, Michael J., and Paul A. Cox. *Plants, People, and Culture: The Science of Ethnobotany*. New York: Scientific American Library, 1996.

Balston, Catherine. "Guaraná: The Edible 'Eyes of the Amazon.'" BBC Travel, April 29, 2021. www.bbc.com/travel/story/20210428-guaran-the-edible-eyes-of-the-amazon ?referer=https%3A%2F%2Fwww.bbc.com%2Fnews%2Fworld-latin-america-36028247.

Barbosa, Gabriela Ferreira. "Almanaques de farmácia: corpo e saúde na construção do Brasil (1937–1945)." Paper presented at XXVII Simpósio Nacional de História, Natal, RJ, June 22 to 26, 2013. São Paulo: Associação Nacional dos Professores Universitários de História, 2013. www.snh2013.anpuh.org/resources/anais/27/1364949280_ARQUIVO _Almanaquesdefarmacia.pdf.

Barbosa, Luiz C. *Guardians of the Brazilian Rainforest: Environmental Organizations and Development*. London: Routledge, 2015.

Barreiro, José Carlos. *Imaginário e viajantes no Brasil do século XIX: cultura e cotidiano, tradição e resistência*. São Paulo: Editora Universidade Estadual Paulista, 2002.

Barros, Roque Spencer Maciel de. *A evolução do pensamento de Pereira Barreto*. São Paulo: Editorial Grijalbo, 1967.

Barthes, Roland. *Mythologies*. Translated by Annette Lavers. New York: Hill and Wang, 1972.

———. "Toward a Psychosociology of Contemporary Food Consumption." In *Food and Culture: A Reader*, edited by Carole Counihan and Penny van Esterik, 23–31. New York: Routledge, 2013.

Batista, Djalma. *O complexo da Amazônia: análise do processo de desenvolvimento*. 2nd ed. Manaus: Editora Valer; Editora INPA; Editora da Universidade Federal do Amazonas, 2007.

Batista Filho, Malaquias, and Anete Rissin. "A transição nutricional no Brasil: *tendências regionais e temporais*." *Cadernos de saúde pública* 19, suppl. 1 (2003): 181–91.

Bauer, Ralph, and Marcy Norton. "Introduction: Entangled Trajectories; Indigenous and European Histories." *Colonial Latin American Review* 26, no. 1 (2017): 1–17.

Baumann, Thomas W., Brigitte Schulthess, and Karin Hänni. "Guaraná (*Paullinia cupana*) Rewards Seed Dispersers without Intoxicating Them by Caffeine." *Phytochemistry* 39, no. 5 (1995): 1063–70.

Beattie, Peter M. *The Tribute of Blood: Army, Honor, Race, and Nation in Brazil, 1864–1945*. Durham, NC: Duke University Press, 2001.

Beaufort, Bastien. "La mercatique transatlantique d'un végétal psychoactif: le guaraná entre remède et aliment (1840–1921)." *Confins* 35 (2018). https://doi.org/10.4000/confins.13215.

———. "Le *Waraná* des Indiens Sateré Mawé: plante amazonienne en voie de globalisation et extension des frontières du commerce équitable." *Revue internationale des études du développement* 4, no. 240 (2019): 95–121.

Beck, Hans T. "Caffeine, Alcohol, and Sweeteners." In *The Cultural History of Plants*, edited by Ghillean Prance and Mark Nesbitt, 173–90. New York: Routledge, 2005.

Begliomini, Helio. "Luiz Pereira Barreto (1840–1923) presidente (1895–1896) e patrono da cadeira n° 1." *Biografias de acadêmicos*. Academia de Medicina de São Paulo, September 10, 2011. www.academiamedicinasaopaulo.org.br/biografias/1/BIOGRAFIA-LUIZ-PEREIRA -BARRETO.pdf.

Beinart, William, and Karen Middleton. "Plant Transfers in Historical Perspective: A Review Article." *Environment and History* 10 (2004): 3–29.

Belasco, Warren J. *Appetite for Change: How the Counterculture Took on the Food Industry*. Ithaca, NY: Cornell University Press, 2006.

Belik, Daniel. "Indigenous Routes: Interfluves and Interpreters in the Upper Tapajós River (c. 1750–1950)." PhD diss., St. Andrews University, 2018.

Belik, Walter. *The Food Industry in Brazil: Towards a Restructuring?* London: Institute of Latin American Studies, 1994.

Bell, Catherine. *Ritual Theory, Ritual Practice*. New York: Oxford University Press, 1992.

Belluzzo, Ana Maria de Morais. *O Brasil dos viajantes*. 2nd ed. São Paulo/Rio de Janeiro: Metalivros/Objetiva, 1999.

Belluzzo, Rosa. *Nem garfo, nem faca: à mesa com os cronistas e viajantes*. São Paulo: Editora Senac São Paulo, 2019.

Belluzzo, Rosa, and Marina Heck. *Doces sabores*. São Paulo: Studio Nobel, 2002.

Benchimol, Samuel. *Navegação e transporte na Amazônia*. Manaus: Governo do Estado do Amazonas, 1995.

Bender, George A. "Henry Hurd Rusby: Scientific Explorer, Societal Crusader, Scholastic Innovator." *Pharmacy in History* 23, no. 2 (1981): 71–85.

Bennett, Tony. *The Birth of the Museum: History, Theory, Politics*. London: Routledge, 1995.

Bergmann, Linda S. "A Troubled Marriage of Discourses: Science Writing and Travel Narrative in Louis and Elizabeth Agassiz's *A Journey in Brazil*." *Journal of American Culture* 18, no. 2 (Summer 1995): 83–88.

Berkhofer, Robert F., Jr. *The White Man's Indian: Images of the American Indian from Columbus to the Present.* New York: Vintage Books, 1979.

Bermejo, J. E. Hernández, and J. León, eds. Preface to *Neglected Crops: 1492 from a Different Perspective,* xix–xxi. Rome: Food and Agriculture Organization of the United Nations, 1994.

Bernardelli, Giorgio. "The Missionary of the Sateré-Mawé." *PIME: Missionaries since 1850.* Pontifical Institute for Foreign Missions, May 29, 2019. www.pimeusa.org/2019/05/the -missionary-of-the-satere-mawe.

Besse, Susan K. *Restructuring Patriarchy: The Modernization of Gender Inequality in Brazil, 1914–1940.* Chapel Hill: University of North Carolina Press, 1996.

Bezerra, José Arimatea Barros. "Educação alimentar e a constituição de trabalhadores fortes, robustos e produtivos: análise da produção científica em nutrição no Brasil, 1934–1941." *História, ciências, saúde—Manguinhos* 19, no. 1 (January–March 2012): 157–79.

Bittencourt, Agnello. *Dicionário amazonense de biografias: vultos do passado.* Rio de Janeiro: Conquista, 1973.

Bliss, A. Richard, Jr. "Proposed Vegetable Drug Deletions." *Journal of the American Pharmaceutical Association* 9, no. 8 (August 1920): 767–71.

Booth, D. A. "Influences on Human Fluid Consumption." In *Thirst: Physiological and Psychological Aspects,* edited by David J. Ramsay and David Booth, 53–73. London: Springer-Verlag, 1991.

Borges, Dain. "Healing and Mischief: Witchcraft in Brazilian Law and Literature, 1890–1922." In *Crime and Punishment in Latin America: Law and Society Since Late Colonial Times,* edited by Ricardo D. Salvatore, Carlos Aguirre, and Gilbert M. Joseph, 181–210. Durham, NC: Duke University Press, 2001.

Borges, Luiz Carlos, and Manuela Bretas de Medina, Livia Nascimento Monteiro. "Ciência, imaginário e civilização em Couto de Magalhães." *Revista Brasileira de História da Ciência* 5, no. 2 (July–December 2012): 250–66.

Borrás, Maria Rosa Lozano. *Plantas da Amazônia: Medicinais ou mágicas—plantas comercializadas no Mercado Municipal Adolpho Lisboa.* Manaus: Editora Valer, Governo do Estado do Amazonas, 2003.

Bourdieu, Pierre. *Distinction: A Social Critique of the Judgment of Taste.* Translated by Richard Nice. London: Routledge, 2010.

Bowler, Tim. "The Brazilian Recipe for Brewing Success." BBC News, July 14, 2008.

Bradburd, Daniel, and William Jankowiak. "Drugs, Desire, and European Economic Expansion." In *Drugs, Labor, and Colonial Expansion,* edited by William Jankowiak and Daniel Bradburd, 3–30. Tucson: University of Arizona Press, 2003.

Braga, Isabel Mendes Drumond. *Sabores do Brasil em Portugal: descobrir e transformar novos alimentos (séculos XVI–XXI).* São Paulo: Editora Senac, 2010.

Brandt, S. A., A.M.G. de Castro, D.A.S. Carmo, M.R.A. Junqueira, J. S. Milagre, I. C. Araújo, and J.R.O. *Avaliação do mercado brasileiro de guaraná.* Manaus: ACAR-Amazonas, 1973.

Breen, Benjamin. *The Age of Intoxication: Origins of the Global Drug Trade.* Philadelphia: University of Pennsylvania Press, 2019.

Breitbach, Ulrike B., Michael Niehues, Norberto P. Lopes, Jair E. Q. Faria, and Maria G. L. Brandão. "Amazonian Medicinal Plants Described by C.F.P. von Martius in the 19th Century." *Journal of Ethnopharmacology* 147, no. 1 (May 2013): 180–89.

Brice, William R., and Silvia F. de M. Figueirôa. "Charles Hartt, Louis Agassiz, and the Controversy over Pleistocene Glaciation in Brazil." *History of Science* 39 (2001): 161–84.

Brinkmann, Sören. "Leite e modernidade: ideologia e políticas de alimentação na era Vargas." *História, ciências, saúde—Manguinhos* 21, no. 1 (January–March 2014): 1–17.

Brito, Mariana Reis de, E. M. Nic Lughadha, Luiz Fernando Dias Duarte, and L. de Senna-Valle. "Exchange of Useful Plants between Brazil and England in the Second Half of the Nineteenth Century: Glaziou and the Botanists of the Royal Botanic Gardens, Kew." *Kew Bulletin* 70, no. 4 (2015): 1–10.

Brockway, Lucile H. *Science and Colonial Expansion: The Role of the British Royal Botanic Gardens.* New York: Academic Press, 1979.

Brown, Michael F. "Can Culture Be Copyrighted?" *Current Anthropology* 39, no. 2 (1998): 193–222.

———. "Facing the State, Facing the World: Amazonia's Native Leaders and the New Politics of Identity." *L'Homme* 33, no. 126–28 (1993): 307–26.

———. *Who Owns Native Culture?* Cambridge, MA: Harvard University Press, 2003.

Browne, Janet. "Biogeography and Empire." In *Cultures of Natural History*, edited by N. Jardine, J. A. Secord, and E. C. Spary, 305–21. Cambridge: Cambridge University Press, 1996.

Brunk, Conrad G. "Philosophical and Ethical Issues: Toward the Creation of 'Ethical Space.'" In *The Ethics of Cultural Appropriation*, edited by James O. Young and Conrad G. Brunk, 161–72. Chichester, UK: Wiley-Blackwell, 2009.

Bruschini, Maria Cristina Aranha. *Mulher e trabalho: uma avaliação da década da mulher.* São Paulo: Nobel; Conselho Estadual da Condição Feminina, 1985.

———. "Work and Gender in Brazil in the Last Ten Years." *Cadernos de pesquisa* 37, no. 132 (September–December 2007): 537–72. www.scielo.br/scielo.php?script=sci_arttext&pid=S0100-15742007000300003&lng=en&nrm=iso&tlng=en.

Bryant, Raymond L., and Michael K. Goodman. "Consuming Narratives: The Political Ecology of 'Alternative' Consumption." *Transactions of the Institute of British Geographers* 29 (2004): 344–66.

Bulmer-Thomas, Victor. *The Economic History of Latin America since Independence.* Cambridge: Cambridge University Press, 2014.

Burbach, Roger, and Patricia Flynn. *Agribusiness in the Americas.* New York: Monthly Review Press, 1980.

Burke, Brian J. "Cooperatives for 'Fair Globalization'? Indigenous People, Cooperatives, and Corporate Social Responsibility in the Brazilian Amazon." *Latin American Perspectives* 37, no. 6 (November 2010): 30–52.

Burns, E. Bradford. *A History of Brazil.* 2nd ed. New York: Columbia University Press, 1970.

Cabral, J. Irineu. *Sol da manhã: memória da Embrapa.* Brasília: UNESCO, 2005.

Cabral, Umberlândia. "Um em cada quatro adultos do país estava obeso em 2019." *Agência IBGE Notícias*, October 21, 2020. https://web.archive.org/web/20210817205026

/https://agenciadenoticias.ibge.gov.br/agencia-noticias/2012-agencia-de-noticias
/noticias/29204-um-em-cada-quatro-adultos-do-pais-estava-obeso-em-2019.

Cagle, Hugh. *Assembling the Tropics: Science and Medicine in Portugal's Empire, 1450–1700.*
Cambridge: Cambridge University Press, 2018.

Calainho, Daniela Buono. "Jesuítas e medicina no Brasil colonial." *Tempo* 19 (2005): 61–75.

Candido, Antônio. "The Brazilian Family." In *Brazil: Portrait of Half a Continent*, edited by
T. Lynn Smith, 291–312. New York: Dryden Press, 1951.

Cañizares-Esguerra, Jorge. "How Derivative Was Humboldt? Microcosmic Nature
Narratives in Early Modern Spanish America and (Other) Origins of Humboldt's
Ecological Sensibilities." In *Colonial Botany: Science, Commerce, and Politics in the Early
Modern World*, edited by Londa Schiebinger and Claudia Swan, 148–67. Philadelphia:
University of Pennsylvania Press, 2005.

———. "Iberian Science in the Renaissance: Ignored How Much Longer?" *Perspectives on
Science* 12, no. 1 (2004): 86–124.

Capobianco, João. *Avaliação e identificação de ações prioritárias para a conservação,
utilização sustentável e repartição dos benefícios da biodiversidade na Amazônia brasileira.*
Brasília: Ministério do Meio Ambiente, 2002.

Cardoso, Antonio Alexandre Isidio. "O Eldorado dos deserdados: indígenas, escravos,
mirantes, regatões e o avanço rumo ao Oeste Amazônico no século XIX." PhD diss.,
Universidade de São Paulo, 2018.

Carlyle, Thomas. *Heroes, Hero Worship and the Heroic in History.* New York: Charles
Scribner's Sons, 1841.

Carneiro, Henrique. *Bebida, abstinência e temperança.* São Paulo: Editora Senac São Paulo,
2010.

———. "O corpo sedento: bebidas na história do Brasil." In *História do corpo no Brasil*,
edited by Mary del Priore and Marcia Amantino, 131–56. São Paulo: Editora UNESP, 2011.

———. "Proibição da maconha: racismo e violência no Brasil." *Cahiers des Amériques
Latins* 92 (2019): 132–52.

———. "O saber fitoterápico indígena e os naturalistas europeus." *Fronteiras* 13, no. 23
(January–June 2011): 13–32.

———. "Transformações do significado da palavra 'droga': das especiarias coloniais ao
proibicionismo contemporâneo." In *Álcool e drogas na história do Brasil*, edited by
Renato Pinto Venâncio and Henrique Carneiro, 11–28. Belo Horizonte: Editora PUC
Minas, 2005.

Carone, Edgar. *A evolução industrial de São Paulo.* São Paulo: Editora Senac São Paulo,
2001.

Carvalho, J. A., and L. R. Wong. "Fertility Transition in Brazil: Causes and
Consequences." *Notas Población* 20, no. 56 (December 1992): 107–41.

Carvalho Júnior, Almir Diniz de. "Índios cristãos no cotidiano das colônias do norte
(século XVII e XVIII)." *Revista de História* 168 (January–June 2013): 69–99.

———. "A ordem da missão e os jogos da ação: conflitos, estratégias e armadilhas na
Amazônia do século XVIII." *Tempo* 19, no. 35 (2013): 23–41.

———. "Visão do diabo: crenças e rituais ameríndios sob a ótica dos jesuítas na
Amazônia colonial, séculos 17 e 18." In *Amazônia e outros temas*, edited by Sidney
Antonio da Silva, 159–94. Manaus: EDUA, 2010.

Carvalhosa, Paulo Emendabili Souza Barros de. "Monumento a Luiz Pereira Barreto." Galileo Emendabili—esculpindo São Paulo. May 8, 2013. https://web.archive.org/web /20180619140718/https://www.galileoemendabili.net/monumento-a-luiz-pereira -barreto.

Cascudo, Luís da Câmara. "Esfriando bebidas." In *Antologia da alimentação no Brasil,* edited by Luís da Câmara Cascudo, 178–79. Rio de Janeiro: Livros Técnicos e Científicos, 1977.

———. *História da alimentação no Brasil.* 2 vols. São Paulo: Editora da Universidade de São Paulo, 1983.

Castelnau-L'Etoile, Charlotte de. "The Uses of Shamanism: Evangelizing Strategies and Missionary Models in Seventeenth-Century Brazil." In *The Jesuits: Cultures, Sciences and the Arts,* Vol. 2, edited by John O'Malley, 616–37. Toronto: University of Toronto Press, 2006.

Castro, Eduardo Viveiros de. *A inconstância da alma selvagem e outros ensaios de antropologia.* São Paulo: Cosac & Naify, 2002.

———. *From the Enemy's Point of View: Humanity and Divinity in an Amazonian Society.* Translated by Catherine V. Howard. Chicago: University of Chicago Press, 1992.

Caulfield, Sueann. *In Defense of Honor: Sexual Morality, Modernity, and Nation in early Twentieth-Century Brazil.* Durham, NC: Duke University Press, 2000.

Certeau, Michel de. *The Practice of Everyday Life.* Translated by Steven Rendall. Berkeley: University of California Press, 1988.

———. *The Writing of History.* Translated by Tom Conley. New York: Columbia University Press, 1988.

Certeau, Michel de, Luce Giard, and Pierre Mayol. *The Practice of Everyday Life.* Vol. 2, *Living and Cooking,* translated by Timothy J. Tomasik. Minneapolis: University of Minnesota Press, 1998.

Chalhoub, Sidney. *Trabalho, lar e botequim: o cotidiano dos trabalhadores no Rio de Janeiro da belle époque.* São Paulo: Brasiliense, 1986.

"A chama do coração: Uma releitura das obras de Caio Miranda." Caravansarai. Accessed April 16, 2022, www.caravansarai.com.br/LivChamaDoCoracaoAutor.htm.

Chambers, David Wade, and Richard Gillespie. "Locality in the History of Science: Colonial Science, Technoscience, and Indigenous Knowledge." *Osiris* 15 (2000): 221–40.

Chambouleyron, Rafael. "Cacao, Bark-Clove and Agriculture in the Portuguese Amazon Region in the Seventeenth and Early Eighteenth Century," *Luso-Brazilian Review* 51, no. 1 (2014): 1–35.

———. "Indian Freedom and Indian Slavery in the Portuguese Amazon (1640–1755)." In *Building the Atlantic Empires: Unfree Labor and Imperial States in the Political Economy of Capitalism,* edited by John Donoghue and Evelyn P. Jennings, 54–71. Leiden: Brill, 2015.

Chambouleyron, Rafael, Benedito Costa Barbosa, Fernanda Aires Bombardi, and Claudia Rocha de Sousa. "'Formidável contágio': epidemias, trabalho e recrutamento na Amazônia colonial, 1660–1750." *História, ciências, saúde—Manguinhos* 18, no. 4 (October–December 2011): 987–1004.

Chauí, Marilena de Souza. *Brasil: mito fundador e sociedade autoritária.* São Paulo: Fundação Perseu Abramo, 2001.

Clement, Charles R. "Crops of the Amazon and Orinoco Regions: Their Origin, Decline and Future." In *Neglected Crops: 1492 from a Different Perspective*, edited by J. E. Hernández Bermejo and J. León, 195–203. Rome: Food and Agriculture Organization of the United Nations, 1994.

———. "1492 and the Loss of Amazonian Crop Genetic Resources." Pt. 1, "The Relationship between Domestication and Human Population Decline." *Economic Botany* 53, no. 2 (1999): 188–202.

———. "1492 and the Loss of Amazonian Crop Genetic Resources." Pt. 2, "Crop Biogeography at Contact." *Economic Botany* 53, no. 2 (1999): 203–16.

Clement, Charles R., Michelly de Cristo-Araújo, Geo Coppens D'Eeckenbrugge, Alessandro Alves Pereira, and Doriane Picanço-Rodrigues. "Origin and Domestication of Native Amazonian Crops." *Diversity* 2, no. 1 (2010): 88–90.

Clément, Daniel. "The Historical Foundations of Ethnobiology (1860–1899)." *Journal of Ethnobiology* 18, no. 2 (Winter 1998): 161–87.

Coccia, Emanuele. *The Life of Plants: A Metaphysics of Mixture*. Translated by Dylan J. Montanari. Cambridge: Polity Press, 2019.

Coe, Kathryn, and Craig T. Palmer. "The Words of Our Ancestors: Kinship, Tradition, and Moral Codes." *World Cultures eJournal* 16, no. 1 (2008): 1–31.

Coimbra, Carlos E., Ricardo Ventura Santos, James R. Welch, Andrey Moreira Cardoso, Mirian Carvalho de Souza, Luiza Garnelo, Elias Rass, et al. "The First National Survey of Indigenous People's Health and Nutrition in Brazil: Rationale, Methodology, and Overview of Results." *BMC Public Health* 13, no. 52 (2013): 1–19.

Congretel, Mélanie, Geoffroy Filoche, Henrique dos Santos Pereira, and Florence Pinton. "Found Again in Translation? Standardizing the Authenticity of Guaraná among the Sateré-Mawé People (Brazilian Amazon)." *HAU: Journal of Ethnographic Theory* 11, no. 2 (2021): 579–600.

Congretel, Mélanie, and Florence Pinton. "Local Knowledge, Know-How and Knowledge Mobilized in a Globalized World: A New Approach of Indigenous Local Ecological Knowledge." *People and Nature* 2 (2020): 527–43.

Conklin, Beth A., and Laura R. Graham. "The Shifting Middle Ground: Amazonian Indians and Eco-Politics." *American Anthropologist* 97, no. 4 (December 1995): 695–710.

Cook, Ian, and Philip Crang. "The World on a Plate: Culinary Culture, Displacement, and Geographical Knowledges." *Journal of Material Culture* 1, no. 2 (1996): 131–53.

Cook, Ian, Philip Crang, and Mark Thorpe. "Tropics of Consumption: 'Getting with the Fetish' of 'Exotic' Fruit?" In *Geographies of Commodity Chains*, edited by Alex Hughes and Suzanne Reimer, 173–92. London: Routledge, 2004.

Cordiviola, Alfredo. *Richard Burton: A Traveller in Brazil, 1865–1868*. Lewiston, NY: Edwin Mellen Press, 2001.

Corrêa, Manoel Pio, and Leonam de Azeredo Pena. *Dicionário das plantas úteis do Brasil*. Vol. 3. Rio de Janeiro, Ministério da Agricultura, 1984.

Corrêa, Maria Pinheiro Fernandes, Aloizio de Arruda Pinto, and Walda Corrêa dos Santos. *Guaraná: resumos informativos*. Brasília: Embrapa, CNPq, 1979.

Corrêa, Paulo, and Cristiane Schmidt. "Public Research Organizations and Agricultural Development in Brazil: How Did Embrapa Get It Right?" *World Bank Economic Premise*

145 (June 2014). https://documents.worldbank.org/en/publication/documents
-reports/documentdetail/156191468236982040/public-research-organizations-and
-agricultural-development-in-brazil-how-did-embrapa-get-it-right.

Costa, Hideraldo. *Cultura, trabalho e luta social na Amazônia: discurso dos viajantes-século
19*. Manaus: Editora Valer, 2013.

Costa, Jurandir Freire. *Órdem médica e norma familiar*. Rio de Janeiro: Graal, 1999.

Costa, Kelerson Semerene. "Intervenções humanas na natureza amazônica (século XVII
ao XIX)." *Ciência & ambiente* 33 (July–December 2006): 81–96.

Costa, Palmira Fontes da, and Henrique Leitão, "Portuguese Imperial Science, 1450–1800:
A Historiographical Review." In *Science in the Spanish and Portuguese Empires, 1500–1800*,
edited by Daniela Bleichmar, Paula de Vos, Kristin Huffine, and Kevin Sheehan, 35–53.
Stanford, CA: Stanford University Press, 2008.

Courtwright, David T. *The Age of Addiction: How Bad Habits Became Big Business.*
Cambridge, MA: Harvard University Press, 2019.

———. *Forces of Habit: Drugs and the Making of the Modern World*. Cambridge, MA:
Harvard University Press, 2001.

Crane, Peter. "Can We Save the Charismatic Megaflora?" *Oryx* 49, no. 3 (2015): 377–78.

Crawford, Matthew James. *The Andean Wonder Drug: Cinchona Bark and Imperial
Science in the Spanish Atlantic, 1630–1800*. Pittsburgh: University of Pittsburgh Press,
2016.

Cribelli, Teresa. *Industrial Forests and Mechanical Marvels: Modernization in Nineteenth-
Century Brazil*. Cambridge: Cambridge University Press, 2016.

———. "'These Industrial Forests': Economic Nationalism and the Search for Agro-
Industrial Commodities in Nineteenth-Century Brazil." *Journal of Latin American
Studies* 45, no. 3 (2013): 545–79.

Croce, Paul Jerome. *Science and Religion in the Era of William James*. Chapel Hill:
University of North Carolina Press, 1995.

Crowe, Ivan. "The Hunter-Gatherers." In *The Cultural History of Plants*, edited by Ghillean
Prance and Mark Nesbitt, 3–12. New York: Routledge, 2005.

Cruz, Graziela Fregonez Baptista. *Fabricação de refrigerantes*. Rio de Janeiro: Redetec,
2012.

Cunha, Manuela Carneiro da. "Antidomestication in the Amazon: Swidden and Its Foes."
HAU: Journal of Ethnographic Theory 9, no. 1 (2019): 126–36.

———. *"Culture" and Culture: Traditional Knowledge and Intellectual Rights*. Chicago:
Prickly Paradigm Press, 2009.

———. *Índios no Brasil: história, direitos, e cidadania*. São Paulo: Claro Enigma, 2012.

———. "Política indigenista no século XIX." In *História dos Índios no Brasil*, edited by
Manuela Carneiro da Cunha, 133–54. São Paulo: Companhia das Letras, 1992.

Cunha, Manuela Carneiro da, and Mauro W. B. de Almeida. "Indigenous People,
Traditional People, and Conservation in the Amazon." *Daedalus* 129, no. 2 (Spring
2000): 315–38.

Cytrynowicz, Roney, and Monica Musatti Cytrynowicz. *Indústria farmacêutica no Brasil:
memória iconográfica*. São Paulo: Narrativa Um, 2018.

Dantes, Maria Amélia M., ed. *Espaços da ciência no Brasil: 1800–1930*. Rio de Janeiro:
Editora Fiocruz, 2001.

Davidson, David M. "How the Brazilian West Was Won: Freelance and State on the Mato Grosso Frontier." In *Colonial Roots of Modern Brazil: Papers of the Newberry Library Conference,* edited by Dauril Alden, 61–106. Berkeley: University of California Press, 1973.

Dávila, Jerry. *Diploma of Whiteness: Race and Social Policy in Brazil, 1917–1945.* Durham, NC: Duke University Press, 2003.

Davis, Shelton H. *Victims of the Miracle: Development and the Indians of Brazil.* Cambridge: Cambridge University Press, 1977.

Dawson, Alexander S. *The Peyote Effect: From the Inquisition to the War on Drugs.* Berkeley, CA: University of California Press, 2018.

DDB-Brasil. "Guaraná Antarctica: 10 Million Fans." Ad Age. January 21, 2013. https://adage.com/creativity/work/10-million-fans/30475.

Deaecto, Marisa Midori. *Comércio e vida urbana na cidade de São Paulo (1889–1930).* São Paulo: Editora Senac São Paulo, 2002.

Deloria, Philip J. *Playing Indian.* New Haven, CT: Yale University Press, 1999.

Delson, Roberta Marx. "The Beginnings of Professionalization in the Brazilian Military: The Eighteenth-Century Corps of Engineers." *Americas* 51, no. 4 (1995): 555–74.

Denevan, William M. "Estimating Amazonian Indian Numbers in 1492." *Journal of Latin American Geography* 13, no. 2 (2014): 207–21.

———. "The Pristine Myth: The Landscape of the Americas in 1492." *Annals of the Association of American Geographers* 82, no. 3 (September 1992): 369–85.

Dent, Rosanna. "Studying Indigenous Brazil: The Xavante and the Human Sciences, 1958–2015." PhD diss., University of Pennsylvania, 2017.

Diamond, Seymour, Roger K. Cady, Merle L. Diamond, Mark W. Green, and Vincent T. Martin, eds. *Headache and Migraine Biology and Management.* San Diego: Elsevier Science and Technology, 2015.

Dias, Camila Loureiro. "Jesuit Maps and Political Discourse: The Amazon River of Father Samuel Fritz." *Americas* 69, no. 1 (July 2012): 95–116.

Dias, Carolina Carmona. "O Movimento Slow Food no Brasil e a valorização dos biomas brasileiros." Master's thesis, Universidade de Coimbra, 2018.

Dias, Maria Odila Silva. *Power and Everyday Life: The Lives of Working Women in Nineteenth-Century Brazil.* Translated by Ann Frost. New Brunswick, NJ: Rutgers University Press, 1995.

Diegues, Antônio Carlos Santana. *O mito moderno da natureza intocada.* 5th ed. São Paulo: Editora Hucitec, 2004.

Dietz, Lawrence. *Soda Pop: The History, Advertising, Art and Memorabilia of Soft Drinks in America.* New York: Simon and Schuster, 1973.

Domingues, Ângela. "Os conceitos de guerra justa de resgate e os ameríndios do Norte do Brasil." In *Brasil: colonização e escravidão,* edited by Maria Beatriz Nizza da Silva, 45–56. Rio de Janeiro: Nova Fronteira, 1999.

———. *Viagens de exploração geográfica na Amazônia em finais do século XVIII: política, ciência e aventura.* Lisbon: Secretaria Regional do Turismo, Cultura e Emigração; Centro de Estudos de História do Atlântico, 1991.

Domingues, Heloisa M. Bertol. "As ciências naturais e a construção da nação brasileira." *Revista de História* 135 (1996): 41–60.

Donati, Kelly. "The Pleasure of Diversity in Slow Food's Ethics of Taste." *Food, Culture and Society* 8, no. 2 (September 2005): 227–42.

Donovan, Kevin P. "'Development' as If *We Have Never Been Modern*: Fragments of a Latourian Development Studies." *Development and Change* 45, no. 5 (September 2014): 869–94.

Dória, Carlos Alberto. "Beyond Rice Neutrality: Beans as Patria, Locus, and Domus in the Brazilian Culinary System." In *Rice and Beans: A Unique Dish in a Hundred Places*, edited by Richard Wilk and Livia Barbosa, 121–36. New York: Berg, 2012.

———. *A formação da culinária brasileira: escritos sobre a cozinha inzoneira.* São Paulo: Três Estrelas, 2014.

Douglas, Mary. "Deciphering a Meal." *Daedalus* 101, no. 1 (1972): 61–81.

Douglas, Mary, and Baron Isherwood. *The World of Goods: Towards an Anthropology of Consumption.* Rev. ed. London: Routledge, 1996.

Dove, Michael R. "Center, Periphery and Bio-Diversity: A Paradox of Governance and a Developmental Challenge." In *Valuing Local Knowledge: Indigenous People and Intellectual Property Rights*, edited by Stephen Brush and Doreen Stabinsky, 41–67. Washington, DC: Island Press, 1996.

———. "Indigenous People and Environmental Politics." *Annual Review of Anthropology* 35 (2006): 191–208.

Drayton, Richard. *Nature's Government: Science, Imperial Britain, and the "Improvement" of the World.* New Haven, CT: Yale University Press, 2001.

Duarte, Regina Horta. *Activist Biology: The National Museum, Politics and Nation Building in Brazil.* Translated by Diane Grosklaus Whitty. Tucson: University of Arizona Press, 2016.

———. "Between the National and the Universal: Natural History Networks in Latin America in the Nineteenth and Twentieth Centuries." *Isis* 104 (2013): 777–87.

Dutra, Eliana de Freitas. *O ardil totalitário: imaginário político no Brasil dos anos 30.* Rio de Janeiro: Editora UFRJ; Belo Horizonte: Editora UFMG, 1997.

Edler, Flavio Coelho. *Boticas & pharmácias: uma história ilustrada da farmácia no Brasil.* Rio de Janeiro: Casa da Palavra, 2006.

———. "Medical Knowledge and Professional Power: From the Luso-Brazilian Context to Imperial Brazil." In *Biomedicine as a Contested Site: Some Revelations in Imperial Contexts*, edited by Poonam Bala, 45–66. Lanham, MD: Lexington Books, 2009.

———. "Plantas nativas do Brasil nas farmacopeias portuguesas e europeias, séculos XVII–XVIII." In *Usos e circulação de plantas no Brasil, séculos XVI–XIX*, edited by Lorelai Kury, 96–137. Rio de Janeiro: Andrea Jakobsson Estúdio, 2013.

Edmundo, Luiz. "Bebia-se no Rio de Janeiro de 1900." In *Antologia da alimentação no Brasil*, edited by Luís da Câmara Cascudo, 107–9. Rio de Janeiro: Livros Técnicos e Científicos, 1977.

Elisabetsky, Elaine, and Patricia Shanley. "Ethnopharmacology in the Brazilian Amazon." *Pharmacology & Therapeutics* 64, no. 2 (1994): 201–14.

Elkin, Noah. "Promoting a New Brazil: National Expositions and Images of Modernity, 1861–1922." PhD diss., Rutgers University, 1999.

Elmore, Bartow J. *Citizen Coke: The Making of Coca-Cola Capitalism.* New York: W. W. Norton, 2015.

Emmi, Marilia Ferreira. "Raízes italianas no desenvolvimento da Amazônia, 1870–1950: pioneirismo econômico e identidade." PhD diss., Universidade Federal do Pará, 2007.

Emmins, Colin, "Soft Drinks." In *The Cambridge World History of Food*, edited by Kenneth F. Kiple and Kriemhild Coneè Ornelas, 702–12. Cambridge: Cambridge University Press, 2000.

Enríquez, Gonzalo, Maria Amélia da Silva, and Eugênia Cabral. *Biodiversidade da Amazônia: usos e potencialidades dos mais importantes produtos naturais do Pará.* Belém: NUMA, UFPA, 2003.

Erickson, H. T., Maria Pinheiro F. Corrêa, and José Ricardo Escobar. "Guaraná (*Paullinia cupana*) as a Commercial Crop in Brazilian Amazonia." *Economic Botany* 38, no. 3 (1984): 273–86.

Estes, J. Worth. "The Pharmacology of Nineteenth-Century Patent Medicines." *Pharmacy in History* 30, no. 1 (1988): 3–18.

———. "The Therapeutic Crisis of the Eighteenth Century." In *The Inside Story of Medicines: A Symposium*, edited by Gregory Higby and Elaine Stroud, 31–50. Madison: American Institute of the History of Pharmacy, 1997.

Evenson, R. E., and D. Gollin. "Assessing the Impact of the Green Revolution, 1960 to 2000." *Science* 300, no. 5620 (May 2003): 758–62.

Fabian, Johannes. *Time and the Other: How Anthropology Makes Its Object.* New York: Columbia University Press, 2002.

Faraco, Raphael. *Maués: terra, gente e memórias.* Manaus: Editora Valer, 2006.

Farge, Arlette. *The Allure of the Archives.* Translated by Thomas Scott-Railton. New Haven, CT: Yale University Press, 2015.

Fausto, Carlos, and Michael Heckenberger. Introduction to *Time and Memory in Indigenous Amazonia: Anthropological Perspectives*, edited by Carlos Fausto and Michael Heckenberger, 1–42. Gainesville: University Press of Florida, 2007.

Feliciano, Paula de Oliveira. "Literatura e construção de uma brasilidade pela culinária (1840–1960)." *Jangada* 11 (January–June 2018): 142–55.

Fernandes, João Azevedo. *Selvagens bebedeiras: álcool, embriaguez e contatos culturais no Brasil colonial (séculos XVI–XVIII).* São Paulo: Alameda, 2011.

Fernandes, Tania Maria. "Medicamentos no Brasil: entre naturais e sintéticos (1920 a 2000)." *Revista Fitos* 7, no. 2 (April–June 2012): 119–24. www.arca.fiocruz.br/bitstream /icict/19202/2/7.pdf.

———. *Plantas medicinais: memória da ciência no Brasil.* Rio de Janeiro: Editora Fiocruz, 2004.

Ferreira, Gerson André Albuquerque. "Wará: ensaios sobre as interferências do comércio justo na formação política das lideranças Sateré-Mawé." PhD diss., Universidade Federal do Amazonas, 2017.

Ferreira, Vanessa Alves, and Rosana Magalhães. "Obesidade e pobreza: o aparente paradoxo; Um estudo com mulheres da Favela da Rocinha, Rio de Janeiro, Brasil." *Cadernos de Saúde Pública* 21, no. 6 (November–December 2005): 1792–1800.

Fico, Carlos. *Reinventando o otimismo: ditadura, propaganda e imaginário social no Brasil.* Rio de Janeiro: Fundação Getúlio Vargas, Editora, 1997.

Figueroa, Alba. "Guaraná, a máquina do tempo dos Sateré-Mawé." *Boletim do Museu Paraense Emílio Goeldi: Ciências humanas* 11, no. 1 (January–April 2016): 55–85.

Figueiredo, Betânia Gonçalves. "O arranjo das drogas nas boticas e farmácias mineiras entre os séculos XVIII e XIX." In *Álcool e drogas na história do Brasil*, edited by Renato Pinto Venâncio and Henrique Carneiro, 141–54. São Paulo: Alameda, 2005.

Filoche, Geoffroy. "Making the Difference with a Common Plant: The Recovery of Guaraná by the Sateré-Mawé (Brazil)." In *The Commons, Plant Breeding and Agricultural Research: Challenges for Food Security and Agrobiodiversity*, edited by Fabien Girard and Christine Frison, 173–84. London: Routledge, 2018.

Filoche, Geoffroy, and Florence Pinton. "Who Owns Guaraná? Legal Strategies, Development Policies and Agricultural Practices in Brazilian Amazonia." *Journal of Agrarian Change* 14, no. 3 (2014): 380–99.

Fioravanti, Carlos. "Luzeia: The Superguaraná." *Pesquisa Fapesp* 203 (January 2013). https://revistapesquisa.fapesp.br/en/luzeia-the-superguarana.

Food and Agriculture Organization of the United Nations. "Staple Foods: What Do People Eat?" *Food and People: Dimensions of Need*. Rome: FAO, 1995. www.fao.org/3/u8480e/U8480E07.htm#Staple%20foods%20What%20do%20people%20eat.

Food and Agriculture Organization of the United Nations and Institut National de la Recherche Agronomique. *Constructing Markets for Agroecology: An Analysis of Diverse Options for Marketing Products from Agroecology*. Rome: FAO/INRA, 2018. www.fao.org/3/I8605EN/i8605en.pdf.

Foster, Robert J. *Coca-Globalization: Following Soft Drinks from New York to New Guinea*. New York: Palgrave Macmillan, 2008.

Fraboni, Maurizio. "Waraná: o legítimo guaraná dos Sateré-Mawé." In *Povos indígenas no Brasil, 1996/2000*, edited by Carlos Alberto Ricardo, 469–71. São Paulo: Instituto Socioambiental, 2000.

Fraboni, Maurizio, and Obadias Batista. "Esclarecimento: para que serve uma fortaleza." *Notícias Slow Food*. Terra Madre Brasil: November 17, 2008. http://terramadre.slowfood brasil.com/esclarecimento-para-que-serve-uma-fortaleza.

Franco, José Luiz de Andrade, and José Augusto Drummond. *Proteção à natureza e identidade nacional no Brasil, anos 1920–1940*. Rio de Janeiro: Editora Fiocruz, 2009.

Freire, Diego. "Guaraná Found to Have Higher Anti-Oxidant Potential Than Green Tea," *Agência FAPESP*. Fundação de Amparo à Pesquisa do Estado de São Paulo: August 17, 2016. https://agencia.fapesp.br/guarana-found-to-have-higher-anti-oxidant-potential-than-green-tea/23763.

Freitas, Andreia de. *A estrutura de mercado do segmento de fitoterápicos no contexto atual da indústria farmacêutica brasileira*. Brasília: Ministério de Saúde, 2007.

Freyre, Gilberto. *Açúcar: em torno da etnografia, da história, e da sociologia do doce no Nordeste canavieiro do Brasil*. Recife: Editora Massangana, 1987.

Friedman, Jonathan. "Myth, History and Political Identity." *Cultural Anthropology* 7, no. 2 (May 1992): 194–210.

Fry, Peter. *Para inglês ver: identidade e política na cultura brasileira*. Rio de Janeiro: Zahar, 1982.

Furquim, Luiz Fernando. "O consumidor e os meios de comunicação." In *História da propaganda no Brasil*, edited by Renato Castelo Branco, Rodolfo Lima Martensen, and Fernando Reis, 286–87. São Paulo: T.A. Queiroz, 1990.

Furst, Lilian R. *Before Freud: Hysteria and Hypnosis in Later Nineteenth-Century Psychiatric Cases*. Lewisburg, PA: Bucknell University Press, 2008.

Furtado, Júnia Ferreira. "Tropical Empiricism: Making Medical Knowledge in Colonial Brazil." In *Science and Empire in the Atlantic World,* edited by James Delbourgo and Nicholas Dew, 127–51. New York: Routledge, 2007.

Gabriel, Joseph M. "Indian Secrets, Indian Cures, and the *Pharmacopoeia of the United States of America.*" In *Drugs on the Page: Pharmacopoeias and Healing Knowledge in the Early Modern Atlantic World,* edited by Matthew James Crawford and Joseph M. Gabriel, 240–62. Pittsburgh: University of Pittsburgh Press, 2019.

———. "A Thing Patented Is a Thing Divulged: Francis E. Stewart, George S. Davis, and the Legitimization of Intellectual Property Right in Pharmaceutical Manufacturing, 1879–1911." *Journal of the History of Medicine and Allied Sciences* 64, no. 2 (April 2009): 135–72.

Garcia, Roosevelt. "Dez curiosidades sobre a Tubaína." *Memória.* Veja São Paulo, September 26, 2017. https://vejasp.abril.com.br/blog/memoria/dez-curiosidades-sobre -a-tubaina.

Garfield, Seth. *Indigenous Struggle at the Heart of Brazil: State Policy, Frontier Expansion, and the Xavante Indians, 1937–1988.* Durham, NC: Duke University Press, 2001.

———. *In Search of the Amazon: Brazil, the United States, and the Nature of a Region.* Durham, NC: Duke University Press, 2013.

Garfinkel, Harold. *Studies in Ethnomethodology.* Englewood Cliffs, NJ: Prentice-Hall, 1967.

Geertz, Clifford. *The Interpretation of Cultures: Selected Essays.* New York: Basic Books, 1973.

Gerassi-Navarro, Nina. "Picturing the Tropics from Humboldt to Darwin." In *Entangled Knowledge: Scientific Discourses and Cultural Difference,* edited by Klaus Hock and Gesa Mackenthun, 201–29. Münster: Waxmann, 2012.

Gertner, David, Rosane Gertner, and Dennis Guthery. "Coca-Cola's Marketing Challenges in Brazil: The Tubaínas War." *Thunderbird International Business Review* (March–April 2005): 231–54.

Gesteira, Heloísa Meireles. "A América portuguesa e a circulação de plantas, séculos XVI–XVIII." In *Usos e circulação de plantas no Brasil, séculos XVI–XIX,* edited by Lorelai Kury, 12–51. Rio de Janeiro: Andrea Jakobsson Estúdio, 2013.

Getz, Christy, and Aimee Shreck. "What Organic and Fair Trade Labels Do Not Tell Us: Towards a Place-Based Understanding of Certification." *International Journal of Consumer Studies* 30, no. 5 (2006): 490–501.

Giassullo, Gia, and Peter Freedman. *The Soda Fountain: Floats, Sundaes, Egg Creams and More.* Berkeley: Ten Speed Press, 2014.

Giddens, Anthony. *The Consequences of Modernity.* Cambridge: Polity Press, 1990.

———. *The Constitution of Society: Outline of the Theory of Structuration.* Berkeley: University of California Press, 1984.

Gijswijt-Hofstra, Marijke. Introduction to *Cultures of Neurasthenia from Beard to the First World War,* edited by Marijke Gijswijt-Hofstra and Roy Porter, 1–30. Amsterdam: Rodopi, 2001.

Giorgetti, Melina, Lucia Rossi, and Eliana Rodrigues. "Brazilian Plants with Possible Action on the Central Nervous System—a Study of Historical Sources from the 16th to 19th Century." *Revista Brasileira de Faramacognosia* 21, no. 3 (May–June 2011): 537–55.

Glick, Thomas. Introduction to *A Recepção do Darwinismo no Brasil*, edited by Heloisa Maria Bertol Domingues, Magali Romero Sá, and Thomas Glick, 19–28. Rio de Janeiro: Editora Fiocruz, 2003.

Goffman, Erving. *Gender Advertisements*. New York: Harper and Row, 1979.

Gollner, Adam. *The Fruit-Hunters: A Story of Nature, Adventure, Commerce and Obsession*. New York: Scribner, 2008.

Gomes, Denise Maria Cavalcante. "Indigenous Societies in Brazil before the European Arrival." *Oxford Research Encyclopedia for Latin American History*. Oxford: Oxford University Press, 2018. https://doi.org/10.1093/acrefore/9780199366439.013.558.

Gomes, Elir Jesus. *Jesus: sua vida, seu sonho*. São Luís: Lithograf, 2006.

Gomes, Mario Luiz. "Vendendo saúde! Revisando os antigos almanaques de farmácia." *História, ciências, saúde—Manguinhos* 13, no. 4 (December 2006): 1007–18.

Gómez, Miguel I., Christopher B. Barrett, Terri Raney, Per Pinstrup-Andersen, Janice Meerman, André Croppenstedt, Sarah Lowder, et al. "Post-Green Revolution Food Systems and the Triple Burden of Malnutrition." *Food Policy* 42 (2013): 129–38.

Goodman, David, and Michael Redclift. *Refashioning Nature: Food, Ecology and Culture*. London: Routledge, 1991.

Goodman, Jordan. "Excitania: or, How Enlightenment Europe Took to Soft Drugs." In *Consuming Habits: Global and Historical Perspectives on How Cultures Define Drugs*, edited by Jordan Goodman, Paul E. Lovejoy, and Andrew Sherratt, 121–41. New York: Routledge, 2007.

Goodman, Michael K. "Reading Fair Trade: Political Ecological Imaginary and the Moral Economy of Fair Trade Foods." *Political Geography* 23, no. 7 (September 2004): 891–915.

Gootenberg, Paul. *Andean Cocaine: The Making of a Global Drug*. Chapel Hill: University of North Carolina Press, 2008.

Gottlieb, O. R., and W. B. Mors. "Fitoquímica amazônica: uma apreciação em perspectiva." *Interciência* 3 (1978): 252–63.

Gould, Stephen Jay. *The Mismeasure of Man*. New York: Norton, 1993.

Graham, Richard. *Britain and the Onset of Modernization in Brazil, 1850–1914*. Cambridge: Cambridge University Press, 1968.

———. *Feeding the City: From Street Market to Liberal Reform in Salvador, Brazil, 1780–1860*. Austin: University of Texas Press, 2010.

Graham, Sandra Lauderdale. *House and Street: The Domestic World of Servants and Masters in Nineteenth-Century Rio de Janeiro*. Austin: University of Texas Press, 1992.

Green, James N. *We Cannot Remain Silent: Opposition to the Brazilian Military Dictatorship in the United States*. Durham, NC: Duke University Press, 2010.

Greenway, John L. "'Nervous Disease' and Electric Medicine." In *Pseudo-Science and Society in Nineteenth-Century America*, edited by Arthur Wrobel, 47–73. Lexington: University Press of Kentucky, 1987.

Gregório, Vitor Marcos. "Uma face de Jano: A navegação do rio Amazonas e a formação do Estado brasileiro (1838–1867)." Master's thesis, Universidade de São Paulo, 2008.

Gross, Anna Sophie. "As Brazilian Agribusinesss Booms, Family Farms Feed the Nation." *Mongabay Series: Amazon Agribusiness*. Mongabay: January 17, 2019. https://news.mongabay.com/2019/01/as-brazilian-agribusiness-booms-family-farms-feed-the-nation.

Guimarães, Maria Regina Cotrim. *Civilizando as artes de curar: Chernoviz e os manuais de medicina popular no Império*. Rio de Janeiro: Fiocruz, 2016.

Guzmán, Tracy Devine. *Native and National in Brazil: Indigeneity after Independence*. Chapel Hill: University of North Carolina Press, 2013.

Haag, Carlos. "The Day on Which Brazil Said 'No' to the United States." *Revista FAPESP* 156 (February 2009): 80–85.

———. "The Secret Photos of Professor Agassiz." *Revista FAPESP* 175 (September 2010): 80–85.

Hall, Clarence W. *Adventurers for God*. New York: Harper & Brothers, 1959.

Hall, Colin, Michael James, and Tim Baird. "Forests and Trees as Charismatic Mega-Flora: Implications for Heritage Tourism and Conservation." *Journal of Heritage Tourism* 6, no. 4 (November 2011): 309–23.

Harris, Mark. "The Making of Regional Systems: The Tapajós/Madeira and Trombetas/Nhamundá Regions in the Lower Brazilian Amazon, Seventeenth and Eighteenth Centuries." *Ethnohistory* 65, no. 4 (October 2018): 621–45.

———. *Rebellion on the Amazon: The Cabanagem, Race, and Popular Culture in the North of Brazil, 1798–1840*. New York: Cambridge University Press, 2010.

Harris, Steven J. "Jesuit Scientific Activity in the Overseas Missions, 1540–1773." *Isis* 96, no. 1 (March 2005): 71–79.

Hartmann, Tekla. *A nomenclatura botânica dos Boróro: materiais para um ensaio etnobotânico*. São Paulo: Instituto de Estudos Brasileiros, 1967.

Headrick, Daniel R. *The Tentacles of Progress: Technology Transfer in the Age of Imperialism, 1850–1940*. New York: Oxford University Press, 1988.

Hecht, Susanna B. *The Scramble for the Amazon and the "Lost Paradise" of Euclides da Cunha*. Chicago: University of Chicago Press, 2013.

Heckenberger, Michael, and Eduardo Góes Neves. "Amazonian Archaeology." *Annual Review of Anthropology* 38 (2009): 251–66.

Hemming, John. *Die If You Must: Brazilian Indians in the Twentieth Century*. London: Macmillan, 2003.

———. *Naturalists in Paradise: Wallace, Bates and Spruce in the Amazon*. New York: Thames & Hudson, 2015.

Henman, Anthony. "Guaraná (*Paullinia cupana* var. *sorbilis*): Ecological and Social Perspectives on an Economic Plant of the Central Amazon Basin." *Journal of Ethnopharmacology* 6, no. 3 (November 1982): 311–28.

———. *O guaraná: sua cultura, propriedades, formas de preparação e uso*. São Paulo: Global, 1983.

Henrique, Márcio Couto. "Presente de branco: a perspectiva indígena dos brindes da civilização (Amazônia, século XIX)." *Revista Brasileira de História* 37, no. 75 (2017): 195–216.

———. "Sobre a (in)visibilidade dos índios da Amazônia (século XIX)." In *Os oitocentos na Amazônia: política, trabalho e cultura*, edited by Magda Maria de Oliveira Ricci and Maria de Nazaré Sarges, 109–40. Belém: Editora Açaí, 2013.

———. "O soldado-civilizador: Couto de Magalhães e os índios no Brasil do século XIX." In *Militares e educação em Portugal e no Brasil*, edited by Claudia Alves and Maria de Araújo Nepomuceno, 45–83. Rio de Janeiro: FAPERJ; Quartet, 2010.

Henrique, Márcio Couto, and Laura Trindade de Morais. "Estradas líquidas, comércio sólido: índios e regatões na Amazônia (século XIX)." *Revista História* 171 (July–December 2014): 49–82.

Herold, Marc W. "Ice in the Tropics: the Export of 'Crystal Blocks of Yankee Coldness' to India and Brazil." *Revista Espaço Acadêmico* 11, no. 126 (November 2011): 162–77.

Herzog, Tamar. "Dialoguing with Barbarians: What Natives Said and How Europeans Responded in Late-Seventeenth- and Eighteenth-Century Portuguese America." In *Justice in a New World: Negotiating Legal Intelligibility in British, Iberian, and Indigenous America*, edited by Brian Owensby and Richard Ross, 61–88. New York: New York University Press, 2018.

Hill, Andrew J. "Developmental Issues in Attitudes to Food and Diet." *Proceedings of the Nutrition Society* 61, no. 2 (May 2002): 259–66.

Hill, Jonathan D. Introduction to *Rethinking History and Myth: Indigenous South American Perspectives on the Past*, edited by Jonathan D. Hill, 1–17. Urbana: University of Illinois Press, 1988.

Hirsch, Eric. "Betelnut 'Bisnis' and Cosmology: A View from Papua New Guinea." In *Consuming Habits: Global and Historical Perspectives on How Cultures Define Drugs*, edited by Jordan Goodman, Paul E. Lovejoy, and Andrew Sherratt, 86–97. New York: Routledge, 2007.

Hirtz, Frank. "It Takes Modern Means to Be Traditional: On Recognizing Indigenous Cultural Communities in the Philippines." *Development and Change* 34, no. 5 (November 2003): 887–914.

Hobsbawm, Eric J. *The Age of Empire, 1875–1914*. New York: Vintage, 1989.

———. *Age of Extremes: The Short Twentieth Century, 1914–1991*. New York: Vintage, 1996.

Hobsbawm, Eric, and Terence Ranger, eds. *The Invention of Tradition*. Cambridge: Cambridge University Press, 1992.

Hochstetler, Kathryn, and Margaret E. Keck. *Greening Brazil: Environmental Activism in State and Society*. Durham, NC: Duke University Press, 2007.

Hoefle, Milton. "The Early History of Parke-Davis and Company." *Bulletin of the History of Chemistry* 25, no. 1 (2000): 28–34.

Hoehne, F. C. *Plantas e substâncias vegetais tóxicas e medicinais*. São Paulo: Graphicars, 1939.

Holanda, Sérgio Buarque de. *Caminhos e fronteiras*. São Paulo: Companhia das Letras, 1995.

———. *Visão do paraíso: os motivos edênicos no descobrimento e colonização do Brasil*. 4th ed. São Paulo: Companhia Editora Nacional, 1985.

Holmila, Marja, and Kirsimarja Raitasalo. "Gender Differences in Drinking: Why Do They Still Exist?" *Addiction* 100 (2005): 1763–69.

Holway, Tatiana. *The Flower of Empire: An Amazonian Water Lily, the Quest to Make It Bloom, and the World It Created*. Oxford: Oxford University Press, 2013.

Homma, Alfredo Kingo Oyama. "Guaraná: passado, presente, e futuro." In *Extrativismo vegetal na Amazônia: história, ecologia, economia e domesticação*, edited by Alfredo Kingo Oyama Homma, 307–20. Brasília: Embrapa, 2014.

———. "Uso, valorização e experiências exitosas com recursos genéticos vegetais na Amazônia." Paper presented at the II Congresso Brasileiro de Recursos Genéticos,

Belém, PA, September 24–28, 2012. www.alice.cnptia.embrapa.br/bitstream/doc /950546/1/2.pdf.

Homma, Alfredo Kingo Oyama, Marilene Corrêa da Silva Freitas, and Aldenor da Silva Ferreira. "As concessões de terras para os japoneses na Amazônia na década de 1920." In *Imigração japonesa na Amazônia: contribuição na agricultura e vínculo com o desenvolvimento regional*, edited by Alfredo Kingo Oyama Homma, Aldenador da Silva Ferreira, Marilene Corrêa da Silva Freitas, and Therezinha de Jesus Pinto Frase, 135–63. Manaus: Edua, 2011.

hooks, bell. *Black Looks: Race and Representation*. London: Turnaround, 1992.

Hopkins, Michael J. G. "Modelling the Known and Unknown Plant Biodiversity of the Amazon Basin." *Journal of Biogeography* 34 (2007): 1400–1411.

Hornborg, Alf. "Animism, Fetishism, and Objectivism as Strategies for Knowing (or Not Knowing) the World." *Ethnos* 71, no. 1 (March 2006): 21–32.

———. "Technology as Fetish: Marx, Latour, and the Cultural Foundations of Capitalism." *Theory, Culture & Society* 31, no. 4 (2014): 119–40.

"How Many Are They?" Povos indígenas no Brasil, February 16, 2018. https://pib.socio ambiental.org/en/How_many_are_they%3F.

Huber, Bridget. "Slow Food Nation: How Brazil Challenged the Junk Food Industry and Became a Global Leader in the Battle against Obesity." *Food and Environment Reporting Network*. July 28, 2016. https://thefern.org/2016/07/brazil.

Hugh-Jones, Stephen. "Coca, Beer, Cigars, and Yagé: Meals and Anti-Meals in an Amerindian Community." In *Consuming Habits: Global and Historical Perspectives on How Cultures Define Drugs*, edited by Jordan Goodman, Paul E. Lovejoy, and Andrew Sherratt, 86–97. New York: Routledge, 2007.

———. "Yesterday's Luxuries, Tomorrow's Necessities: Business and Barter in Northwest Amazonia." In *Barter, Exchange and Value: An Anthropological Approach*, edited by Caroline Humphrey and Stephen Hugh-Jones, 42–74. Cambridge: Cambridge University Press, 1992.

Ibáñez-Bonillo, Pablo. "Processos de guerra justa en la Amazonía portuguesa (siglo XVII)." In *Os indígenas e as justiças no mundo ibero-americano (sécs. XVI–XIX)*, edited by Ângela Domingues, Maria Leônia Chaves de Resende, and Pedro Cardim, 241–72. Lisbon: Centro de História da Universidade de Lisboa, 2019.

Instituto Brasileiro de Economia, Centro de Estatística Econômica. *Food Consumption in Brazil: Family Budget Surveys in the Early 1960's*. Jerusalem: Israel Program for Scientific Translations for the U.S. Department of Agriculture, Economic Research Service, 1970.

Irmscher, Christoph. *Louis Agassiz: Creator of American Science*. Boston: Houghton Mifflin Harcourt, 2013.

———. "Mr. Agassiz's 'Photographic Saloon.'" In *To Make Their Own Way in the World: The Enduring Legacy of the Zealy Daguerreotypes*, edited by Ilisa Barbash, Molly Rogers, and Deborah Willis, 205–31. New York: Aperture, 2000.

Ishii, Raquel Alves. "Viagens do 'homem que virou rio': narrativas, traduções e percursos de William Chandless pelas Amazônias no século XIX." Master's thesis, Universidade Federal do Acre, 2011.

Jacobs, Andrew, and Matt Richtel. "How Big Business Got Brazil Hooked on Junk Food." *New York Times*, September 16, 2017.

Jaeckel, Volker. "Antônio Vieira e João Felipe Bettendorff—dois missionários que marcaram a história da Amazônia do século XVII." In *Estudos da AIL em literatura, história, e cultura brasileiras*, edited by Raquel Bello Vázquez, Roberto Samartim, Elias J. Torres Feijó, and Manuel Brio-Semedo, 173–78. Coimbra: Associação Internacional de Lusitanistas Editora, 2015.

Jamieson, Ross W. "The Essence of Commodification: Caffeine Dependencies in the Early Modern World." *Journal of Social History* 35, no. 2 (2001): 269–94.

Janiga-Perkins, Constance G. "Pero de Magalhães Gândavo's *História da Província Santa Cruz*: Paradise, Providence, and How Best to Turn a Profit." *South Atlantic Review* 57, no. 2 (May 1992): 29–44.

Jardim, Marina Silva, Antonio Carlos Sequeira Fernandes, and Vera Maria Medina da Fonseca. "Silva Coutinho: uma trajetória profissional e sua contribuição às coleções geológicas do Museu Nacional." *História, ciências, saúde—Manguinhos* 20, no. 2 (April–June 2013): 457–79.

Jardine, Nicholas, and Emma Spary. "The Natures of Cultural History." In *Cultures of Natural History*, edited by N. Jardine, J. A. Secord, and E. C. Spary, 3–12. Cambridge: Cambridge University Press, 1996.

Jarnagin, Laura. *A Confluence of Transatlantic Networks: Elites, Capitalism, and Confederate Migration to Brazil*. Tuscaloosa: University of Alabama Press, 2014.

Jaszi, Peter, and Martha Woodmansee. "Beyond Authorship: Refiguring Rights in Traditional Culture and Bioknowledge." In *Scientific Authorship: Credit and Intellectual Property in Science*, edited by Mario Biagioli and Peter Galison, 195–223. New York: Routledge, 2003.

Kapfhammer, Wolfgang. "Amazonian Pain: Indigenous Ontologies and Western Eco-Spirituality." *Indiana* 29 (2012): 145–69.

———. "Divine Child and Trademark: Economy, Morality, and Cultural Sustainability of a Guaraná Project among the Sateré-Mawé, Brazil." In *Native Christians: Modes and Effects of Christianity among Indigenous Peoples of the Americas*, edited by Aparecida Vilaça and Robin Wright, 211–28. Farnham: Ashgate, 2009.

———. "De 'Sateré puro' (*Sateré sese*) ao 'novo Sateré' (*Sateré pakup*): mitopraxis no movimento evangélico entre os Sateré-Mawé." In *Transformando os deuses*. Vol. 2, *Igrejas evangélicas, pentecostais e neopentecostais entre os povos indígenas no Brasil*, edited by Robin Wright, 101–40. Campinas: UNICAMP, 2004.

Kapfhammer, Wolfgang, and Luiza Garnelo. "Programas sociais e Agência Indígena entre os Sateré-Mawé do Baixo Amazonas no Brasil." *Mundo Amazônico* 10, no. 1 (2019): 125–54.

Keneni, Gemechu, Endashaw Bekele, and Muhammad Imtiaz. "Genetic Vulnerability of Modern Crop Cultivars: Causes, Mechanisms and Remedies." *International Journal of Plant Research* 2, no. 3 (May 2012): 69–79.

Kern, Daniela. "'The Amazonian Idol': The Naissance of a National Symbol in the Empire of Brazil (1848–1885)." In *Empires and Nations from the Eighteenth to the Twentieth Century*, Vol. 1, edited by Antonello Biagini and Giovanna Motta, 214–21. Newcastle upon Tyne: Cambridge Scholars, 2014.

Kerr-Corrêa, Florence, Andrea M. Hegedus, Alessandra F. Sanches, Luzia Trinca, Ligia Regina Sansigolo Kerr, Adriana Tucci, et al. "Differences in Drinking Patterns between Men and Women in Brazil." In *Alcohol, Gender and Drinking Problems: Perspectives from*

Low and Middle Income Countries, edited by Isidore S. Obot and Robin Room, 49–68. Geneva: World Health Organization, 2005.

Kewer, Christina da Costa, Euler Esteves Ribeiro, Ednéa Aguiar Maia Ribeiro, Rafael Noal Moresco, Maria Izabel de Ugalde Marques da Rocha, Greice Franciele Feyl dos Santos Montagner, Michel Mansur Machado, et al. "Habitual Intake of Guaraná and Metabolic Morbidities: An Epidemiological Study of an Elderly Amazonian Population." *Phytotherapy Research* 25, no. 9 (2011): 1367–74.

Kingsland, Sharon E. *The Evolution of American Ecology, 1890–2000*. Baltimore: Johns Hopkins University Press, 2008.

Klein, Herbert S., and Francisco Vidal Luna. *Feeding the World: Brazil's Transformation into a Modern Agricultural Economy*. Cambridge: Cambridge University Press, 2018.

———. *Modern Brazil: A Social History*. New York: Cambridge University Press, 2020.

Kodama, Kaori. "Os estudos etnográficos no Instituto Histórico e Geográfico Brasileiro (1840–1860): história, viagens e questão indígena." *Boletim do Museu Paraense Emílio Goeldi* 5, no. 2 (May–August 2010): 253–72.

Kopytoff, Igor. "The Cultural Biography of Things: Commoditization as Process." In *The Social Life of Things: Commodities in Cultural Perspective*, edited by Arjun Appadurai, 64–92. Cambridge: Cambridge University Press, 1986.

Krug, Cristiane, Guaraci D. Cordeiro, Irmgard Schäffler, Claudia I. Silva, Reisla Oliveira, Clemens Schlindwein, Stefan Dötterl, et al. "Nocturnal Bee Pollinators Are Attracted to Guaraná Flowers by Their Scents." *Frontiers in Plant Science* 9, no. 1072 (2018): 1–6. www .ncbi.nlm.nih.gov/pmc/articles/PMC6080595.

Kury, Lorelai. "A sereia amazônica dos Agassiz: zoologia e racismo na *Viagem ao Brasil*." *Revista Brasileira de História* 21, no. 41 (2001): 157–72.

———. "Plantas sem fronteiras: jardins, livros e viagens, séculos XVIII–XIX." In *Usos e circulação de plantas no Brasil*, edited by Lorelai Kury, 228–90. Rio de Janeiro: Andrea Jakobsson Estúdio, 2013.

———. "Viajantes-naturalistas no Brasil oitocentista: experiência, relato e imagem." *História, ciências, saúde–Manguinhos* 8 (2001): 863–80.

Kury, Lorelai, and Magali Romero Sá. "Flora brasileira: um percurso histórico." In *Flora brasileira: história, arte & ciência*, edited by Ana Cecilia Impellizieri Martins, 18–57. Rio de Janeiro: Casa da Palavra, 2009.

Lambert, Jacques. *Os dois Brasis*. São Paulo: Companhia Editora Nacional, 1970.

Laraia, Barbara A. "Food Insecurity and Chronic Disease." *Advances in Nutrition* 4, no. 2 (March 2013): 203–212.

Lathrap, Donald W. "The Antiquity and Importance of Long-Distance Trade Relationships in the Moist Tropics of Pre-Columbian South America." *World Archaeology* 5, no. 2 (1973): 170–86.

Latour, Bruno. *We Have Never Been Modern*. Translated by Catherine Porter. Cambridge, MA: Harvard University Press, 1993.

Latour, Bruno, Denise Milstein, Isaac Marrero-Guillamón, and Israel Rodríguez-Giralt. "Down to Earth Social Movements: An Interview with Bruno Latour." *Social Movement Studies* 17, no. 3 (2018): 353–61.

Laudan, Rachel. *Cuisine and Empire: Cooking in World History*. Berkeley: University of California Press, 2013.

————. "A Plea for Culinary Modernism: Why We Should Love New, Fast, Processed Food." *Gastronomica: The Journal of Food and Culture* 1, no. 1 (Winter 2001): 36–44.

Lea, R. A. W. "Processing and Packaging." In *The Chemistry and Technology of Soft Drinks and Fruit Juices*, edited by Philip R. Ashurst, 85–102. Sheffield: Sheffield Academic Press, 1998.

Leal, Claudio Murilo. "Guaraná." In *100 palavras para conhecer melhor o Brasil*, edited by Andréia N. Ghelman and Arnaldo Niskier, 165. Rio de Janeiro: Instituto Antares, 2008.

Lears, Jackson T. J. *Fables of Abundance: A Cultural History of Advertising in America*. New York: Basic Books, 1994.

Leite, Bruno Martins Boto. "Verdes que em vosso tempo se mostrou, Das boticas jesuíticas da província do Brasil, séculos XVII–XVIII." In *Usos e circulação de plantas no Brasil, séculos XVI–XIX*, edited by Lorelai Kury, 54–93. Rio de Janeiro: Andrea Jakobsson Estúdio, 2013.

León, J. "Plant Genetic Resources of the New World." In *Neglected Crops: 1492 from a Different Perspective*, edited by J. E. Hernández Bermejo and J. León, 3–11. Rome: Food and Agriculture Organization of the United Nations, 1994.

Lesch, John E. "Conceptual Change in an Empirical Science: The Discovery of the First Alkaloids." *Historical Studies in the Physical Sciences* 11, no. 2 (1981): 305–28.

Leta, Jacqueline. "As mulheres na ciência brasileira: crescimento, contrastes, e um perfil de sucesso." *Estudos Avançados* 17, no. 49 (2003): 271–84.

Lévêque, Christian. *A biodiversidade*. Translated by Waldo Mermelstein. Florianópolis: EDUSC, 1999.

Levin, Judith. *Soda and Fizzy Drinks: A Global History*. London: Reaktion Books, 2021.

Levis, Carolina, Bernardo M. Flores, Priscila A. Moreira, Bruno G. Luize, Rubana P. Alves, Juliano Franco-Moraes, Juliana Lins, Evelien Konings, et al. "How People Domesticated Amazonian Forests." *Frontiers in Ecology and Evolution* 5, no. 171 (January 2018): 1–21.

Levis, Carolina, F. R. C. Costa, F. Bongers, M. Peña-Claros, C. R. Clement, A. B. Junqueira, E. G. Neves, E. K. Tamanaha, et al. "Persistent Effects of Pre-Columbian Plant Domestication on Amazonian Forest Composition." *Science* 355, no. 6328 (2017): 925–31.

Lévi-Strauss, Claude. *The Raw and the Cooked*. Translated by John Weightman and Doreen Weightman. New York: Harper & Row, 1969.

————. *The Savage Mind*. Translated by John Weightman and Doreen Weightman. Chicago: University of Chicago Press, 1966.

————. *Tristes Tropiques*. Translated by John Russell. New York: Criterion Books, 1961.

Levy-Costa, Renata Bertazzi, Rosely Sichieri, Nézio dos Santos Pontes, and Carlos Augusto Monteiro. "Disponibilidade domiciliar de alimentos no Brasil: distribuição e evolução (1974–2003)." *Revista de Saúde Pública* 39, no. 4 (2005): 530–40.

Lewin, Louis. *Phantastica: A Classic Survey on the Use and Abuse of Mind-Altering Plants*. Translated by P. H. A. Wirth. Rochester, VT: Park Street Press, 1998.

Liebenau, Jonathan. *Medical Science and Medical Industry: The Formation of the American Pharmaceutical Industry*. Baltimore: Johns Hopkins University Press, 1987.

Lima, Natalia da Silva, Erica de Paula Numata, Leonardo Mendes de Souza Mesquita, Pollyana Hammoud Dias, Wagner Vilegas, Alessandra Gambero, and Marcelo Lima Ribeiro. "Modulatory Effects of Guaraná (*Paullinia cupana*) on Adipogenesis." *Nutrients* 9, no. 635 (2017): 1–11.

Linstroth, J. P. "Conflict Avoidance among the Sateré-Mawé of Manaus, Brazil, and Peacemaking Behaviours among Amazonian Amerindians." *Creating the Third Force: Indigenous Processes of Peacemaking*, edited by Hemdesa Tuso and Maureen P. Flaherty, 249–76. Lanham, MD: Lexington Books, 2018.

Lisboa, Karen Macknow. *A nova Atlântida de Spix e Martius: natureza e civilização na "Viagem pelo Brasil (1817–1820)."* São Paulo: Editora Hucitec, 1997.

Locatelli, Piero. "Agreement to Reduce Sugar in Brazil Excludes Main Products." *O joio e o trigo.* December 6, 2018. https://ojoioeotrigo.com.br/2018/12/agreement-to-reduce -sugar-in-brazil-excludes-main-products.

Lopes, Maria Margaret. *O Brasil descobre a pesquisa científica: os museus e as ciências naturais no século XIX.* São Paulo: Editora Hucitec, 1997.

Lorenz, Sônia da Silva. *Sateré-Mawé: os filhos do guaraná.* São Paulo: Centro de Trabalho Indigenista, 1992.

Losada, Janaína Zito, and José Augusto Drummond. "Espíritos cheios de bichos: A fauna nas viagens de Louis Agassiz e Richard Francis Burton pelo Brasil oitocentista." *Varia História* 31, no. 55 (January–April 2015): 253–84.

Lotti, Ariane. "The Commoditization of Products and Taste: Slow Food and the Conservation of Agrobiodiversity." *Agriculture and Human Values* 27 (2010): 71–83.

Lovejoy, Paul E. "Kola in the History of West Africa." *Cahiers d'études Africaines* 20, no. 77–78 (1980): 97–134.

Ludwig, Armin K. *Brazil: A Handbook of Historical Statistics.* Boston: G. K. Hall, 1985.

Lurie, Edward. *Louis Agassiz: A Life in Science.* Chicago: University of Chicago Press, 1960.

Luz, Nícia Villela. *A Amazônia para os negros americanos (as origens de uma controvérsia internacional).* Rio de Janeiro: Editora Saga, 1968.

MacClancy, Jeremy. *Consuming Culture: Why You Eat What You Eat.* New York: Henry Holt, 1993.

Macêdo, Sidiana da Consolação Ferreira de. "A cozinha mestiça: uma história da alimentação em Belém (fins do século XIX a meados do século XX)." PhD diss., Universidade Federal do Pará, 2016.

Machado, Maria Helena P. T. "A ciência norte-americana visita a Amazônia: entre o criacionismo cristão e o poligenismo 'degeneracionista.'" *Revista da USP* 75 (September–November 2007): 68–75.

———. "Um mitógrafo no Império: a construção dos mitos da história nacionalista do século XIX." *Estudos históricos* 14, no. 25 (2000): 63–80.

———. "Nineteenth-Century Scientific Travel and Racial Photography: The Formation of Louis Agassiz's Brazilian Collection." *Mirror of Race*, May 8, 2012. http://mirrorofrace .org/machado.

Machado, Othon. "Contribuição ao estudo das plantas medicinais do Brasil—o guaraná." *Rodriguésia* 10, no. 20 (December 1946): 89–110.

Magnoli, Demétrio. *O corpo da pátria: imaginação geográfica e política externa no Brasil, 1808–1912.* São Paulo: Editora UNESP/Moderna, 1997.

Makuta, Glenn. *Biodiversidade, arca do gosto e fortalezas: um guia para entender o que são, como se relacionam com o que comemos, e como podemos apoiá-los.* São Paulo: Associação Slow Food do Brasil, 2018.

Marchi, Victorio De. *De duas, uma: a fusão na mesa.* São Paulo: Bella Editora, 2018.

Marcondes, Pyr. *Uma história da propaganda brasileira: as melhores campanhas, gênios da criação, personagens.* Rio de Janeiro: Ediouro, 2002.

Marcus, George E. "Ethnography in/of the World System: The Emergence of Multi-Sited Ethnography." *Annual Review of Anthropology* 24 (1995): 95–117.

Marques, Teresa Cristina Novaes. *A cerveja e a cidade do Rio de Janeiro: de 1888 ao início dos anos 1930.* Brasília: Editora da Universidade de Brasília, 2014.

Marques, Vera Regina Beltrão. *Natureza em boiões: medicinas e boticários no Brasil setecentista.* Campinas: Editora da Unicamp, 1999.

Martha, Geraldo B., Jr., Elisio Contini, and Eliseu Alves. "Embrapa: Its Origins and Changes." In *The Regional Impact of National Policies: The Case of Brazil,* edited by Werner Baer, 204–26. Cheltenham, UK: Edward Elgar, 2012.

Martins, Ana Luiza. "Da fantasia à História: folheando páginas revisteiras." *História* 22, no. 1 (2003): 59–71.

Matos, Maria Izilda Santos de. *Meu lar é um botequim: alcoolismo e masculinidade.* São Paulo: Companhia Editora Nacional, 2000.

Mayer, Sidney Luiz. "Jesuítas no estado do Maranhão e Grão Pará: convergências e divergências entre Antôno Vieira e João Filipe Bettendorff na aplicação da liberdade dos Índios." Master's thesis, Universidade do Vale do Rio dos Sinos, 2010.

Mbembe, Achille. *Necropolitics.* Durham, NC: Duke University Press, 2019.

McCann, Bryan. *Hello, Hello Brazil: Popular Music in the Making of Modern Brazil.* Durham, NC: Duke University Press, 2004.

McCook, Stuart. "'Squares of Tropic Summer': The Wardian Case, Victorian Horticulture, and the Logistics of Global Plant Transfers, 1770–1910." In *Global Scientific Practice in an Age of Revolutions, 1750–1850,* edited by Patrick Manning and Daniel Rood, 199–215. Pittsburgh: University of Pittsburgh Press, 2016.

McEwan, Colin. "Seats of Power: Axiality and Access to Invisible Worlds." In *Unknown Amazon: Culture in Nature in Ancient Brazil,* edited by Colin McEwan, Cristiana Barreto, and Eduardo Neves, 176–97. London: British Museum Press, 2001.

McNamara, Brooks. "The Indian Medicine Show." *Educational Theatre Journal* 23, no. 4 (December 1971): 431–45.

McTavish, Jan R. *Pain and Profits: The History of the Headache and Its Remedies in America.* New Brunswick, NJ: Rutgers University Press, 2004.

Medeiros, Fernando Saboia de. *A liberdade da navegação do Amazonas (relações entre o império e os Estados Unidos da América).* São Paulo: Companhia Editora Nacional, 1938.

Meggers, Betty. *Amazonia: Man and Culture in a Counterfeit Paradise.* Chicago: Aldine-Atherton, 1971.

Megill, Allan. "'Big History' Old and New: Presuppositions, Limits, Alternatives." *Journal of the Philosophy of History* 9, no. 2 (August 2015): 306–26.

Mello-Leitão, Cândido de. *História das expedições científicas no Brasil.* São Paulo: Companhia Editora Nacional, 1941.

Melo, Angelita Cristine. "Pharmacy in Brazil: Progress and Challenges on the Road to Expanding Clinical Practice." *Canadian Journal of Hospital Pharmacy* 70, no. 5 (September–October 2017): 381–90.

Melo, Joaquim. *SPI: a política indigenista no Amazonas*. Manaus: Governo do Estado do Amazonas, Secretaria de Estado de Cultura, 2009.

Mendes, Amando. *Amazônia econômica: problema brasileiro*. 2nd ed. Rio de Janeiro: A Noite, 1941.

Mendes, Fúlvio Rieli, and Elisaldo A. Carlini. "Brazilian Plants as Possible Adaptogens: An Ethnopharmacological Survey of Books Edited in Brazil." *Journal of Ethnopharmacology* 109, no. 3 (2007): 493–500.

Meneley, Anne. "Hope in the Ruins: Seeds, Plants, and Possibilities of Regeneration." *EPE: Nature and Space* 4, no. 1 (2021): 158–72.

Menéndez, Miguel A. "A área Madeira-Tapajós: situação de contato e relações entre colonizador e indígenas." In *História dos índios no Brasil*, edited by Manuela Carneiro da Cunha, 281–296. São Paulo: Companhia das Letras, 1992.

———. "Contribuição ao estudo das relações tribais na área Tapajós-Madeira." *Revista de Antropologia* 27/28 (1984/85): 271–86.

———. "Uma contribuição para a etno-história da área Madeira-Tapajós." *Revista do Museu Paulista* 28 (1981/82): 289–388.

Mengel, Alex Alexandre. "Modernização da agricultura e pesquisa no Brasil: a Empresa Brasileira de Pesquisa Agropecuária—Embrapa." PhD diss., Universidade Federal Rural do Rio de Janeiro, 2015.

Merchant, Carolyn. *The Death of Nature: Women, Ecology, and the Scientific Revolution*. San Francisco: Harper & Row, 1979.

Meurer-Grimes, B., A. Berkov, and H. Beck. "Theobromine, Theophylline, and Caffeine in 42 Samples and Products of Guaraná (*Paullinia cupana*, Sapindaceae)." *Economic Botany* 52, no. 3 (1998): 293–301.

Michiles, Aurélio. "Sobre a obra *O sangue da terra*: memórias inapagáveis." Associação Cultural Video Brasil (2014). http://site.videobrasil.org.br/pt/canalvb/video/1791184/Aurelio_Michiles_Memorias_Inapagaveis.

Michiles, Ronaldo José. "A cadeia produtiva do guaraná: um estudo com o guaraná no município de Maués." PhD diss., Universidade Federal do Amazonas, 2010.

Mignolo, Walter D. *The Darker Side of Western Modernity: Global Futures, Decolonial Options*. Durham, NC: Duke University Press, 2011.

Miki, Yuko. *Frontiers of Citizenship: A Black and Indigenous History of Postcolonial Brazil*. Cambridge: Cambridge University Press, 2018.

Milanesio, Natalia. *Workers Go Shopping in Argentina: The Rise of Popular Consumer Culture*. Albuquerque: University of New Mexico, 2013.

Miller, Bruce Granville, and Gustavo Menezes, "Anthropological Experts and the Legal System: Brazil and Canada." *American Indian Quarterly* 39, no. 4 (2015): 391–430.

Miller, Theresa L. *Plant Kin: A Multispecies Ethnography in Indigenous Brazil*. Austin: University of Texas Press, 2019.

Mintz, Sidney W. "Food and Its Relationship to Concepts of Power." In *Food and Agrarian Orders in the World-Economy*, edited by Philip McMichael, 3–13. London: Praeger Books, 1995.

———. *Sweetness and Power: The Place of Sugar in Modern History*. New York: Viking, 1985.

———. *Tasting Food, Tasting Freedom: Excursions into Eating, Culture, and the Past*. Boston: Beacon Press, 1996.

Mitchell, Cristina. "Ultra-Processed Foods Are Driving the Obesity Epidemic in Latin America, Says New PAHO/WHO Report." Pan-American Health Organization, September 1, 2015. www.paho.org/hq/index.php?option=com_content&view =article&id=11180:ultra-processed-foods&Itemid=1926&lang=en.

Moeran, Brian. "Business, Anthropology and Magical Systems: The Case of Advertising." In *Ethnographic Praxis in Industry Conference Proceedings*, edited by Maria Bezaitis, Alexandra Mack, and Ken Anderson, 119–32. New York City: American Anthropological Association, 2014.

Moeran, Brian, and Timothy De Waal Malefyt. "Performing Magical Capitalism." *Perspectives*. EPIC: Advancing the Value of Ethnography in Industry. October 26, 2016. www.epicpeople.org/performing-magical-capitalism.

Mondini, Lenise, and Carlos Augusto Monteiro. "Mudanças no padrão de alimentação da população urbana brasileira (1962–1988)." *Revista de Saúde Pública* 28, no. 6 (1994): 433–39.

Montagne, Michael. "The Pharmakon Phenomenon: Cultural Conceptions of Drugs and Drug Use." In *Contested Ground: Public Purpose and Private Interest in the Regulation of Prescription Drugs*, edited by Peter Davis, 11–25. New York: Oxford University Press, 1996.

Montanari, Massimo. *Food Is Culture*. Translated by Albert Sonnenfeld. New York: Columbia University Press, 2006.

Monteiro, Carlos Augusto. "Nutrition and Health: The Issue Is Not Food, nor Health, So Much as Processing." *Public Health Nutrition* 12, no. 5 (2009): 729–31.

Monteiro, Carlos Augusto, Wolney Conde, and Barry Popkin. "Income-Specific Trends in Obesity in Brazil, 1975–2003." *American Journal of Public Health* 97, no. 10 (October 2007): 1808–12.

———. "Trends in Under- and Overnutrition in Brazil." In *The Nutrition Transition: Diet and Disease in the Developing World*, edited by Benjamin Caballero and Barry M. Popkin, 234–37. London: Academic Press, 2002.

Monteiro, Carlos Augusto, Renata Bertazzi Levy, Rafael Moreira Claro, Inês Rugani Ribeiro de Castro, and Geoffrey Cannon. "Increasing Consumption of Ultra-Processed Foods and Likely Impact on Human Health: Evidence from Brazil." *Public Health Nutrition* 14, no. 1 (December 2010): 5–10.

Monteiro, Carlos Augusto, L. Mondini, A. L. M. Souza, B. M. Popkin. "Da desnutrição para a obesidade: a transição nutricional no Brasil." In *Velhos e novos males da saúde no Brasil: a evolução do país e de suas doenças*, 2nd ed., edited by Carlos Augusto Monteiro, 247–55. São Paulo: Editora Hucitec, 2000.

Monteiro, John Manuel. "As 'raças' indígenas no pensamento brasileiro do Império." In *Raça, ciência e sociedade*, edited by Marcos Chor Maio and Ricardo Ventura Santos, 15–22. Rio de Janeiro: Fiocruz/CCBB, 1996.

———. *Tupis, tapuias e historiadores: estudos de história indígena e do indigenismo*. Tese Livre-Docência, Universidade Estadual de Campinas, 2001.

Monteiro, Mario Ypiranga. *Antropogeografia do guaraná*. Manaus: Instituto Nacional de Pesquisas da Amazônia, 1965.

Monteleone, Joana. *Sabores urbanos: alimentação, sociabilidade, e consumo - São Paulo, 1828–1910*. São Paulo: Alameda, 2015.

Moraes, Antonio Carlos Robert. "O sertão: um 'outro' geográfico." *Terra Brasilis*, no. 4–5 (2003): 1–8.

Morais, Isabela. "Um cardápio gordo em casa e na TV: publicidade para o público infantil, aliada à má educação alimentar da família coloca em risco a saúde de crianças e adolescentes." *Espaço Aberto / USP* 136 (March 2012): 14–18.

Moreira, Ildeu, and Luisa Massarani. "The Naturalists and the Popularization of Science." Paper Presented at 7th International Conference on Public Communication of Science and Technology (PCST), Cape Town, South Africa, December 4–7, 2002.

Moreira, Vânia. "O ofício do historiador e os índios: sobre uma querela no Império." *Revista Brasileira de História* 30, no. 59 (2010): 53–72.

Moreira Neto, Carlos de Araújo. *Índios da Amazônia, de maioria a minoria (1750–1850)*. Petrópolis: Vozes, 1988.

Morelle, Rebecca. "Key Report Makes New Tally for Number of World's Plants." *BBC News*, May 10, 2016. www.bbc.com/news/science-environment-36230858.

Mori, Scott A., Amy Berkov, Carol A. Gracie, and Edmund F. Hecklau, eds. *Tropical Plant Collecting: From the Field to the Internet*. Florianópolis: TECC Editora, 2011.

Mori, Scott A., and Flora Castano Ferreira. "A Distinguished Brazilian Botanist, João Barbosa Rodrigues (1842–1909)." *Brittonia* 39, no. 1 (January–March 2011): 73–85.

Morley, John E. "A Brief History of Geriatrics." *Journal of Gerontology: Series A* 59, no. 11 (November 2004): 1132–52.

Motoyama, Shozo, Francisco Assis de Queiroz, and Milton Vargas. "1964–1985: sob o signo do desenvolvimento." In *Prelúdio para uma história: ciência e tecnologia no Brasil*, edited by Shozo Motoyama, 319–85. São Paulo: Editora da Universidade de São Paulo, 2004.

Motta, Rodrigo Patto Sá. *As universidades e o regime militar: cultura política brasileira e modernização autoritária*. Rio de Janeiro: Zahar, 2014.

Moustakas, Dimitrios, Michael Mezzio, Branden R. Rodriguez, Mic Andre Constable, Margaret E. Mulligan, Evelyn B. Voura. "Guaraná Provides Additional Stimulation over Caffeine Alone in the Planarian Model." *PLoS One* 10, no. 4 (April 2015): 1–17.

Moya, Sergio Delgado. *Delirious Consumption: Aesthetics and Consumer Capitalism in Mexico and Brazil*. Austin: University of Texas Press, 2017.

Mueller, Bernardo, and Charles Mueller. "The Political Economy of the Brazilian Model of Agricultural Development: Institutions versus Sectoral Policy." *Quarterly Review of Economics and Finance* 62 (2016): 12–20.

Mukharji, Projit Bihari. "Vishalyakarani as *Eupatorium ayapana*: Retro-Botanizing, Embedded Traditions, and Multiple Historicities of Plants in Colonial Bengal, 1890–1940." *Journal of Asian Studies* 73, no. 1 (February 2014): 65–87.

Myers, Justin. "The Logic of the Gift: The Possibilities and Limitations of Carlo Petrini's Slow Food Alternative." *Agriculture and Human Values* 30 (2013): 405–15.

Nascimento, Douglas. "Monumento a Luiz Pereira Barreto." São Paulo Antiga, February 24, 2017. www.saopauloantiga.com.br/monumento-a-luiz-pereira-barreto.

Nascimento Filho, Firmino José do. "Interação genótipos x ambientes, adaptabilidade, estabilidade e repetibilidade em clones de guaraná (*Paullinia cupana* var. *sorbilis* [Mart.] Ducke)." PhD diss., Universidade Federal de Viçosa, 2003.

Nazaré, Raimunda Fátima Ribeiro de, and Francisco José Câmara Figueirêdo. *Contribuição ao estudo do guaraná*. Belém: EMRAPA-CPATU, 1982.

Nehring, Ryan. "Yield of Dreams: Marching West and the Politics of Scientific Knowledge in the Brazilian Agricultural Research Corporation (Embrapa)." *Geoforum* 77 (December 2016): 206–17.

Nepomuceno, Rosa. *O jardim de D. João*. Rio de Janeiro: Casa da Palavra, 2007.

Néri, Priscila. "A guerra pelo guaraná da Amazônia: Coca-Cola e AmBev investem pesado para alcançar maior produtividade e qualidade." *O Estado de São Paulo*, December 7, 2003.

Nestle, Marion. *Soda Politics: Taking on Big Soda (and Winning)*. New York: Oxford University Press, 2015.

Neves, Eduardo Góes. *Arqueologia da Amazônia*. Rio de Janeiro: Jorge Zahar, 2006.

Neves, Margarida de Souza. *As vitrines do progresso: o Brasil nas Exposições Internacionais*. Rio de Janeiro: PUC-RJ/FINEP/CNPq, 1986.

Nimuendajú, Curt. "The Maué and Arapium." In *Handbook of South American Indians*, Vol. 3, edited by Julian H. Steward, 245–54. Washington, DC: Government Printing Office, 1948.

Nixon, Rob. *Slow Violence and the Environmentalism of the Poor*. Cambridge, MA: Harvard University Press, 2011.

Norton, Marcy. *Sacred Gifts, Profane Pleasures: A History of Tobacco and Chocolate in the Atlantic World*. Ithaca, NY: Cornell University Press, 2008.

———. "Subaltern Technologies and Early Modernity in the Atlantic World." *Colonial Latin American Review* 26, no. 1 (2017): 18–38.

———. "Tasting Empire: Chocolate and the European Internalization of Mesoamerican Aesthetics." *American Historical Review* 111, no. 3 (June 2006): 660–91.

Nova, Vera Lucia C. Casa. "Leituras de almanaques de farmácia: Biotônico Fontoura e a saúde da mulher." PhD diss., Universidade Federal do Rio de Janeiro, 1990.

Nunes, Francivaldo Alves. "O 'valor' das terras amazônicas no século XIX: questões sobre agricultura e extrativismo." *Saeculum-Revista de História* 26 (Jan–Jun 2012): 93–102.

Nygren, Anja. "Local Knowledge in the Environment-Development Discourse: From Dichotomies to Situated Knowledges." *Critique of Anthropology* 19, no. 3 (1999): 267–88.

O'Brien, Thomas F. *The Century of U.S. Capitalism in Latin America*. Albuquerque: University of New Mexico Press, 1999.

Offer, Avner. "Between the Gift and the Market: The Economy of Regard." *Economic History Review* 3 (1997): 450–76.

Oliveira, Daniel Coelho de. "Comida, carisma e prazer: um estudo sobre a constituição do Slow Food no Brasil." PhD diss., Universidade Federal Rural do Rio de Janeiro, 2013.

Oliveira, João Pacheco de. *O nascimento do Brasil e outros ensaios: "pacificação" regime tutelar e formação de alteridades*. Rio de Janeiro: Contra Capa, 2016.

Oliveira, Roberto Cardoso de. *O índio e o mundo dos brancos: a situação dos Tukúna do Alto Solimões*. São Paulo: Difusão Européia do Livro, 1964.

Oliven, Ruben George, and Rosana Pinheiro-Machado. "From 'Country of the Future' to Emergent Country: Popular Consumption in Brazil." In *Consumer Culture in Latin*

America, edited by John Sinclair and Anna Cristina Pertierra, 53–65. New York: Palgrave Macmillan, 2012.

Oliver, Graciela de Souza. "Debates científicos e a produção do vinho paulista, 1890–1930." *Revista Brasileira de História* 27, no. 54 (December 2007): 239–60.

Oliver, José R. "The Archaeology of Forest Foraging and Agricultural Production in Amazonia." In *Unknown Amazon: Culture in Nature in Ancient Brazil,* edited by Colin McEwan, Cristiana Barreto, and Eduardo Neves, 50–85. London: British Museum Press, 2001.

O'Neill, Darcy. "History of the Soda Fountain." Art of Drink, August 23, 2014. www .artofdrink.com/soda/history-of-the-soda-fountain.

Oreskes, Naomi. "Objectivity or Heroism? On the Invisibility of Women in Science." *Osiris* 11 (1996): 87–113.

Ormindo, Paulo. "Imagens para a ciência." In *Natureza, ciência e arte na "Viagem pelo Brasil" de Spix e Martius, 1817–1820,* edited by Alda Heizer and Paulo Armindo, 67–76. Rio de Janeiro: Andrea Jakobsson Estúdio, 2018.

Ortiz, Renato. *A moderna tradição brasileira.* São Paulo: Editora Brasiliense, 1988.

Osseo-Asare, Abena. *Bitter Roots: The Search for Healing Plants in Africa.* Chicago: University of Chicago Press, 2014.

Otavo, Okezi. *Progressive Mothers, Better Babies: Race, Public Health, and the State in Brazil, 1850–1945.* Austin: University of Texas Press, 2016.

Owensby, Brian. *Intimate Ironies: Modernity and the Making of Middle-Class Lives in Brazil.* Stanford, CA: Stanford University Press, 1999.

Padley, Tom. "God's Ongoing Work among the Sateré-Maué Tribe in the Amazon." *Alliance for Renewal Churches,* January 2010. https://arcchurch.org/wp/blog/the-satare -maue-tribe-in-the-amazon.

Pádua, José Augusto. "Flora e nação: um país no espelho." In *Flora brasileira: história, arte e ciência,* edited by Ana Cecilia Impellizieri Martins, 92–127. Rio de Janeiro: Casa da Palavra, 2009.

———. *Um sopro de destruição: pensamento político e crítica ambiental no Brasil escravista (1786–1888).* Rio de Janeiro: Jorge Zahar, 2002.

Pan-American Health Organization. *Ultra-Processed Food and Drink Products in Latin America: Trends, Impact on Obesity, Policy Implications.* Washington, DC: PAHO, 2015. https://iris.paho.org/bitstream/handle/10665.2/7699/9789275118641_eng.pdf.

"Panorama do setor." *Revista ABIR* (2019/2020): 10–13.

Parascandola, John. "Alkaloids to Arsenicals: Systematic Drug Discovery before the First World War." In *The Inside Story of Medicines,* edited by Gregory Higby and Elaine Stroud, 72–92. Madison: American Institute of the History of Pharmacy, 1997.

Pariona, Amber. "Who Are the Charismatic Megafauna of the World?" World Atlas, August 25, 2017. www.worldatlas.com/articles/who-are-the-charismatic-megafauna-of -the-world.html.

Parkin, Katherine J. *Food Is Love: Advertising and Gender Roles in Modern America.* Philadelphia: University of Pennsylvania Press, 2011.

Patel, Raj. "The Long Green Revolution." *Journal of Peasant Studies* 40, no. 1 (2013): 1–63.

Patiño, Víctor Manuel. *Plantas cultivadas y animales domésticos en América equinoccial.* Vol. 3, *Fibras, medicinas, misceláneas.* Cali: Imprenta Departamental, 1967.

Paton, Lucy Allen. *Elizabeth Cary Agassiz: A Biography*. Boston: Houghton Mifflin, 1919.

Peard, Julyan. *Race, Place, and Medicine: The Idea of the Tropics in Nineteenth-Century Brazil*. Durham, NC: Duke University Press, 2000.

Peirano, Mariza G. S. "Anthropology with No Guilt: A View from Brazil." In *Other People's Anthropologies: Ethnographic Practice on the Margins*, edited by Aleksandar Bošković, 186–98. New York: Berghahn Books, 2008.

Pels, Peter. Introduction to *Magic and Modernity: Interfaces of Revelation and Concealment*, edited by Brigit Meyer and Peter Pels, 1–38. Stanford, CA: Stanford University Press, 2003.

Pendergrast, Mark. *For God, Country, and Coca-Cola: The Unauthorized History of the Great American Soft Drink and the Company That Makes It*. New York: Scribner's, 1993.

Pereira, Antutérpio Dias. "O viver escravo em Cuiabá: relações sociais, solidariedade, e autonomia (1831–1888)." PhD diss., Universidade Federal da Grande Dourados, 2016.

Pereira, Nunes. *Os índios Maués*. Rio de Janeiro: Edição da Organização Simões, 1954.

———. *Panorama da alimentação indígena: comidas, bebidas e tóxicos na Amazônia brasileira*. Rio de Janeiro: Livraria São José, 1974.

Pereira, Rosangela A., Amanda M. Souza, Kiyah J. Duffey, Rosely Sichieri, and Barry M. Popkin. "Beverages Consumption in Brazil: Results from the first National Dietary Survey." *Public Health Nutrition* 18, no. 7 (May 2015): 1164–72.

Petersen, James B., Eduardo Neves, and Michael J. Heckenberger. "Gift from the Past: Terra Preta and Prehistoric Amerindian Occupation in Amazonia." In *Unknown Amazon: Culture in Nature in Ancient Brazil*, edited by Colin McEwan, Cristiana Barreto, and Eduardo Neves, 86–105. London: British Museum Press, 2001.

Pilcher, Jeffrey M. "The Embodied Imagination in Recent Writings on Food History." *American Historical Review* 121, no. 3 (2016): 861–87.

Pingali, Prabhu. "Green Revolution: Impacts, Limits, and the Path Ahead." *Proceedings of the National Academy of Sciences of the United States of America* 109, no. 31 (2012): 12302–8.

Pinstrup-Andersen, Per, and Derrill D. Watson II. *Food Policy for Developing Countries: The Role of Government in Global, National, and Local Food Systems*. Ithaca, NY: Cornell University Press, 2003.

Pires, João Murça. "O guaraná." Unpublished manuscript. Belém: Instituto Agronômico do Norte, 1949.

———. "Guaraná e cupana." *Revista da Sociedade de Agrônomos e Veterinários do Pará* 1, no. 3 (December 1949): 9–20.

Pivetta, Marcos. "Guaraná DNA." *Pesquisa Fapesp* 145 (March 2008): 60–61.

Poblacion, Ana Paula, John T. Cook, Leticia Marín-León, Ana Maria Segall-Corrêa, Jonas A.C. Silveira, Tulio Konstantyner, and José Augusto A.C. Taddei, "Food Insecurity and the Negative Impact on Brazilian Children's Health—Why Does Food Security Matter for Our Future Prosperity? Brazilian National Survey (PNDS 2006/07)." *Food and Nutrition Bulletin* 37, no. 4 (2016): 585–98.

Pollan, Michael. *The Botany of Desire: A Plant's-Eye View of the World*. New York: Random House, 2001.

———. *Caffeine: How Caffeine Created the Modern World*. Newark: Audible Originals, 2020.

Popkin, Barry M., and Corinna Hawkes. "Sweetening of the Global Diet, Particularly Beverages: Patterns, Trends, and Policy Responses." *Lancet Diabetes and Endocrinology* 4 (2016): 174–86.

Popkin, Barry M., and Michelle Mendez. "The Rapid Shifts in Stages of the Nutrition Transition: The Global Obesity Epidemic." In *Globalization and Health*, edited by Ichiro Kawachi and Sarah Wamala, 68–80. Oxford: Oxford University Press, 2009.

Porter, Roy. "The Patient's View: Doing Medical History from Below." *Theory and Society* 14, no. 2 (March 1985): 175–98.

Porto, P. Campos. "Plantas indígenas e exóticas provenientes da Amazônia, cultivadas no Jardim Botânico do Rio de Janeiro." *Rodriguésia* 2, no. 5 (June–September 1936): 93–157.

Prado Júnior, Caio. *História econômica do Brasil*. 21st ed. São Paulo: Editora Brasiliense, 1978.

Prance, Ghillean T. "Forest Refuges: Evidence from Woody Angiosperms." In *Biological Diversification in the Tropics: Proceedings of the Fifth International Symposium of the Association for Tropical Biology*, edited by G. T. Prance, 137–58. New York: Columbia University Press, 1982.

———. "The Increased Importance of Ethnobotany and Underexploited Plants in a Changing Amazon." In *Man's Impact on Forest and Rivers*, edited by John Hemming, 129–36. Vol. 1 of *Changes in the Amazon Basin*. Manchester: Manchester University Press, 1985.

———. "João Murça Pires (1917–1944)." *Taxon* 44, no. 2 (November 1995): 653–54.

———. "The Seeds of Time." In *The Cultural History of Plants*, edited by Ghillean Prance and Mark Nesbitt, 1–2. New York: Routledge, 2005.

Pratt, Mary Louise. *Imperial Eyes: Travel Writing and Transculturation*. London: Routledge, 1991.

Prazeres, Leandro. "Índios denunciam ação ilegal de ONG francesa no Amazonas." Povos Indigenas no Brasil. Insituto Socioambiental and Noticias Uol, November 12, 2008. www.pib.socioambiental.org/en/Not%C3%ADcias?id=62125.

Previdelli, Fabio. "O ateu, com fama de comunista, que inventou o Guaraná Jesus." Aventuras na História. Perfil, November 30, 2019. https://aventurasnahistoria.uol.com .br/noticias/almanaque/o-ateu-com-fama-de-comunista-que-inventou-o-guarana -jesus.phtml.

Putnam, Lara. "The Transnational and the Text-Searchable: Digitized Sources and the Shadows They Cast." *American Historical Review* 121, no. 2 (2016): 377–402.

Raby, Megan. *American Tropics: The Caribbean Roots of Biodiversity Science*. Chapel Hill: University of North Carolina Press, 2017.

Raminelli, Ronald. *Imagens da colonização: a representação do índio de Caminha a Vieira*. Rio de Janeiro: Jorge Zahar, 1996.

Ramos, Alcida Rita. *Indigenism: Ethnic Politics in Brazil*. Madison: University of Wisconsin Press, 1998.

Ramos, Ricardo. "1500–1930: Vídeo-clipe das nossas raízes." In *História da propaganda no Brasil*, edited by Renato Castelo Branco, Rodolfo Lima Martensen, and Fernando Reis, 1–6. São Paulo: T.A. Queiroz, 1990.

Rappaport, Joanne. *The Politics of Memory: Native Historical Interpretation in the Colombian Andes*. Durham, NC: Duke University Press, 1998.

Raynolds, Laura T. "Re-embedding Global Agriculture: The International Organic and Fair Trade Movements." *Agriculture and Human Values* 17 (2000): 297–309.

Reardon, Thomas, Spencer Hudson, and Julio Berdegué. "'Proactive Fast-Tracking' Diffusion of Supermarkets in Developing Countries: Implications for Market Institutions and Trade." *Journal of Economic Geography* 7 (2007): 399–431.

Reardon, Thomas, and C. Peter Timmer. "The Economics of the Food System Revolution." *Annual Review of Resource Economics* 4, no. 1 (2012): 225–64.

Reardon, Thomas, C. Peter Timmer, Christopher B. Barrett, and Julio Berdegué. "The Rise of Supermarkets in Africa, Asia, and Latin America." *American Journal of Agricultural Economics* 85, no. 5 (December 2003): 1140–46.

Reis, Artur Cesar Ferreira. *História do Amazonas*. Belo Horizonte: Editora Itatiaia, 1989.

Renn, Jürgen, and Malcolm D. Hyman. Introduction to *The Globalization of Knowledge in History*, edited by Jürgen Renn, 15–44. Edition Open Access, 2012.

Revilla, Juan. *Plantas da Amazônia: oportunidades econômicas e sustentáveis*. 3rd ed. Manaus: Programa de Desenvolvimento Empresarial e Tecnológico, 2000.

Rial, Carmen Sílvia Moraes. "Racial and Ethnic Stereotypes in Brazilian Advertising," *Antropologia em Primeira Mão* 44 (2001): 1–18.

Ribeiro, Darcy. *Línguas e culturas indígenas do Brasil*. Rio de Janeiro: Centro Brasileiro de Pesquisas Educacionais, 1957.

Ribeiro, Márcia Moisés, *A ciência dos trópicos: a arte médica no Brasil do século XVIII*. São Paulo: Editora Hucitec, 1997.

Ribeiro, Ricardo Ferreira. "Tortuosas raízes medicinais: as mágicas origens da farmacopéia popular brasileira e sua trajetória pelo mundo." In *Álcool e drogas na história do Brasil*, edited by Renato Pinto Venâncio and Henrique Carneiro, 155–84. São Paulo: Alameda; Belo Horizonte: Editora PUC Minas, 2005.

Ricardo, Beto and Fany Ricardo, eds. *Povos Indígenas no Brasil, 2001–2005*. São Paulo: Instituto Socioambiental, 2013.

Rios, Marlene Dobkin de, and David E. Smith. "The Function of Drug Rituals in Human Society: Continuities and Changes." *Journal of Psychedelic Drugs* 3 (1977): 269–75.

Risse, Guenter B. "The Road to Twentieth-Century Therapeutics: Shifting Perspectives and Approaches." In *The Inside Story of Medicines*, edited by Gregory Higby and Elaine Stroud, 51–73. Madison: American Institute of the History of Pharmacy, 1997.

Rodgers, Andrew Denny, III. *American Botany, 1873–1892: Decades of Transition*. Princeton, NJ: Princeton University Press, 1944.

Rodrigues, Jaime. "Alimentação popular em São Paulo (1920 a 1950)—políticas públicas, discursos técnicos, e práticas profissionais." *Anais do Museu Paulista* 15, no. 2 (July–December 2007): 221–55.

Rodrigues, Renan Albuquerque, Aluízio da Silva Ribeiro Neto, Maria de Lourdes Ferreira da Silva. "Saberes indígenas e ressignificação no processo identitário dos Sateré-Mawé/AM." *Espaço Ameríndio* 8, no. 2 (July–December 2014): 206–29.

Roiter, Márcio Alves. "Panorama modernista: *influência* indígena no art déco brasileiro." *Textos do Brasil* 19 (2012): 74–89.

Roller, Heather F. *Amazonian Routes: Indigenous Mobility and Colonial Communities in Northern Brazil*. Stanford, CA: Stanford University Press, 2014.

————. *Contact Strategies: Histories of Native Autonomy in Brazil*. Stanford, CA: Stanford University Press, 2021.

————. "River Guides, Geographical Informants, and Colonial Field Agents in the Portuguese Amazon." *Colonial Latin American Review* 21, no. 1 (2012): 101–26.

Rose, Nikolas. "Authority and the Genealogy of Subjectivity." In *Detraditionalization: Critical Reflections on Authority and Identity*, edited by Paul Heelas, Scott Lash, and Paul Morris, 294–327. Cambridge: Blackwell, 1996.

Rosemberg, Fulvia, and Regina Pahim Pinto. *A educação da mulher*. São Paulo: Nobel, Conselho Estadual da Condição Feminina, 1985.

Rosenberg, Charles E. *No Other Gods: On Science and American Social Thought*. Baltimore: Johns Hopkins University Press, 1976.

————. "The Therapeutic Revolution: Medicine, Meaning, and Social Change in Nineteenth-Century America." *Perspectives in Biology and Medicine* (Summer 1977): 485–506.

Rossi-Wilcox, Susan M. "Henry Hurd Rusby: A Biographical Sketch and Selectively Annotated Bibliography." *Harvard Papers in Botany* 1, no. 4 (January 1993): 1–30.

Roth, Cassia. *A Miscarriage of Justice: Women's Reproductive Lives and the Law in Early Twentieth-Century Brazil*. Stanford, CA: Stanford University Press, 2020.

Rottenburg, Richard. "On Juridico-Political Foundations of Meta-Codes." In *The Globalization of Knowledge in History*, edited by Jürgen Renn, 483–500. Berlin: Max-Planck-Gesellschaft zur Förderung der Wissenschaften, 2012.

Rottenburg, Richard, and Sally Engle Merry. "A World of Indicators: The Making of Governmental Knowledge through Quantification." In *The World of Indicators: The Making of Governmental Knowledge Through Quantification*, edited by Richard Rottenburg, Sally E. Merry, Sung-Joon Park, and Johanna Mugler, 1–33. Cambridge: Cambridge University Press, 2015.

Rtveladze, Ketevan, Tim Marsh, Laura Webber, Fanny Kilpi, David Levy, Wolney Conde, Klim McPherson, et al. "Health and Economic Burden of Obesity in Brazil." *PLoS One* 8, no. 7 (July 2013): 1–10.

Ruschel, Alaides Puppin. "Women in Agricultural Science in Brazil." In *The Role of Women in the Development of Science and Technology in the Third World*, edited by A. M. Faruqui, M. H. A. Hassan and G. Sandri, 661–67. Singapore: World Scientific, 1991.

Russell-Wood, A. J. R. *The Portuguese Empire, 1415–1808: A World on the Move*. Baltimore: Johns Hopkins University Press, 1998.

Ryan, Ted. "Coca-Cola in Brazil." Coca-Cola Company, December 4, 2012. www.coca-colacompany.com/stories/coca-cola-in-brazil.

Sá, Dominichi Miranda de. *A ciência como profissão: médicos, bacharéis e cientistas no Brasil (1895–1935)*. Rio de Janeiro: Editora Fiocruz, 2006.

Saba, Roberto. *American Mirror: The United States and Brazil in the Age of Emancipation*. Princeton, NJ: Princeton University Press, 2021.

Safier, Neil. "Global Knowledge on the Move: Itineraries, Amerindian Narratives, and Deep Histories of Science." *Isis* 101, no. 1 (March 2010): 133–45.

Sahlins, Marshall. *Culture and Practical Reason*. Chicago: University of Chicago Press, 1976.

————. "On the Culture of Material Value and the Cosmography of Riches." *HAU: Journal of Ethnographic Theory* 3, no. 2 (2013): 161–95.

————. "What Is Anthropological Enlightenment? Some Lessons of the Twentieth Century." *Annual Review of Anthropology* 28, no. 1 (1999): 1–23.

Samoggia, Antonella, Pietro Landuzzi, and Carmen Enriqueta Vicién. "Market Expansion of Caffeine-Containing Products: Italian and Argentinian Yerba Mate Consumer Behavior and Health Perception." *International Journal of Environmental Research and Public Health* 18, no. 15 (July 23, 2021). doi: 10.3390/ijerph18158117.

Sampaio, Gabriela dos Reis. *Nas trincheiras da cura: as diferentes medicinas no Rio de Janeiro imperial.* Campinas: UNICAMP, CECULT, IFCH, 2001.

Sanjad, Nelson. "Portugal e os intercâmbios vegetais no mundo ultramarino: as origens da rede luso-brasileira de jardins botânicos, 1750–1800." In *Múltiplas faces da história das ciências na Amazônia,* edited by José Jerônimo de Alencar Alves, 77–101. Belém: Editora UFPA, 2005.

Sanjad, Nelson, Ermelinda Pataca, and Rafael Rogério Nascimento dos Santos. "Knowledge and Circulation of Plants: Unveiling the Participation of Amazonian Indigenous Peoples in the Construction of Eighteenth and Nineteenth Century Botany." *HoST—Journal of History of Science and Technology* 15, no. 1 (June 2021): 11–38.

Santana, José Carlos Barreto de. "Euclides da Cunha e a Amazônia: visão mediada pela ciência." *História, ciências, saúde—Manguinhos* 6 (Sept. 2000): 901–17.

Sant'Anna, Denise Bernuzzi de. *Gordos, magros e obesos: a história do peso no Brasil.* São Paulo: Estação Liberdade, 2016.

Santos, Araci Alves, and José Celso Torres. "O catálogo de produtos naturais e industriais da primeira exposição colonial." *Anais do 13º Seminário Nacional de História da Ciência e da Tecnologia, Universidade de São Paulo (USP), September 2012.* São Paulo: Sociedade Brasileira de História da Ciência, 2012. www.13snhct.sbhc.org.br/resources/anais/10/1345058460_ARQUIVO_TrabalhoCatalogo-JoseCelsoTorres.pdf.

Santos, Boaventura de Sousa. *Epistemologies of the South: Justice against Epistemicide.* New York: Routledge, 2014.

Santos, Breno Machado dos. "Os jesuítas no Maranhão e Grão-Pará seiscentista: uma análise sobre os escritos dos protagonistas da missão." PhD diss., Universidade Federal de Juiz de Fora, 2013.

Santos, Fernando Sérgio Dumas dos. "Alcoolismo: algumas reflexões acerca do imaginário de uma doença." *PHYSIS—Revista de Saúde* 3, no. 2 (1993): 75–95.

Santos, Francisco Jorge dos. *Além da conquista: guerra e rebeliões indígenas na Amazônia pombalina.* 2nd ed. Manaus: Editora da Universidade do Amazonas, 2002.

Santos, Laura Carvalho dos. "Antonio Moniz de Souza, o 'Homem da Natureza Brasileira': ciência e plantas medicinais no início do século XIX." *História, ciências, saúde—Manguinhos* 15, no. 4 (October–December 2008): 1025–38.

Santos, Luís Cláudio Villafañe G. *O Brasil entre a América e a Europa: o Império e o interamericanismo (do Congresso do Panamá à Conferência de Washington).* São Paulo: UNESP, 2004.

Santos, Nadja Paraense dos, Angelo C. Pinto, and Ricardo Bicca de Alencastro. "Theodoro Peckolt: naturalista e farmacêutico do Brasil imperial." *Química Nova* 21, no. 5 (1998): 666–70.

Santos Filho, Lycurgo de Castro. *História geral da medicina brasileira.* Vol. 1. São Paulo: Editora da Universidade de São Paulo, 1977.

Santos-Granero, Fernando. Introduction to *The Occult Life of Things: Native Amazonian Theories of Materiality and Personhood,* edited by Fernando Santos-Granero, 1–29. Tucson: University of Arizona Press, 2009.

Saouma, Edouard. Foreword to *Neglected Crops: 1492 from a Different Perspective,* edited by J. E. Hernández Bermejo and J. León, v–vi. Rome: Food and Agriculture Organization of the United Nations, 1994.

"Sateré Mawé." Povos Indígenas no Brasil. March 26, 2018. https://pib.socioambiental.org /en/Povo:Sater%C3%A9_Maw%C3%A9.

Scarano, Fabio Rubio. "Patrimônio florístico brasileiro: *ciência* e biodiversidade." In *Flora brasileira: história, arte e ciência,* edited by Ana Cecilia Impellizieri Martins, 68–86. Rio de Janeiro: Casa da Palavra, 2009.

Scarpin, Paula. "Cinema, guaraná e comunistas." *Revista Piauí* 9 (2007). https://piaui.folha .uol.com.br/materia/cinema-guarana-e-comunistas.

Schiebinger, Londa. *Plants and Empire: Colonial Bioprospecting in the Atlantic World.* Cambridge, MA: Harvard University Press, 2004.

Schiebinger, Londa, and Claudia Swan. Introduction to *Colonial Botany: Science, Commerce, and Politics in the Early Modern World,* edited by Londa Schiebinger and Claudia Swan, 1–16. Philadelphia: University of Pennsylvania Press, 2005.

Schimpl, Flávia Camila, José Ferreira da Silva, José Francisco de Carvalho Gonçalves, Paulo Mazzafera. "Guaraná: Revisiting a Highly Caffeinated Plant from the Amazon." *Journal of Ethnopharmacology* 150, no. 1 (2013): 14–31.

Schivelbusch, Wolfgang. *Tastes of Paradise: A Social History of Spices, Stimulants, and Intoxicants.* Translated by David Jacobson. New York: Pantheon Books, 1992.

Schlothauer, Andreas. "Munduruku and Apiaká Featherwork in the Johann Natterer Collection." *Archiv Weltmuseum Wien* 63–64 (2013–2014): 132–61.

Schmidt, Frederico. *O guaraná, sua cultura e indústria.* Rio de Janeiro: Imprensa Nacional, 1941.

Schor, Juliet B. "In Defense of Consumer Critique: Revisiting the Consumption Debates of the Twentieth Century." *Annals of the American Academy* 611 (May 2007): 16–30.

Schuster, Sven. "The 'Brazilian Native' on Display: Indianist Artwork and Ethnographic Exhibits at the World's Fairs, 1862–1889." *Journal of the International Association of Research Institutes in the History of Art,* July 2015. www.riha-journal.org/articles/2015 /2015-jul-sep/schuster-the-brazilian-native-on-display.

Schwarcz, Lilia Moritz. *The Spectacle of the Races: Scientists, Institutions, and the Race Question in Brazil, 1870–1930.* Translated by Leland Guyer. New York: Hill and Wang, 1999.

Schweickardt, Júlio Cesar. *Ciência, nação e região: as doenças tropicais e o saneamento no estado do Amazonas, 1890–1939.* Rio de Janeiro: Editora Fiocruz; Fapeam, 2011.

Secord, James A. "Knowledge in Transit." *Isis* 95, no. 4 (December 2004): 654–72.

"The Secret Science of Soda." American Chemical Society. Accessed March 28, 2018. www.acs.org/content/acs/en/education/whatischemistry/adventures-in-chemistry /secret-science-stuff/soda-pop.html.

Sena, Ernesto Cerveira de. *Entre anarquizadores e pessoas de costumes: a dinâmica política nas fronteiras do Império: Mato Grosso (1834–1870).* Cuiabá: Carlini & Caniato; Editora da Universidade Federal de Mato Grosso, 2009.

Sherratt, Andrew. "Alcohol and Its Alternatives: Symbol and Substance in Pre-Industrial Cultures." In *Consuming Habits: Global and Historical Perspectives on How Cultures Define Drugs*, edited by Jordan Goodman, Paul E. Lovejoy, and Andrew Sherratt, 11–45. New York: Routledge, 2007.

———. Introduction to *Consuming Habits: Global and Historical Perspectives on How Cultures Define Drugs*, edited by Jordan Goodman, Paul E. Lovejoy, and Andrew Sherratt, 1–10. New York: Routledge, 2007.

Shortt, S. E. D. "Physicians, Science, and Status: Issues in the Professionalization of Anglo-American Medicine in the Nineteenth Century." *Medical History* 27, no. 1 (1983): 51–68.

Silva, Hiram Reis da. *Desafiando o Rio-Mar: descendo o Solimões*. Porto Alegre: EDIPUCRS, 2010.

Silva, João Luiz Máximo da. *Cozinha modelo: o impacto do gás e da eletricidade na casa paulistana (1870–1930)*. São Paulo: EDUSP, 2008.

Silva, Joaquim Caldeira da. "Eu vi os supermercados nascerem," In *História da propaganda no Brasil*, edited by Renato Castelo Branco, Rodolfo Lima Martensen, and Fernando Reis, 278–85. São Paulo: T. A. Queiroz, 1990.

Silva, Nil Castro da. "Culinária e alimentação em Gilberto Freyre: raça, identidade e modernidade." *Latin American Research Review* 49, no. 3 (2014): 3–22.

Silva Filho, Wellington Bernardelli. "Entre as mezinhas lusitanas e plantas brasileiras: iatroquímica, galenismo e flora medicinal da América portuguesa do século XVIII nas farmacopeias do frei João de Jesus Maria." PhD diss., Universidade de Lisboa, 2017.

———. "Medicinal Plants of Brazil in the Pharmacopoeia of the Friar João de Jesus Maria." In *Cross-Cultural Exchange and the Circulation of Knowledge in the First Global Age*, edited by Amélia Polónia, Fabiano Brachi, Gisele Cristina da Conceição, and Monique Palma 207–22. Porto: Edições Afrontamento, 2018.

Simão, André Luciano. "Modernização e civilização em debate: proposta(s) positivista(s), embate e ideias de ação política ao final do século XIX." PhD diss., Universidade de São Paulo: 2013.

Simon, Marcelo Fragomeni, and Fernando Luis Garagorry. "The Expansion of Agriculture in the Brazilian Amazon." *Environmental Conservation* 32, no. 3 (2005): 203–12.

Sinclair, John. "The Advertising Industry in Latin America: A Contemporary Overview." In *Consumer Culture in Latin America*, edited by John Sinclair and Anna Cristina Pertierra, 35–50. New York: Palgrave Macmillan, 2012.

Sinclair, John, and Anna Cristina Pertierra. "Understanding Consumer Culture in Latin America: An Introduction." In *Consumer Culture in Latin America*, edited by John Sinclair and Anna Cristina Pertierra, 1–13. New York: Palgrave Macmillan, 2012.

Siqueira, Elisabeth. *História de Mato Grosso: da ancestralidade aos dias atuais*. Cuiabá: Entrelinhas, 2002.

Siqueira, Vera Beatriz. "Natural Contrasts: Images of Brazilian Flora from Tropical Exuberance to Rustic Landscape." In *Flora brasileira: história, arte e ciência*, edited by Ana Cecilia Impellizieri Martins, 157–64. Rio de Janeiro: Casa da Palavra, 2009.

Sivulka, Juliann, *Soap, Sex and Cigarettes: A Cultural History of American Advertising*. 2nd ed. Boston: Wadsworth Cengage Learning, 2012.

Skidmore, Thomas E. *Black into White: Race and Nationality in Brazilian Thought*. New York: Oxford University Press, 1974.

Skirycz, Aleksandra, Sywlia Kierszniowska, Michaël Méret, Lothar Willmitzer, and George Tzotzos. "Medicinal Bioprospecting of the Amazon Rainforest: A Modern Eldorado?" *Trends in Biotechnology* 34, no. 10 (April 2016): 781–90.

Slater, Candace. *Dance of the Dolphin: Transformation and Disenchantment in the Amazonian Imagination.* Chicago: University of Chicago Press, 1994.

"Slow Food Brazil on the Front Line in the Fight to Save Biodiversity," Slow Food Foundation for Biodiversity, December 5, 2016. https://www.fondazioneslowfood.com /en/slow-food-brazil-the-front-line-the-fight-to-save-biodiversity/.

Smail, Daniel Lord. *On Deep History and the Brain.* Berkeley: University of California Press, 2008.

Smith, Woodruff D. "From Coffeehouse to Parlour: The Consumption of Coffee, Tea, and Sugar in North-Western Europe in the Seventeenth and Eighteenth Centuries." In *Consuming Habits: Global and Historical Perspectives on How Cultures Define Drugs,* edited by Jordan Goodman, Paul E. Lovejoy, and Andrew Sherratt, 142–57. New York: Routledge, 2007.

Soejarto, D. D., and N. R. Farnsworth. "Tropical Rain Forests: Potential Source of New Drugs." *Perspectives in Biology and Medicine* 32, no. 2 (Winter 1989): 244–56.

Soihet, Rachel. *Condição feminina e formas de violência: mulheres pobres e ordem urbana, 1890–1920.* Rio de Janeiro: Forense Universitária, 1989.

Soluri, John. *Banana Cultures: Agriculture, Consumption, and Environmental Change in Honduras and the United States.* Austin: University of Texas Press, 2005.

Sommer, Barbara A. "Colony of the Sertão: Amazonian Expeditions and the Indian Slave Trade." *Americas* 61, no. 3 (2005): 401–28.

Sonnedecker, Glenn, David L. Cowen, and Gregory J. Higby, eds. *Drugstore Memories: American Pharmacists Recall Life behind the Counter, 1824–1933.* Madison, WI: American Institute of the History of Pharmacy, 2002.

Sousa Neto, Manoel Fernandes de. *Planos para o Império: os planos de viação do Segundo Reinado (1869–1889).* São Paulo: Editora Alameda, 2012.

Souza, Amanda de M., Rosangela A. Pereira, Edna M. Yokoo, Renata B. Levy, and Rosely Sichieri. "Most Consumed Foods in Brazil: National Dietary Survey 2008–2009." *Revista de Saúde Pública* 47, suppl. 1 (2013): 190–99.

Souza, Geraldo Horácio de Paula. "Aspectos do problema da água de alimentação em São Paulo." *Arquivos de Higiene e Saúde Pública* 1, no. 2 (1936): 109–24.

Souza, Laura de Mello e. *The Devil and the Land of the Holy Cross: Witchcraft, Slavery, and Popular Religion in Colonial Brazil.* Translated by Diane Grosklaus Whitty. Austin: University of Texas Press, 2004.

Souza, Ricardo Luiz de. "Cachaça, vinho, cerveja da colônia ao século XX." *Estudos Históricos* 33, no. 1 (January–June 2004): 56–75.

Spillane, Joseph. *Cocaine: From Medical Marvel to Modern Menace in the United States, 1884–1920.* Baltimore: Johns Hopkins University Press, 2000.

Stasi, Luiz Claudio di, Elza Maria Guimarães Santos, Claudenice Moreira dos Santos, and Clélia Akiko Hiruma. *Plantas medicinais na Amazônia.* São Paulo: Editora UNESP, 1989.

Stavenhagen, Rodolfo. "Ethnodevelopment: A Neglected Dimension in Development Thinking." In *Development Studies: Critique and Renewal,* edited by Raymond Apthorpe and András Kráhl, 71–94. Leiden: E. J. Brill, 1986.

"Stella Firm Buys Budweiser Brewer." BBC News, July 14, 2008. http://news.bbc.co.uk/1 /hi/7504643.stm.

Stepan, Nancy Leys. *Picturing Tropical Nature*. Ithaca, NY: Cornell University Press, 2001.

———. "Race and Gender: The Role of Analogy in Science." *Isis* 77, no. 2 (June 1986): 261–77.

Stirn, Matt. "Yaupon: The Rebirth of America's Forgotten Tea." BBC Travel, February 24, 2021, https://www.bbc.com/travel/article/20210223-yaupon-the-rebirth-of-americas -forgotten-tea.

Suk, Lena Oak. "'Only the Fragile Sex Admitted': The Women's Restaurant in 1920s São Paulo, Brazil." *Journal of Social History* 51, no. 3 (Spring 2018): 592–620.

Tansey, James, and Steve Rayner. "Cultural Theory and Risk." In *Handbook of Risk and Crisis Communication*, edited by Robert L. Heath and H. Dan O'Hair, 53–79. New York: Routledge, 2018.

Taylor, R. B. "Ingredients." In *The Chemistry and Technology of Soft Drinks and Fruit Juices*, edited by Philip R. Ashurst, 16–54. Sheffield: Sheffield Academic Press, 1998.

Tempass, Mártian César. "O Brasil e a sua culinária indígena." In *Culturas indígenas*, edited by Ministério das Relações Exteriores, 117–29. Brasília: Gráfica Brasil, 2012.

Temporão, José Gomes. *A propaganda de medicamentos e o mito da saúde*. Rio de Janeiro: Graal, 1986.

Tinsman, Heidi. *Buying into the Regime: Grapes and Consumption in Cold War Chile and the United States*. Durham, NC: Duke University Press, 2014.

Tocchini, R. P. "Alguns aspectos sobre o guaraná (*Paullinia cupana* var. *sorbilis* Ducke) e sua relação com o refrigerante guaraná." *Boletim do Instituto de Tecnologia de Alimentos* 54 (1977): 41–54.

Tomes, Nancy. *Remaking the American Patient: How Madison Avenue and Modern Medicine Turned Patients into Consumers*. Chapel Hill: University of North Carolina Press, 2016.

Topik, Steven C., and Allen Wells, eds. *The Second Conquest of Latin America: Coffee, Henequen, and Oil during the Export Boom, 1850–1930*. Austin: University of Texas Press, 1998.

Torre, Oscar de la. *The People of the River: Nature and Identity in Black Amazonia, 1835–1945*. Chapel Hill: University of North Carolina Press, 2018.

Toscano, Frederico de Oliveira. "The Only Thing Like Coca-Cola Is Coca-Cola Itself: Agency of Matter and Food Culture in the City of Recife in the 1940s." Paper presented at the Dublin Gastronomy Symposium, May 31, 2016. https://arrow.tudublin.ie/dgs /2016/May31/8.

———. "Yes, nós temos Coca-Cola: o ideal da fartura norte-americana na mesa do Nordeste, 1930–1964." PhD diss., Universidade de São Paulo, 2019.

Tota, Antônio Pedro. *The Seduction of Brazil: The Americanization of Brazil during World War II*. Translated by Lorena B. Ellis. Austin: University of Texas Press, 2009.

Trouillot, Michel-Rolph. "The Otherwise Modern: Caribbean Lessons from the Savage Slot." In *Critically Modern: Alternatives, Alterities, Anthropologies*, edited by Bruce M. Knauft, 220–40. Bloomington: Indiana University Press, 2002.

———. *Silencing the Past: Power and the Production of History*. Boston: Beacon Press, 1995.

Tsing, Anna Lowenhaupt. *The Mushroom at the End of the World: On the Possibility of Life in Capitalist Ruins*. Princeton, NJ: Princeton University Press, 2015.

Turnbull, David. "Local Knowledge and Comparative Scientific Tradition." *Knowledge and Policy* 6 (1993–1994): 29–54.

Turner, Terence. "The Crisis of Late Structuralism. Perspectivism and Animism: Rethinking Culture, Nature, Spirit, and Bodiliness." *Tipití: Journal of the Society for the Anthropology of Lowland South America* 7, no. 1 (2009): 3–42.

———. "Ethno-Ethnohistory: Myth and History in Native South American Representations of Contact with Western Society." In *Rethinking History and Myth: Indigenous South American Perspectives on the Past*, edited by Jonathan Hill, 235–81. Urbana: University of Illinois Press, 1988.

Tyler, Varro E. "The Recent History of Pharmacognosy." In *The Inside Story of Medicines*, edited by Gregory Higby and Elaine Stroud, 160–71. Madison, WI: American Institute of the History of Pharmacy, 1997.

Uggé, Enrique. *Mitología Sateré-Maué*. Translated by María Victoria de Vela. Buenos Aires: Colección 500 años, 1991.

———. *Sateré-Maué: Los Pueblos Indios en sus Mitos*. Quito: Abya-Yala Ediciones, 1993.

Utsumi, Igor. "Brazilian Soda Market." Brazil Business. Fujikawa, May 2, 2014. https://thebrazilbusiness.com/article/brazilian-soda-market.

Van der Geest, Sjaak, Susan Reynolds Whyte, and Anita Hardon. "The Anthropology of Pharmaceuticals: A Biographical Approach." *Annual Review of Anthropology* 21 (1996): 153–78.

Van Valen, Gary. *Indigenous Agency in the Amazon: The Mojos in Liberal and Rubber-Boom Bolivia, 1842–1932*. Tucson: University of Arizona Press, 2013.

Vasconcelos, Francisco de Assis Guedes de, Mariana Perrelli Vasconcelos, and Iris Helena Vasconcelos. "Fome, comida, e bebida na música popular brasileira: um breve ensaio." *História, ciências, saúde—Manguinhos* 22, no. 3 (July–September 2015): 723–41.

"Veja como é produzido o refrigerante de guaraná." UOL Economia. January 14, 2013. https://economia.uol.com.br/album/2013/01/14/veja-como-e-produzido-o-guarana.htm?foto=6.

Velho, Lea, and John Krige. "Publication and Citation Practices of Brazilian Agricultural Scientists." *Social Studies of Science* 14 (1984): 45–62.

Viana, Jorge. "Manoel Urbano da Encarnação." *Senador Jorge Viana, PT-AC*. Accessed January 27, 2019. https://web.archive.org/web/20190127100828/http://www.jorgeviana.com.br/index.php?option=com_content&view=article&id=130%20&Itemid=48.

Vianna, Helio. "O que comia o imperador." In *Antologia da alimentação no Brasil*, edited by Luís da Câmara Cascudo, 147–51. Rio de Janeiro: Livros Técnicos e Científicos, 1977.

Vignoli, Clara. "Manejo de *Paullinia cupana* var. *sorbilis* (Mart.) Ducke (Sapindaceae) em sistemas agroflorestais na etnia Sateré-Mawé, Terra Indígena Andirá-Marau." Master's thesis, Instituto Nacional de Pesquisas da Amazônia, 2016.

Vultos da geografia do Brasil: coletânea das ilustrações publicadas na Revista Brasileira de Geografia. Rio de Janeiro: Serviço gráfico IBGE, 1943.

Walker, Timothy D. "Acquisition and Circulation of Medical Knowledge within the Early Modern Portuguese Colonial Empire." In *Science in the Spanish and Portuguese Empires*,

1500–1800, edited by Daniela Bleichmar, Paula de Vos, Kristin Huffine, and Kevin Sheehan, 247–70. Stanford, CA: Stanford University Press, 2008.

———. "Establishing Cacao Plantation Culture in the Atlantic World: Portuguese Colonial Cacao Cultivation in Brazil and West Africa, c. 1580–1912." In *Chocolate: History, Culture, and Heritage*, edited by Louis E. Grivetti and Howard-Yana Shapiro, 543–58. Hoboken: Wiley, 2009.

———. "The Medicines Trade in the Portuguese Atlantic World: Acquisition and Dissemination of Healing Knowledge from Brazil (c. 1580–1800)." *Social History of Medicine* 26, no. 3 (2013): 403–31.

"Waranà: A Tale of Indigenous Resistance." Slow Food Foundation for Biodiversity, February 26, 2019. https://www.fondazioneslowfood.com/en/warana-a-tale-of -indigenous-resistance/.

Warner, John Harley. "Science in Medicine." *Osiris* 1 (1985): 37–58.

Warren, John. "Why Do We Consume Only a Tiny Fraction of the World's Edible Plants?" World Economic Forum, January 15, 2016. www.weforum.org/agenda/2016/01/why-do -we-consume-only-a-tiny-fraction-of-the-world-s-edible-plants.

Weckerle, Caroline S., Verena Timbul, and Philip Blumenshine, "Medicinal, Stimulant, and Ritual Plant Use: An Ethnobotany of Caffeine-Containing Plants." In *Plants, Health, and Healing: On the Interface of Ethnobotany and Medical Anthropology*, edited by Elisabeth Hsu and Stephen Harris, 262–301. New York: Bergahn Books, 2010.

Weinberg, Bennett Alan, and Bonnie K. Bealer. *The World of Caffeine: The Science and Culture of the World's Most Popular Drug*. New York: Routledge, 2001.

Weinstein, Barbara. *The Amazon Rubber Boom, 1850–1920*. Stanford, CA: Stanford University Press, 1983.

———. *The Color of Modernity: São Paulo and the Making of Race and Nation in Brazil*. Durham, NC: Duke University Press, 2015.

———. *For Social Peace in Brazil: Industrialists and the Remaking of the Working Class in São Paulo, 1920–1964*. Chapel Hill: University of North Carolina Press, 1996.

White, Richard. *The Middle Ground: Indians, Empires, and Republics in the Great Lakes Region, 1650–1815*. Cambridge: Cambridge University Press, 1991.

Whitehead, Neil L. Introduction to *Histories and Historicities in Amazonia*, edited by Neil L. Whitehead, vii–xx. Lincoln: University of Nebraska Press, 2003.

Whitt, Laurelyn. *Science, Colonialism, and Indigenous Peoples: The Cultural Politics of Law and Knowledge*. Cambridge: Cambridge University Press, 2009.

Whitt, Laurie Ann. "Cultural Imperialism and the Marketing of Native America." *American Indian Culture and Research Journal* 19, no. 3 (1995): 1–31.

Whyte, Susan Reynolds, Sjaak van der Geest, and Anita Hardon. *Social Lives of Medicines*. Cambridge: Cambridge University Press, 2002.

Williams, David B. "A Wrangle over Darwin: How Evolution Evolved in America." *Harvard Magazine*, September 1, 1998. www.harvardmagazine.com/sites/default/files /html/1998/09/darwin.html.

Williams, David E., and Susan M. Fraser. "Henry Hurd Rusby: The Father of Economic Botany at the New York Botanical Garden." *Brittonia* 44, no. 3 (1992): 273–79.

Williams, Raymond. "Advertising: The Magic System." In *Problems in Materialism and Culture: Selected Essays*, 170–95. London: Verso, 1980.

Wilsnack, Richard W., Sharon C. Wilsnack, Arlinda F. Kristjanson, Nancy D. Vogeltanz-Holm, and Gerhard Gmel. "Gender and Alcohol Consumption: Patterns from the Multinational GENACIS Project." *Addiction* 104, no. 9 (September 2009): 1487–500.

Winsor, Mary P. *Reading the Shape of Nature: Comparative Zoology at the Agassiz Museum.* Chicago: University of Chicago Press, 1991.

Wohlleben, Peter. *The Hidden Life of Trees: What They Feel, How they Communicate.* Translated by Jane Billinghurst. Vancouver: Greystone Books, 2015.

Wolfe, Patrick. "Settler Colonialism and the Elimination of the Native." *Journal of Genocide Research* 8, no. 4 (2006): 386–409.

Woodard, James P. *Brazil's Revolution in Commerce: Creating Consumer Capitalism in the American Century.* Chapel Hill: University of North Carolina Press, 2020.

———. "Marketing Modernity: The J. Walter Thompson Company and North American Advertising in Brazil, 1929–1939." *Hispanic American Historical Review* 82, no. 2 (2002): 257–90.

Woortmann, Klaas. "A comida, a família e a construção do gênero feminino." *Revista de Ciências Sociais* 29, no. 1 (1986): 103–30.

Wright, Robin M., and Manuela Carneiro da Cunha. "Destruction, Resistance, and Transformation—Southern, Coastal, and Northern Brazil (1580–1890)." In *The Cambridge History of the Native Peoples of the Americas,* edited by Frank Salomon and Stuart B. Schwartz, 287–381. Cambridge: Cambridge University Press, 1999.

Wright, Robert M., Wolfgang Kapfhammer, and Flavio Braune Wiik. "The Clash of Cosmographies: Indigenous Societies and Project Collaboration—Three Ethnographic Cases (Kaingang, Sateré-Mawé, Baniwa)." *Vibrant—Virtual Brazilian Anthropology* 9, no. 1 (2012): 384–450.

Yamada, Masaaki. "Japanese Immigrant Agroforestry in the Brazilian Amazon: A Case Study of Sustainable Rural Development in the Tropics." PhD diss., University of Florida, 1999.

Yoquinto, Luke. "The Truth about Guaraná." Live Science, May 30, 2013. www.livescience.com/36119-truth-guarana.html.

Young, James O., and Conrad G. Brunk. Introduction to *The Ethics of Cultural Appropriation,* edited by James O. Young and Conrad G. Brunk, 1–10. Chichester, UK: Wiley-Blackwell, 2009.

Yunes, João. "The Population of Brazil." *Revista de Saúde Pública* 6, no. 4 (1972): 393–404.

Zylberstajn, Décio. "Agribusiness Systems Analysis: Origin, Evolution and Research Perspectives." *Revista de Administração* 52, no. 1 (January–March 2017): 114–17.

Websites

Google Books Ngram Viewer
https://books.google.com/ngrams/graph?content=guaraná&year_start=1800&year_end=2000&corpus=15&smoothing=3&share=&direct_url=t1%3B%2Cguaraná%3B%2Cco

Guaraná Antarctica on Facebook
www.facebook.com/GuaranaAntarctica

Guayapi
  www.guayapi.com/en
Museu da Pessoa
  https://acervo.museudapessoa.org/pt/entenda/portfolio/publicacoes/tematicas
    -diversas/memoria-dos-brasileiros-saberes-e-fazeres-o-guarana-de-maues-2007
Portal dos Filhos do Waraná
  www.nusoken.com
Propagandas Históricas
  www.propagandashistoricas.com.br

Documentary Films

Araújo, Joaquim Gonçalves de Araújo, and Silvino Santo, dirs. *No paiz do Amazonas.*
  J.G. Araújo Produções Cinematográficas, 1922.
Michiles, Aurélio, dir. *Guaraná: olho de gente.* Vídeo Céuvagem, 1983.
———. *O sangue da terra.* Centro de Trabalho Indigenista, 1984.

Index